D1016989

HOW WARS ARE WON

HOW WARS ARE WON

The 13 Rules of War—

From Ancient Greece to the War on Terror

Bevin Alexander

Crown Publishers • New York

Published by Crown Publishers, New York, New York.
Member of the Crown Publishing Group, a division of Random House, Inc.
www.randomhouse.com

CROWN is a trademark and the Crown colophon is a registered trademark of
Random House, Inc.

Printed in the United States of America

Design by Leonard Henderson

Maps by Jeffrey L. Ward

Library of Congress Cataloging-in-Publication Data

Alexander, Bevin.
How wars are won: the 13 rules of war—from ancient Greece
to the war on terror / Bevin Alexander.
1. War. 2. Military art and science. I. Title.
U21.2 .A416 2002
355.02–dc21   2002006665

ISBN 0-609-61039-2

10 9 8 7 6 5 4 3 2

First Edition

Contents

CONTENTS

List of Maps

HOW WARS ARE WON

Introduction

The New Kind of War

THE ATTACK ON the World Trade Center and the Pentagon on September 11, 2001, dramatically changed the face of war. Suddenly war ceased to be primarily an enterprise employing military weapons against expectant armies, and changed to include lethal blows with civilian devices against innocent people.

This is a new kind of war in that no warriors previously had employed such a weapon as an airliner loaded with passengers and jet fuel, but it is also the most ancient kind of war in that the strikes were ambushes, a tactic used in war from Stone Age times onward. Ambushes are designed to inflict the most damage at the least cost, to hit unwary, vulnerable targets, preferably those without means of defense.

September 11 will therefore go down in history as the moment when the world ceased to think of warfare exclusively as conventional clashes of massive, sophisticated weapons on the battlefield, and reverted to seeing war in its rawest, truest, and oldest form, characterized by small groups of warriors striking by surprise, or at night, against the actual or psychological rear of the enemy. Ravaging defenseless civilians, hit-and-run raids, sudden assaults on ill-defended places, hiding in inaccessible lairs, all these and more are the centuries-old elements of irregular warfare: the strategies of the snare and of refusal to meet the main military strength of the enemy in open battle. The specific ancient rule the terrorists followed was to avoid the enemy's strength and strike at weakness.[1]

Other terrorists will surely employ other rules of war by innovating other techniques of engagement, and using other devices to carry out their aims. Since the rules the terrorists use are universal, the civilized world must use the same rules to defeat them. The distinction now is that the rules and tactics will be played out in a much different fashion and in much different arenas from those seen in the huge wars and battlefields of the twentieth century.

Future wars are likely to be more limited, more specific in purpose. They will likely resemble guerrilla operations. Such conflicts are now largely being conducted by disaffected groups or factions *within* states, such as the Basques in Spain, the Tamils in Sri Lanka, and various rebel groups in Colombia. But the irregular methods that characterize these struggles—and have marked partisan war since prehistoric times—are being refined into a radically new type of warfare that pays little attention to national boundaries or to the old rules of orthodox war.

In coming to terms with the motives of the terrorists, we will do well to remember that war is essentially a political act to secure an aim; this was as true in Paleolithic times as it is today. One tribe ousting another from a hunting ground 20,000 years ago was executing a political act no less than the Allies preventing Germany from conquering Europe in World War II.

Likewise, the United States fought the Persian Gulf War of 1991 to keep Saddam Hussein from getting control of the oil supply of the Middle East. The purpose was not, as was advertised by the first Bush administration, to preserve the freedom of the autocratic little oil sheikdom of Kuwait.

This connection of war with politics is frequently misunderstood. Yet war is a military act *only* to the extent that military forces are needed to carry out a nation's political goal. The most memorable quotation from Carl von Clausewitz, the nineteenth-century Prussian author of the influential study *On War,* is "war is only a continuation of state policy by other means."[2] That's why the French premier in the First World War, Georges Clemenceau, said "wars are too important to be left to the generals." There can be no more graphic an example of war as politics than the destruction of the World Trade Center and the dreadful damage to the Pentagon.

The attack of September 11 focused attention on partisan or unorthodox war. But no matter what kind of war we face in the future, whether from terrorists or more traditional armed forces, in formulating effective responses we can draw lessons and devise tactics using military rules or maxims whose origins go back beyond recorded time. The key defining feature of terrorist war is surprise, and we may not be able to predict exactly where or how our enemies will strike in the future. But we *can* understand their methods and techniques, and we *can* construct systems to defend against their blows and root them out of their holes.

Even before the terrorist strikes, war had changed profoundly in recent years. By the mid-1990s, military planners had determined that massive, world-scale wars no longer could be fought. The Persian Gulf War of 1991 showed that modern conventional weapons had become so accurate and so deadly that human beings would simply not be able to survive in appreciable numbers on traditional battlefields. With the subsequent completion of the satellite-directed Global Positioning System, or GPS, the vulnerability of troops on the battlefield has become even greater because bombs and missiles can be sent with almost pinpoint accuracy to practically any spot on earth.

This means that the huge weapons and massive collisions of millions of men in battle, which characterized the two world wars of 1914–1918 and 1939–1945, have now passed away.

The development of nuclear weapons from 1945 onward had already created enormous doubts about the possibility of fighting large wars. When the United States and the Soviet Union came within an eye blink of nuclear confrontation in 1962, during the Cuban missile crisis, every responsible person realized that nuclear weapons could *not* be used in war. Any nuclear strike would lead to counterstrikes that could accelerate beyond human capacity to control. This reality forced people everywhere to step back from the abyss.[3]

But only since the Gulf War have military leaders finally abandoned the concept that wars could still be fought between formal armies arrayed against each other using conventional, or nonnuclear, weapons. Traditional fire-and-maneuver tactics of individual military units, whether infantry, artillery, armor, or combinations of the three, are now out of date. Today in almost any environment, including mountains, troops massed in even small groups are extremely vulnerable. Even if masked, they can usually be seen by aerial photographs, satellite scanners, unmanned aerial vehicles (UAVs), aircraft, or helicopters. Once detected, they can be precisely located by GPS and hit with bombs, missiles, or shells directed by laser, infrared, acoustic, or radar homing signals.

The vulnerability of traditional military units has led to a great deal of deliberation as to how military operations can be carried out in the future. The most obvious casualty has been the idea of *any* war between comparably or equally armed opponents. In other words, direct collisions like those between the Russians and the Germans in 1941–1945 could have only one outcome under present-day conditions: each side would inflict immense casualties, immobilize the other, and bring about stalemate.

Another fact became evident in the Persian Gulf War: a nation like the United States with leading-edge, or state-of-the-art, military technology can destroy in short order an opponent with less advanced technology. In the gulf, the Iraqi forces, deploying weapons a generation behind American arms, were virtually eradicated in a hundred hours.

At first blush, the overwhelming superiority of American military power seemed to ensure that nobody henceforth could seriously or effectively challenge any American move. With the demise of the Soviet Union in 1991, no comparably equipped military organization existed in the world, and none was being contemplated.[4] But as we learned in the attacks of September 11, American military superiority did not in fact make the United States immune either to attacks or to military pressure.

We experienced a vivid glimpse into the uncharted future from the U.S. debacle in Somalia. Somalia was a failed state that had degenerated into anarchy caused by internecine conflict among warlords, and was stricken with famine by 1992. In an effort to ameliorate the famine, the United States began shipping in thousands of tons of food, and landed troops to ensure fair distribution. More ominously from the viewpoint of the Somali people, the United States also commenced a program of "nation building" in 1993, seeking to create a country in the image of the United States. Nations, however, must evolve out of the genius of their own people. Outsiders, no matter how well intentioned, cannot impose their values and their institutions on a people who have no knowledge of them or any experience in their development or implementation.

The untenable situation came to a head when clansmen ambushed U.S. Army Rangers trying to rescue a downed helicopter crew in Mogadishu on October 3, 1993. They killed eighteen Americans, wounded seventy-three, and dragged the body of an American through the streets with ropes. The attack demonstrated perfectly how a guerrilla trap can be sprung. The Rangers did not possess armor, and this contributed greatly to their losses. Even heavy weapons are, however, no guarantee of victory for a unit isolated in the midst of a hostile city. In tight urban areas, attackers can find ample opportunities to approach armored vehicles and destroy them with unsophisticated weapons (like satchel charges of explosives).[5]

It's only a small step in theory, though a vast leap in magnitude, from the murder of eighteen on the streets of Mogadishu in 1993 to the murder of thousands in the towers of Manhattan in 2001. In both cases, our opponents found ways to shun American military strength and strike directly at American institutions and people. The lesson the Somalis taught was adapted by the Middle Eastern terrorists who attacked on September 11.

The terrorists came in, as it were, *under* the defensive shield of the United States. By seizing commercial aircraft on routine flights, they managed to avoid suspicion until they diverted the planes toward New York City and northern Virginia, allowing them enough time to hit the targets before the military's defensive system could respond. If the terrorists had used military aircraft and approached from the Atlantic Ocean, they would have been spotted at once and shot down.

The terrorists thus neutralized or evaded existing safeguards. An early example of the same principle is the Battle of Hastings in 1066. William of Normandy used weapons unfamiliar to the Anglo-Saxons to conquer the English king Harold and seize all of England. Most historians have held that Harold lost because his army was exhausted by fighting a battle with Norwegians in northern England only days before William landed on the south coast. This is not true. Harold lost because his forces were armed with pikes, axes, and swords, whereas William's army possessed two superior weapons: the bow and armored cavalry. Nowadays we would call Hastings a clash between *asymmetrical* armies. In other words, William conquered England because the new weapons his forces used neutralized the defenses of the Anglo-Saxons.

France and the United States failed in their efforts to control Vietnam from 1945 to 1975 for much the same reason that Harold failed at Hastings. Both countries tried to fight a traditional, or conventional, war against the Vietnamese Communist forces, but the Communists insisted on fighting a guerrilla war. That is to say the Vietnamese used different weapons, and with those weapons they were superior. They, like the September 11 terrorists, eluded strength and struck at weakness.

In most cases the Vietnamese refused to engage in pitched battles because they knew they would lose them, since they possessed few heavy weapons. Instead they adopted a policy of ambushing supply columns, surrounding and annihilating small outposts, and making surprise strikes at night on enemy installations. When French or American search-and-destroy missions went into the field, the Vietnamese fought long enough to inflict losses, but then vanished into the forests. Their methods inflicted a steady and unrelenting drain on manpower as well as on the resolve of the French and American people.

The Vietnamese never won a major military victory against the Americans (though they did against the French at Dien Bien Phu in 1954). But they did not have to. The morale of the people at home was their real target. When opposition at home became overwhelming, the French and American governments withdrew.

Although, as the examples above show, the methods or techniques of war must be tailored to existing challenges, warfare itself has followed the same set of rules or maxims from the Stone Age to the present. This is because the aim of war is constant. War is an act of violence to impose one's will on another. It is an organized effort by a cell, band, tribe, nation, or coalition to force another group to do what it does not want to do.

The purpose of this book is to elucidate these key rules of war, identifying along the way those that are likely to be most relevant in future combat.[6] Although conditions, arms, and the ways soldiers fight have varied greatly over the millennia, the problems commanders face and the solutions they reach are fundamentally identical. The method Alexander the Great employed to defeat the Indian king Porus in 326 B.C. is the same method a company of soldiers can use to win a firefight today.

A commander must decide which rule must be applied to solve a particular problem, and that solution must vary according to the particular circumstances the commander faces. All the rules of war are consistently valid, but in any given situation, following one may bring victory, while following another would bring defeat.

Remarkably enough, this has not always been understood. Antoine-Henri Jomini, a Swiss officer who served in the Napoleonic wars and who wrote a widely heralded interpretation of Napoleon Bonaparte's methods, said Napoleon won quick, decisive victories by the ferocious application of concentrated military force against a weak, sensitive point.[*] This was true. But Jomini believed he had discovered in Napoleon's campaigns a unique "scientific" method of conducting war in all cases, and he implied that anyone who mastered it could follow it to victory.

His conclusion was simplistic in the extreme, for *how* Napoleon managed to concentrate his force and *where* he found the weak point to strike were the keys to his generalship. Napoleon knew that at any specific juncture he might employ any of several maxims. But the first might bring little advantage, the second stalemate, the third defeat, and only the fourth victory.

Napoleon was a supreme military artist. He understood not only which rule best suited a given situation, but also how it should be carried out, and he was acutely aware that the manner in which he implemented the rule would spell the difference between success and failure. Like Michelangelo, who saw the finished form of David hidden within a block

---

*In this book Napoleon Bonaparte is called Bonaparte in references up to December 2, 1804, when he placed the emperor's crown on his own head, and as Napoleon thereafter.

of raw marble, Napoleon saw in the terrain, lines of supply, locations of troops, roads, weather, the situation of the opposing general, and other factors before him the finished shape of a campaign or battle and how it could be decided.

Like Napoleon, a great captain is one who understands the changes under way that are affecting how war is conducted. This has *not* been a common accomplishment of military leaders. Over the ages, commanders have most often failed to perceive the transformations of war, and both soldiers and civilians have suffered greatly because of their blindness. If the French nobility had heeded the devastating killing power of the English longbow at Crécy in 1346, they would not have fought a Hundred Years War. If commanders in the American Civil War had recognized the range of the Minié-ball rifle and the defensive power of field fortifications, 600,000 men would not have died in battles that were among the bloodiest in history. If generals in World War I had calculated the effects of the terrible trinity of machine gun, quick-firing artillery, and fortifications, they would not have destroyed nearly a whole generation of European youth. There is every reason to believe, however, that a profound new understanding of the challenges the world faces from terrorism has in fact been brought about by the ghastly attacks of September 11.

Whatever form warfare takes in the future, it will involve the application of strategy and tactics, the twin divisions of warfare that have existed from the start. The word *strategy* is taken from the Greek word for "general," *strategos*. It is primarily the art of the general, and refers most appropriately to the plan behind a whole campaign or war. *Tactics* refers to the methods for winning victories on the battlefield or in close combat. While the specifics of strategy and tactics are, of course, crucial to the outcome of any war, it is the underlying rules of war that are the fundamental keys to victory.

Strategy and tactics must be designed to take advantage of the wisdom embodied in the rules. No single rule is always applicable in any given situation; rather the rules offer guidelines for finding solutions in whatever circumstance a commander finds himself. The commander must evaluate every new situation with great care, and *then* choose the rule or rules he must employ to achieve success. The rules of war relate to solving *specific* problems as they arise, and are not *general* rules always to be applied in all situations. In fact, applying a rule in the wrong situation can lead to disaster.

Since warfare has always had the same purpose—to force an opponent to do something against his will—most if not all of the rules or methods by which this force can be achieved were worked out in conflicts fought before the dawn of history. Ancient pictorial records that have survived show clashes and military organizations. For example, the first fully formed phalanx, or massed body of spear-carrying infantry, appears on the Sumerian "Stele of Vultures," which dates from the third millennium B.C. In addition, storytellers transmitted by voice the traditions of the past and recounted tales of ancient wars.

After the alphabet was invented in the West and logographic symbols in China, much of this received wisdom was put down in writing.[7] Magnificent examples are the Greek bard Homer's *Iliad* and *Odyssey*, which preserved stories told by ancient Greeks before they learned to write. Thereafter, writers composed histories and narratives that described events and wars in their own times, and that drew on the accumulated wisdom inherited from the past.

These authors—some of the most famous are the Greeks Herodotus, Thucydides, and Xenophon—gave insights into the rules of war. But only one ancient writer, the great Chinese strategist Sun Tzu, produced an orderly, coherent, comprehensive summary or analysis of the rules. Sun Tzu probably inherited most if not all of his ideas from the past, but his own interpretation of them, written or assembled around 400 B.C., constitutes the most profound, succinct, and systematic treatise ever produced on the prosecution of successful war.

Sun Tzu believed careful planning and accurate information about the enemy were the keys to victory, while a commander's primary target was the mind of the opposing general. All war, according to Sun Tzu, is based on deception. The successful general must conceal his dispositions and intent. He feigns incapacity. When near, he makes it appear he is far away; when far away, that he is near. The general approaches his objective indirectly. Make an uproar in the east, but attack in the west. The general seeks a quick victory, not lengthy campaigns; extended operations exhaust the treasury and the troops. The commander attacks only when the situation assures him victory. By threatening in many directions, he seeks to disperse the enemy to defend everywhere. If defending everywhere, the enemy is weak everywhere. When the enemy prepares to defend in many places, "those I have to fight in any one place will be few." The way to avoid what is strong is to strike what is weak. As water seeks the easiest path to the sea, so armies should avoid obstacles and seek avenues of least resistance.

Sun Tzu postulated two forces—the *zheng* element, which fixes the enemy in place, and the *qi* element, which flanks or encircles the enemy, either actually or psychologically. The *zheng* (ordinary) element is direct and more obvious; the *qi* (extraordinary) is indirect, unexpected, distracting, or unorthodox. Using both elements ensures that decisive blows will fall where the enemy does not anticipate them, and is least prepared. However, the two forces are fluid. As factors change, the *zheng* effort can be transformed into the *qi* and the *qi* into the *zheng*.

Napoleon never drew up a theory of war, but his campaigns reveal six principal admonitions: rely on the offensive; pursue a defeated enemy; trust in speed to economize on time; bring about strategic surprise; concentrate superior force on the battlefield, especially at the decisive point of attack; and until the time of attack, protect forces by a "well-reasoned and circumspect" defense.[8]

As warfare moves into a period of revolutionary change, these rules will remain as relevant as they have always been. Some will likely be less useful, owing to technological innovations, though perhaps enterprising commanders will find ways to bring them into the twenty-first century. As the essential thirteen rules of war are introduced, this book will attempt to highlight which of the rules are likely to be most effective in waging the new war and provide glimpses of the way in which the rules might be applied.

Bevin Alexander

1

The Revolution in Warfare

TWO UNRELATED DEVELOPMENTS have fused to produce a true revolution in warfare. The first is highly accurate and extremely powerful weapons. The second is the discovery that modern conventional armies can be defeated by guerrilla methods.

Each development occurred independently, but their combined effect is almost certain to create a new type of combat by small units that operate in conjunction with one another, but function far more independently than existing military forces. There will be less distinction than in the past between orthodox military operations, guerrilla methods, and terrorist strikes. Motivations for each will differ, but they will function much the same.

The traditional battlefield will disappear, and combat will take on more the nature of sudden, surprise blows on unsuspecting targets, and equally surprise counterstrikes by defending forces. In this it will resemble present-day guerrilla and terrorist clashes. Distances at which forces operate will be great, because troops must be dispersed over wide tracts of territory, and—to prevent being destroyed by standoff missiles and bombs—they will remain hidden until prepared to strike.

The long-established structure of armies in a descending order of size from corps to divisions, regiments, and battalions will not persist much longer. Existing military organizations were designed for sustained operations on the linear battlefields or main lines of resistance (MLRs) of the twentieth century. As such battle lines are now obsolete, military structures designed to fight on these lines are also obsolete. At the same time, the capacity of modern computers, radios, and television to provide to all military elements simultaneously and in split seconds target data and precise details about one's own forces and enemy forces makes the old structural or command divisions not only unnecessary but barriers to quick action.

With the disappearance of the heavily defended front line, troops can move at will in all directions, and everywhere will be the rear of the enemy. Clashes may occur at many different places, and make no clear distinctions between front or rear, or even, unfortunately, between soldier and civilian.

The reason customary battlefields will vanish is that soldiers no longer can survive on them. In the past quarter century, but especially in the past decade, nonnuclear weapons have become so accurate and so powerful that practically any target anywhere can be hit by standoff weapons.

Single tanks, cannons, and vehicles, and small bodies of troops now can be found, precisely located, and destroyed by weapons fired from helicopters, aircraft, gunships, cannons, missile launchers, or even individual soldiers manning handheld weapons.[1] Missiles and "smart" bombs can be guided to specific targets by inerrant radar, laser, infrared, acoustic, or other homing devices. While "dumb" bombs that fall where they are dropped still exist, and sometimes miss their targets, as does fire aimed by soldiers, weapons are far more accurate and battlefields far more deadly today than they were in World War II or the Korean War.[2]

All this was demonstrated by the collapse of the Taliban government in the second week of November 2001 after only a few weeks of targeted bombing and strikes by attack aircraft, AC-130 gunships, and other weapons.[3]

Numerous programs are under way to locate enemy forces with even greater precision and to make combat even more lethal. The Pentagon is developing highly computerized command centers that can be located continents away from any war zone. These command centers will collect data from sensors and surveillance systems such as satellites and unmanned aerial vehicles (UAVs), and use the information to strike enemy targets with bombs and rockets fired by aircraft, missile launchers, and artillery.

Devices to detect the presence of even tiny enemy elements are already extremely effective, and will become more foolproof in coming years. Among the most important advances are ground sensors and UAVs, or aerial drones. Ground sensors can be dropped from planes into enemy territory. Once on the ground, the sensors sprout antennae and send back to command centers pictures and infrared images showing the precise locations of enemy vehicles and soldiers. Aerial drones range in size and scope from the high altitude Global Hawk, which can fly virtually around the world, taking close-up pictures of enemy installations, to small tactical "hummingbird" drones only nine inches long, which can give troops in close-combat situations quick birds'-eye views of the enemy ahead.

The army is developing a small all-terrain vehicle that can serve as the personal robot of an individual soldier, following him wherever he goes, and carrying his weapons, ammunition, explosives, and food.

New strike weapons include the small "hornet" canister that can be dropped by soldiers or from trucks and can detect and classify enemy vehicles as they pass, then strike them with armor-piercing projectiles. The air force is developing a whole family of UAVs that can serve as attack platforms. In Afghanistan the Predator UAV's video cameras not only located and passed on to other aircraft precise information about enemy forces, but also launched Hellfire missiles at targets itself. The next generation of UAV strike weapons includes the X-45, a thirty-foot-long unmanned combat aerial vehicle that will carry twelve bombs. At first the aircraft will ask human controllers for permission to bomb targets. By 2010 the Pentagon expects X-45s to attack independently anything within designated "kill boxes."[4]

Large concentrations of troops and weapons now are targets for destruction, not marks of power, and they no longer will exist. Dispersion will be the aim in future conflicts. Troops will operate in much smaller groupings because they offer much smaller and less lucrative targets. Weapons will be lethal, but lighter. Main battle tanks and huge cannons are becoming increasingly a liability. Mobility will be essential, and much movement will be by helicopter, which is faster than travel on land because it is not bound by roads.[5]

Military units, to survive, must not only be small, but highly mobile, self-contained, and autonomous. Accordingly, the lessons learned in guerrilla warfare, which largely operates with separate detachments of a few to a few hundred men, will have vast significance in determining a new type of regular military force and developing new types of strategy and tactics.

In 2000, John Arquilla and David Ronfeldt wrote for the Rand Corporation a study, *Swarming and the Future of Conflict*, that encapsulates much of the advanced thinking about armies and how they must fight wars today. Arquilla and Ronfeldt postulated small "pods" or modest-sized teams that would "swarm" around an enemy target on all sides—either directly as attacking troops, or by fire delivered from artillery, missile, attack helicopter, or other aerial "pods" miles away.

In other words, infantry "pods" might assault an enemy position directly on two or three sides, in close coordination with an artillery or missile "pod" positioned five or six miles distant, or army Apache attack helicopter or air force AC-130 gunship "pods" overhead. Artillery gunners would strike targets pointed out by the infantry, while the aircraft might also hit such targets, or might go after targets they located themselves.

Several pods would be formed into a "cluster," the main tactical unit. Clusters might function alone or with other clusters. In any event, pods or clusters, using instantaneous modern communication systems, would strike hard, quick blows, disperse quickly, then recombine for another strike as necessary. One cluster or as many as needed would be assigned to complete a mission. All would be tied together in an all-channel communications network, in which everyone was connected to everyone else. This would allow any unit to collaborate with any other unit, wherever located, and permit coordinated attacks or strikes that in existing military formations would be impossible.[6]

Instant communications combined with great mobility and high flexibility are the keys to the success of swarming tactics.[7] If carried out properly, small units in constant communication with one another could attack an enemy on all sides simultaneously. This has been a largely unattainable goal for orthodox armies, because of the difficulty in communicating rapidly with intermediate or lower headquarters, and getting them to make quick changes in mission or direction.

The problem has bedeviled armies for centuries. Just prior to the battle of Waterloo in June 1815, for example, Napoleon sent off Marshal Emmanuel de Grouchy with a large corps to keep the Prussians from joining the British. But Grouchy merely followed on the tail of the Prussians, and Napoleon was unable to communicate with him in time to interpose Grouchy's corps *between* the Prussians and the British. That is the principal reason Napoleon lost Waterloo.

The new warfare also will require officers to embrace change and new ideas, and cease holding on doggedly to preconceived theories and orthodox solutions. There no longer will be a place for the familiar "Colonel Blimp," the rigid, by-the-book officer determined to do things as they have always been done. One example of the kind of thinking that must vanish occurred in the early stages of World War II. German commanders discovered their 88-mm antiaircraft gun, designed to shoot down high-flying enemy aircraft, was, in fact, the best weapon they possessed to penetrate armor. This gun became the great "tank-buster" in the German army. General Erwin Rommel used it extensively against the British in the desert war in Libya and Egypt. The British had a nearly identical antiaircraft gun, a 3.7-inch cannon that had as high a muzzle velocity as the 88. Their top command, however, refused to use it in an antitank role. It had been designed as an antiaircraft gun, and that was what it remained.

Changes in technology and tactics can be difficult for traditional officers to accept, but they open avenues to success for those who can think creatively. Since super-accurate weapons and high mobility will force military units to disperse widely, the officer who can accomplish missions without constant supervision and instruction will have high value. Another factor in the new warfare, instantaneous communications, will make it possible for numerous autonomous elements to work together efficiently, even when they are far apart. Thus commanders who can see their tasks as part of a larger goal or objective and who can cooperate with other detached elements will be successful. In other words, the new warfare will place far more emphasis on original thinking, independent action, and individual responsibility by officers down to the lowest level.

A good example of the new kind of thinking was the extremely effective work of small special forces units in Afghanistan in the fall of 2001. These outfits, operating on the ground and relying on their own initiative, located Taliban and Al Qaeda targets with the help of friendly Afghan tribesmen, and directed accurate strikes by bombs and shellfire from American aircraft overhead.

The face of battle will be transformed. It will be spread over a much larger surface, will employ weapons that nearly always hit their targets, and will demand officers and soldiers who are more accountable and reliable than has ever been required in the past. But the element that makes for victory—essentially the application of superior force at a crucial point—will continue as before. The commander who can see how to bring this about under the altered conditions prevailing today will be successful.

Swarming advocates the dispersal of a wide number of small maneuver units over a battle space, along with the devolution of a great deal of command and control authority from senior officers to those small units. This implies, of course, highly responsible and skilled junior officers, and a profound shift away from the top-heavy headquarters structure of armies commanded by often-distant senior commanders that has existed for many years.

Perhaps the most extreme example of overcentralized control and micromanagement was President Lyndon B. Johnson, who sometimes personally directed local engagements by battalions and smaller units in the Vietnam War, while he sat half a world away in the White House.

The idea of pods and clusters may be more comprehensible if the pod is thought of as a platoon or team of thirty to fifty men and a cluster as a company of three or four platoons. Each team in a given cluster might have the same mission, or the teams might have different missions. Arquilla and Ronfeldt assume that clusters would keep the same teams.

Thus clusters, and not individual teams, would be assembled for a given mission.

Several clusters might be detailed to destroy, say, a terrorist camp discovered in Somalia. Once the task was completed, the clusters would move to another mission. In other words, clusters could combine and recombine in as large or as small numbers as needed, and only as often and for as long as necessary.

There is no inherent reason why teams from one cluster could not be joined temporarily with teams in another cluster to accomplish a specific job. Thus clusters could be variable in size, especially as each pod would be self-sufficient, autonomous, and supplied directly. This is not done at present. Small units now have to get their food, ammunition, fuel, and other needs from a logistic system organized around much larger military organizations.

Arquilla and Ronfeldt recognize that the concept they propose would require a novel, innovative system of logistics. "For swarming," they write, "these goods and services will have to be delivered not to fixed locations, but to an ever-shifting set of small forces almost constantly on the move."[8]

The idea of pods and clusters resembles intellectually the *Kampfgruppen*, or mixed battle groups, of guns, armor, infantry, and sometimes engineers that the Germans developed in 1940. A battle group formed with forces and size needed to carry out a specific mission, and dissolved when it was completed. *Kampfgruppen* were flexible but effective, and dominated German tactical operations for the remainder of World War II.

The idea also resembles the battle teams that the Communist guerrillas used against the French and the Americans in Vietnam. Although the Communists often structured their forces in battalions, regiments, and divisions, or "field forces," the soldiers usually fought as members of small platoon-sized teams, with several teams working together to attack an enemy base or position.

Under the proposed system, individual teams might have designated missions or jobs, such as infantry assault, defense against tanks or aircraft, long-range artillery or missile bombardment, or helicopter strikes. Others might combine missions, in the fashion of light infantry units today—having the primary task of attacking enemy positions with automatic weapons, grenade launchers, and high explosives, but also armed with antitank and antiaircraft missiles, mortars, and mine detectors. But all, whether single-purpose or multipurpose, would be connected in a cluster so that any could be called upon in time of need to assist any other.

Arquilla and Ronfeldt propose that the teams would largely employ light fighting vehicles. The army has the fully tracked M-113 armored personnel carrier (APC) and Bradley fighting vehicle in a number of configurations. Both can deflect most small-arms fire and light shrapnel. The Bradley's armaments include 25-mm cannons, machine guns, Stinger air-defense missiles, and TOW antitank missiles.[9] The army also has fielded a wheeled "interim armored vehicle" (IAV), which can carry nine soldiers and a crew of two or a turreted 105-mm gun and its crew.

One school of thought believes primary tactical movement should be by helicopter, not on the ground. This school, led by army Major Anthony M. Coroalles, holds that the only way to restore mobility is by employing helicopters—that is, using air-assault infantry and light artillery as the maneuver force.[10] Throughout history, faster armies have won because their elements could reach decisive points before the enemy or, by concentrating an overwhelming force, could evict smaller enemy forces from these places.

Using choppers to carry and protect them, air-delivered troops can move at ten times the speed of any land weapon. Helicopter refueling and maintenance can be provided well to the rear, thus choppers are logistically less vulnerable than fighting vehicles, which must have these elements brought up to them. Also, helicopters can fly over the enemy and overwhelm a force.[11]

The mode of transportation will resolve itself into the best vehicle for the mission. In cases where American forces have to travel long distances over difficult terrain to strike, the choice will be helicopters or the new V-22 Osprey, a tilt-engine transport hybrid between a helicopter and a fixed-wing airplane.[12] In cases where distances are small and roads plentiful, ground vehicles may be as good or better. And ground and helicopter forces will doubtless work in conjunction in many circumstances.[13]

Swarming, or attacking on all sides, was probably the normal way of fighting by hunter-gatherer tribes in the Stone Age, since it is essentially an ambush. But it has been difficult to bring it about in conventional warfare—because of the rigid structure of military organizations[14] and the inadequacy, until very recent times, of communications on the battlefield.

The model formula for orthodox war is called the convergent assault; this is normally a two-direction attack, whereas swarming is an omnidirectional attack. In the convergent assault, the commander divides his force into two or more segments. Ideally, one segment attacks the target from one direction, while another segment attacks the same target from a different direction. Sometimes a part of the force "fixes" the enemy in place or distracts him while the other part maneuvers to gain surprise and break up the defense.

The convergent assault is mentioned in the Bible (2 Samuel 5:22–25), and was used by Alexander the Great and Hannibal. It has been the canonical solution for a long time. In part this has been because it could be used by small detachments and large armies alike, and could succeed against familiar as well as unexpected obstacles.

For example, it finally broke the tactical impasse along the western front in World War I caused by the immense power of the machine gun, heavy field fortifications, and accurate, fast-firing artillery. These weapons virtually stopped movement in the first year of the war. In 1915, however, a German captain, Willy Martin Rohr, developed "infiltration" or "storm troop" tactics. One small group of soldiers held down an enemy trench position or strong point with heavy directed fire by automatic weapons, mortars, and sometimes cannons, while one or more well-trained teams of eight to twelve "storm troopers," working in conjunction, infiltrated the trench line or sneaked up on the strong point, and "rolled it up" with grenades, small-arms fire, and sometimes flamethrowers. This fire-and-maneuver system overcame enemy guns and fortifications, returned movement to the battlefield, and became the fundamental method of tactical engagements for the rest of the century.[15]

Swarming is a variation on fire-and-maneuver, but is an advance over it, made possible by flexible military units and instant communications. High speed and mobility, though assets, are not essential to the theory.

Swarming has profound implications for use against terrorist groups and training sites in countries harboring them, and against hostile formal military forces in those countries. Clusters could encircle and destroy a camp or a force discovered in remote or isolated areas, or close in on a compound within a city and eliminate it, with far more facility than conventional forces. Targets of these types are likely to be fleeting, and will require prompt and decisive action. In October 2001, for example, an unmanned aerial vehicle spotted a terrorist group, possibly including Osama bin Laden, traveling on a road in Afghanistan, but American forces did not have time to launch a strike before it vanished. Pods or teams could move much faster because they would not have to wait for higher command to design a full-fledged operation or go through several headquarters to get clearance. Clusters and pods, with command authority already delegated to them, could respond at once to opportunities as they appeared.

Swarming has less significance for actions against clandestine cells within democratic countries. These cells are far too small to have capability for defense, must strike by surprise, and possess little hope of surviving except by chance. Terrorist blows within democratic states will almost always be suicide missions, or underhanded sneak ventures like the anthrax-laden letters sent through the U.S. mails in autumn 2001. Since such strikes can rarely be predicted in advance, action against them must primarily be *preventive*. This means essentially detective work by police and intelligence services to root out the cells and the terrorists before they can strike.

Lessons from the Past

Some armies in the past worked out routines that incorporated swarming and could be performed without direct control or coordination by a commander. But this approach required highly trained soldiers who could be depended upon to follow prior instructions precisely.

Numerous tribes of the steppes of inner Eurasia developed such internal discipline and were highly successful. They were mounted archers and had in their horses the sort of speed and flexibility that Arquilla and Ronfeldt envision in mobile teams.

The horsemen surrounded an enemy force, not coming to grips with it, but firing arrows into the massed bodies of infantry or cavalry. The horsemen used the compound bow, consisting of a layer of sinew on the back and a layer of horn on the inner surface or belly, with a frame of wood in the middle. The bow could exert a pull of well over a hundred pounds, although it was short enough to be wielded easily by a man on horseback. Arrows could kill at 300 yards and, equipped with sharp metal points, could penetrate the thickest armor.

The horse archers could materialize before an enemy force, unleash a storm of arrows, attack to the front, sides, and rear, and disappear, without ever coming into collision with infantry swords or spears or even, in many cases, with cavalry armed with javelins or spears. A favorite technique was the feint. Combining the speed of the horse with a refined system of control and timing, horsemen rushed forward in a furious charge, then, pretending the onslaught had failed, withdrew, seemingly in panic and sometimes over the horizon. Only the most controlled troops could withstand the urge to rush after the supposedly fleeing horsemen, and, in the process, go beyond their supports, lose their tight battle order, and allow units or individuals to become separated. Then the horse archers suddenly regrouped, turned on the advancing enemy, and destroyed the disorganized soldiers one unit or soldier at a time.

During the Battle of Britain in 1940, the British Royal Air Force used swarming tactics to defeat heavy German Luftwaffe bomber assaults against England. British radar, developed prior to the war, could track German bombers from the moment they took off from bases in western Europe. This allowed RAF fighters to mass in advance, and attack each bomber flight from all sides when it came within a target box or sector. It was this combination of radar and omnidirectional fighter strikes that caused staggering losses to the Luftwaffe and preserved Britain from invasion.[16]

Chinese forces used another variant of swarming when they intervened in the Korean War in late 1950. The Chinese had no air power and were armed only with rifles, machine guns, hand grenades, and mortars. Against the much more heavily armed Americans, they adapted a technique they had used against the Nationalists in the Chinese civil war of

1946–1949. The Chinese generally attacked at night and tried to close in on a small troop position—generally a platoon—and then attacked it with local superiority in numbers. The usual method was to infiltrate small units, from a platoon of fifty men to a company of 200, split into separate detachments. While one team cut off the escape route of the Americans, others struck both the front and the flanks in concerted assaults. The attacks continued on all sides until the defenders were destroyed or forced to withdraw. The Chinese then crept forward to the open flank of the next platoon position, and repeated the tactics.[17]

These examples demonstrate that the idea of swarming and a new, smaller unit structure for military forces embody techniques and principles that reach back to the earliest days of warfare. In the chapters that follow, we will examine these principles, showing how they succeeded in previous wars and how they may be employed in the future.

2

Striking at Enemy Weakness

T HE RULE OF war that is most directly relevant to the current war on terrorism is the maxim to exploit an enemy's weakness, while nullifying his strength. International terrorism is based on this rule, as is guerrilla warfare. Though they share this same principle, international terrorism differs from guerrilla war in a deep-seated way, and the difference will be the key to the war against terrorism. International terrorism has one great strength: it makes sneak attacks on unsuspecting people, and thus is difficult to prevent. But it also has one profound weakness: it operates as clandestine cells in an alien environment, and thus can be isolated.

Though international terrorism copies the strategy and tactics of guerrilla warfare, it differs fundamentally in that international terrorism is fought in the *enemy's* land. True guerrilla warfare is fought in one's *own* land. Terrorism accordingly is offensive, aimed at forcing a distant enemy to accept terrorist dictates. Guerrilla conflict is primarily defensive, aimed at neutralizing a foreign invader or weakening a domestic enemy.

International terrorism is a new type of war, therefore, not because it targets helpless citizens, but because it seeks to achieve political goals across a distance. Transferring a conflict from the Middle East to the people of the United States is unique, and distinguishes it from other wars. The principal aim of the terrorists is not to destroy the United

States, but to transform the Middle East, to drive the West out of it, and to overturn the liberal or secular Moslem governments there.

In waging this war, international terrorism mimics guerrilla methods because these are the easiest for small covert cells to use. The nature of guerrilla war is to avoid an enemy's strength by refusing to fight pitched battles, and guerrilla war achieves its power by striking vulnerable targets that are ill-defended or not defended at all. International terrorism does the same.

But the projection of irregular-type warfare over a great distance—that is, from its source in the Middle East to the United States—has resulted in the counterprojection of something quite akin to irregular war by the United States and Britain, *also* over a great distance—back to the Middle East. This demonstrates the far-reaching, radical, unprecedented nature of the new form of war. It also points to the ultimate irrationality of the terrorist campaign, since it seeks an intrinsically unattainable goal—to alter the political behavior of a foreign land by skulking attacks on its citizens.[1]

The main driving force of international terrorism is anger for wrongs its leaders feel other countries have perpetrated on their people. The category of international terrorist forces includes not only the Al Qaeda group associated with Osama bin Laden, but also the Irish Republican Army (IRA), which has attacked targets in England, and the suicide bombers of Palestine associated with Hamas, Islamic Jihad, and Yasir Arafat's Palestinian Authority, who have been attacking civilians and soldiers in Israel. All three are essentially engaged with killing foreigners. The Palestinian suicide bombers argue that the land of Israel belongs to them, but in fact they are operating in a territory peopled by Israelis.

The major focus of the struggle against international terrorism is on the Al Qaeda network, because of the strikes of September 11. But it's important to understand that Al Qaeda is an example of a type, and has antecedents that go far back in time. The Middle East was the scene of one of the worst terrorist movements ever, the Assassins (Nizari Ismailis), a politico-religious Islamic movement that started in 1094 in a dispute over who would be caliph (religious governor and successor to

Mohammed). The movement of the Assassins evolved into a war of murder waged by Iranian terrorists against Iraqis and Syrians.

Al Qaeda complains that Middle Eastern people have suffered at the hands of the West for centuries, and directs its greatest animus against the United States, not only because it is the major Western power, but also because the United States has been so active in Middle Eastern affairs, most notably supporting Israel and moderate states in the Middle East, and leading a coalition against Iraq in the Persian Gulf War of 1991. But Al Qaeda also opposes the liberal or secular Moslem states of the region that have cooperated with the West and that seek to bring the Middle East into the world economy and the community of nations.

In trying to evict the West from the Middle East, Al Qaeda activists see Islam, the main religion of the region, as their vehicle. They, along with some other Moslems, maintain that the aim of Islam is to wipe out other religious beliefs and to create states based on Islamic law. Accordingly the terrorists wish to turn Islam into a militant, aggressive, despotic movement that attacks not only the West but also moderate Moslem states. On the other hand, a large number of Moslems hold that Islam does not teach such a radical, exclusionary doctrine, and that its overriding message is peace.

The terrorists' goals are foolishly ambitious. To reconstruct Islam in their dictatorial image is an enormous, probably impossible task. A program to force the United States and other Western nations out of the Middle East by random acts of terror is even more illogical because the capacity of the West to resist and to inflict retribution is immensely greater than the terrorists' capacity to inflict damage.

This is all the more the case because the terrorists have deliberately narrowed their support base in their home region to radical or extremist fringe groups, such as the Taliban of Afghanistan. As Middle East observer Judith Miller states, these groups are increasingly fragmented and diverse, and represent no unified force.[2] In this fact lies the great vulnerability and the key difference between them and a true guerrilla war.

Al Qaeda, the IRA, and Palestinian suicide bombers are not fundamentally strong. But their disciples are dedicated and resilient, and have adopted a rule of war—avoiding strength and striking at weakness—that is difficult to defeat. Guerrilla methods, however, while practically invincible when employed properly *within* one's own country, have tremendous weaknesses when used as the terrorists are using them, in a foreign land. International terrorism will be hard to root out; in democratic states where people can move freely, it may be impossible to prevent terrorist attacks entirely.[3] But terrorism does not possess the inherent capacity for victory that true guerrilla warfare possesses.

The aim of international terrorists is to create fear in the hope that this fear will cause their enemy to yield to certain demands or relinquish control over territory, or, as the terrorists see things, over their way of life. This is a delusion. Attacks on defenseless people are seen everywhere as cowardly, and arouse anger, not fear.[4] That anger mobilizes populations against them, as we have seen in the wake of the September 11 attacks.

Those attacks focused law enforcement as never before on finding terrorists, and both the police and the FBI have vast resources to bring to bear. Domestic hiding places have never been entirely secure because terrorists are not *part* of the community. Now they are more likely to arouse suspicion or at least curiosity. Ordinary observant citizens are more inclined to provide leads that police can pursue, while efforts at ferreting out cells by paid informants or tipsters have mushroomed. The hunt for terrorists *within* targeted countries will be largely carried out as a police mission, along the lines of rounding up fugitives or suspects. The scale is increased, but the methods are part of orthodox police work, and a great deal of progress can be made in this way.

Precisely because of their vulnerability abroad, however, terrorists must center their ultimate leadership in countries or regions that offer support and protection to them. That is why terrorism must be pursued to its *sources*, the headquarters where leaders plan and organize strikes, wherever they are located. Through close surveillance and good intelligence work, as well as international cooperation, these supposedly safe harbors can be found and the cells rooted out. In the future, no state will openly endorse terrorism, because it would thereby invite military, economic, and diplomatic retaliation of the fiercest kind. Terrorism will enjoy only covert support at best. And this hidden assistance will come solely from radical states or dictators outside the norms of civilized behavior. As such, these terrorist sympathizers can be isolated and dealt with.

Methods to destroy terrorism, aside from pressure on host countries, will include hunting down and eliminating furtive cells within democratic countries by police and intelligence services; cutting off the money supply of the movements through international financial channels; spying on suspected groups; targeting leaders for assassination or capture; and striking located hard targets, bases, or training sites by military special forces units or by standoff weapons such as cruise missiles and aircraft.[5]

Might terrorists be able to establish bases of cover within democratic countries? Since the Vietnam War, specialists in think tanks have conjectured how small American forces might function in hostile territory, a mission somewhat parallel in its requirements to those of terrorist cells in democratic countries. The theory was that the Americans would remain hidden in out-of-the-way places, be supplied clandestinely by air, provide intelligence for the Pentagon, and make quick strikes at isolated enemy positions or installations. These proposals always have had an aura of fantasy, however, because experience has shown they won't work.

During the late stages of World War II, small Allied teams, mostly British and American (the "Jedburghs"), joined the French resistance or Maquis in occupied France, helping them carry out strikes against the Germans and providing intelligence for the Allied invasion in June 1944. Those teams, however, depended upon the protection of the French underground. The few teams unable to reach local help were destroyed by the Germans or had to evacuate quickly.

The closest Americans have come to a force that remotely resembles the structure of terrorist cells was Detachment 101 of the Office of Strategic Services (OSS), the predecessor of the Central Intelligence Agency. This unit dropped into Japanese-occupied northern Burma in mid-1943. It recruited Kachin tribesmen to form an intelligence and irregular force, and operated for a number of months behind enemy lines. Detachment 101 was somewhat successful, but it was not a true guerrilla force operating in enemy territory, because it survived only with the support and protection of the Kachins, who lived in mountainous areas where the Japanese seldom ventured.

Could something resembling the Kachins provide a hiding place in democratic countries for terrorists? In other words, could Middle Eastern terrorists disappear into a community largely made up of Moslems? Not likely. For, unlike the Kachins, such a community is not isolated geographically, and few of its members support the murderous aims of terrorists. The probability of discovery in a Moslem neighborhood would be in reality no lower than elsewhere.

Accordingly, international terrorists will never have domestic support. They always will be regarded as predatory monsters who should be destroyed, not harbored. Terrorist cells in democratic countries must be clandestine in the strictest sense, limited to a few trusted accomplices, and hidden from the rest of society. Such cells have great vulnerability, because any activity that draws the slightest attention will be regarded by observers as suspicious, and will invite police investigation.

While the use of the strike-at-weakness rule by terrorists is, therefore, ultimately irrational and will have counterproductive effects, its employment by true guerrilla forces can be extremely effective. Successful guerrillas enjoy the support of natives in their own countries. It is this that gives them strength. The concept was expressed best by Mao Zedong (1893–1976), who focused the world's attention on the movement. Guerrillas, he said, are fishes who swim in the sea of the people.[6] They are able to disappear into the population when not engaged in hostilities, and thus cannot be singled out and destroyed. This is an extremely powerful asset, and explains why their type of warfare is successful only *at home.*

Mao Zedong Creates a Doctrine

In order to see the devastating potential of the rule to strike at the enemy's weakness while nullifying his strength, we can find no better example than that of the guerrilla war waged by Mao Zedong. Guerrilla war is an alternate form of conflict that has run alongside conventional war from the earliest days of organized armies 4,500 or more years ago. In fact, it is the original, most primitive form of war.

The lives of prehistoric people may not have been wholly "solitary, poor, nasty, brutish and short," as the seventeenth-century English philosopher Thomas Hobbes maintained, but they definitely involved guerrilla-like war. Excavations of Paleolithic cemeteries in Europe and Egypt give ample proof of methodical killings of men, women, and children. And there is solid evidence that raids, ambushes, and surprise attacks on settlements constituted a major component of tribal warfare.[7]

Irregular or guerrilla war is, in fact, the most successful form of conflict, but for most of recorded history it received little notice. The great campaigns and battles of conventional armies from ancient Sumerian and Egyptian times onward were so dramatic and decisive in determining the rise and fall of states and empires that they inspired the majority of literature, history, and art. The obscure, mostly anonymous, and largely unrecorded clashes that settled the fates of tribes and peoples elsewhere on earth seemed insignificant by comparison. Even when a famous commander came to grief against tribes that refused to fight orthodox battles—as happened to Alexander the Great in central Asia in 329 B.C.[8]—historians and military men tended to explain the defeat away as an accident or chance event.

Despite countless examples through the centuries of decisive victories following a policy of avoiding battle, the concept did not affect mainstream thinking about war or its practice until the last half of the twentieth century. And it got attention then only because orthodox generals using the most modern conventional weapons lost wars to irregular warriors who refused to fight standard battles. The scene of their exposure to a new way of thinking was Vietnam from 1945 to 1975.

But it was Mao Zedong who produced the intellectual basis, theory, and procedures for successful modern guerrilla war. Mao developed his ideas during the two-decade struggle that ended in 1949 for control of China between the Communists and the Nationalists.[9] The Communist leader Vo Nyugen Giap used Mao's teachings to develop the tactics and strategy that defeated first the French and then the Americans in Vietnam.

Mao was quick to acknowledge, however, that the Chinese strategist Sun Tzu, in his *Art of War*, written about 400 B.C., gave him practically all the ideas he incorporated into his theory. Sun Tzu's axioms or admonitions make no distinction between orthodox and irregular war; they apply to any form of conflict, and thus demonstrate that all kinds of war follow the same principles.

The primary aim of Mao's system was to direct small but frequent violent attacks against enemy towns, bases, depots, and lines of communication. Attacks occurred in many different places and at unexpected times. The goal was to force the enemy to disperse his forces widely and in small detachments to protect vital points. Even guarded, these positions remained vulnerable, because the enemy could not predict which position Mao's forces would attack. The purpose was to confuse the enemy, make him uneasy and insecure, and therefore demoralize him.[10] This was a process of nullifying the enemy's strength.

Although Mao developed bases for his forces in out-of-the-way places, notably a small rural soviet in the Wuyi Mountains of southeastern China around the city of Ruijin in 1928–1934, he ruled that all such refuges had to be abandoned if the enemy surrounded them and forced the guerrillas into a defensive battle that they must win or die. "The tactics of defense have no place in the realm of guerrilla warfare," he wrote.[11]

Since a country or movement engaged in guerrilla warfare abandons the concept of a formal military line of resistance, the enemy can move throughout the country's entire territory. Consequently, everywhere is in the rear of the enemy. That is why guerrillas, without a defended region of their own, must depend upon the people for food, support, refuge, and spying on the enemy's movements. To gain the backing of the peasants, who made up 80 percent of the Chinese population, Mao seized the fields of rich gentry landlords, divided them among peasant families, and reduced high taxes and high interest on loans, which had kept peasants in poverty for centuries.

Mao also insisted that guerrillas cannot defend specific places. Their strength lies at the other extreme. They can strike fast and hard with small forces against vulnerable enemy targets, and then get away. In contrast, conventional armies are locked into defense of their lines of communication and supply, bases, airfields, ports, garrisons, outposts, and occupied cities. If an orthodox army's supply line is cut, its means of subsistence are lost. The traditional army will go to any lengths to protect its supplies and depots. This forces armies to disperse, and gives guerrillas innumerable targets at which they can strike. It is not necessary to actually destroy those targets; merely the threat of attack keeps the enemy army divided and largely inactive.

Guerrillas thus have the initiative. They can select when, where, and how to attack. The side that holds the initiative has liberty of action, and can dictate events. The supporting population provides eyes and ears to tell guerrillas where enemy forces are located. With superior information, guerrillas can engage under conditions of their own choosing. In attacks they seek maximum surprise and overwhelming superiority in numbers. They decoy the enemy to believe they are going to hit a point in one direction, but actually strike a target in a different direction. They use ambushes or approach covertly in darkness. Attacks are sudden, sharp, vicious, and of short duration, and the forces get away to safety fast.

Vietnam: Successful Irregular War

In Giap (born 1912), the Vietnamese Communists possessed a great general, who applied the teachings of Mao to free Vietnam from French colonial rule, then to break American support of the reactionary government of South Vietnam in Saigon (now Ho Chi Minh City). Giap summarized his operations by repeating the classic definition of guerrilla warfare: avoiding the enemy where he was strong, and attacking him where he was weak.

Giap urged his men to exhaust the enemy by small victories. The main objective was to destroy enemy manpower. To achieve this, he stressed the tactical principles of "initiative, flexibility, rapidity, surprise, suddenness of attack and retreat."[12]

In order to carry this plan out, Giap trained his soldiers to concentrate quickly, take battle positions at once, and depart fast to avoid being spotted and attacked. The usual pattern was to arouse enemy suspicions at one or more false attack points, and then to strike at a wholly unexpected place. In battles against the French especially, the Communists leaked misleading information to double agents, and marched forces toward a pretended target, but then moved stealthily at night in the real direction of attack, avoiding villages and inhabited areas to reduce chances of being detected.

The Communists generally approached a French position by infiltration at night. The soldiers usually moved individually and at wide intervals. This technique concealed them from air attack, and normally from ground detection. It also unnerved French forces. The Communists were so stealthy that they sometimes infiltrated right through an enemy position, and were able to attack it on two or more sides.

The actual onslaught normally opened with a small engineer, or sapper, force that crept to a critical point and blew a breach with dynamite, sometimes tied on the end of a bamboo pole inserted into wire entanglements. Behind were assault infantry units, which rushed in and tried to overwhelm the French post. In reserve was another force with the mission of covering the shock troops with fire, assisting them in the attack if successful, or protecting their retreat if repulsed.

The French relied on roads to move troops and deliver food, ammunition, and other supplies. The Communists therefore possessed ready-made opportunities for ambush. They often generated ambushes by besieging a French outpost, making no serious effort to capture it, but inducing the French to send a rescue expedition from the nearest base. They then set up a blocking position, and attacked the relief column as it came by. The French were never able to prevent such ambushes, and feared them till the end of the war.

Throughout the war, the Communists gained strength from the people, who regularly hid them, and the Communists, in turn, promised to give the peasants land and reduce their taxes and interest on loans, as well as to end forced labor. The Communists also assassinated leaders who opposed them. On the whole the populace supported the Communists because they were attempting to drive out the imperial French and achieve Vietnamese independence.

The French abandoned Indochina (Vietnam, Laos, Cambodia) in May 1954 at the Geneva conference after suffering the staggering loss of 13,000 troops at Dien Bien Phu in northwestern Vietnam, an isolated base that the Communists surrounded and forced to surrender.

The Western powers and the Communist bloc agreed at Geneva to divide Vietnam "temporarily" along the seventeenth parallel, the Communists controlling the north, and a reactionary government under a Roman Catholic bachelor, Ngo Dinh Diem, ruling the south. The stated aim was to hold an all-Vietnam election in two years to reunite the country. But Diem knew he would lose any free election and refused to hold it, instead purging all the Communists he could find and suppressing the Buddhists, the majority faith in the country. These moves set off a new revolt in the south. With the Communists about to take over, the United States encouraged a coup by South Vietnamese generals in November 1963. The result was the assassination of Diem and the first of a series of military regimes, which represented no popular forces, and depended entirely on American support.

President Lyndon B. Johnson decided to assume conduct of the war early in 1965. But American doctrine was focused on fighting a "mid-intensity" (nonnuclear) war against the Soviet Union. This type of conflict emphasized heavy weapons, direct confrontation of the enemy, set-piece battles, high expenditures of ammunition, bombs, and missiles, and occupation of enemy territory. American military commanders wanted to carry out search-and-destroy missions in Vietnam, and maintained the belief, articulated by Lieutenant General Lionel C. McGarr, chief of the U.S. Army's advisory group in Vietnam (1960–62), that the objective was to "find, fix, fight, and finish the enemy."[13] American commanders never overcame the conviction that "finishing" the enemy in battle was their goal.[14]

U.S. military leaders found it difficult to understand the "low-intensity conflict" being waged by the Communists, which depended upon lightly armed infantry and firepower restraint, and was unconcerned with holding ground. American military leadership was never able to resolve this contradiction, trying to the last to fight a conventional war against the Vietcong, or VC (Vietnamese Communists). But such a war was always elusive, because the Vietcong usually refused to meet American forces in pitched battles.

Even in the cases when they did engage U.S. forces, they withdrew after inflicting casualties. This was Giap's primary aim. The Communist leaders were prepared to lose ten Vietnamese soldiers to one American. They were convinced the American people would not sustain even that ratio of losses indefinitely, and would demand withdrawal from the war.

The American search-and-destroy tactical system was immensely counterproductive. The basic plan was to make contact with the enemy, then withdraw, so that bombers, attack helicopters, and artillery could blast the enemy. As one American general described the procedure, "You don't fight this fellow rifle to rifle. You locate him and back away. Blow hell out of him, and then police up."[15]

For one thing, the practice was unbelievably expensive (the United States used twice as many tons of explosives in Vietnam as in all of its campaigns in World War II), and seldom hit the Vietcong or North Vietnamese. The Communist soldiers normally got away before the shells and bombs began to land. Meanwhile, many thousands of innocent civilians died or were injured.

Lieutenant Colonel John Paul Vann, a U.S. Army adviser, expressed the immense frustration that this sort of war generated among Americans. The Vietcong could be whipped, he asserted, "if they would only stand and fight."[16]

Yet this was exactly what the Communists would *not* do. And the American military leaders—like the French leaders before them—were unable to transform their thinking or their tactics to deal with the reality they faced.

The search-and-destroy objective soon came into conflict with the U.S. Army's obligation to defend the many army and air force bases in Vietnam. By 1966 about half of American combat forces were protecting base areas and lines of communications. The proportion of static defensive troops never went below 40 percent.[17]

The military also needed large numbers of service troops to deliver ammunition, food, fuel, and other supplies, and to maintain and repair vast numbers of vehicles, aircraft, and weapons. Americans thus were dispersed all over the country at heavily defended bases. As a consequence, they could not field any more fighting troops than the Vietcong and North Vietnamese. And since they could not determine where, when, or in what strength the enemy would attack, those troops assumed a largely passive role.

The great strength of the American army, extremely heavy firepower, was therefore wasted because the Communists did not wait around to be pounded by American shells, missiles, and bombs. U.S. forces might "find" Communist units, but they seldom could "fix, fight, and finish" them.

The silhouette of the kind of war the Americans would face emerged as early as the summer and fall of 1965, in the early stages of U.S. intervention, but went unrecognized. General Giap baited the American commander, General William C. Westmoreland, with a prize he couldn't resist, an openly committed North Vietnamese regular army division of 10,000 men in the heavily forested, sparsely inhabited mountains of central Vietnam, near the Cambodian border. Giap made threatening gestures to send this division to the sea, and cut South Vietnam in half.

This was the kind of war American commanders dreamed about. Here was an enemy who could be found, fixed, fought, and finished. Or so they thought.

The Communist division, or "field force," under General Chu Hoy Man was located about thirty-five miles southwest of the town of Pleiku, a South Vietnamese stronghold. Man had positioned his men in and around a limestone massif full of springs called Chu Pong, 2,400 feet above sea level, and 1,200 feet above the surrounding rolling plateau.[18]

General Man opened his campaign to lure the Americans into the highlands by sending a regiment to surround a U.S. outpost at the village of Duc Co, thirteen miles north of Chu Pong. Duc Co was garrisoned by thirteen Americans and 400 Montagnards, who were mercenaries from mountain tribes. General Man's aim was not to capture Duc Co, but to lure a relief column out, so he could ambush it. On August 9 he succeeded: an armored South Vietnamese task force left Pleiku. The North

Vietnamese assaulted it but couldn't destroy it because it was protected by American-made M-41 tanks mounting 76-mm guns and M-113 armored personnel carriers (APCs). General Man pulled his regiment back to Chu Pong.

Man then sent two regiments against another American-Montagnard outpost at the village of Plei Me, twenty-five miles south of Pleiku. One regiment assaulted the outpost on October 19, while the other regiment set up a trap on the dirt road connecting Plei Me with the highway to Pleiku.

The Plei Me attack was extremely violent, but again the aim was not to capture the post. The Communists used automatic weapons, 82-mm mortars, 75-mm recoilless rifles, and rocket launchers to bombard the compound, destroying several bunkers, while sappers blew a hole in the razor-wire outer fence with dynamite. The Communist commander deliberately limited the infantry assault through the opening to a size large enough to make the defenders think they were about to be overrun, but not large enough actually to do so. The assaulting soldiers died in a hail of gunfire.

The next morning American bombers pounded the enemy around the outpost, causing many casualties, but costing four bombers, an attack helicopter, and seven C-123 supply ships destroyed by ground fire.

Meanwhile the second North Vietnamese regiment ambushed a South Vietnamese relief column sent from Pleiku, and armed with tanks and APCs. The ambush on October 23 happened in a dense forest about eighteen miles south of Pleiku. The tanks and APCs beat off the assault, but not before a great deal of damage had been done. The ferocity of the attack so stunned the South Vietnamese commander that he refused to move for two days, until artillery of the U.S. 1st Cavalry Division (Airmobile), dropped by helicopter nearby, delivered shell concentrations ahead of the column as it crept on to Plei Me.

The 1st Cavalry was the only division in the U.S. Army that was fully mobile by helicopters, and its commander, Brigadier General Harry W. O. Kinnard, dispersed helicopters over a wide region in an intensive search for the North Vietnamese. Some troops dropped from UH-1D Hueys lift helicopters ("slicks") into small open areas (landing zones, or LZs) in the forest, and then patrolled outward. When soldiers or choppers found enemy soldiers, a "rapid-reaction force" at a rear base or LZ was to land on or near the enemy to bring him to battle. The infantry were to be supported by Huey attack helicopters ("hogs") mounting machine guns and rockets, as well as air force bombers. Kinnard also planned to drop 105-mm howitzers (with a range of 13,000 meters) into nearby landing zones by medium-lift CH-47 Chinook choppers to provide artillery support.

The North Vietnamese had not expected to be spied on so effectively, and the helicopters caught many of them in the open, especially as foliage was light because it was the dry season. The first American success occurred on November 1, when helicopters spotted men west of Plei Me. A platoon dropped at an LZ nearby, and seized a North Vietnamese hospital, killing fifteen and capturing forty-three. A North Vietnamese battalion trying to retreat in the vicinity sent a small detachment to strike the platoon, killing seven and wounding nineteen, allowing the battalion to get away, then breaking contact itself and vanishing.

Over the next several days, 1st Cavalry Division troops collided with several small North Vietnamese detachments retreating westward. The Communists fought as long as they wanted to, then withdrew, leaving an empty battlefield. The Americans only afterward recognized the ploy being used against them.

Meanwhile a Vietcong detachment moved up on a brigade headquarters and helicopter laager at a tea plantation eight miles southwest of Pleiku. On the night of November 12, 1965, it dropped a hundred 60-mm and 82-mm mortar rounds on the plantation, damaging a number of choppers, and killing seven and wounding twenty-three men. The attack demonstrated the vulnerability of American positions to sneak attacks, and led commanders to keep substantial portions of their combat strength guarding rear "forts" in "Indian Country." Thus began the dispersal of American forces to defensive "forts" all over the country—any one of which could be attacked by the Vietcong.

American commanders eventually recognized that the North Vietnamese were retreating back to Chu Pong, and early on November 14 a battalion commander, Lieutenant Colonel Harold Moore, spotted from a helicopter an open space, about a hundred yards wide, at the foot of Chu Pong. He dubbed it "X-ray" and at once began sending in elements of his battalion by helicopter to occupy the space and spread out from it to seize Chu Pong. One company started up a finger ridge leading to the top of the mountain.

North Vietnamese outposts saw the Americans as they landed, and General Man sent elements of his division down the slope. The Americans met withering small-arms and mortar fire, and were stopped cold. Colonel Moore sent another company to assist the first, but it too was halted by heavy fire. Meanwhile U.S. artillery and air force spotters in helicopters directed fire and air strikes on the lower portions of Chu Pong. But the strikes had little effect on the enemy, who infiltrated the landing zone itself, and began lacing it with fire, while North Vietnamese gunners shot down a propeller-driven A-1E Skyraider.

As the last of Moore's battalion came in, enemy fire disabled two helicopters. Wounded men piled up at the battalion command post. Enemy fire prevented practically any movement.

Next morning another company landed at X-ray to reinforce Colonel Moore's men, while a full battalion under Lieutenant Colonel Robert Tully landed during the night at a clearing, code-named Victor, about two miles southeast, and moved overland to X-ray early in the morning.

At first light North Vietnamese forces launched a fierce frontal attack against the Americans on the lower slopes of Chu Pong. American firepower held the enemy off, though some got so close that they engaged Americans in hand-to-hand fighting. Around 9:00 A.M., the North Vietnamese began withdrawing, using snipers tied in trees to cover their retreat.

Then, during the night of November 15–16, the North Vietnamese mounted numerous small probes and a single company-sized attack that got nowhere. Early on the morning of November 16 the Americans discovered that the enemy had vanished. General Man had used the nighttime attacks to cover his withdrawal. The Americans had lost seventy men dead and 121 wounded, but they counted the bodies of 834 enemy, and estimated that 500 more were dead and others wounded.

On November 17 the Americans abandoned X-ray. The same day, however, a North Vietnamese regiment ambushed the 2nd Battalion of the 7th Cavalry Regiment as it was marching overland to LZ Albany, about four miles north of X-ray. The ambush came near to being a massacre. The Americans suffered 151 killed, 121 wounded, and four missing, although the Vietnamese lost about 400 men before withdrawing. The last engagement was on November 18, when a Vietcong battalion struck LZ Columbus, three miles northeast of X-ray, disabling two helicopters, killing three and wounding thirteen soldiers.

On November 19 helicopters pulled all Americans out of LZ Albany and LZ Columbus. The Chu Pong campaign was over.

The Americans listed 1,300 enemy dead, against 224 American dead. Perhaps the Americans were overzealous in their body count of the enemy, but Communist losses clearly were greater than American, and General Westmoreland took the results as a victory. To him it seemed the Americans could win a war of attrition quickly.

Yet ominous lessons were not learned. The first was that U.S. forces had responded only to enemy action. They had initiated the strike itself, but everything else had been a reaction to North Vietnamese moves. The second was that the enemy forces disengaged exactly when and how they wanted, holding Americans in place till they got away. The Communists could decide how long they wished to fight, and how many casualties they were willing to accept. The initiative was firmly in Communist hands. The Communists also learned a lesson on Chu Pong: American firepower was greater than they could bear, and they quickly reverted to their tried-and-true strategy of guerrilla strikes by small forces.

The Communists challenged American forces head-on only once more, in the Tet offensive beginning January 31, 1968, when more than 70,000 Communist soldiers surged into a hundred South Vietnamese cities, including Saigon. Though the Tet offensive failed, it demonstrated that the Communists had not been defeated, and caused President Johnson's subsequent refusal to stand for reelection. American disillusionment with the war followed, leading to withdrawal of American forces, and the surrender of South Vietnam in 1975.

Guerrilla Successes Through History

In the last quarter of the twentieth century a number of studies and books advocated change in American military doctrine to reflect the lessons taught in Vietnam. But until the Soviet Union collapsed in 1991, the fixation on mid-intensity war and huge conventional battles with heavy weapons prevailed. In the decade following, military brass undertook some restructuring, but progress was slow and reticence great. Only the events of September 11, 2001, at last convinced military leaders that they faced a new kind of war, and that the military's entire approach had to be altered radically.

Because this recognition has now come, we need to examine how this type of war was fought in the past to learn how we can win it today. When Rome, for example, could not challenge the cavalry of the great Carthaginian general Hannibal in 217 B.C., Quintus Fabius Maximus remained in the hills where Hannibal's horsemen were ineffective, and launched repeated guerrilla attacks that kept Rome's allies loyal and prevented Hannibal from founding a base in Italy. His methods gave the world the concept of "Fabian strategy."[19]

Another remarkable case of the effective use of guerrilla tactics is Scotland, which preserved its independence from England by following for 250 years, with occasional lapses, the "testament" of Robert the Bruce (1274–1329). For years Robert had seen the brave "schiltrons," or massed bodies of Scottish spearmen, shattered by arrow storms from English longbows followed by charges of English armored knights. He admonished the Scots to abandon this direct challenge, maintain the defensive, fight only in strong positions among hills and morasses, trust to retirement into the woods rather than fortifying castles, ravage the open country in front of the advancing enemy, and confine their attacks to night surprises and ambushes.[20] When the Scots did this, the English could get nowhere. When they faced the English head-to-head, as occasionally happened after taking bad advice, they lost.

Another important success in irregular war—conducted by a French leader, Constable Bertrand du Guesclin—could have ended the Hundred

Years War if French leaders had heeded the lesson. They did not, and the war dragged on another half century. The French had discovered that they would lose if they continued to attack English knights lined up on foot with lances poised and English longbows arrayed on either side, as had happened in the disastrous battles of Crécy in 1346 and Poitiers in 1356. Longbow arrows could penetrate French armor with devastating effect, and the wall of lances could stop cavalry charges.

In a land of few archers, the French could not counter English long-bows directly. So, when a nine-year truce ended in 1369, Constable du Guesclin realized he had to avoid battle. Wherever English armies appeared, Guesclin sacrificed the countryside, and sent the people behind the walls of towns or castles.[21] When the English passed by, Guesclin's forces emerged to hang on their rear, cutting off foraging parties, killing stragglers, and destroying isolated detachments.

Using this strategy, even the most formidable English campaigns accomplished nothing. For example, in 1373, John of Gaunt led an English army across France from Calais to Bordeaux. He captured no town and won no engagement. The French refused to fight. The English burned a broad swath through central France, but arrived at Bordeaux in the autumn cold, hungry, low in numbers, almost destitute of horses, and riddled with dysentery and fever.

Meanwhile Guesclin besieged English-held castles or towns where the garrisons were weak. If no succor came, he captured them. If it did, he withdrew and struck another weakly held English post. Guesclin made surprise attacks at night on unsuspecting enemy units or ill-defended towns, and ambushed parties on the roads. But he refused to attack any English force, even one smaller, if it had time to form up in a good defensive position, and throw out archers on either wing.

The system regained huge tracts of territory, and the effect on public opinion in England was precisely that of the indecisive results in Vietnam in the United States. Ministers were accused of mismanaging the war, some were charged with malice or treason, more troops were sent to France but achieved nothing, and an immense wave of dissatisfaction swept over the country.[22]

The French had found the formula to beat the English. But Guesclin died in 1380, and the aristocracy returned to their old habits, leading in 1415, at Agincourt, to a headlong attack against another English army arrayed with knights in the middle with lances and bowmen on the flanks with longbows. And, once again, the French chivalry suffered devastating defeat. A peasant girl, Joan of Arc (1412–1431), at last relieved the English siege of Orleans in 1429 and inspired the French people to drive out the English.

One of the most decisive collisions in history between conventional and irregular forces occurred in 1808–1814 between the armies of Napoleon and the people of Spain. Napoleon occupied Spain and Portugal in 1807, and placed his brother Joseph on the Spanish throne, propped up by French bayonets. Spanish officials showed little resistance, but the people revolted on May 2, 1808, and embarked on a *guerrilla* (Spanish for "little war"). From this the world derived the generic word for this kind of war.

Local insurgents formed small independent bands that struck at isolated French garrisons, towns, and supply columns. When French forces pursued them, they vanished into the rough Spanish sierras. French garrisons in cities and forts could only be supplied with food and ammunition by powerful French columns, which could withstand repeated ambushes on the roads. By 1812 the French had been virtually immobilized by these elusive bands, and vast tracts of Spain were free of French troops. This made the British campaign to reconquer the Iberian peninsula much easier.

One of the most famous of the guerrilla leaders was Francisco Espoy y Mina, who operated in the difficult country bordering Navarre and Aragon in northern Spain. Frequently Mina was beset on all sides by flying columns of enemy troops. Mina dispersed his bands into small parties that escaped on goat paths in the mountains that only they could follow. After the enemy passed, they descended on convoys or blockhouses that held French garrisons. Mina was pursued often by forces many times his own, but never could be caught.

Guerrillas often seized important urban places, and could be ousted only after the French mounted major offensives. One such occasion was

August 14–15, 1811, when another chieftain, Juan Diaz Porlier, drove the French garrison out of Santander on the Bay of Biscay, caused hundreds of casualties, and withdrew only when strong French reinforcements arrived.

As Sir Charles Oman, the great historian of the Peninsular War, wrote, "Lightly moving guerrilla bands, unhampered by a base to defend or a train to weigh them down, and well served as to intelligence by the residents of the countryside, can paralyze the action of an infinitely larger number of regular troops."[23]

When Sir Charles wrote these words in 1908, he noted—as practically no one else did at the time or for well over half a century thereafter—that the Boer War of 1899–1902 remarkably resembled the Spanish guerrilla war in almost every aspect, including its success and implications for the future.

The British were largely able to portray to the world that they won the Boer War, between themselves and two tiny Dutch-speaking republics, Transvaal and the Orange Free State, deep in the interior of South Africa. In fact, the British were thoroughly bested by the Boers, Dutch for "farmer," who fought a guerrilla war from 1900 to 1902 with never more than 15,000 men, which tied up a British army of 250,000 troops.

The Boers gained virtually everything they were fighting for—the promise of independence, retention of their Afrikaans dialect as an official language, and continued suppression of the much more numerous blacks of the country. The British advertised as a victory the Boers' agreement to recognize the British king as their sovereign. But this was more symbolic than real, because the British also agreed to give back to the Boers control of their country, and, in 1910, granted them and the British in South Africa dominion status, or complete independence.[24]

Military commanders saw few military lessons in the guerrilla warfare in Spain and South Africa, and they also largely ignored the significance of another astonishing victory of irregular fighters, in Arabia during World War I. This campaign was the intellectual creation of a legendary English officer, T. E. Lawrence, or Lawrence of Arabia (1888–1935).[25] An honors history graduate of Oxford University in 1910, Lawrence, who spoke Arabic fluently, was posted in 1916 to assist Hussein, sharif of Mecca, in his revolt against the Turks, who had occupied Arabia for centuries. The Turks were enemies of the British. They, with German help, were entrenched at Gaza in Palestine, attempting to seize the Suez Canal.

The British had instigated the revolt mainly to get the Arabs to eliminate the 25,000-man Turkish garrison at Medina, and wanted Lawrence to persuade Hussein to mobilize an Arab army to break the Turks' supply line, the Damascus-Medina railway, and then attack and destroy the garrison.

Such an idea was an illusion. It would require the Arabs not only to recruit an army, but also to acquire and learn to use heavy weapons. The British were unlikely to provide such weapons. Moreover, the Arabs had no generals skilled in conventional war, while the Bedouin tribal structure rendered the Arabs incapable of the military discipline and organization necessary to confront the Turks in open battle.

Something the British army leaders did not see was that the best place for the Medina garrison was Medina, because there it contributed nothing to the war. The Arabs at most could only *evict* the garrison, in which case it would move up to reinforce the Turkish-German army at Gaza.

The Achilles' heel of the Turks was the Damascus-Medina railway. Yet it should not, as the British command in Cairo demanded, be cut permanently. Instead, Lawrence believed the line should be sabotaged regularly but kept barely open, just capable of feeding the Medina garrison. This would force the Turks to devote most of their strength to defending the line, leaving little energy for other actions. Lawrence was sure the Turks would remain in Medina for as long as possible. As Moslems, their possession of the holy city confirmed their legitimacy as the sovereign power. Accordingly, keeping the garrison at Medina would have the same effect as placing the 25,000 men in a prisoner-of-war camp.

Lawrence realized he could use the existing skills of the Bedouins to come out of their natural environment, the Arabian Desert, through which much of the railway line ran, and, with light arms and few more skills than they already possessed as desert mounted men, break the railway, disappear rapidly into the desert, and reappear at some other place, repeatedly. This would create a military stalemate.

Unlike a conventional army, Lawrence wrote, the Bedouins could be "an influence, an idea, a thing intangible, invulnerable, without front or back, drifting about like a gas." In comparison with the Bedouin who "might be a vapor, blowing where he listed," conventional armies are "like plants, immobile, firm-rooted, nourished through long stems to the head."[26] That is, an invading army can only survive if it is regularly replenished with food, ammunition, and other supplies delivered from a distant source.

Although the British command at Cairo balked, Lawrence carried out this policy, repeatedly breaking the railway line using simple explosives, and keeping the garrison at Medina until the British army cracked through the Turkish-German line in Palestine in 1918 and forced Turkey out of the war.

Irregular forces have provided some of the best examples in history of the rule to strike at enemy weakness while keeping the enemy's strength useless. These lessons remain pertinent because the aim of avoiding what is strong and striking what is weak is as important as it has ever been.

3

Defend, Then Attack

IN ORDINARY MILITARY encounters, one side generally attacks because it thinks it's stronger, and the other defends because it feels it's weaker. In such cases the defender usually hopes merely to fend off destruction, or to gain enough time to withdraw the rest of his forces. There is, however, a much more successful method available to a defender who has a better weapon or who employs a superior tactical system.

If a commander has either, he has the opportunity to defend so successfully that the attacker is weakened and demoralized, whereupon the defender can *then* go over to the attack himself and defeat or destroy the enemy. The rule of war involved here is to gain possession of a better weapon or a better tactical system, induce the enemy to launch a fruitless attack, and then to attack oneself.

Some great commanders have understood this rule well. Even when they could employ no better weapons than their enemies, they have tried to make their tactical methods or their armies better, or, if not better, *different*, so that their enemies would be baffled or uncertain when encountering them.

But this has not been the case for the great run of commanders throughout history. As a rule they have failed to understand the need for a unique advantage, and—to avoid being surprised themselves—have strived to make their armies *like* the armies they opposed, in weapons as well as techniques. If one side developed a new and more effective tactic or weapon, the other side tried to copy it. When the Persian king Darius discovered Alexander the Great's cavalry were armed with a long lance superior to his own horsemen's short javelins, he attempted to adopt it, but was unable to complete the transition before his armies were shattered.

Armies consequently have usually aimed for symmetry in arms and in tactics. In practice, however, military leaders have often refused to match the strengths of their enemies, or have failed to recognize the advantages their enemy's weapons or tactics provided. Moreover, most military officers have felt there was an *accepted* way of engaging in combat, and anyone who operated differently was being sneaky or unfair. This explains why regular soldiers have always hated guerrillas or any kind of anomalous, unexpected actions.

A British historian of the Japanese attack in Malaya in December 1941, for example, complained that the Japanese refused to drive down the roads, as they should have done. Instead they infiltrated through the jungles, coming out far to the rear and forming roadblocks, forcing British troops—who *were* on the roads—to surrender. To this Briton, the Japanese were terribly unsportsmanlike.

One of the most baffling arenas for military leaders has been defensive warfare. Imaginative commanders, however, have been able to find ways to overcome the seemingly intractable problem of an inferior force encountering a superior force.

Down the ages, inferior forces have usually had to stand on the defensive to survive against more powerful enemies. Fortunately, defensive weapons historically have been stronger than offensive weapons. In ancient times, city or fortress walls posed barriers to invading armies. The strength of the ancient Greek phalanx—a formidable mass of men armed with long spears and protected by armor—lay in its capacity to defend against a frontal attack by another phalanx or by cavalry. Nothing, neither charging men nor galloping horses, could penetrate a forest of leveled spears projecting from a solid phalanx. The phalanx's only weaknesses were its need to operate on level ground, and its inability to turn to face a threat on its flanks. In later centuries, single-shot muskets with attached bayonets formed the basis for defense. Salvos of musket fire could often stop attacks by infantry. When cavalry charged, musketeers could form into a square with bayonets pointed outward and generally stop the assault.

But a defense, even if successful, can rarely produce a decision. Unless the attacking force is broken up, forced to retreat, or destroyed, its power of movement remains, and it can fight other engagements that might bring victory. Hence commanders of weaker forces have always sought ways to transform a defensive standoff into an offensive victory.

The principle of "defend, then attack" has given weaker armies the potential of winning decisive victories. The rule, of course, can be applied by powerful armies as well. But it has been employed more often to transform a dangerous position of weakness into an opportunity for victory. Its success depends not only upon possession of a better weapon or a better tactical system, but also upon an opponent who cannot or does not understand what's happening.

The Byzantines: Belisarius and Narses

Two of the greatest generals who mastered the principle of defending, then attacking, were the Byzantines Belisarius (A.D. 505–565) and Narses (born A.D. 478). They served Justinian (483–565), the greatest of the Eastern Roman, or Byzantine, emperors. Born in the Balkans to an Illyrian peasant, and married to the famous Theodora, a former courtesan and dancer, Justinian—primarily owing to the military actions of Belisarius and Narses—held the eastern frontier against Persian attacks, and recovered portions of Africa, Italy, and Spain that had been lost to barbarian invasions.

Byzantium, with its capital in Constantinople (modern-day Istanbul), was the eastern, Greek-speaking half of the Roman Empire that survived after the Western Empire, with its capital in Rome, disintegrated in the fourth and fifth centuries from barbarian incursions. The barbarian tribes—Franks, Burgundians, Vandals, Angles and Saxons, Goths, and others—carved out impermanent kingdoms, fought among themselves, and submerged the classical civilization of the West in the Dark Ages that lasted until about the year 1000.

The Eastern Empire survived largely because the walls of Constantinople were virtually invulnerable, and because Justinian adopted a defensive strategy that relied on the army created by Belisarius and Narses. This army came to depend on the cataphract, a formidable armored warrior who originated at the time of Justinian. He was mounted on a large warhorse and carried a long lance, a sword, and a powerful compound bow of laminated bone, wood, and sinew. This bow had been developed in the Eurasian steppes, and was short enough for the cataphract to wield on horseback.

Belisarius and Narses could scarcely have been more different. Belisarius, a soldier since boyhood, was tall, well-built, handsome, rash, inventive, and full of ambition. Narses was a court eunuch, short, lean, wizened, calculating, a flatterer, dissembler, and sinister intriguer. Both were able, but Narses, though he only occasionally served as a general, was probably the better of the two. Narses was far more influential with Justinian than Belisarius, because he, being a eunuch, could never set up a dynasty and replace Justinian on the throne, while Belisarius always posed that threat.

Justinian never gave either commander adequate forces for the immense tasks he assigned them. But he always gave Belisarius the least. That motivated Belisarius to devise new ways to defeat enemies who usually far outnumbered him.

In December 536, after conquering Sicily and southern Italy, Belisarius entered Rome with 5,000 men, and two months later was besieged there by 20,000 Ostrogoths ("eastern Goths"), a fierce Germanic people who had occupied most of Italy. The Ostrogoths controlled present-day Ukraine until A.D. 370, when the Huns, a violent and predatory tribe from deeper into the Eurasian steppes, conquered them. The Hunnish empire collapsed in 453, and the Ostrogoths moved into Italy, where they were ruled ably by their king Theodoric from 493 to his death in 526. His departure destabilized the kingdom, but the newly elected king Wittigis was seeking to restore Ostrogoth power, while Justinian was trying to demolish it and regain Italy for the empire.

A group of Gothic cavalry nearly killed Belisarius the day after he arrived at Rome. The Byzantine general had left a garrison to hold the fortified Salarian Bridge over the Anio River outside the city. When a body of Goths reached the bridge, the garrison took to its heels, but didn't tell Belisarius. Next morning Belisarius, with 1,000 cavalry, rode toward the bridge, and was set upon by a large force of Goths. He survived by a near miracle, and galloped back into Rome.

Though his situation looked precarious, particularly because the Goths outnumbered his forces many times over, Belisarius had already spotted their two fundamental weaknesses. They were inept at besieging walled cities, and their horsemen were armed only with swords and spears.

The first weakness determined Belisarius's strategy. He knew he could not meet the Goths in open battle because his army was so tiny it would be overwhelmed. Accordingly, he made the utmost of Rome's walls and fortifications. The only way the Goths could capture a fortified city like Rome was by starving it out. This took time, and in the siege of Rome the Goths wore themselves down. Poor sanitation in the camps they built brought on disease and sickness, but their greatest weakness was that they soon consumed all the food in the immediate vicinity, and had to send small groups to forage far over the countryside. These journeys not only exhausted the Goths, but Belisarius dispatched long-range raids that pounced on isolated detachments and killed many men. As the siege continued, the Goths became steadily weaker.

The second Gothic tactical weakness—their inadequate arms—determined Belisarius's battle methods. All the mounted Byzantines were archers, employing the compound bow. None of the Gothic cavalry could use the bow and arrow. The Goths had archers, employing a short bow weaker than the compound bow. But archers were foot soldiers, and could enter battle only under the cover of heavily armed cavalry. Though Belisarius had to remain on the defensive, he had a superior weapon. If he could induce the Goths to attack, he could so weaken them that he could then go over to attack himself and win. Belisarius understood well the principle of defend, then attack.

The Gothic cavalry could protect themselves only if they were able to get in close to Byzantine cavalry, where they could use their hand weapons, while the Byzantine mounted archers would have insufficient space to draw their bows. Belisarius thus saw that his bowmen had to remain out of reach, and do their damage at a distance.

Belisarius put this knowledge to good use. He sent 200 of his cavalry to seize a hill a short distance beyond the Salarian Gate. When the Goths came to engage, he told his men to fight at a distance with bows and arrows only. Under no circumstances were they to use spears and swords. When their arrows were exhausted, they were to hurry back behind the nearby Roman walls.

A strong force of Goths charged up the hillside to dislodge the intruders. But the Byzantines poured flight after flight of arrows into the densely packed enemy, pulling away from the few who were able to get close. When the Byzantines ran out of arrows, they galloped back to Rome, followed by the Gothic cavalry, who recoiled before arrow-firing catapults and bowmen mounted on the walls.

Belisarius repeated the tactic twice more in the following days, with identical results, causing huge Gothic losses. The significance of the superior Byzantine weapon—the compound bow of laminated bone, wood, and sinew—was lost on King Wittigis. He decided that if the Byzantines could come out, draw an attack, and win, so could his cavalry. Accordingly, Wittigis ordered 500 horsemen to seize a hill outside the range of the catapults on the walls, and wait for the Byzantines to attack. Belisarius sent out 1,000 mounted archers, who rode round and round the massed Gothic cavalry, coming nowhere close, but decimating them with arrows.[1]

Belisarius thus overcame his shortage of manpower by weakening the Goths with a combination of small tactical engagements and a long, fruitless siege. Not only did Belisarius force the Goths to give up their siege of Rome, but, by using the same methods, ousted them from other Italian cities. By 541, five years after Belisarius entered Italy, the Goths had lost all but the northern part of the country, including their capital, Ravenna. Exasperated, they deposed Wittigis. Justinian, fearing Belisarius might use his victory to set up a rival empire in the west, recalled the general and sent him to fight the Persians on the eastern frontier.

Over the next nine years the Goths, under a new king, Totila, were successful in recapturing much of Italy against incompetent Byzantine commanders.[2] At last in 552, Justinian dispatched Narses to Italy. Narses, now seventy-five years old, used a different version of the defend-then-attack principle than Belisarius. But his method was also successful, and Narses drove the Goths out of Italy.[3]

Although Narses had 20,000 men, the largest Byzantine army ever sent into Italy, it was still less than half the size of Totila's forces, located at Rome. Nevertheless, Narses resolved to meet the Gothic army in battle and destroy it. He marched around the head of the Adriatic Sea, then traveled nearly 300 miles through Italy to the vicinity of Gubbio in Umbria, about a hundred miles north of Rome. Meanwhile Totila advanced toward him, massing his army about thirteen miles south of Narses at Taginae (now Gualdo Tadino), and the next day advanced within two bowshots of the Byzantine line.

Totila drew up the whole of his cavalry in front, with his infantry— who were also the only Goths who wielded bows—in the rear. The bowmen should have been placed ahead of or to the side of the horsemen, where they could have shot their arrows. Located behind the cavalry, they served no tactical purpose. Apparently Totila expected to win by a single mounted charge that would break the Byzantine center with Gothic spears and swords, and hoped his infantry could follow behind to complete the destruction of the enemy.

To meet this frontal attack, Narses already had a superior weapon, the compound bow that Belisarius had used to such good effect. But he introduced in addition a novel order of battle—and thus employed a superior tactical system. His tactic was a perfect expression of the defend-then-attack principle. The formation was probably Narses's own invention, since it had never been recorded before. Narses dismounted 8,000 of his horsemen and formed them in a solid phalanx in the center of the field. They presented a bristling hedge of spears. On each flank, or wing, he drew up 4,000 foot archers, and each wing was thrown forward—that is, the archers lined up at an angle turning outward, in this fashion:

Totila was probably baffled by the Byzantine formation, and delayed attacking for several hours, hoping his enemy would break ranks for dinner. But Narses had anticipated this eventuality, and kept his men in ranks. He allowed them to eat a small meal while standing.

Sometime in the afternoon the Gothic cavalry advanced to attack. They took no notice of the Byzantine archers on each wing, but charged straight at the leveled spears of the massed dismounted cavalry. As they advanced they found themselves half encircled by the enemy bowmen on either flank and exposed to a rain of arrows from both sides.

The Gothic squadrons in the center reached the phalanx, where they collided with Byzantines in the front ranks kneeling with spear butts fixed in the earth, and pointed upward toward the bellies of the oncoming horses. Meanwhile the Byzantine men behind the front rank leveled their spears over the heads of the men kneeling in front of them. The Goths could not break through this formation, while the squadrons on the flanks were raked by flights of arrows. Hundreds of Goths fell, and riderless horses galloped over the battlefield.

The Goths withdrew in disorder, and never organized another formal charge. Individual leaders gathered groups and improvised small assaults, but all were thwarted by arrow storms. Chaos reigned for several hours, until toward evening the Byzantines began to advance. The Gothic cavalry fell back on their own infantry, who did not stand fast in the face of the frantic horses and the menacing Byzantines. They broke ranks and fled, and the Gothic army disintegrated. About 6,000 Goths died that day, and all who were captured were massacred. Totila was mortally wounded and died a short distance from the field.

The battle of Taginae marked the demise of the Ostrogoths. Immediately after the battle, Narses set out to exterminate the remaining

Gothic warriors. Within two years the few remnants that survived left Italy and disappeared from history. All this had come about because Narses followed the principle of defend, then attack. He was able to do this because he took advantage of his superior weapon, the compound bow, and because he devised a superior tactical system—archers thrown out on either flank.

Crécy: How an Idea Changed History

Eight centuries after Taginae, an English army applied a superior weapon—this time the longbow—deployed in a tactical formation new and baffling to the enemy but almost identical to that which Narses had used, and won a great victory over a much larger army of French chivalry at Crécy in northern France in 1346. This was another example of the brilliant employment of the defend-then-attack principle, and had vast repercussions, because for many years the French could find no way to overcome the superior weapon and the superior tactical formation they encountered.

The English hoped to use the principle to capture the French throne, join it to the English crown, and create a huge empire on both sides of the English Channel. The conflict they initiated, known as the Hundred Years War, ultimately failed because the French finally gave up their attempts to win battles, and retreated to their walled and fortified castles and towns. These places had to be captured one at a time, which usually involved long and expensive sieges that wore the English army down.

Nevertheless, the brilliance in the way the English fought brought them military renown, and the war turned England into a great power and an arbiter of European affairs.

What set off this spectacular chain of events was the simple but powerful longbow—along with the vision of one man, King Edward III (1312–1377).

The longbow was not an English invention. It was developed by native Celts in Wales, and first aroused attention in 1182, during one of the numerous English attempts to subdue the land, when Welsh arrows pen-

etrated an oak door four inches thick.[4] Edward III's grandfather, Edward I
(1239–1307), was the first ruler to recognize the importance of the
weapon, and he began pushing English yeoman farmers to wield it. The
longbow was made of a six-foot length of elm or yew; its three-foot arrow
could penetrate two layers of a knight's armor at 250 yards. It was not as
powerful as the Eurasian compound bow used by the Byzantines, but
compared to the crossbow, the main stringed weapon in use in western
Europe, it could shoot twice as fast, twice as far, and had equal power.

Edward I used the longbow effectively in wars in which he tried to
conquer the Welsh and the Scots, but an obscure battle in 1332, twenty-
five years after Edward I died, first displayed a radical new way to
employ the weapon. The battle was at Dupplin Muir in Scotland. After
virtually destroying an English army at Bannockburn, near Stirling, in
1314, the Scots slowly drove the English out of their country. According
to peace terms in 1328, a few Scottish noblemen who had sided with the
English were entitled to recover their Scottish fiefs or manors, but the
Scottish people considered them renegades and refused. The only way
the nobles could get back their land was by force. So, with a hired
English detachment of longbow archers, they advanced into Scotland,
and at Dupplin Muir on the River Earn near Perth they encountered a
large, closely packed body of Scottish foot soldiers armed with pikes
and swords. This body advanced on the enemy, who had pulled up on a
hillside with the armored Scottish knights dismounted, their lances leveled, in a single mass in the center. Longbow archers were drawn out in
a thin line on either flank, thrown forward, so that the whole invading
force resembled a half-moon.

The Scots advanced up the hillside, ignored the archers on either
flank, made straight for the knights in the center, and struck them so
hard that they were driven back in places. But the knights barely managed to hold. As the opposing forces stood pressed together, their spears
locked, the English archers closed in on either side, pouring deadly shafts
into the Scots, and driving them in toward the middle. The Scots, crushed
together, unable to wield their weapons, at last broke and ran away.

The records don't show who came up with the innovative arrange-
ment. It's unlikely the inventors knew about Narses's formation at

Taginae.[5] In any event, the battle of Dupplin Muir was the turning point of English arms. King Edward III used the same formation at the battle of Halidon Hill, near Berwick, a year later, and handed the Scots another crushing defeat. Edward III had become king in 1327 when his mother, Queen Isabella, and her lover Roger Mortimer deposed his father Edward II, a man of limited capability and strong attachments to unsavory and grasping favorites.

When the war against France commenced in 1337, Edward realized he could never match the numbers of men-at-arms the French could place in the field, and had to stand on the defensive. A defense could seldom bring victory, but a defensive system like that at Dupplin Muir might transform his prospects, especially as no one on the Continent had ever seen a formation like that.

His task was made easier because, on the Continent, the knight on horseback had become the absolute standard of battle. Especially in France, the fiery and undisciplined knights disdained all other kinds of warriors, and believed the zenith of warfare was to crash headlong with horses and lances against an opposing body of similarly armed knights.

After inconclusive engagements in France for nine years, Edward landed with about 2,400 horse and 12,000 foot soldiers, all English or Welsh, at La Hogue in Normandy in July 1346. He had no particular strategic plan, but immediately began ravaging the countryside, quickly capturing Caen, and then trying to seize Rouen on the Seine River. But he found all the bridges on the lower Seine broken. Meanwhile his fleet absconded back to England, and Philip VI of France (1293–1350) gathered a great army at Paris, and prepared to go after the English.

The closest place of relative safety was Flanders (present-day western Belgium), and Edward marched past the French army at Paris, and got his forces across the Seine on a hastily repaired bridge near St.-Germain-en-Laye. On August 24, with the French close behind, he made a dangerous passage of the Somme River at a ford below the town of Abbeville. Two short marches onward and a few miles south of Calais on the English Channel, Edward found a defensive position that pleased him. He turned about and resolved to strike a blow.

On August 26, 1347, Edward drew up his army in three divisions, or units, two in the front line, and one in reserve, facing southeast, in the direction of Abbeville, along a low ridgeline running from the village of Crécy on the southwest to the hamlet of Wadicourt at the northeast end. The large forest of Crécy, which was impenetrable, blocked Edward's western flank, forcing the French to approach from the southeast. The country north of Wadicourt, on Edward's left (or northeastern) flank, was more open, and King Philip might have maneuvered in this direction. But his impatient nobility were eager to attack as soon as they had seen the English massed on the Crécy-Wadicourt ridgeline, and Philip never had a chance to reconnoiter such a flanking move.

Each English division was formed up in the half-moon shape from Dupplin Muir. The dismounted men-at-arms were in the center wielding lances, with archers turned outward on each flank. Edward took his post just above Crécy at a windmill (where today a charming small wooden tower allows observers to look out over the entire field of battle, virtually unchanged from 1346).

Four French knights, detailed by Philip to scout ahead, reached a village a couple miles southeast of Crécy, saw the English ahead, and rode back to report. Since the afternoon was now far advanced, they advised the king to defer battle till the morrow. Philip agreed and called for a halt of his army of 30,000 men. But the lords would have none of Philip's caution, and were determined to attack. When the vanguard spotted the enemy, it drew back to form in battle formation, only to encounter masses of knights and nobles pressing from the rear, creating great disorder and confusion.

The French never managed to formulate a clear plan of attack. Each contingent of mounted French men-at-arms or knights scrambled to the front as best it could, jostling to find space. Only a force of mercenary infantry, crossbowmen from Genoa, got forward in a body and deployed a few hundred yards from the English on a parallel ridgeline.

Meanwhile Philip reached the front and saw his army was now so close to the enemy that it was impossible to withdraw in safety. Incensed at seeing the English army standing defiantly on the slope ahead, Philip ordered his men to attack.

The Genoese descended first into the depression between the two ridges—the *Vallée des Clercs*—got into alignment, then let fly their bolts. But their missiles fell short. The English longbowmen took one pace forward, drew their arrows to their heads, and shot so fast and close that it seemed to observers like a snowstorm beating on the Genoese. Arrows nailed helmets to heads, pierced breasts, and felled the whole first line of crossbowmen in the opening moment. The Genoese, confounded by a weapon they'd never seen before, stood their ground only a short time, then reeled backward in disorder.

As this was happening, the advanced group of mounted French knights, armed with long lances and swords, were moving forward to attack under the Count of Alençon. The Genoese careened into them. Thinking they were fleeing out of cowardice, the count ordered his horsemen to trample the crossbowmen or slash their way through with swords. This mad attempt to ride down their own infantry brought the whole line of French chivalry to a halt at the foot of the ridge where the English were arrayed.

English longbow shafts rained down on the French horsemen and archers in their confusion. Nearly every arrow struck a horse or man. Hundreds of men fell. Some animals went mad, rushing sideways, or rearing, or backing up. At this moment the charge of the main body of mounted French men-at-arms pushed into the mass, creating even more chaos, and falling under the same unrelenting hail of arrows. A few knights managed to extricate themselves and launch charges at the English men-at-arms, but the arrow storm never stopped, and these warriors, too, fell back into the seething mass in the *Vallée des Clercs* and along the slopes.

By far the greatest loss to the French came from the English longbowmen, who maintained their positions on the flanks all through the engagement. Yet the assaults of the French were always directed at the dismounted men-at-arms. None succeeded, although on occasion a few French reached the English knights, where they were always repelled.

As the battle went on, the French assaults became more and more haphazard, but still the barons in the rear rushed forward, trying to get into the fight. The French made fifteen or sixteen separate attacks that day, continuing long after nightfall. It was midnight before the last broken bands of French horsemen ceased to dash against the impenetrable English line.

The English made no attempt to pursue. Exhausted, they lay down in their ranks to snatch a few hours' rest. On the morning of August 27, through the mist the English could spot piles of corpses in the valley and on the hillside. King Edward sent 500 men-at-arms and 2,000 archers to push forward into the French position and beyond. They collided with a late-arriving group of French horsemen commanded by the Archbishop of Rouen. The English scattered them with much slaughter.

During the whole battle, about 1,500 knights and lords were killed. Some infantry died, especially the Genoese, but few of the French infantry, mainly peasants, ill-armed and ill-led, came into contact with the English. Instead, they fled in the night. Total English losses were two knights, one squire, and forty men-at-arms and archers.

Until the victory at Crécy, English arms had no great standing on the Continent. Now the reputation of the English soared. They had shattered the most formidable chivalry in Europe, a force three times the size of their own army.

King Edward had introduced two innovations to Continental warfare. He had dismounted his armored knights, and lined them up on foot like an ancient Greek phalanx. Their lance points bristling in a lethal hedge, the men-at-arms presented a defensive barrier that could stop man or beast, and could hold ground. He followed exactly the principle of defend, then attack, for he not only ushered in a new tactical formation—dismounted men-at-arms—but he also combined it with a superior weapon: missile power, or the ability of the bow and arrow to strike at a distance. His defense was so formidable that the French were beaten and their forces scattered even before the English advanced to the attack the next morning.

After the battle of Crécy, the French nobility appreciated the lethal power of English arrows, but, with few peasants or townsmen who practiced archery, they could not imitate the tactic effectively.[6] And although in future engagements they also dismounted their men-at-arms and sent their horses to the rear, they did not copy Edward's method of forming them into a solid, immovable phalanx. Instead, the French *attacked* on foot. The English formation was splendid in a *defensive* situation, where the men-at-arms had only to hold their position. But it was foolhardy to send men in attack on foot because they would suffer much longer under a hail of longbow shafts than would a force on horseback.

The situation became all the more hopeless because the French—in a wrongheaded attempt to nullify the penetrating power of the longbow—began greatly to *increase* the armor of men-at-arms, exchanging chain mail for plate. Armor became far too heavy to march a mile on foot, scramble through bushes and briers and sometimes mud, then assault a well-guarded position. Oftentimes the knights arrived so exhausted they could scarcely lift their heavy lances or swords. A peculiarity of this period was the danger a knight faced if he ever fell, for, bearing such great weight, he could seldom stand back up without help. Stalled knights could easily be killed or taken prisoner.

Consequently, ten years later, at Poitiers in 1356, the French suffered yet another defeat much like Crécy, and they still repeated the same mistakes with the same outcome at the battle of Agincourt in 1415.

With the tactics developed by Edward III, the English remained virtually invincible for as long as the French insisted on headlong attacks. These victories permitted England to control a large part of France for a number of years, but their hold was always ephemeral. This was because dismounted knights and longbow archers achieved victories *only* if the French challenged them in battle. At last the French moved to a better strategy. They took advantage of the fact that—in this era before cannons had become powerful enough to knock down thick stone or brick walls—castles and walled towns could usually be captured only by starving the inhabitants. Since every siege took many men and much time, conquest of towns and castles became an exhausting, expensive, impossible task, especially as a subdued town or castle might subsequently be seized by a defiant group of Frenchmen and have to be captured all over again.

The Civil War: Countering a New Weapon

The English longbow did not survive long after the Hundred Years War. It was superseded by the musket, which fired a gunpowder-propelled metal bullet or ball that was accurate to about a hundred yards. This was a shorter range than the longbow, but almost anyone could be taught to load and fire a musket, whereas drawing a bow required great strength, and aiming it called for great skill.

In the decade before the American Civil War, a new infantry hand weapon appeared, the single-shot Minié-ball rifle, which had four times the range of the musket and revolutionized warfare—although few commanders on either side recognized this fact.

One commander did, Confederate General Thomas J. "Stonewall" Jackson, and he combined the vastly increased killing power of the rifle with a new variation of the defend-then-attack principle to devise a way to win the war for the South.[7]

Though Jackson's concepts brought spectacular results on the few occasions they were practiced, he was unsuccessful in persuading his commander, Robert E. Lee, to adopt them fully. And when Jackson was mortally wounded at Chancellorsville in May 1863, Lee reverted to the extremely costly headlong assault tactics of nearly all the commanders in the Civil War. As a result, by the time the war ended, 600,000 Americans had died, one person in sixty in the entire population, not to speak of enormous numbers who were maimed and crippled.[8]

Jackson was unable to influence Confederate tactics till the second year of the war. By that time he realized the methods being used were causing disaster, especially to the Southerners, who had only one-third the manpower of the North.[9]

Tactics in the war came straight out of the Mexican War, which had ended thirteen years before. Soldiers formed up in close-ordered lines, two men deep, and moved forward to attack the enemy standing in identical formations. With muskets, this made sense. Soldiers had to approach within a hundred yards, often closer, before muskets had much effect. Both attackers and defenders also fought standing up, because reloading single-shot muskets and rifles was virtually impossible lying on the ground.[10]

Attacking forces thus *had* to remain exposed. Defending troops in theory might shield themselves behind barricades or fortifications, but doctrine rejected this because troops so located could not form up quickly to counterattack if their enemy was defeated. Furthermore, commanders believed troops behind barricades would be reluctant to abandon them and go over to the attack.[11]

Consequently, soldiers both attacked and defended in closely packed lines. They did not build field fortifications, and, once the Minié-ball rifle came into existence, were shot down in appalling numbers.

Stonewall Jackson witnessed this carnage at the battle of First Manassas in July 1861, where his brigade had stood "like a stone wall" in the midst of a flood of fleeing Confederates who could not withstand the storm of Union rifle fire. Jackson's unyielding brigade was the rock around which the Confederate army rallied. This won the battle for the South and gave Jackson the name he will bear forever. However, Stonewall Jackson was more deeply impressed by the battles of the Seven Days, June 26–July 2, 1862, just east of Richmond, when the new senior Confederate commander, Robert E. Lee, ordered headlong attacks against defending Union troops, and lost a quarter of his entire army.

Jackson had already tried four times to persuade the Confederate president, Jefferson Davis, to abandon head-to-head confrontations, sweep behind Washington, cut off its rail communications and hence its food supply, force Abraham Lincoln's government to vacate, and take the war to the Northern people. If Northern cities were occupied and factories destroyed, he was convinced, the North would concede the South independence. But Davis did not want to invade the North, and hoped the Northern people would tire of the war and grant peace.

Jackson knew this was not going to happen. Despairing of changing Davis's mind, he looked for other ways to defeat the North. Lee's concept of war offered no hope at all. Although Jackson soon became Lee's principal lieutenant as well as his most cogent adviser, he could not alter Lee's conviction that the best way to fight a battle was to attack his enemy head-on, to try to *force* a decision. Lee never fully grasped the fact that the Minié ball had changed battle fundamentally, though five out of six attacks in the war failed.

Lee's method of frontal attacks most decidedly had not worked in the Seven Days, for all he had done was drive the Union army into a strong defensive position along the James River. There Lee could not evict it, and it remained a great threat.

Jackson saw in the results of the Seven Days, however, the possibility for a new application of the defend-then-attack principle. Since an army on the defensive armed with the Minié-ball rifle could inflict terrible casualties on an attacker, the solution was to defend, and then, once heavy casualties had been inflicted on the enemy, to attack. Jackson worked out his new system immediately after the Seven Days.

The first goal, Jackson saw, was to place the Union army in a position where it *had* to attack. Jackson realized that this could be done in one of three ways: marching on the Federal rear; taking up a position that blocked Federal advance; or moving to a position that threatened a vital Federal possession. In any of these cases, the Union commander would have to attack in hopes of evicting the Confederate army.

Once the Federals were maneuvered so that they had to accept battle, Jackson planned to locate Confederate troops in a preselected, strong defensive position anchored by cannons, with at least one unobstructed flank around which the Rebels could subsequently advance. The Seven Days had proved that an attack would fail against such a position, causing enormous casualties and demoralizing the survivors. Then the Confederates could move swiftly on the open flank of the unnerved Union army, and either drive it into disorderly retreat, or pin it against some terrain feature, and force it to surrender.[12]

It's virtually certain Jackson did not discuss this idea in detail with Lee. He recognized Lee's aggressive disposition for head-on attacks, and instead recommended a series of specific actions that would lead to the strategy he had conceived. Prior to the battle of Chancellorsville in May 1863, where he was mortally wounded, Jackson made four such recommendations, all of which Lee either rejected entirely or carried out too slowly to be fully effective.

Jackson's first effort came in mid-August 1862 when he tried to get Lee to swing around the unguarded eastern flank of John Pope's army on the Rapidan River north of Orange, Virginia, and force it against the Rapidan or the Blue Ridge Mountains just to the west. There Pope would have either to attack or surrender. Lee accepted Jackson's idea but moved so slowly that Pope got wind of the trap, and hurriedly retreated to the Rappahannock River, twenty miles north.[13]

Jackson's second effort came shortly afterward. Pope had a solid position along the Rappahannock. If he remained there much longer, heavy Union reinforcements would double the size of his army and permit him to drive on to Richmond. To oust him quickly, Lee directed his cavalry chief, Jeb Stuart, to destroy a railway bridge a few miles north of the river, and thereby cut off Pope's supplies. But Stuart's efforts failed. Lee now told Jackson to break the Union line with his infantry corps. Jackson took the opportunity to strike far deeper than Lee had intended—in fact a strategic descent all the way to Manassas Junction, twenty-five miles north of the river, and just twenty-two miles from Washington. Lee's aim had been merely to force Pope to retreat. Jackson's aim, not articulated to Lee, was to place his corps close enough to the Union capital to threaten it, thus obliging Pope to abandon the Rappahannock line and come after him. In addition, Jackson believed his location, so deep into Union-held territory, would appear to Pope to be a chance to destroy Jackson's corps before Lee could rescue it.

Pope fell completely for the bait, moved on Manassas to "bag" Jackson, and was baffled to find Jackson had vanished. Still falling for the ruse, Pope was then delighted to discover that Jackson was apparently cowering in an isolated and vulnerable position along an unfinished railway embankment at Groveton, a few miles west of Manassas. But Jackson had selected this position with great care, because it was only a few miles northeast of Gainesville, and he had learned that Lee was approaching Gainesville through Thoroughfare Gap in the Bull Run Mountains just to the west.

Jackson was sure his troops could stop Pope's attacks, and they did, over a two-day period—the battle of Second Manassas, August 29–30,

1862. Union troops attacked frontally against the Rebels holding the railway embankment, but were stopped time after time by their rifle fire and by cannons moved up close to the line and firing canister, which blasted a lethal cloud of metal bullets and fragments into the advancing Federal masses.

These failures caused heavy Union casualties and accomplished precisely what Jackson had anticipated. The Federals were demoralized, depressed, and ripe for an attack around their western flank by Lee, whose army had arrived there by way of Thoroughfare Gap about noon on the first day of the battle. Lee had remained there, inactive, all the while Jackson was being assailed. If Lee had attacked early on the afternoon of the first day, or the morning or early afternoon of the second day, the Union army could not have escaped. It possessed only a single route for retreat, a stone bridge over Bull Run, just to the east. But Lee, who wanted only to maneuver Pope out of Virginia, not fight him, delayed attacking until late on the second day. By then it was too late to cut Pope off from the stone bridge. Thus, despite heavy losses, the Federal army escaped.

Jackson's third effort came immediately afterward, when Lee decided to invade Maryland. Lee planned to move first to Frederick, forty miles northwest of Washington. George B. McClellan, who had replaced Pope, would regard this as a threat to Washington, and would press toward Frederick. Lee then intended to march across South Mountain into the Cumberland Valley, just west of Frederick. His aim was to draw the Union army away from its main supply points, then to drive on to Harrisburg, Pennsylvania, and destroy the long railroad bridge over the Susquehanna River there.

Jackson thought this plan would accomplish little. He proposed instead that the Confederate army stay east of South Mountain and maneuver north of Washington. Abraham Lincoln was certain to insist that McClellan keep the Union army between Lee and Washington. The Confederates would then be free to march either toward Baltimore or Philadelphia, forcing McClellan to attack. The Confederates could choose a readily defensible position with an open flank, as at Groveton.

Jackson was sure the Federal attack would fail, and the Rebels could then sweep around McClellan's flank and possibly destroy his army.

Lee, however, rejected Jackson's proposal. As a result, McClellan advanced into the Cumberland Valley and pressed Lee back. Lee's best course thereafter would have been to return to Virginia, for no hope of gain remained. Instead he decided to fight at Sharpsburg, Maryland, twenty miles west of Frederick and just north of the Potomac River. However, Lee's army was less than half the size of McClellan's, and was backed against the Potomac with no possibility of maneuver. The battle of Antietam, which followed on September 17, 1862, was the bloodiest day of the Civil War. Lee stopped McClellan, who, like Pope at Second Manassas, sacrificed his men in repeated frontal assaults against the massed rifles and guns of the Confederates. But Lee could not exploit this success, because he had insufficient space to launch a counterattack against McClellan's flank. Antietam was a disaster for the Confederacy because it gave Lincoln the opportunity he needed to issue the Emancipation Proclamation, which turned the war into a moral crusade.[14]

Jackson's fourth attempt to persuade Lee to adopt his strategy came prior to the battle of Fredericksburg in December 1862. After Antietam the two hostile armies had moved to this town on the Rappahannock River, fifty-five miles north of Richmond, the Confederate capital. Lincoln had finally realized McClellan was incompetent, and had replaced him with Ambrose E. Burnside, who planned to attack Fredericksburg to open a path to Richmond. Jackson saw that the Confederates could not gain a decision at Fredericksburg. They could stop a Union assault, but would have no space to swing around the defeated army and break it apart. The key was Stafford Heights, an elevation directly across the Rappahannock from the town. Here Federal artillery could dominate every inch of the battlefield and spoil any Confederate move on the Union flank.

Jackson proposed that the Confederates move back from their position guarding Fredericksburg to a point on the North Anna River about twenty-five miles south. Here there *was* room for maneuver, and a chance, after Burnside had attacked and failed, to swing around him, cut off his supplies and line of retreat, and destroy his army. But again

Lee rejected his idea, and decided to fight at Fredericksburg. Jackson told General D. H. Hill that there "we will whip the enemy but gain no fruits of victory."[15] He was right. The Federals suffered 12,600 casualties in frontal assaults that were as hopeless as they were gruesome. Confederates standing behind a stone wall on the "sunken road" were almost impervious to Union fire, while their rifles stopped every one of the twelve Federal charges. The South lost 5,300 men, but achieved nothing. The North retained the initiative, and could easily replace its losses.

After Fredericksburg, Lincoln saw that Burnside was no better a general than McClellan, and replaced him with "Fighting Joe" Hooker, an officer with little depth or subtlety, but whose aggressiveness Lincoln hoped would serve to break through Confederate barriers and drive on to Richmond. Hooker performed even worse than Burnside. In early May 1863, trying to oust Lee from Fredericksburg, Hooker advanced a large Union force on the crossroads of Chancellorsville, a few miles west of the town, in early May 1863, but was shattered by a march on his flank by Stonewall Jackson's corps, and forced to retreat. Jackson was mortally wounded in the battle, however, and Lee lost his spectacular generalship and counsel.[16]

Gettysburg: Willfully Ignoring Reality

Only a month after Chancellorsville, Robert E. Lee decided to advance into Pennsylvania. He told a reluctant Jefferson Davis his purpose was to tap the abundant food supplies of the region, but his real aim was to seek a decision in the war. But the lesson Jackson had been trying to teach him— to defend in order to weaken the enemy, then attack—had not sunk in.[17]

Lee is one of the supreme examples in history of a commander who disregards the circumstances he finds himself in, and continues on a policy that is bound to result in disaster. Although most of the senior officers on both sides were unable to fathom the problem presented by the Minié-ball rifle, Lee had been offered a solution time after time by Stonewall Jackson, and time after time he had rejected it.

The value of the defensive approach was no secret in the Army of Northern Virginia. James Longstreet, a corps commander, and Porter Alexander, his artillery chief, most certainly knew it. Alexander remarked, "When all our corps were together, what could successfully attack us?"[18] Longstreet believed he had extracted from Lee a promise to maintain the tactical defensive in Pennsylvania, and Lee actually intended to do so. As events were to show, however, he reverted to his old offensive habit the moment he faced a challenge.

The strength of the defense had actually become even greater by 1863. Field fortifications were now standard because officers recognized they could stop bullets. At the same time cannons, especially nimble twelve-pounder Napoleons (named after Napoleon III, not the emperor), sometimes moved up alongside defending troops, where they spewed out canister at oncoming enemy. This trinity—the Minié-ball rifle, field fortifications, and canister-armed cannons—now was making it virtually impossible to attack and win.

Lee set his army in motion northward on June 10, 1863. On June 27, Richard S. Ewell's troops occupied Carlisle, Pennsylvania, seventy-five miles north of the Potomac and only eighteen miles west of Harrisburg, the state capital. His cavalry skirmished only four miles from the city. Meanwhile, Jubal Early's division pressed through York, and occupied Wrightsville on the Susquehanna, twenty miles southeast of Harrisburg. The remainder of the Army of Northern Virginia was to the west, moving up through the Cumberland Valley toward Ewell.

On June 28 one of Longstreet's spies reported that the Union army under George G. Meade—who had replaced Hooker—was at Frederick and South Mountain, a few miles west. In other words, Meade was fifty-five miles south of Ewell's troops at Carlisle. Yet Lee reacted in a strange and destructive manner. He at once called off Ewell's march on Harrisburg, and ordered the entire Confederate army to concentrate thirty miles south of Carlisle at Gettysburg.

Lee's decision to turn back south was a terrible mistake. He occupied a superb strategic position at Carlisle and at Wrightsville, on the Susquehanna. The Union army at Frederick and South Mountain was so

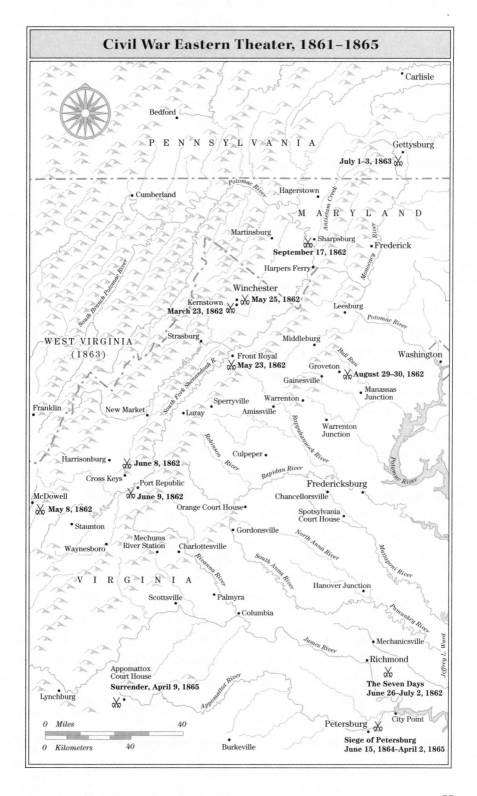

Civil War Eastern Theater, 1861–1865

Carlisle

Bedford

P E N N S Y L V A N I A

Gettysburg
July 1–3, 1863

Potomac River

Cumberland   Hagerstown

M A R Y L A N D

Antietam Creek

Martinsburg   Sharpsburg
                September 17, 1862   Frederick

Monocacy River

Harpers Ferry

Winchester
Kernstown   May 25, 1862
March 23, 1862   Leesburg

Potomac River

Strasburg   Middleburg

WEST VIRGINIA
(1863)   Bull Run   Washington
                        Front Royal
                        May 23, 1862   Groveton
South Fork Shenandoah R.   August 29–30, 1862
                                Gainesville
                                            Manassas
                        Sperryville   Junction
Franklin   New Market   Warrenton
                    Luray   Amissville
                                            Warrenton
                                            Junction
Robinson River

Rappahannock River

Harrisonburg   June 8, 1862   Culpeper
Cross Keys   Rapidan River
        Port Republic   Fredericksburg
McDowell   June 9, 1862   Orange Court House   Chancellorsville
May 8, 1862   Spotsylvania
                                        Court House
    Staunton   Gordonsville
                                North Anna River
    Mechums
Waynesboro River Station Charlottesville
                            Rivanna River   South Anna River
                                            Hanover Junction
V I R G I N I A
            Scottsville   Palmyra   Mattaponi River

            Columbia   Pomunkey River

                        James River   Mechanicsville

                                        Richmond
    Appomattox   Jeffrey L. Ward
    Court House
    Surrender, April 9, 1865   The Seven Days
Lynchburg   June 26–July 2, 1862
                                Appomattox River

0   Miles   40
                                        City Point
0   Kilometers   40   Burkeville   Petersburg
                                Siege of Petersburg
                                June 15, 1864–April 2, 1865

69

far south it constituted no immediate threat. Lee had a great opportunity to turn his back on this army, seize Harrisburg, break the bridges on the Susquehanna, turn the river into a moat, and strike out on the undefended road to Philadelphia, the Union's second city, with 600,000 inhabitants, much industry, and located astride the main north-south railroad arteries of the North. The North had no troops to stop this move. Taking Philadelphia would have won the war for the South.[19]

Even if Lee could not bring himself to march on Philadelphia, he should have concentrated his army somewhere near Carlisle. There he would have had ample time to scout out and occupy a formidable defensive position, build powerful entrenchments, and reconnoiter effective turning routes. The Union army would have been compelled to assault, and almost surely would have been defeated.

Instead, in the rush back to Gettysburg, Lee's troops had to endure hard and exhausting marches. He had no chance to reconnoiter a suitable battlefield, or even to know what lay in front of him.

Accordingly, A. P. Hill's corps, moving from Cashtown, a few miles west, bumped into a wild and disorderly fight on July 1 on the western edge of Gettysburg. And Lee, who had said he intended to stand on the defensive and let the Federals attack, now ordered a full-scale assault. By the end of the day, after fearful casualties, the Confederates had ousted the outnumbered Union forces from Gettysburg, and from Seminary Ridge just to the west of the town. The Union army began to concentrate on Cemetery Hill and Ridge immediately to the south of the town and a mile opposite Seminary Ridge.

Cemetery Hill and Ridge was a magnificent defensive position because it was elevated and presented completely open fields of fire along every possible avenue of attack from the west, where the Confederate army was located. Longstreet saw, the moment he rode up in the afternoon, that under no circumstances should it be assaulted. He quickly came up with a solution that would have forced the Federals to attack Lee's army, and relieved the Rebels from the impossible task of assaulting Cemetery Hill and Ridge.

"All we have to do," Longstreet told Lee, "is to throw our army around by their left [south], and we shall interpose between the Federal army and Washington. We can get in a strong position and wait, and if they fail to attack us we shall have everything in condition to move back tomorrow night in the direction of Washington." He thought, however, that the Federals would be compelled to come after the Confederates. "When they attack," Longstreet said, "we shall beat them."

"No," Lee replied, pointing to Cemetery Ridge, "the enemy is there, and I am going to attack him there." Longstreet responded, "If he is there tomorrow, it will be because he *wants* you to attack him."

But Lee would not listen. And on July 2 he ordered a massive attack on the southern reaches of Cemetery Ridge. After a day of constant assaults and immense casualties, the Army of Northern Virginia had been gravely weakened, but had gained nothing significant. On this day the scales tilted against the South. There was one chance to retain some Confederate power: to withdraw back across the Potomac. But this did not happen.

Instead, on July 3, Lee ordered a direct charge straight against the center of the Union position on Cemetery Ridge. Longstreet tried to talk him out of it, but got nowhere. The impending disaster preyed on Longstreet's conscience and he considered canceling it on his own authority. He aired the dilemma with Porter Alexander, who wrote, "I was too conscious of my own youth and inexperience to express any opinion not directly asked. So I remained silent while Longstreet fought his battle out alone and obeyed his orders."[20]

The attack has gone down in history as Pickett's Charge, named after George Pickett, who commanded part of the force. It was doomed before it started. Sending massed bodies of troops across nearly a mile of open ground against emplaced riflemen and banked cannons was an invitation for destruction. Only a third of the men in the charge even got to Cemetery Ridge, and about half the 13,500 Confederates who made the attack were killed, wounded, or captured. It was an act of lunacy.

Lee lost 27,000 men at Gettysburg, well over a third of his army. He had destroyed the last offensive power of the Confederacy. From that moment on, there was no hope of a Southern victory.

Implications for the Future

The essence of the rule of defend, then attack is to employ either a superior weapon or a superior tactical system, and to use one or both to withstand an attack, then to go over to the offensive after the enemy is weakened and discouraged. Since in the foreseeable future we are likely to encounter principally terrorist strikes, the element of defending *before* attacking is going to be missing in most of the engagements we fight. Nevertheless, the wisdom of the rule—to seek better weapons and better tactics—remains a priority.

But terrorists can obey only half of this admonition, for they are unlikely ever to possess weapons even remotely comparable to those of the United States or other Western powers, let alone superior ones.[21] For that reason they are emphasizing not better arms but better tactics to use against us.

An example is the attack by Moslem extremists against the Indian parliament buildings in New Delhi on December 13, 2001. This, being a terrorist surprise attack, was not preceded by a defensive move, so it doesn't fit the rule of defend, then attack. Even so, the extremists did employ a superior tactical method. They struck an ill-defended target, but one with tremendous political and emotional significance. The aim was to end Indian control of Kashmir, a mostly Moslem region. The terrorists were seeking to destabilize India, and possibly foment war between Moslems and Hindus. They did not succeed, but by a relatively small act they caused India to blame Pakistan for failing to control terrorists in its territory, and led the two powers to the brink of war.

The Palestinian suicide bombers who attacked Israeli civilians and soldiers in 2001 and 2002 likewise employed superior tactics and gained extraordinary results, killing and maiming hundreds of Israelis. Their assaults, however, led Israel to undertake extreme retaliatory measures, which only increased tensions. The purpose of *any* tactical operation should be to advance the strategic goal of the attacking force, otherwise the tactical operation is meaningless. The true aim of the suicide bombers is unclear. If they are bent on the outright eradication of Israel, then they will gain nothing because continued suicide bombings will only increase the resolve of the Israelis to defend themselves. If, on the other hand, their aim is to force a division of the Holy Land into two separate, independent states, Israel and Palestine, their tactical success might induce Israel to yield in order to end the killings. Such a solution would require the terrorist groups to accept a land-for-peace agreement, and the Israelis to give up settlements they have built in the midst of Palestinian communities on the West Bank and in Gaza.

Beyond the present-day concerns we have about fighting terrorism, the defend-then-attack principle has implications on a broader, more conceptual level. The experiences of the historical figures described in this chapter provide lessons about how we can discern dangers and exploit opportunities in situations where we must defend before going over to the offensive. We are not going to be more powerful than the forces we oppose in every case. An enemy may find the opportunity to concentrate a superior force against us, or he may surprise one of our isolated units. Consequently, the rule is as important as ever.

Robert E. Lee's case especially is a cautionary tale. Lee was a model of honor, integrity, and devotion to duty to his men, and the battle methods he employed were enshrined in the successes of the Mexican War, in which he had been a hero. Other leaders found it difficult if not impossible to criticize him, even as disasters accumulated from his first days as commander.

Our real models for the future should be officers like the four commanders above who studied their problems with logic, creativity, and imagination, and came up with original solutions. Lee, on the other hand, should show us that we must question concepts presented as axiomatic *because* they succeeded in the past.

The new kind of war we face will challenge the ideas that have guided armies over the past two centuries. Our problems may be fully as inexplicable on first sight as those of Belisarius with a tiny army facing a host of fierce Goths, or of Civil War officers seeing lines of their men go down at ranges of 200 yards. The answer is original thought focused on addressing the problem at hand. There will be answers. But they may not be what has been done before.

4

Holding One Place, Striking Another

PROBABLY THE OLDEST tactical device on earth is to attract attention in one place with some gesture, while taking decisive action elsewhere. Every magician employs the tactic with sleight-of-hand and distraction. A quarterback fakes a handoff to a running back, then fades back to pass. A pitcher throws a couple of wide curve balls, then drills a strike right over the plate. A politician draws attention to a lucrative contract he's landed for a local industry, but downplays his vote to raise taxes. In war, this tactical device is at the heart of the principle of holding at one place while striking at another. It is one of the most successful battle methods.

The Chinese strategist Sun Tzu summarized its essential nature 2,500 years ago when he spoke of the *zheng* element, which fixes the enemy in place, and the *qi* element, which flanks or encircles the enemy, whether physically or psychologically (see Introduction). *Zheng* is the direct or more obvious move against which the enemy girds himself, *qi* the indirect, unexpected move that defeats him. If the *qi* succeeds beyond all expectation, however, it can be transformed into the *zheng* and the *zheng* into the *qi*. The two are mutually supportive forces; they interact between and depend upon each other.

This combination has always been important, because it is often instrumental in achieving the commander's single greatest imperative—

hitting a decisive point with a force powerful enough to vanquish opposition. To reach this point, except when he possesses overwhelming strength, a commander must deceive his enemy so that the blow is not foreseen, or he must hold the enemy at another place with enough force to keep him from moving.

In contemporary military terminology, the principle of holding in one place and striking at another is called the convergent assault. It can be practiced at all levels, but is most often seen at and below the battalion level (about a thousand men) in a tactic called "fire and maneuver." One of many techniques for using this tactic is to have one group ("fire") to direct machine guns, artillery, mortars, or rockets on the enemy force to hold it down, while another group ("maneuver") approaches the enemy from one direction and still another unit (also "maneuver") approaches it from the other. In this situation the base of fire is Sun Tzu's *zheng*, and the two maneuver units together are his *qi*.

Swarming (see chapter 1) is actually a convergent assault of this kind. It differs from the classic approach in that it permits virtually simultaneous strikes on all sides of an enemy position.

The principle of holding at one place and striking at another is more significant than ever today. Distraction and guile are essential in the new kind of war. Quick communications can alert an enemy to danger. Mobile forces can move with speed to counter a known strike or avoid it, while super-accurate weapons can break up an attack if it is spotted in time. In the Gardez operation in eastern Afghanistan in February and March 2002, American forces employed a variation of this rule. Finding a group of Al Qaeda operatives holed up in caves in a mountain valley, they assaulted the position heavily with bombing from aircraft. While the enemy was shielding himself from the bombs, special forces troops and their Afghan allies swept around all sides of the position, cutting off retreat, then closed in on the cave complexes, destroying them. In the past this same concept has spawned a thousand variations, but the one that has come down to us as *the* model or prime example was carried out by the Swedish king Gustavus Adolphus in the seventeenth century.

Gustavus Adolphus on the Lech, 1632

Gustavus Adolphus conceived his masterpiece when he discovered a German Imperial army emplaced on the Lech River in Bavaria on April 16, 1632.[1]

The battle came midway in the Thirty Years War, which had started in 1618 as a religious conflict between Roman Catholics and Protestants. The war soon degenerated into an effort by the Catholic Ferdinand II of Austria to transform the virtually impotent Holy Roman Empire, of which he was emperor, into a powerful centralized state of which he would be the actual sovereign. At the time the empire was a congeries of little German territories that wanted to keep their independence. By 1630 the Catholic Imperial army had swept aside most Protestant or independent opposition and was close to conquering all of Germany. This alarmed King Gustavus Adolphus of Sweden because it threatened Swedish hegemony in the Baltic Sea. In response, Gustavus took a strong army to northern Germany in 1630.

Gustavus won the battle of Breitenfeld in Saxony, against the Imperial army under Marshal Johan de Tilly, on September 17, 1631. He then over-wintered along the Rhine River and, on April 10, 1632, stormed Donau-wörth, the most westerly fortress in Bavaria, on the Danube River. Having been beaten once by Gustavus in open battle, Tilly elected not to challenge him again, and withdrew the Imperial army about ten miles eastward, emplacing it in a formidable defensive position along the eastern bank of the north-flowing Lech River, just before it debouched into the Danube.

Gustavus wanted to defeat Tilly, but he also wanted to defeat a new Imperial army now forming in Moravia under Albrecht von Wallenstein. He was confident he could defeat both armies. Once this was done, he believed Ferdinand would give up his ambitions, Germany would return to its divided condition of 1618, and Sweden could annex enough territory along the Baltic to dominate that sea. But these hopes rested on his opponents meeting him in open battle. As events were to show, neither was willing to oblige.

To create what he considered an impregnable position, Tilly had bro-

ken all the bridges on the Lech as far as Augsburg, nearly thirty miles
south, and along the low-lying bank of his position he had built strong
redoubts joined by trenches and anchored by heavy cannons at intervals.

Gustavus had two obvious choices: he could force Tilly to vacate his
position by crossing the Lech well to the south, turning back north to the
Danube, blocking Tilly from his line of retreat to Austria, and forcing him
to fight in the open field; or Gustavus could cross the Lech only a few
miles to the south, then swing back and lock Tilly in his corner where he
could not get food, thus also forcing him to come out and fight.

But either choice would take time, and Gustavus decided on a bold
and unexpected stroke to defeat Tilly quickly, because he expected
Wallenstein to march on him shortly, and he wanted to dispose of Tilly's
army before encountering Wallenstein. The plan he adopted was a perfect example of *zheng* and *qi*.

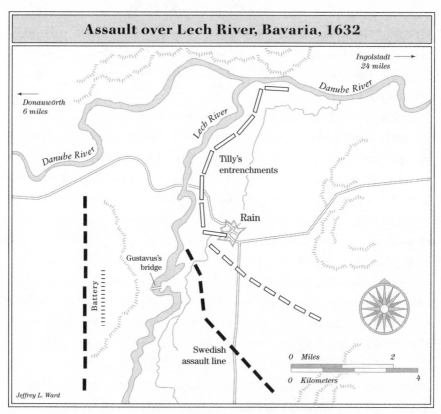

Assault over Lech River, Bavaria, 1632

First, Gustavus made threatening gestures against Tilly's army *(zheng)*, which convinced Tilly that Gustavus might attempt to force the river frontally. Tilly accordingly held his troops in readiness behind their fortifications.

Meanwhile, Gustavus set up seventy-two cannons on an elevation above the west bank of the Lech five miles south of the Danube. These guns cannonaded the space across the river, discouraging Imperial forces from moving into it. Then, directly east of the cannons in a river bend out of sight of Tilly's army, Swedish engineers constructed a pontoon bridge out of boats and planking. Under a thick cloud of smoke caused by burning wet straw, 300 Finnish soldiers crossed the bridge and established a fortified bridgehead on the eastern bank about a mile south of Tilly's fortifications. Tilly soon discovered the Finns, but the detachment was small, and the Swedish cannons across the river caused him to avoid assaulting. On the next night, April 14–15, the main body of Swedish infantry crossed the bridge, some of the artillery following, while cavalry forded the stream a little farther south and moved up alongside the infantry. All these movements represented the indirect, unexpected approach, or *qi*.

Now it was too late to dislodge the enemy on his flank, but Tilly made the effort, sending in desperate infantry and cavalry charges on April 16. All were thrown back, the infantry caught in a deadly crossfire between the Swedish guns on the other side of the river and those on the eastern bank. The Imperial army lost 4,000 men killed, wounded, and captured, including Tilly, who was mortally wounded. The Swedes lost only a quarter as many. The Imperial survivors fled back to their fortifications, and during the night retreated eastward.

Despite the brilliance of this victory, Gustavus proved his strategic sense was gravely lacking when he did not pursue the defeated army, and thus lost the chance of destroying it. The survivors ultimately joined Wallenstein. Accordingly, Gustavus's victory on the Lech, though a model of tactical engagement, had no strategic consequences.

Gustavus now compounded this error by an even greater strategic blunder. He commenced devastations of the Bavarian countryside in hopes of drawing Wallenstein into battle. But Wallenstein, wary of Gustavus's tactical brilliance, ignored the depredations and—believing Gustavus was more concerned about his supply and communications line back through Saxony to Sweden—joined the Imperial ally, Maximilian of Bavaria, in east-central Bavaria at the town of Amberg. This position potentially threatened the Swedish supply line.

But Wallenstein, at Amberg, had left unprotected the road to Vienna, capital of the empire and seat of Ferdinand. Gustavus's close friend and Swedish chancellor, Axel Oxenstierna, pleaded with the king by letter to ignore the threat to his supply line, requisition food from enemy sources, continue down the Danube, and seize Vienna. It didn't matter, he wrote, if northern Germany were to be lost if Gustavus could occupy the heart of the empire. Surely, in order to get the Swedes to evacuate Austria, Emperor Ferdinand would hurriedly sign a favorable peace treaty.

But Gustavus for some inexplicable reason was unwilling to take the risk. Had he captured Vienna, the empire would have been in an impossible position. His army could have lived indefinitely off confiscated supplies. And if Wallenstein had marched to relieve the city, he would likely have been defeated by Gustavus's tactical skill. Gustavus forfeited an opportunity for a great, war-ending victory. Instead he moved to Nuremberg, west of Amberg, and entrenched, again hoping he could entice Wallenstein into battle. But Wallenstein declined, moving to nearby Fürth and likewise entrenching.

For six weeks the two armies faced each other, both getting hungrier by the day. But Wallenstein refused to come out of his fortifications. In desperation, Gustavus ordered a direct assault. It failed, with heavy casualties, and Gustavus, his army now desperate for food, did what Oxenstierna had begged him to do nearly three months before—he struck out for Vienna on September 18, 1632, hoping Wallenstein would come after him and at last meet him in open battle.

But Wallenstein again refused to take the bait, and instead turned north into Saxony, a state that was an ally of Sweden. He captured Leipzig, commenced despoiling the Saxon countryside, and broke Gustavus's line of communications. Once again Gustavus valued his communications more than a strategic descent on the enemy homeland. He turned hurriedly north, marching 165 miles in eighteen days. On November 6, 1632, he again proved his mastery of battle tactics when he at last caught Wallenstein in a position in which he had to fight or be destroyed. Gustavus won the battle of Lützen, southwest of Leipzig. But he died in the fighting. The Imperial army re-formed with new troops, and the political situation in Germany went unchanged.

Gustavus Adolphus is one of the premier examples in history of a commander who can win battles but cannot win wars. Winning great tactical engagements is only a tool to reach a political goal. That is the aim of war. Gustavus's victory on the Lech had no consequences, and neither did his other tactical victories. He was one of the great masters of the principle of holding one place and striking another, but his triumphs in battle were never translated into political gains.

Jena, 1806: Converging by Accident

In the century and a half between Gustavus Adolphus and Napoleon Bonaparte, the principle of holding in one place and striking at another generally fell out of favor because armies became too expensive for rulers to risk heavy losses of troops except in unusual circumstances.

During this period, rulers resorted to professional armies, abandoning the temporary armies hired for a single campaign that had marked the Thirty Years War and had led to terrible consequences. In this conflict, armies were largely raised by military contractors, or condottiere, who recruited soldiers and sold their services to a ruler. The armies subsisted by forcible extractions from the people, and were undisciplined, poorly trained, and loyal to their captains, as opposed to the ruler who hired them. They were so rapacious, murderous, and destructive that they threatened to shatter civilization in Europe. In Germany more than 8 million civilians died at the hands of mercenaries, and entire districts were depopulated.

To prevent such outrages from recurring, kings turned to new professional armies deliberately kept apart from civilians lest the soldiers commit violence against them. In addition, the men were subjected to

ferocious discipline, and denied any freedom so as to discourage deser-
tion. Soldiers were required to swear allegiance directly to the rulers
themselves. But since few decent men were willing to serve under such
onerous and humiliating conditions, the armies were recruited from the
dregs of society. To keep these men quiescent and obedient, rulers
looked after their physical welfare, providing warm uniforms and bar-
racks, and feeding them regularly from magazines, or stores kept in
fortresses.

Such armies cost lots of money, and rulers hated to expend them in
battle. Accordingly, the major military objective during the period
became not battle, but attempting to maneuver into a position between
the enemy and his supply magazines, therefore forcing him to retreat.
Maneuvering remained the principal military action until the French
Revolution of 1789 created volunteer armies composed of patriotic citizens who lived off the country and who would not desert at the first
opportunity. The loyal, dedicated spirit of these citizen formations carried over into the armies of Napoleon, and permitted him to march his
troops longer and faster than professional armies tied to magazines, and
to embark on wars not of maneuver, but of annihilation.

Between Gustavus and Napoleon, occasional major battles were
fought, but only a few commanders, notably Frederick the Great of
Prussia in the middle of the eighteenth century, used decisive battle as
an instrument of policy. Frederick's tactics incurred enormous casualties, but they won stunning victories and raised Prussia to a great power.
His tactics had elements of holding in one place and striking at another,
but Frederick largely followed the principle of landing an overwhelming
blow (see chapter 10).

As Napoleon began his conquest of Europe, Prussia foolishly
remained neutral. When Napoleon seized the Austrian capital of Vienna,
and virtually destroyed a combined Russian-Austrian army at Austerlitz
in Moravia in December 1805, the Prussian king, Frederick William III, at
last realized he faced another major power in central Europe. He didn't
like it, and decided to act.[2]

Unfortunately, the Prussian military had not evolved one bit from
its inflexible magazine-fed structure of the eighteenth century. For the

fast-marching soldiers of France, who found their victuals on the way, this fossil of an army was dangerous only if collided with directly.[3]

To defeat the Prussian army, Napoleon decided to march around it. In the event, the battle he fought at Jena and nearby Auerstädt in central Germany became one of the greatest examples in history of the principle of holding in one place and striking at another.

For Prussia to challenge France in 1806 was suicidal. The French Grand Army was much larger than the Prussian field army (180,000 versus 130,000 men), and at this time the French were cantoned all the way from Frankfurt to south Germany, a distance of more than eighty miles, and were within two weeks' march of the Prussian frontier.

After August 9, 1806, when Prussia mobilized, the senior generals could not decide on a strategy. What Frederick William should have done was to emplace his army behind the Elbe River and wait for the Russians, who'd signaled their interest in helping. Instead the senior commanders ordered a general movement southwest through Saxony and the Thuringian Forest to the Saale River.

In the first days of October, Napoleon secretly concentrated his army along the Main River, to the south of the Saale, and then began to move north. His aim was to get all the way to Berlin, 200 miles to the northeast, before the Russians could arrive. If he had moved directly from the west (that is, from France), he would have pushed the Prussians back *on* Berlin and Russian assistance. By coming from the south instead, he hoped to separate the main Prussian forces *from* their capital, their supply lines, and the Russians.

The Grand Army advanced in three columns, each containing two corps, on a front of forty miles. The columns were near enough to one another to assist if the need arose. This giant *bataillon carré* ("battalion square") displaced the few Prussian outposts that had reached the Saale by the time the French got there, and then advanced toward the towns of Jena and Weimar to the north, with the entire Prussian army moving back in the face of the French advance.

By October 12 the advance guard, under Marshal Louis-Nicolas Davout, a corps of 26,000 men, had swept around and beyond Jena, bypassing the

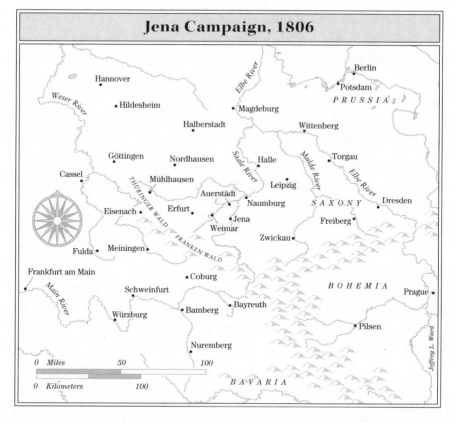

Jena Campaign, 1806

left, or eastern, flank of the Prussian army. This endangered the main Prussian lines of communication to the cities of Leipzig, Halle, and Berlin.

Napoleon heard from prisoner-of-war interrogations that the Prussians were concentrating at Erfurt, twenty-six miles west of Jena. He concluded that they planned either to accept battle there or withdraw to Halle, sixty miles northeast, and from there to Magdeburg on the Elbe River.

Accordingly Napoleon decided to launch the bulk of his army directly through Jena to Erfurt, while sending Davout in a turning movement to block the Prussians from retreating northward. Napoleon planned a classic battle of convergence, or holding at one place and striking at another. His main body detailed to drive on Jena-Erfurt was the *zheng*, or direct, force, while Davout's force advancing on the Prussians from the north was the *qi*, or indirect, force.

But the actual situation developed differently. As things turned out, the Prussians were not concentrated at Erfurt, as Napoleon had been told, but rather were more dispersed in the Erfurt-Jena region. When, on October 12, King Frederick William learned that Davout had occupied Naumburg, to his north, the news stunned him, because he saw his line of retreat could be cut off. At a council of war he decided the army must withdraw northward to the Elbe, taking a route by way of Auerstädt, just to the southwest of Davout's forces at Naumburg. While Karl Wilhelm Ferdinand, Duke of Brunswick, started north with 70,000 men on the morning of October 13 (the king coming along), Prince Friedrich Ludwig Hohenlohe, with 50,000 men, was ordered to guard the flank of the army under Brunswick. When Brunswick had passed Auerstädt, Hohenlohe was to pull behind as rear guard.

Meanwhile, Napoleon, believing the whole Prussian army was concentrated around Erfurt, marched most of his army just west of Jena on October 13. Hohenlohe had no inkling he would soon face 100,000 French troops, and positioned only part of his force to guard against an advance from Jena, keeping the bulk to the west around Weimar.

Early on October 14, French troops marched westward from Jena through fog, driving the Prussians out of several villages. Napoleon, though thinking the Prussians were only a delaying force, nevertheless applied strong pressure, and since the Prussians were hopelessly outnumbered, they fell back in great disorder northwest. By 4:00 P.M. the battle was over and pursuit began. Marshal Joachim Murat's cavalry spread over the countryside, taking thousands of prisoners. Prussian fugitives streamed northeast in hopes of reaching the main army under Brunswick.

But Brunswick, the king, and their 70,000 men were having troubles of their own. On the night of October 13 they bivouacked at Auerstädt. Brunswick planned to march northeast the next day to Freiberg and Halle. But Davout at nearby Naumburg got the news of Brunswick's movement, and he advanced the next morning to challenge the Prussians. In doing so, he transformed his small body of 26,000 men from the diversionary *qi* force to the holding *zheng* force, attempting to keep Brunswick in place so that Napoleon could come up with his superior force and deal the decisive blow. Despite his inferior numbers, Davout, in a fierce series of actions, did manage to hold the Prussians, and actually began pushing them back southwestward.

Frederick William, who had heard nothing of Hohenlohe's debacle at Jena, decided to fall back on Hohenlohe, whom he assumed was coming behind. So the 70,000-man main army of Prussia withdrew from the field of Auerstädt before a force so much weaker that no one, including Napoleon himself, could believe it at first.

The retreat began at 12:30 P.M. on October 14, 1806. The Prussians soon met panic-stricken survivors of the Jena battle, and chaos spread, with reports that the French were on their heels. Unit after unit broke and scattered across country. On this day alone the French captured 25,000 Prussians, while the residue fled pell-mell toward the Elbe and points north.

Napoleon had won one of the most decisive battles ever recorded of holding at one place and striking at another. Yet the tactics had been turned upside down. The Prussians at Jena were not the main force, as Napoleon thought, but only the rear guard. The main force was actually at Auerstädt. Davout's *qi* force had been transformed into the *zheng* force, and Napoleon's *zheng* had become the *qi* that pressed on the Prussian rear and drove it into disintegration.

The battle thus shows the tremendous flexibility of the principle, provided it's carried out by resourceful commanders. In this case Napoleon was blessed with Davout, who understood he had been placed inadvertently in the role of the holding force, though he had far fewer troops than the enemy. Davout did not hesitate to act, thereby achieving a tremendous victory. The example shows vividly the extreme importance of responsible, reliable officers at every level, for in the stress of battle, it is too late to assess whether an officer at a point that has suddenly become crucial is up to the job.

On October 15, Napoleon's forces launched the most famous cavalry roundup in history. French horsemen spread out all over the North German Plain, demanding surrenders everywhere, and getting them. The Prussian army virtually evaporated. On October 27, Napoleon entered Berlin in triumph, and the Prussian king retreated into East Prussia, where he and the remnants of his army found bare support from the

Russians. The next year at Friedland, Napoleon beat the Russians, too, and signed a peace with the czar.

Kum River Line, Korea, July 1950

At the end of World War II in 1945, the Soviet Union and the United States divided Korea at the thirty-eighth parallel for purposes of accepting the surrender of Japanese forces. This temporary division turned into a political boundary between a Communist state to the north and an American client state to the south. On June 25, 1950, Kim Il Sung, dictator of North Korea, launched a massive invasion of South Korea with the intention of reuniting the peninsula. North Korean divisions, led by Soviet-made T-34 tanks with heavy armor and mounting high-velocity 85-mm guns, drove South Korean defenders in increasing disorder southward.

The United States quickly came to the assistance of the South Koreans, but the only American troops available were four divisions occupying Japan. The Americans required time in order to deploy in strength, and the burden of the initial defense fell on the extremely understrength 24th Infantry Division, occupying the Japanese island of Kyushu, nearest to Korea.[4]

The first American element to engage the North Koreans was the tiny 540-man Task Force Smith, which set up a barrier to block the main highway near Osan, about twenty miles south of Seoul, on July 5, 1950, but had to retreat after a massive North Korean assault.[5]

Other elements arrived soon, but by July 13 the division had been pushed back south fifty miles to the west-flowing Kum River, a line that 8th Army commander Walton H. Walter wanted to hold long enough for other divisions to arrive. He also wanted to shield the important city of Taejon, fifteen miles south. The engagements along the Kum River on July 14–16, 1950, constitute some of the most enlightening examples in modern times of holding in one place and striking another—both in how to execute the principle, and in how inexperienced and unskilled soldiers can be overwhelmed by it.

There were two main approaches for the North Koreans to Taejon:

through the village of Taepyong-ni on the Kum directly north of the city, and through the village of Kongju, eight miles west. The North Koreans had two divisions, each with 6,000 men.

William F. Dean, the 24th Division commander, was in charge of the defending forces along the river, and he committed the two-battalion 34th Infantry Regiment, with 2,000 men, supported by the 63rd Field Artillery Battalion, to hold at Kongju to the west, and the two-battalion 19th Infantry Regiment along with three artillery battalions, totaling 3,400 men, to shield the direct route through Taepyong-ni. The 19th Infantry had just arrived and had seen no action.

Each regiment deployed on either side of the broken bridge at each village, with artillery and reserves lined up on the road leading south. This would have been acceptable if the Americans had possessed supporting forces on both flanks. But they did not. The two regiments were essentially isolated at each village.

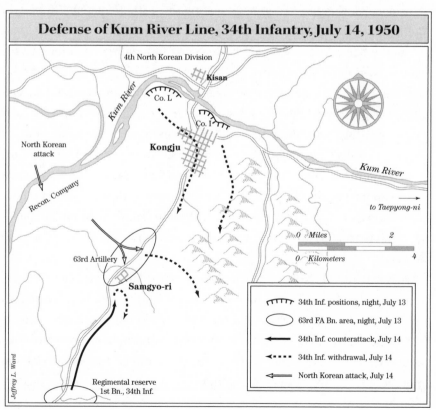

Defense of Kum River Line, 34th Infantry, July 14, 1950

4th North Korean Division

Kisan

Kum River

Co. L

Co. I

Kongju

North Korean attack

Kum River

Recon. Company

to Taepyong-ni

0 Miles 2

63rd Artillery

0 Kilometers 4

Samgyo-ri

Jeffrey L. Ward

Regimental reserve
1st Bn., 34th Inf.

34th Inf. positions, night, July 13

63rd FA Bn. area, night, July 13

34th Inf. counterattack, July 14

34th Inf. withdrawal, July 14

North Korean attack, July 14

The U.S. commanders should have anticipated that they could readily be flanked on both sides of Kongju and Taepyong-ni. Since they were outnumbered, a better policy would have been a "hedgehog" defense at both places, in which infantry were arrayed in a tight circle, with mortars and artillery inside. This would not have prevented the North Koreans from crossing the river, but would have blocked their supplies and stopped their movement onward, and given the 8th Army time to organize a stronger defense at Taejon. The hedgehogs then could have retreated, aided by American air power, as moving fortresses, bristling with cannons and machine guns, sending infantry ahead on either flank to rout out any enemy trying to set up roadblocks, and blasting with artillery any heavy obstacle that got in the way. This is precisely how the 1st Marine Division and elements of the 7th Infantry Division retreated from the Chosin (Changjin) Reservoir in North Korea five months later.

Instead, at Kongju the commander of the 34th Regiment, Robert L. Wadlington, placed his 3rd Battalion, with only two line companies (I and L),[6] on the banks of the Kum on both sides of the village, and located his reserve 1st Battalion over seven miles to the south, so far away it would have great difficulty aiding the 3rd Battalion. In addition, the artillery battalion was positioned three miles south of Kongju. This battalion retained communications with the regimental rear command post to the south at Nonsan, but had none with the infantry companies or artillery forward observers on the river. The artillery should have been able to provide direct supporting fire for the infantry, but owing to the lack of communications it was not able to do so. This grotesque failure in command eliminated the possibility of directed fire on any North Koreans assaulting the positions.

Early on July 14, North Korean guns began shelling Company I on the high ground just east of the blown bridge at Kongju, and Company L to the west of the bridge. Shortly after, lookouts reported North Koreans were crossing the river about two miles downstream (southwest) on two barges. With no communication back to the artillery, forward observers could not call in fire. As a result, about 500 enemy troops had crossed by 9:30 A.M.

Meanwhile the companies along the river were coming under considerable artillery and mortar shelling. The commander of Company L decided his position was untenable and withdrew. Company I remained in place, but the damage had been done. The entire left flank of the 34th's position had been abandoned, and the North Koreans promptly advanced. They quickly assaulted the artillery battalion three miles south, overrunning its ten howitzers, and killing or capturing 136 men.

When Wadlington learned of the destruction of the artillery battalion, he ordered the 1st Battalion, in reserve seven miles to the south, to counterattack northward. The infantry was so far in the rear that they took a long while to get up to the North Korean position. Enigmatically, the regimental commander's orders had been to retire if the battalion's mission had not been accomplished by dark.[7] As dusk was at hand, the commander, instead of attacking, promptly retreated back to the starting point, loaded on trucks, and drove south to Nonsan. Company I remained in position all day, undergoing intermittent shelling. It stayed till 9:30 P.M., then fled through the mountains southeast of Kongju and rejoined the regiment.

July 14 was a disaster for American arms. A North Korean effort to hold the two infantry companies on the river with mortar and shell fire alone *(zheng)* had been so successful that one of the companies had actually abandoned its position. Meanwhile, the Americans had made no effort to defend against a *qi* move on the regiment's rear, which had resulted in the annihilation of an artillery battalion and the abandonment of the Kongju position. By the end of the day, the 34th Regiment had withdrawn completely out of the fight.

Meanwhile, the untried 19th Regiment was left alone at Taepyong-ni. At and on both sides of the village three companies were emplaced facing the river. Behind the infantry were three artillery battalions, the 52nd, about three miles south, and the 13th and 11th, two miles south of that.

There were scarcely any reserves. The defection of the 34th had motivated the regimental commander, Colonel Guy S. Meloy Jr., to send Lieutenant Colonel Thomas M. McGrail with a small reserve force to a point six miles on the regiment's left flank. Only Company F remained as a regimental reserve about a mile and a half behind the river.

The Korean attack on the 19th Regiment came at 3:00 A.M. on July 16. A North Korean plane flew over the Kum and dropped a flare, the signal for a general assault. Intense tank and artillery fire opened from the north bank, while Koreans used boats or rafts to get across, or swam.

At daylight they launched a textbook convergent assault. The main holding force attacked straight into the village of Taepyong-ni from the broken bridge and around it *(zheng)*. The Koreans overran parts of the defending infantry companies, and, screaming and firing Soviet PPSh-41 submachine guns ("burp guns"), seized the 1st Battalion command post, half a mile from the river. This stunning advance held the regiment by the throat.

Meanwhile, envelopments were taking place on both flanks *(qi)*. North Koreans circled around on the east, and overran a 4.2-inch mortar battery, while a larger force crossed on the west, and continued on south.

Colonel Meloy organized a counterattack that pulled in every man in both battalion and regimental headquarters, and, despite heavy casual-

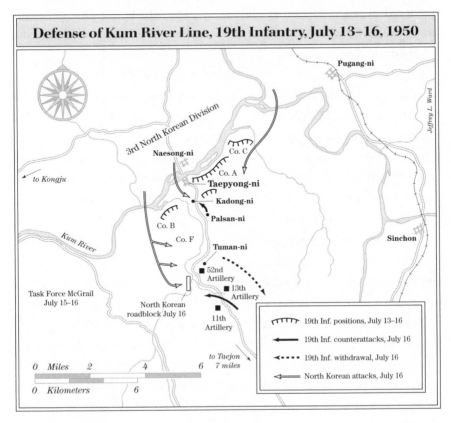

Defense of Kum River Line, 19th Infantry, July 13–16, 1950

Pugang-ni

Jeffrey L. Ward

3rd North Korean Division

to Kongju

Naesong-ni

Co. C

Co. A

Taepyong-ni

Kadong-ni

Palsan-ni

Co. B

Co. F

Kum River

Tuman-ni

Sinchon

52nd Artillery

13th Artillery

Task Force McGrail
July 15–16

North Korean roadblock July 16

11th Artillery

to Taejon
7 miles

19th Inf. positions, July 13–16
19th Inf. counterattacks, July 16
19th Inf. withdrawal, July 16
North Korean attacks, July 16

0   Miles   2   4   6

0   Kilometers   6

ties, regained the battalion command post. This seemed like a victory, but the direct attack into the village was only a decoy, and so was the envelopment to the east. The main effort was being made on the west. This force passed behind the regimental position and set up weapons on high ground above the regiment's only exit road, leading south.

From this elevation a few hundred yards south of the 52nd Artillery, the North Koreans, primarily with machine guns, blocked all movement up and down the road.

When Colonel Meloy heard of the roadblock, he directed Lieutenant Robert E. Nash to somehow get to Colonel McGrail six miles to the west, and tell him to take his force, equipped with M-24 Chaffee light tanks and tracked vehicles bearing four .50-caliber machine guns (quad-mount .50s), and break the block from the south. When Meloy himself got to the north end of the roadblock, he was shot in the calf, and turned over command to Lieutenant Colonel Otho T. Winstead, 1st Battalion chief. Winstead ordered Major Edward L. Logan to organize an attack on the block. On the way back to the river line, Winstead met his death.

Meanwhile, Lieutenant Nash, following Meloy's orders, drove through the roadblock, meeting a curtain of fire, which missed him but punctured a tire, and forced his jeep into a rice paddy. Nash walked to the 13th Artillery below the roadblock, borrowed another jeep, and, after a roundabout journey, found Colonel McGrail.

Meanwhile, Major Logan at the north end of the roadblock got nowhere. M-24 tank commanders, for unexplained reasons, refused to try to silence the North Korean machine guns. But south of the barrier McGrail organized an attack up the road with one M-24 in the lead, followed by four open-topped quad-mounts loaded with soldiers, and a second M-24 bringing up the rear. The force was stopped after a short distance by machine-gun fire. The American weapons returned fire as the infantry jumped into the roadside ditches. North Korean gunfire killed nine of the ten quad-mount gunners. The two M-24s shot off all their ammunition, then went back south. McGrail and most of the infantry crawled back in ditches and eventually got out of enemy fire.

At about 6:00 P.M., officers on the north end of the roadblock commandeered an M-24 to knock aside a pile of smoldering trucks and other vehicles that blocked the road, put Colonel Meloy inside, and, with about twenty vehicles following, ran the roadblock. They got through, but the block closed behind them, leaving about 500 men still on the north. These men set off on foot eastward around the block, as other members of the regiment had already done. Many got through, but many others did not.

The 19th Infantry lost 650 men killed. The 1st Battalion was almost cut in half: 338 out of 785 men perished. The cause, of course, was the enemy roadblock, made possible by the main thrust *(zheng)* on the village, and the two flanking moves *(qi)*. The purpose of the attack was achieved in the first minutes, when the Americans were dislodged from the river line. Yet American losses might not have been so great if leaders had organized a determined attack on the roadblock.[8]

The defeat on the Kum River led to another defeat a few days later at Taejon, and to the withdrawal of the American and South Korean armies to the Pusan perimeter.

Implications for the Future

In the examples above, Tilly and the Prussians thought the blow was going to land at one place, while it actually came at another. The American commanders along the Kum River in Korea also must have *thought* the main North Korean blows were going to come straight down the main road off the broken bridges at Kongju and Taepyong-ni, though it's difficult to understand why. Their dispositions, with their forces arrayed on either side of the road at each place, show they were paying little attention to the danger on their flanks. Neither commander made any effort to form an all-around defense of his position (hedgehog), though this is what the situation screamed for.

It is imperative for officers to think out their situations objectively and logically—to get clear not only the correct or proper tools they have to counter the enemy's expected moves, but also how they might devise *unexpected* defenses of their own.

The examples show how commanders did *not* follow these imperatives. Tilly had boxed himself in a corner between the Lech and the Danube *before* Gustavus Adolphus arrived on the scene. The Prussians had allowed the French to pass by their flank *before* they decided to retreat. In both cases the commanders did not consider the possibility that the enemy commanders would ignore their defensive plans in favor of offensive plans of their own. This, of course, was especially true of the American officers along the Kum River in Korea.

In the future we will face the unexpected and the unpredicted at least as often as in the past. And because actions will be faster, employ deadlier weapons than ever, and be spread over much vaster regions, surprises must be *planned for*, not dealt with on an ad-hoc basis when they materialize.

There is evidence that the American military is thinking hard along this line. For example, the operations in Afghanistan in the fall of 2001 were largely directed by highly trained special forces troops on the ground. These men conferred with friendly Afghan leaders at every juncture to find all intelligence available to determine where the Al Qaeda and Taliban forces were; how they could best be approached and with what weapons; and whether they had means of retreat, and how these could be blocked. In other words, the special forces units determined the best means of getting their job done *before* they called in air strikes. The success of the bombing campaign in Afghanistan in 2001 is due largely to the able advance thinking of these special forces teams.

5

Feigned Retreat

PRETENDING TO BE defeated, running away, and then ambushing the supposedly victorious pursuers has been a rule of war for as long as we have records of human conflict. A case among the Murngin Aborigines of Australia in the 1920s followed this scenario exactly—tribal members faked a rout by another Aboriginal band, and led the pursuers to the tribe's main body concealed in some woods. Chief Red Cloud (1822–1909) of the Oglala Sioux carried out a similar deception that led to the death of eighty-two whites in the Fetterman Massacre in Montana in 1866.[1]

Mao Zedong used the practice to protect the small Communist "Central Soviet" in the Wuyi Mountains of southeastern China in the war against the Nationalists from 1928 to 1934. Mao's forces were far inferior to the pursuing Nationalist troops. Retreating in seeming panic, they would entice a Nationalist unit to follow. Once the unit was isolated within Communist-held territory, the Reds surrounded it with overwhelming force and destroyed it. The Communists in the Vietnam War also used this technique on occasion, retreating before American search-and-destroy forces, then turning on a small unit that had become separated from supporting elements.

This is the rule of feigned retreat. The principle is to draw an enemy out of his defensive positions so that he can be defeated. The rule is extraordinarily difficult to pull off in battle, however, because most troops are demoralized when they are called upon to withdraw, and cannot be turned back into optimistic, aggressive soldiers simply on command of their officers.

Even so, this maxim was used with tremendous effect even by warriors who could not read and write, and had no means of communicating over distances except by flags, smoke signals, and couriers. The concept arose among horse-archers of nomad tribes on the steppes of Eurasia about 2,700 years ago, and attained its zenith there. Feigned retreat and the tactics built around it caused the downfall of sundry states and empires, and threatened the collapse of Europe in the thirteenth century.

The rule has many applications today, not least at the conceptual or strategic level. In future conflict, we can appear to withdraw from a contest or a negotiation, biding our time until our opponent lets down his defenses or exposes a vulnerable position. Then we can strike at a point of weakness. For example, we may accept publicly and at face value the expressed goodwill of a country that professes not to be sheltering terrorists, but that we suspect is actually doing so, in order to create a screen to send in secret intelligence agents to locate where the terrorists are hiding and who is protecting them. We then can confront that country, and demand that it choose which side it is on.

At the tactical level, this rule has a number of applications. Actual or potential enemies, such as lawless clans in Somalia or terrorist groups in Yemen, can easily withdraw into caves, desert places, or the surrounding population, and be difficult to locate and destroy in ordinary military operations. We can pretend that we have given up and are withdrawing, but actually work with friendly native groups or tribes to notify us when the enemy emerges, then strike. This tactic can be a two-edged sword, however, because local tribes may act as though they are American friends only for the money and goods we can supply, but actually be working for the terrorists. The only answer here, as in many other arenas, is eternal vigilance and careful intelligence-gathering to distinguish true from false friends.

Feigned retreat and the military system built around it arose in the steppes of Eurasia because conditions were ripe there. Around the oceanic peripheries of Eurasia, where rainfall was common and rivers and seas offered means of communication, the great civilizations emerged—Babylon, Egypt, Assyria, Greece, Persia, Carthage, Rome to the west, the Indus River civilization to the south, and China to the east. The main characteristics of these civilizations were agriculture, industry, and trade, and permanent habitations in villages and cities. Deep in the vast interior, however, people had to contend with temperature extremes and undependable rainfall, and much hardier societies arose. These tribes of nomads derived their sustenance from herds of cattle, sheep, goats, horses, or camels, which they followed from one grazing ground to another.

While on the periphery people cultivated the same ground and lived in the same houses year after year, in the heartland a polar opposite society arose, characterized by seasonal movements of the people with their flocks. The people lived in felt yurts or other temporary structures that could be broken down in as little as an hour and carried with them. Tribes packed their few possessions on wagons drawn by oxen or camels and driven by children, and set their stock animals in motion in great herds guarded by every able-bodied man and woman. As the brilliant historian of the steppe Stuart Legg writes, "like a great self-contained land fleet sailing slowly across a green ocean,"[2] the tribes moved hundreds of miles over the immense grasslands that stretched from Mongolia in the east to the Ukraine in the west.

Strife was common among the steppe tribes. Droughts and extremely cold winters frequently ruined grazing grounds, forcing the tribes to seek new pastures, and thereby come into conflict with other tribes. Rainfall became progressively scantier from west to east. Down the centuries, the more favorable conditions in the west drew the ambitions of steppe people in this direction, another great cause of upheaval.

These factors created not only tough, hardy, frugal people, but also highly disciplined tribes, fiercely loyal to their own members and hostile to outsiders. To protect themselves against natural disasters and incursions from other people, the steppe tribes developed a cohesive organization subject to the orders of acknowledged chieftains. Each tribe was organized as a war band and functioned along military lines. Obedience to orders and cooperation with other members of the team were inherent.

Sometime around 2500 B.C., tribesmen climbed on horses in the first tentative attempt to ride them. But the horses in that era were small ponies, too weak to carry a man far. None of the technology of riding had been developed. Instead, the horse found an entirely different use. Around 1700 B.C., probably somewhere between the southern end of the Caspian Sea and the Hindu Kush Mountains northwest of India, the horse chariot was invented.

The chariot was a melding of the wheel and oxcart conceived by farmers in the Tigris and Euphrates valley with horses of the steppes, bred by this time into much stronger animals by steppe tribesmen. Two spoked wheels spun on an axle. Pulled by two horses, the chariot could carry two men at good speed, and could turn, circle, and sweep over open ground.

The war chariot was truly revolutionary, however, because it was joined with another element, the compound bow, which was introduced into the Middle East at about this time. No one is sure of its origin, but it probably was invented centuries before in what is now Mongolia. This bow was an ideal chariot weapon because it was both strong and short. The ordinary wooden bow of the Middle East, five or six feet long, which was twice the length of the compound bow, was too awkward, and its pull, or draw, of fifty pounds gave it a range of not more than a hundred yards. The compound bow, composed of laminated wood, horn, and sinew, had a pull of well over a hundred pounds, was deadly at 300 yards, and had an extreme range of 400 yards.

The chariot changed warfare completely. Infantry were staggered by storms of high-velocity arrows fired at them well beyond their ability to retaliate. Archers in chariots could pour arrows into the enemy's front, or swing around to his flank or rear. Wherever the terrain was firm and open, there was no answer to the chariot.

Its effect was rapid. A wave of invasions crashed into the states of the Middle East. They came mostly from the north, from tribes living on the boundary between the desert and cultivated ground. The Hyksos conquered Egypt. The Kassites swept away the kingdom left by Hammurabi in Mesopotamia. The Mitanni set up a state on the upper Euphrates, and the Hittites pushed into Asia Minor and Syria. Around 1500 B.C. the Aryan people drove through the gap between the Caspian and the Pamir mountain range, pushed through the Khyber and other passes, destroyed the Indus River civilization, and in the following centuries surged down the Ganges valley and into the Deccan in the far south of India.

The chariot made little impact on the steppes, however. It was extremely expensive, because it required wood and other materials as well as the especially fine craftsmanship of wheelwrights, leather workers, and smiths, all difficult to find there. The steppe tribes required a cheaper form of mobility, more in harmony with their need for self-sufficiency.

Most likely the emphasis on chariots led to breeding increasingly stronger and bigger strains of horses. Around 900 B.C., horses had become large enough to bear the weight of a man. At about this time, perhaps a bit later, probably north of the Black Sea in the Ukraine, men began to ride horses. Neither stirrups nor true saddles came along for many centuries; only cloths or blankets were available to throw over horses' backs. But within a generation or two, horse and rider had transformed the steppes. The horse made supervision of stock animals quicker and less fatiguing, enlarged the size of controllable herds, and extended possible migration over long distances.

The next step was for the rider to take up the compound bow. When he did so, he changed the course of history. The mounted archer was perfectly adapted to the steppe way of life. He could be equipped at far less cost than a chariot team, and he was superior to it. The cheapness of the bow made the creation of a special class of society devoted to war, as had happened with the chariot, unnecessary.

The mobility of the steppe horse and rider enabled nomad chiefs to develop tactics never known before. Horses could travel across the open spaces for miles in any direction. This freedom of movement established the two pillars of steppe warfare, speed and surprise. Speed determined the way warriors attacked, and it became their armor, since they could withdraw without having to come to blows with the enemy. The innate discipline of the tribe generated extremely controlled and ordered ways to create surprise. Horse archers might materialize on all sides of an enemy, unleash a storm of arrows, attack the front, sides, and rear, and then disappear.

This last technique spawned the feigned retreat. Selected horsemen rushed forward in a furious charge, then, pretending the onslaught had failed, withdrew, seemingly in panic, and sometimes over the horizon. In many cases, enemy forces, thinking they were winning, rushed after the supposedly fleeing horsemen, and lost their own order and cohesion. All at once the horse archers regrouped, encircled isolated elements of the advancing enemy, and destroyed them one by one. Other times, when the enemy troops refused to be drawn into a chase, hours or days might elapse, with nothing to disturb the silence. Then another charge of redoubled violence would come in, often from a new direction. Success thus depended on able generalship, swift and reliable communications, and intelligent cooperation from the ranks.

As steppe warriors developed these tactics on other steppe warriors, they all became more refined and precise as the years went on, and maneuvers like the feigned retreat, unthinkable in other armies, became matters of routine.

The steppe peoples had always lusted after the riches of the civilized states of the Eurasian coastlines; now they had the means to satisfy their avarice. Steppe horsemen burst out of the heartland upon the civilizations of the periphery. Sometimes the explosions came from tribes bent on plunder living along the frontiers. At other times the friction among tribes extending across much of Eurasia created movements of entire peoples, sometimes forcing tribes to flee into regions of settled civilization.

One of the most notable of these early steppe movements was in the seventh century B.C. The Scythians, an Iranian people, drove an eastern-European people, the Cimmerians, out of the western Ukraine and regions farther west. The Cimmerians, fleeing for their lives, ravaged Asia Minor and shook the power of Assyria, an oppressive military state that held down most of the Middle East. The Scythians, seeing Assyrian power waning, formed an alliance with the Medes of Persia and the

Babylonians, and, in 612 B.C. they razed the Assyrian capital of Nineveh on the upper Tigris River, and destroyed Assyria. The offensive power of the horse archer had tipped the balance of power. The Scythians loaded up their loot and returned to their homes, but remained a latent threat.

A century later, Darius, third in the line of Persian kings who had conquered everything from the Indus and Jaxartes (Syr Darya) rivers in the east to the Nile in the west, set out to secure control of the eastern Mediterranean from the Greeks. But the Greeks' main source of grain was the northern rim of the Black Sea, and the Scythians possessed the grainfields and the ports there. Darius wanted to deprive the Greeks of their food supply, and also eliminate the possibility that the Scythians might repeat against Persia what they had inflicted on Assyria.

With a large army, Darius crossed the Danube and advanced eastward into the grasslands in 512 B.C. In response the Scythians then embarked on the greatest feigned retreat in history. The main body—men, women, and children—withdrew in three columns. Meanwhile, scouts and raiders rode around the Persian army, probing for weak spots or isolated detachments. When they found one, they swarmed all around it, covered the enemy with arrows, and destroyed it, or wheeled away if help arrived. The Scythians also burned all grain and fodder in front of the Persians, destroyed sources of water, fired every settlement, and slaughtered most of the cattle, while Scythian marauders circled continuously around the Persian army, taking a steady toll. Persian morale began to sag, and rations ran low.

Even when Darius had advanced beyond the Dniester River, close to a thousand miles from his supply base and source of reinforcements, the Scythians continued to withdraw into the featureless distance. Exasperated, Darius sent a message to the Scythians: either stand up and fight or negotiate an agreement. But the Scythians refused to do either. Knowing his troops were seriously weakening, and aware of his vulnerability because of his distance from supplies, Darius could do nothing but turn back. All the way to the Danube the Scythians harassed his retreat. Darius never challenged the Scythians again. He learned the bitter lesson that unkempt men on shaggy ponies were more than a match for the greatest army of the world. Other leaders in later times had to learn this all over again.

Manzikert: Death Blow to an Empire

As the technology of warfare evolved, the civilizations of the Middle East adopted the mounted archer as a means of self-defense, and so did China, but to a lesser degree. But Rome, Greece, and Carthage did not. Part of the reason was the relative lack of pastures in the Mediterranean lands, and part was a decided preference for the heavily armored infantryman equipped with spear or sword.[3] But the principal reason was that, in the crucial periods of their development, the civilizations to the west simply did not encounter the horse-archer.

For this lack of technological evolution Rome paid a fearful price. Its legions overcame many challenges as they expanded and defended the frontiers of the empire, but they could not stand up to the horse-archer. Three-quarters of a 40,000-man Roman army was killed or captured at the battle of Carrhae in Mesopotamia in 53 B.C. by Parthians wielding the compound bow. This defeat stopped the eastward expansion of Rome, and left it exposed to repeated attacks from Persia. These threats destabilized the eastern frontier from that day forward and contributed to the empire's fall.

The Roman Empire's successor in the east, the Byzantine, or Eastern Roman Empire, with its capital at Constantinople, built its entire military system around a new type of horseman, a heavily armored cavalryman on a large horse, who carried a sword, lance, and compound bow. This cataphract (from the Greek for "clad in full armor") was a partial merging of the two kinds of warrior who had arisen on the steppe—the horse-archer riding fast horses and wearing little or no armor, and heavy cavalry, the invention of an extremely pugnacious people, the Sarmatians, who evicted the Scythians from the region north of the Black Sea.[4]

The Sarmatians are known as one of the few peoples who required their young women to go into combat. Their great contribution to warfare was the heavy cavalryman—direct ancestor of the knight on horseback, who dominated western Europe for a thousand years. The Sarmatians developed a larger and more powerful horse. This permitted them to clothe some of their men in comparatively heavy armor and equip them with long spears or lances, whose length gave them a decisive advantage in close combat over shorter spears or swords. They thus gave birth to a shock weapon that could be thrown in to rout a cornered foe or one weakened by arrow storms.

The cataphract was the only successful combination ever invented of archer and lancer. Though his strength was formidable, he also had serious weaknesses. He rode a big horse weighed down with armor, and was therefore slower and less maneuverable than light cavalry, or horsemen not so weighed down. He had to wield both a bow and a lance, each requiring special skills.

Since light horsemen had the capability of riding around the cataphract and defeating him, the Byzantines only preserved the effectiveness of this warrior—and thereby maintained their empire—by developing outstanding tactics. They divided their forces into a fighting line, a smaller supporting line, a reserve behind the second line, and detachments on both wings, either to turn the enemy's flank or to protect the main body. With this formation, and because the cataphracts also had the compound bow, it was difficult for light horsemen to penetrate far enough to do much damage. The Byzantines made as many as five charges against an enemy that was pressing. These shocks were the key to victory. It's obvious that such a system could succeed only if an enemy was attacking. In retreat, lighter horsemen could outrun the cataphracts with ease.[5]

But defense was exactly what the Byzantine system was designed for. The paramount aim of Byzantium was not to expand, but to preserve the lands it already held. For centuries this policy worked reasonably well, despite ferocious challenges from barbarians coming into the Balkans, as well as Persia pressing from the east, and the Arabs driving from the south. By the mid-eleventh century, nearly 600 years after the Eastern Empire had definitely separated from Rome, Byzantium still ruled the Balkans south of the Danube and nearly all of Anatolia, or Asia Minor.

But grave weaknesses in the administration of the empire had developed. The court was riven for centuries by rulers and would-be rulers whose intrigues, murders, schemes, and revolts distracted the state almost to the point of dissolution. Rich people seized land from yeoman farmers who had been the mainstay of the state and the source of its soldiers. The government more and more hired mercenary soldiers, who were often unreliable, and the quality of training and performance sank. A vital skill, archery, upon which the defensive strength of the army rested, declined. One observer noted that barbarian archers on one side of the Euphrates River could hit Byzantine soldiers on the other while remaining untouched themselves.

Byzantium therefore was vulnerable to the emergence of a new enemy who could exploit the declining defensive power of the Eastern Roman army, and to a new leader who could take advantage of the debilitated leadership in Constantinople. Such an enemy arose in the middle of the eleventh century, the Seljuk Turks, a fierce tribal people who burst out of the steppes. A leader and superb field commander also arose among them, Alp Arslan.

The Seljuks had already adopted the Moslem religion, and in 1034 they crossed the Oxus River (Amu Darya) and overran the Iranian plateau, Iraq, and Azerbaijan. In 1063, Alp Arslan defeated rival claimants, became sultan, or king, of all the Seljuks, and moved against Armenia, a Byzantine-controlled buffer state in eastern Anatolia. After a twenty-five-day siege, Alp captured the Armenian capital of Ani in 1064, burned it to the ground, and massacred the inhabitants. He then moved forty miles west and seized Kars, another large Armenian city.

The Seljuks' strategic purpose was to depopulate the country in order to create grazing space for their herds. The army had no standard organization, but consisted of individual archer-horseman bands under a chief, who gained his position by bravery and daring, and by finding abundant plunder for his men. Alp Arslan knew this system of raids and devastation offered the Seljuks a better chance for success than pitched battles with the Byzantine army.

Byzantium was ruled throughout this period by a series of profligate emperors and feckless bureaucrats, and their response to the Seljuk incursion was virtually nil. As a result, Turkish bands raided deep into Anatolia with impunity. The Byzantine emperor Constantine X died in 1067, and his wife Eudocia married the son of a distinguished military family, who took the throne on January 1, 1068, as Romanus IV Diogenes.

He was courageous but impetuous, and before long, Eudocia's son Michael, and Constantine's brother, John Ducas, intrigued against him and drew large parts of the army to their side.

In 1068, Romanus at last led the Byzantine army out in response to the Turks, but he was baffled by their evasive tactics, and his own forces rarely acted in concert. The next year much the same thing happened. Romanus campaigned over large parts of Anatolia, chasing the Turks, but they, after ravaging the countryside, escaped. In 1070, Alp Arslan besieged and captured the Byzantine city of Manzikert, north of Lake Van in eastern Anatolia, and also took Khilat (Ahlat), thirty miles south on the lake shore.

Romanus was infuriated, and early in 1071 he formed an army and marched to Erzurum (Theodosiopolis), about a hundred miles northwest of Manzikert. At the time, Alp Arslan was at Aleppo, in northern Syria, 400 miles to the southwest, and Romanus figured he could recapture the two localities before Alp could respond. Besides, Romanus did not fear the Seljuks. In previous operations they had withdrawn rather than challenge the Byzantine army.

Upon reaching the region north of Manzikert in August 1071, Romanus divided his army. He sent more than half of his force, including many of the best troops and all the infantry, under a leading general, Joseph Tarchaniotes, to recapture Khilat. He kept the remainder of his force to seize Manzikert.

Manzikert surrendered without a fight, but at Khilat things went badly wrong. Ever since he'd learned Romanus was advancing on Manzikert, Alp Arslan had been on the march toward the two cities, assembling an army as he went. As the Byzantines moved on Khilat from the north, they collided with the 10,000-man advance force of Alp's 40,000-man army. This larger part of the Byzantine army turned tail and fled, retreating well over 200 miles west, all the way back to Melitene on the Euphrates River, and entirely out of the campaign. The reason was probably treachery on the part of Tarchaniotes, who also did not inform Romanus of his retreat.

Romanus's own first encounter with the Turks near Manzikert was a minor disaster. It was also a superb example of the use of feigned retreat. This skirmish should have warned Romanus of the effectiveness of the tactic, but did not. Foragers reported that they had been beset by Turks, and Romanus dispatched a small group to drive them off. But Turkish archers shot at the Byzantines from a distance, and refused to leave. Romanus now sent a reconnaissance in force under Basilacius, a hotheaded, reckless officer. He charged furiously, and the Turks fled. Basilacius pressed after them till he had gone so far that he lost sight of the Byzantine camp. The Turks now snapped the trap shut. They encircled the force, captured Basilacius, and killed almost all of his men.

With this warning Romanus should have acted with great caution in future encounters with the Turks. Indeed, in his manual *Tactica*, issued in 900, the Byzantine emperor Leo the Wise had laid down the proper course for a situation just like the one Romanus faced. His advice was to engage the enemy at close quarters; take advantage of the Byzantines' superior weight and skill at hand-to-hand fighting; keep enemy forces away by arrow storms; beware of heedless pursuit and ambushes; hold forces close together to avoid parts being encircled; never fight with uncovered flanks and rear; and back up on a natural defense like a marsh, river, or defile.

Romanus did none of this. He did, however, on August 19, 1071, draw up his army at Manzikert in the fashion ordained by *Tactica*. That is, he set up his 40,000 men in four separate but closely connected bodies—left wing, right wing, center (which he commanded), and rear guard (commanded by Andronicus Ducas, eldest son of John Ducas, his secret enemy).

If Romanus had remained where he was, on the defensive, he could not have been beaten, and the Turks would ultimately have had to withdraw for lack of supplies. Alp Arslan knew this, and set in motion the standard tactics employed on the steppe for over a thousand years. The Turks made no effort to close with the enemy, or deliver any sort of general attack. Instead large bodies of horse-archers hovered about and shot from various points. The Byzantine cavalry tried to reply, but when the main body sent out skirmishers, they were outnumbered and suffered in the exchange of arrows—especially because Byzantine archery had degenerated so much over the years, while steppe archery had not. A number of men were shot down, and many horses disabled. As the Byzantine troops grew increasingly restive at the protracted fight, Romanus became angry, and in the afternoon he ordered the whole army to advance.

This was madness. The Turks, as they had done countless times before, withdrew before the Byzantines, refusing to come to blows. The entire Eastern Roman system of warfare was built on the knowledge that the heavily armored cataphracts could not outrun light cavalry. The cataphracts could only succeed if they were able to drive the light horsemen against some obstacle, like a river or defile, which would prevent further flight. But on the plains around Manzikert, the Turkish cavalry could withdraw for days and never be cornered.

Romanus took the precaution of keeping all four elements of his army together as they advanced, and especially kept the rear division in place to prevent an attack on his rear. For some time the Byzantine army advanced slowly across the plain, passing the abandoned and empty Turkish camp. But all the while the enemy refused to make a stand, constantly withdrawing.

Dusk came. The men were tired and thirsty. Romanus halted. He was no closer to the Turks than he had been at the outset. But now he realized it was getting dark, and he had failed to provide a guard for his camp. He ordered the army to turn about and return to its starting point. Thus began the disasters. A force that must make quick, unexpected changes can easily fall into disorder. This happened in the turnaround. The retreat order was not exercised with the same precision by all divisions. The elements on the wings got the order late, did not understand the reason, and when they wheeled about did not keep the proper distance or relative position with the center. Gaps opened among several parts of the wings.

The Turks, as was their custom, closed in on the army as it began to retreat, molesting the retiring columns with severe attacks. Romanus then ordered the army to face about again and beat off these assaults. The whole front line did as told, but the rear (now in front) under Andronicus, son of Romanus's secret enemy John Ducas, did not. With deliberate malice, Andronicus continued his march back to camp, abandoning the rest of the army.

The loss of the rear left the remainder of the Byzantine force unprotected against Turks stealing around the wings to strike from behind. The Turks concentrated their efforts on the right wing, because, in trying to face both ways, this force had fallen into disorder. Stunned by one arrow assault after another in the twilight, the right wing at last broke up and fled. This uncovered the center. The Turks at once fell on its flank and rear. The emperor put up a gallant defense, and turned one charge after another. But the left wing eventually became divided from the center. Encircled by horse-archers, it collapsed, and the survivors ran from the field. The Turks now turned on the center from all sides. The center force held out till full darkness, when the Turks finally broke up the columns. This led to a fearful slaughter. Scarcely a man escaped. One of the few was the emperor himself, who was captured.

The destruction of the army at Manzikert was the fatal blow that ultimately led to the collapse of the Byzantine empire. Seljuk raiders flooded the whole of Asia Minor over the next ten years. They were almost unopposed. The Turks had no use for towns, vineyards, and arable land. They wanted a desert for their herds, and they got it. At the end of the period, Anatolia was reduced to wastes. Thirty years later the entire region—where a sturdy yeoman class had farmed and thrived for centuries—was a land of briars and ruins.

The last bastion of the Byzantine empire, the walled city of Constantinople, fell in 1453, when the Seljuks' successors, the Ottoman Turks, beat down the walls with cannons.

The loss at Manzikert was caused in part by treason. But the overwhelming cause was gross failure of leadership, for the army would not have perished if the emperor had not ignored well-known doctrine, advanced into open country where he had cover neither for his flanks nor his rear, and chased a foe who could not be caught. Feigned retreat is a snare, and it needs someone gullible enough to fall into it.

Yet if Byzantium had possessed a responsible government, another leader who knew the rules might have come forward, built a new army, and stopped the Turks. This did not happen because the ruling circles of the empire were corrupt, self-seeking, and unbelievably obtuse. Instead of girding themselves to meet the challenge, they fell to fighting among themselves. In the end Byzantium failed, not because of the mistake of a single emperor, but because it was not fit to survive.

Mongol Invasion of Europe, 1241–1242

Western civilization's focus on the armored knight riding a heavy horse and wielding a lance as his principal weapon had profound social and military effects. The high cost of armor, swords, lances, and warhorses led kings to assign land and serfs to warriors so that those warriors could contribute the means to conduct warfare. Warriors were thereby transformed into a privileged, wealthy aristocracy and the rest of society into a servitor class, except for a small clergy allied to the aristocracy. Europe's reliance on a single form of mounted warrior and the consequent devaluing of inexpensive light cavalry (as well as infantry) had equally stark military consequences when its chivalry came into contact with the greatest army that ever arose on the steppes.

This army was that of the Mongols, who came to power in the last years of the twelfth century under their khan, Genghis. With his principal *orlok*, or marshal, Subedei Bahadur of the Reindeer People, Genghis Khan took all of the knowledge of horsemanship, archery, and dizzying tactics that had matured on the steppes for 1,500 years, combined them with an efficiency and discipline never attained before, carried the speed and the deception of steppe warfare to its extreme limits, and achieved victories on a scale no people or empire ever reached before or after.[6]

In a stunning campaign in 1219–1220, Mongol forces seized Transoxiana between the Oxus (Amu Darya) and Jaxartes (Syr Darya) rivers, and virtually destroyed the powerful Khwarezmian empire of Iran and Afghanistan. In 1221, Subedei, with the assistance of another orlok, Jebe Noyan, led 20,000 men on a two-year reconnaissance and exploratory mission into the western steppes to open a path for further Mongol conquests. This became the greatest cavalry raid in history. The Mongols destroyed opposing armies in the Caucasus mountains and in the western plains, and secured valuable information about the state of defenses in Europe and the prospects for expansion there.

After the death of Genghis in 1227, the Mongols' interest in Europe waned until 1236. At that time the orlok Subedei gained the enthusiasm of

Genghis's successor, Ogedei, to subdue the western steppes of Russia, so that they could be used as a springboard to seize the great grassed plain of Hungary. With this natural prairie as a base and grazing ground for their horses, the Mongols could destroy the nations of Europe one by one.

The Mongol army built by Genghis and his orloks was the most effective war machine on earth. It was based on the traditional strengths of the steppe: extreme mobility and the compound bow. But it possessed two additional elements: an almost foolproof tactical system, which included a refined form of the feigned retreat, and strategic genius, exemplified by Genghis until his death, and by his two chief orloks, Jebe and especially Subedei. The Mongols employed several types of arrows: long-range arrows to strike at a distance, whistling arrows to signal, and incendiary arrows to set fire to wooden buildings and roofs. They also deployed smoke bombs, possibly fueled by petroleum or another oil. With them, or by firing prairies or woodlands, they created smokescreens to conceal their movements.

The Mongol army consisted entirely of cavalry, both the light horsearchers and the heavy cavalry developed by the Sarmatians. At some time before the sixth century the stirrup, invented in India, had spread throughout Eurasia, and a true saddle had been developed. Together the saddle and stirrup gave horsemen a much firmer seat from which to shoot their arrows or deliver lance blows.

Mongol tactics were refined by repeated drills and built on tried techniques, directed by clear signals from the leaders. They were highly efficient, and led to astonishing Mongol success.

The battle formation was in five ranks. Heavy cavalry made up the first two, and was intended for the major blow. The horses were armored, and the men wore iron helmets and cuirasses of oxhide or leather-covered iron scales, and carried twelve-foot lances, and scimitars, battle axes, or maces. Light cavalry, wearing light armor or none at all, and carrying small swords, javelins, and bows, composed the other three ranks.

In Mongol attacks, light troops spread out as skirmishers well ahead of the main body. They formed three groups, a vanguard and two flanks. If the enemy attacked a flank, the light cavalry that met him would automatically become the vanguard, and the other skirmisher units would swing either to the left or right, while the main body wheeled to face the threat.

Once the vanguard was engaged, the light cavalry in the three rear ranks of the main body would advance through the heavy cavalry to join the skirmishers. If the Mongols were advancing, the light troops showered the enemy front with arrows and javelins. If, however, the enemy was advancing, the light troops withdrew before the enemy, shooting arrows over their shoulders. The purpose of the arrow storms, whether the light troops were advancing or withdrawing, was to open the enemy ranks. When this happened, the light horsemen broke away to either flank, leaving a path for the heavy cavalry to gallop in for a devastating blow.

If the light cavalry failed to create the necessary gaps in the enemy line, the Mongol commander would order the light horse on one wing to move around to the enemy's flank on that side and assault it at right angles. At the same time the heavy cavalry would gallop around behind the same flank in a "standard sweep" and make their decisive charge there.

As an integral part of their tactical system, the Mongols raised the feigned retreat to an art. This was their favorite tactic if the enemy was not shattered by an initial attack. They created a special unit, the *mangudai*, that would charge the enemy alone. After a fearsome assault, the mangudai would break ranks and flee in hopes of provoking the enemy to give chase. All light cavalry learned this technique, so if a large mangudai was needed, it could be formed quickly. As had happened for a millennium and a half, unsuspecting enemy units would usually be convinced that they were on the verge of victory, and would spring after the fleeing Mongols. Unseen in the rear, Mongol archers waited. By the time they were upon the archers, the enemy horsemen were spread out, and many would fall to well-aimed bow shots. Disordered and suffering heavy casualties, the enemy would be vulnerable to the Mongol heavy cavalry, which now made its charge.

In 1236, Subedei moved inexorably across the steppes. He subdued the northern Bulgars on the upper Volga River, and the next year the Kipchaks on the lower Volga. His flanks secure, and with an army of 120,000, Subedei then crossed the frozen Volga into Russia in the winter of 1237. For the next three years the Mongols systematically destroyed most of the Russian states, using the frozen rivers in winter as highways to penetrate deep into the country, and avoid the thick forests. In December 1240 Subedei burned Kiev, and massacred most of its people. Russian resistance now collapsed, and the Mongols quickly moved to the Carpathian mountains, dividing Hungary from Russia.

Although European rulers had been aware the Mongols were moving their way for at least two years, they did nothing to prepare. Pope Gregory IX was not sad to see the Eastern Orthodox Christians of Russia destroyed. But when the Mongols reached the border of Hungary, he became concerned for the Catholics of that country. He and the Holy Roman emperor, Frederick II, who ruled much of Germany and Italy, were on the verge of a violent power conflict, however, and could spare little attention to the pleas of the Hungarian king, Bela IV.

Hungary, Poland, and the German Teutonic Knights, now colonizing the Baltic coast of Prussia, Lithuania, and Latvia, were left on their own to take up the defense. But Poland was fragmented into nine principalities, and the Hungarian nobility argued with King Bela for concessions before agreeing to fight.

Through paid spies (they hired Venetians in that role during the western raid of 1221–1222), the Mongols realized Europe was disunited. They were therefore not concerned that, owing to the need to garrison Russia, they could field only 100,000 men to seize Hungary, their first target.

In January 1241, Subedei concentrated the Mongol army north of the Carpathians around Lemberg (Lvov) and Przemysl, near the present-day Polish-Ukrainian border. His intention was to force the Carpathian passes and march on the Hungarian capital, Gran (Esztergom), on the Danube, twenty-five miles northwest of Buda and Pest. But he knew an advance directly into Hungary was dangerous, with the Poles and Germans on his right flank. Subedei had to quell those threats, and also protect against possible drives from the west by the duke of Austria and the king of Bohemia.

He conceived a remarkable strategic plan that diverted the Poles and Germans, and also eliminated the possibility that the Hungarians and their allies could prevent the rapid seizure of all Hungary east of the Danube.

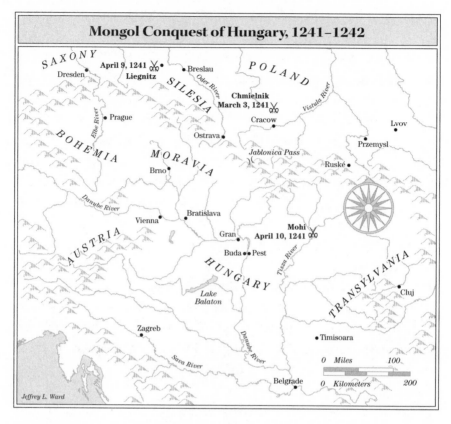

He divided his army into four parts. Three he assigned to the main mission, Hungary, and the fourth to removing danger on his right flank.

This fourth army, under Princes Baidar and Kadan, consisted of two 10,000-man *tumens*, or divisions. It was the first to move, at the beginning of March 1241, crossing the Vistula at Sandomir, which it took by storm. The Poles were completely surprised and had not gathered their forces.

The Mongols' aim was to draw the Poles and Germans away from Hungary by threatening invasion of their homelands. Kadan, with one tumen, moved northwest to spread alarm over as large a part of Poland as possible and threaten German states west of the Oder River. Meanwhile, Baidar, with the other tumen, continued southwest toward the Polish capital of Cracow, burning, pillaging, and drawing attention to himself. When Baidar reached Cracow, however, he turned abruptly around and retreated, as if he were a raiding party returning to base. The chivalry of Poland did not recognize this as a feigned retreat, threw caution to the winds, abandoned the walls of Cracow, drove after the retreating Mongols on their large warhorses, and attacked.

Baidar's men broke and fled, allowing their prisoners to escape. Certain the Mongols were on the run, the Poles chased after them. At Chmielnik, eleven miles from Cracow, a Mongol ambush awaited them. Massed bodies of archers launched clouds of armor-piercing arrows at the Polish warriors, killing most of them. The people of Cracow deserted the town, and the Mongols burned it.

Baidar and Kadan planned to meet at Breslau (Wroclaw), the Silesian capital, but Baidar arrived first, and found the inhabitants had burned their city and taken refuge in the citadel. There Baidar learned that Henry of Silesia had gathered an army of 25,000 at Liegnitz (Legnica), forty miles west. The force was composed of some armored knights, Silesians, Knights Templar and Hospitaller, Teutonic Knights, and some surviving Polish horsemen. But most were Polish, Silesian, and Moravian feudal levies, foot soldiers armed largely with pikes, who were virtually useless for offensive battle.

Baidar also learned that King Wenceslas of Bohemia was marching to join Henry. Sending messages to Kadan and also Subedei, he at once set his tumen in motion for Liegnitz, hoping to get there before Wenceslas. Kadan joined him on the road, and together they arrived at Liegnitz on April 8. The Silesian Henry did not know the Bohemian army was only a day's march away, and marched out on a plain beyond the city to challenge the Mongols.

When the Mongol advance guard appeared in close order, it appeared so small that Henry sent only a modest detachment to meet it. But the group received a terrific onslaught of arrows, and fell back. Henry at once ordered all the rest of his horsemen to attack. The Mongol vanguard broke and fled, and once again the European chivalry chased after the fleeing enemy at a gallop. The charge turned quickly into an extended, disorganized race. Behind a screen of smoke bombs, the Mongol archers were waiting. When the knights came within range, the arrows struck many of them, bringing the charge to a halt. As the knights milled about in confusion, the Mongol heavy cavalry assaulted, killing most of them. The Mongol archers now rode through the smoke screen and shot down the infantry, while other horsemen ran down and killed Henry of Silesia. The Mongols filled nine sacks of right ears cut from the slain and sent them to the nominal commander, Prince Batu, Genghis's grandson.

Wenceslas, however, remained a threat. If his army were added to the Hungarian defenders now mobilizing on the west bank of the Danube, he might tip the balance. Therefore it was important to keep him occupied far to the north.

When Wenceslas heard of the disaster at Liegnitz, he withdrew, collected reinforcements from Thuringia and Saxony, and moved to the Carpathian Mountains sixty miles southeast of Liegnitz, in hopes of luring the Mongols into narrow passes there and destroying them. But Baidar and Kadan reconnoitered the passes, and would not be drawn in.

Determined to ensure that Wenceslas would be no factor in the upcoming collision in Hungary, Baidar and Kadan then made a deep feint to the west, as if planning to invade Germany. Just as they hoped, this drew Wenceslas after them. The Mongols broke into small bodies, rode entirely around the reinforced Bohemian army, and spread out in a wide corridor through Moravia, burning villages and stores and creating a desert to prevent Wenceslas from following.

Once through Moravia, the Mongol princes reassembled their men and turned southeast to join Subedei, ready to fall on the flank of the Austrians if they moved to the aid of Hungary. In a whirlwind campaign, this small force had swept 250 miles across Poland and Silesia and, by threatening to invade Germany, removed any possibility of intervention by Polish, German, Czech, and Austrian forces many times its size. This same small force then managed to ride 300 miles back through Moravia and Hungary to the main body in time to be of service if needed.

Subedei, meanwhile, was setting up the conditions for a giant feigned retreat designed to destroy the Hungarian army massed on the Danube River at Buda and Pest.

First he had to deceive the Hungarians in order to prevent them from throwing effective opposition in his path. To achieve this, Subedei ordered each of the three parts of the main army to enter Hungary from a different direction. The Hungarian king Bela could not concentrate against any one threat, because the other two could drive on his rear or seize important cities or terrain. If Bela divided his force to contain all three threats, the Mongols could reduce two of their own forces and increase the third to overwhelming strength.

Subedei was confident that the Hungarians could not effectively contest any of his three columns, and all could reach the main barrier of the Danube unmolested, and there reunite. In the event, the Mongol columns moved so fast and in such bewildering fashion that King Bela was unable to challenge any of them, and kept his army at Buda and Pest, abandoning all of his kingdom east of the Danube.

The Mongols' right, or northerly, column moved west from Przemysl in early March, shielded on the north by the Vistula and by the flank column of Baidar and Kadan, which had moved a few days before. The right column then turned south through passes of the Carpathians and, in two bodies, swept in a long curving advance to the Danube on March 17, seizing Vac, on the east side of the river between Pest and Gran, and slaughtering the population.

Meanwhile the left, or southerly, column made a great arching sweep to the southeast through Moldavia and Walachia and broke through passes into Transylvania. While part of this column prevented the Transylvanian nobility from bringing forces to aid Bela, another part, under Subedei, raced up the lower Tisza (Theiss) River valley, arriving at Pest on April 3.

The last column to move was the central one containing Prince Batu and the elite guard. This column forced the pass of Ruske in the Carpathians on March 12, and advanced directly on Pest by way of the upper Tisza River valley. The advance guard arrived on the Danube on March 15, and the main body two days later. The movement of the advance guard was one of the fastest in history, 180 miles in three days through enemy country covered with snow.

By April 3, 1241, Subedei had assembled his three columns opposite Buda, on the west bank of the Danube, as well as opposite Pest, on the east bank, where Bela had concentrated his army of 100,000. Subedei remained outnumbered, with about 70,000 men. One column was still in Transylvania, while the northern detachment had not yet fought the battle of Liegnitz. Subedei knew it would be too dangerous to try to forge the river in the face of the assembled Hungarian army, and that the longer he lingered on the banks of the Danube, the more likely other European rulers would be to send reinforcements.

Subedei therefore wanted to draw the Hungarian army away from possible reinforcements and also away from the strong defensive line of the Danube. A threatened attack would do the opposite, concentrating the Hungarian army there.

Accordingly, Subedei commenced a feigned retreat. The Hungarians concluded that the Mongols had been terrified at the size of the army opposing them, and foolishly clamored to pursue the supposedly intimidated foe. The Hungarians thus were lured from the protection of the Danube, as well as from the possibility of reinforcement.

The Mongols retreated slowly, taking six days to reach the Sajo River, about a hundred miles northeast of Buda-Pest. On a heath called Mohi, just west of the Sajo, Batu and Subedei found a good place to turn on their pursuers.

On April 9 the Mongol army rode over the heath, crossed the only bridge over the Sajo, and continued on eastward for ten miles into the thickets around the hills and vineyards of Tokay. In this broken region the Mongols found ample hiding places. When a Hungarian detachment rode into the thickets, they found nothing.

The Hungarians camped on the heath of Mohi. They drew their wagons in a circle girded by chains and ropes, and placed their tents inside. On the Hungarian right, or south, were the marshes of the Tisza River, in front across the heath was the Sajo River, and to the left, or north, were hills and forests.

The battle opened just before dawn on April 10. Batu, with 40,000 men, launched an attack on the bridge over the Sajo. The Hungarians defended fiercely, and the Mongols could make little headway until they brought up catapults and bombarded the Hungarians with fire bombs, forcing them back, and allowing the Mongols to get on the western side.

The Mongols were still sorely pressed, however, outnumbered well over two to one by an enemy that charged repeatedly. Only flights of arrows prevented the Mongols from being overwhelmed. For two hours Batu and his men withstood the massive assaults, losing many men, but utterly absorbing the Hungarians' attention.

While Batu fixed the Hungarian army to the front, Subedei's engineers built a bridge downstream across the Sajo. Now, at the height of the battle at the other bridge, he led 30,000 Mongols onto the southern flank of the enemy army. The Hungarians were stunned, but were able to retreat to their encampment. The Mongols surrounded the encampment, pounded it with arrow storms and catapult missiles, set fire to wagons and tents with incendiary arrows, and shattered Hungarian confidence.

Next the Mongols assembled for a charge, but left a large gap opening on a wide gorge to the west through which the armies had advanced into the heath. The bravest Hungarian knights formed a wedge to meet the charge. But many more Hungarians threw away their weapons and armor to increase their speed, and fled out through the gorge, back toward Buda-Pest. The Mongols killed many of the knights in the wedge with arrows. Only when the survivors became confused and disorganized did the Mongol heavy cavalry charge and destroy them.

The great mass of the Hungarian army retreated westward, believing they were getting away, but actually falling into a trap. The Mongol light cavalry, whose horses were generally faster than the heavy European warhorses, pursued the fugitives on either side, shooting them down like helpless fleeing game. For thirty miles back toward Pest the road was littered with dead. At least 70,000 men died on the battlefield or the flight.

Observers were impressed by the speed, silence, and skill of the Mongol movements, carried out in response to signals with black and white flags. They were also struck by the deadliness of Mongol archery. According to John of Plano Carpini, a contemporary chronicler, the Mongols "wounded and killed many men and horses, and only when other men and horses were worn down by the arrows did they come to close quarters."

After the Sajo River disaster, most Hungarian resistance collapsed. The Mongols pushed up to the Danube and burned Pest, but did not cross the Danube till it froze hard in late December 1241. Then they sacked Buda, destroyed Gran, and sent reconnaissances into Austria and

Croatia. Europe lay open to invasion. No army capable of defeating the Mongols existed. Subedei's plan to subdue each European nation one by one seemed about to get under way.

But on December 11, 1241, a messenger arrived from the Mongol capital, Karakorum, with the news that the khan, Ogedai, had died, and his wife was acting as regent till a new khan could be elected. The Mongol princes were eager to get back to compete for the succession, and started out for home. Batu, whose domain consisted of the new lands the Mongols had conquered to the west, felt he could not hold Hungary but could hold Russia and the Volga valley with Turkomen conscripts. Accordingly the Mongols withdrew early in 1242. Batu returned to his base camp, Sarai, near the Volga sixty miles north of Astrakhan, and there established the capital of a Mongol empire that became known as the Golden Horde.

There was never another opportunity for the Mongols to invade Europe. The Mongol incursion came to seem like a nightmare to the people of Europe, and they invented many myths about how they had defeated and turned back the "Tartars," as they called the Mongols. But they had been saved only by the death of the khan. Had Ogedai survived for a few more years, the history of Europe would have been vastly different.

Implications for the Future

The days of an army actually withdrawing to pull an enemy into an ambush have, of course, passed. Yet the significance of deception has by no means gone away. Ever since September 11, American officials undoubtedly have been dissembling with renegade or former-renegade states, like the Sudan, Libya, Somalia, Yemen, Iraq, and Iran, regarding what our plans and intentions are in the hunt for terrorists. It's also improbable that we are leveling completely with the Palestine Liberation Front, our newfound ally Pakistan, or any of a dozen other states that fear our power but have axes of their own to grind. It is not in American interests to be entirely open with the leaders of any states, except true and trusted friends like Britain, Canada, Australia, and Germany. Indeed, the greatest future of the feigned retreat may lie in the practice of *Realpolitik,* or the unashamed advancement of American interests throughout the world. Until September 11, we tended to think long and hard before we pushed our cases with other countries. Not any longer. Nevertheless, feigned retreat, or *seeming* to go along with policies we don't like until we're ready to change them, will disguise our intentions and disarm our opponents.

Even so, deliberate deception is becoming difficult to bring about in today's world of instant communications, constant conjecture about what is or is not being contemplated, and second-guessing by talking heads on television.

Among the most instructive recurring scenes after the September 11 attacks were the daily briefings at the Pentagon, most often conducted by the secretary of defense, Donald H. Rumsfeld. The room was filled with television and press reporters, some of whom regularly asked the secretary and generals who appeared at the podium precisely what kind of plans they had for military operations, what sort of bombs they expected to use, where they intended to drop them, whether one type of operation or another was going to take place, how many troops were going to be involved, and how and when they were going to be deployed.

The questions went on and on, seeking the most intricate details of future military operations. Few of the questioners seemed to appreciate the implication that everything said was beamed to the world, to ene-mies as well as friends, and that prior knowledge of an attack is an almost sure guarantee of foiling it. Despite being reminded of this by Secretary Rumsfeld and the generals, few reporters appeared to com-prehend that the questions they wanted answered were precisely the kind of information the military must keep secret.

Rather, reporters seemed to expect generals and the secretary to divulge everything because this was a free country, and they represented the free press. Reporters will answer that they were only doing their job. In a sense this is true, because free, unafraid analysis of government actions is the one sure way to prevent dictatorship and oppression. The monstrous societies created by Adolf Hitler and Joseph Stalin showed too well the horrors that can result from censorship and totalitarianism. We cannot, however, expect reporters to be informed of the complexities of a particular military operation. They simply cannot appreciate fully the dangers of divulging details. Governments must accept this lack of perception on the part of most members of the press.

The conflict between free speech and deception in war will not go away. Secrecy is far harder to achieve today than it was in World War II or Korea. The United States gathered a huge naval armada and two full combat divisions for the surprise invasion of Inchon in Korea on September 15, 1950, and the North Koreans had no idea it was going to happen. It's questionable whether a deception of such magnitude could be pulled off today.

Fortunately for the world, operations as large as Inchon are not likely to be needed in the future. Smaller projections of power and smaller military operations may in fact make it easier to achieve secrecy because they will not make as large an imprint. Still, the comment of Confederate general Stonewall Jackson has resonance today. When chided because he would not tell even his closest lieutenants what his plans were, Jackson answered, "If I can deceive my own friends, I can make certain of deceiving the enemy."[7]

6

The Central Position

A COMMANDER HAS always faced an extreme challenge when confronting an enemy decidedly stronger than he is. Although few generals have used the central position, it remains one of the most effective strategies to employ against a stronger enemy.

The rule at work here is to maneuver one's army or force so that it lands between two smaller enemy forces, and then to eliminate one before having to deal with the other. The enemy may be more powerful overall, but if his army is divided, one part at a time may be challenged and beaten.

Instead of consciously applying this rule, most generals over the centuries have aimed for the reverse. They have usually worried that if they got between two enemy forces, they, not the enemy, would be in jeopardy. In a typical situation, a general feared that the enemy forces on either side would converge on his forces. Instead of seeing his location as an advantage, he saw it as a peril.

Because commanders so often have sensed danger and not opportunity in the central position, its execution requires imaginative and confident leaders. For this reason the central position is one challenge where the distinction between bold generals and timid generals is most apparent.

In a complex, intertwined series of campaigns in the Civil War in the spring of 1862, this dichotomy between the leader who seeks the central position and the leader who shuns it was demonstrated in a most dramatic way. One commander, the Confederate general Stonewall Jackson, exploited the central position with amazing results, while the other leader, President Abraham Lincoln, disregarded the central position and allowed great opportunities to slip through his fingers.[1]

After Union forces were defeated at First Manassas, or First Bull Run, in July 1861, President Lincoln appointed George B. McClellan to rebuild the Federal army. By March 1862 his army was twice the size of the Confederate army, and McClellan transported it by boat down the Chesapeake Bay to Fort Monroe, at Hampton on the peninsula between the York and James rivers in Virginia. He then began an advance northwest toward the Confederate capital of Richmond. The intention of this advance was to drive the main Confederate army, under Joseph E. Johnston, out of Richmond and end the war.

Johnston blocked the Union army with a line between the York and James rivers. Although the line was weak, McClellan stopped in front of

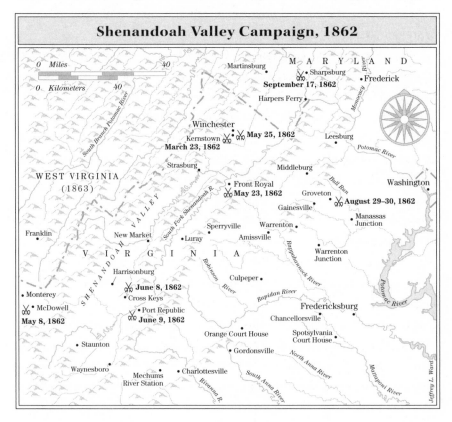

Shenandoah Valley Campaign, 1862

it for a month, and began calling on Lincoln to release Irwin McDowell's 40,000-man corps at Fredericksburg, fifty-five miles north of Richmond, to drive directly on the flank or rear of Johnston's army. Such a move would be decisive, forcing Johnston to abandon Richmond and possibly surrender his whole army.

The Confederacy had no troops to block McDowell. In fact, the only distracting force General Johnston could muster immediately was a tiny 4,600-man army under Stonewall Jackson that was in the northern end of the Shenandoah Valley of Virginia, watching a 23,000-man Union army under Nathaniel B. Banks around Harpers Ferry, on the Potomac River, only a few miles northwest of Washington.

Lincoln had placed such a large force under Banks because he and other Union leaders worried that a Confederate army might burst out of the valley and seize Washington. Jackson's force was much too small to pose any such danger, however, and Johnston feared rather that Lincoln would transfer a large part of Banks's army to assist McClellan on the peninsula.

Since he had no other troops, Johnston abandoned any idea of stopping McDowell from marching on Richmond, and merely instructed Jackson to do what he could to occupy Banks, in order to keep him from detaching troops to McClellan.[2]

Jackson had much greater imagination than Joe Johnston, and he conceived a plan to do far more than merely bottle up Banks in the valley. He also planned to prevent Lincoln from sending McDowell's corps to aid McClellan, and, in addition, to stop yet a third Union army, a 15,000-man force under John C. Frémont, from approaching the valley from the Allegheny Mountains. He achieved all of this in the Shenandoah Valley campaign, one of the most spectacular and successful operations ever recorded of an inferior force defeating much larger forces. The campaign involved two moves from the central position, both of which were decisive.

Jackson's first maneuver was a bold strike on March 23, 1862, with only 3,000 men against a Union force three times larger at Kernstown, four miles below Winchester in the northern end of the Shenandoah Valley. Although Jackson lost the engagement, along with nearly one-quarter of his entire force, Lincoln could not believe Jackson would have made such a move without great reserve strength, and, just as Jackson had hoped, canceled an ordered transfer of part of Banks's army to aid McClellan. Much more important, Lincoln ordered McDowell's corps to remain near Washington—to defend it in the event Jackson struck for the capital.

Thus Jackson's first move, directed against the anxieties of Abraham Lincoln for the security of the capital, was overwhelmingly successful. McDowell was stopped in his tracks. McClellan was irate, and Lincoln reassured him that he would release McDowell as soon as the threat to the capital disappeared.

Banks began moving after Jackson, who had retreated south into the Shenandoah Valley to Harrisonburg, while Frémont advanced toward Banks from the Alleghenies, aiming at the valley town of Staunton, twenty-five miles south of Harrisonburg. Jackson increased his force to 6,000 men by recruiting, while the Confederate president, Jefferson Davis, and his military adviser, Robert E. Lee, gave him access to an 8,000-man division under Richard S. Ewell, resting on the slopes of the Blue Ridge Mountains, just to the east of the valley.

If Frémont and Banks joined, they would have well over twice as many troops as Jackson, and could easily oust him from the valley, and either advance on Richmond from the west, or move over to assist McClellan.

But Jackson was between Banks and Frémont. The key was the town of Staunton. Here the road from Franklin (now in West Virginia), upon which Frémont was marching, met the Valley Pike from Harrisonburg. If Jackson could get to Staunton before either Union commander, he would interpose his army between the two Federal armies, and might strike one before having to deal with the other.

An advance directly on Staunton, however, would alert both Federal commanders to his intent, and induce them to speed up their march, blocking him on both the north and the south somewhere south of Harrisonburg.

Jackson now made one of the most stunning moves in military history. He marched his army, not south toward Staunton, but fifteen miles *east*, and ordered Ewell to join him from the other side of the Blue Ridge Mountains. Yet when Ewell arrived, Jackson's force was already on the march south, and Jackson merely told Ewell to remain where he was, and attack Banks if he marched on Staunton. Jackson now led his small army southeast thirty miles over the Blue Ridge to Mechums River Station on the railroad nine miles west of Charlottesville! In other words, Jackson pulled his troops entirely *out* of the Shenandoah Valley, and deposited them at a point on the railroad that could take them either to Richmond to reinforce Johnston, or to Fredericksburg to confront McDowell.

This completely unexpected move utterly deceived the Union commanders. As Jackson had intended, they concluded the Confederates were going to Richmond or Fredericksburg. With Lincoln's concurrence and despite McClellan's pleas for assistance, the Union secretary of war, Edwin M. Stanton, told McDowell to remain at Fredericksburg until Jackson's intentions were better known. Once again McDowell was halted in his tracks.

The effect of Jackson's march east also had profound effects on Banks and Frémont. Banks assured Stanton that Jackson was "bound for Richmond" and suggested—since he no longer saw any need for an army in the Shenandoah Valley—that his whole force should be sent to McDowell or McClellan. Stanton and Lincoln refused, but did order him to transfer one division to McDowell, leaving Banks with only 10,000 men to defend the valley. At the same time, Frémont's advance commander, Robert H. Milroy, felt no pressing obligation to hurry to Staunton, and remained in the vicinity of Franklin, some forty miles northwest.

When Jackson's men arrived at Mechums River Station, railway cars were waiting for them. When they boarded the cars, however, the train went not east to Richmond, as everyone expected, but *west* to Staunton! In the space of hours Jackson had landed in the central position between Banks and Frémont. And neither army was in a position to assist the other.

Jackson picked up a 2,800-man Rebel force guarding Staunton, and marched west to McDowell, Virginia, halfway to Franklin, where, on May 8, 1862, he defeated Milroy's advance guard and sent it flying. Jackson pursued the defeated Union forces to Franklin and beyond, then turned back east into the Shenandoah Valley and marched on Banks, who had retreated northward to Strasburg, where he built strong fortifications and waited on Jackson's army to attack him frontally.

Jackson sent his cavalry against Banks's positions, making him believe the main Confederate force was coming down on him. Instead, Jackson swung entirely around Strasburg to the east, and marched on Banks's rear base at Winchester, twenty miles north of Strasburg. This turned Banks out of his entrenchments at Strasburg without firing a shot. Banks fled back to Winchester barely ahead of the Confederates, but Jackson defeated him there on May 25, and sent Banks's entire army in headlong flight to the Potomac River.

McDowell at Fredericksburg was now strategically in the central position between Johnston at Richmond and Jackson, who had arrived at Harpers Ferry, on the Potomac. If Lincoln had instructed McDowell to march south to aid McClellen, his presence could have allowed McClellan to destroy Johnston's army. Then McDowell and other Union forces could have turned back on Jackson and destroyed his army as well. But Lincoln was so distracted by Jackson's advance to the Potomac that he made precisely the wrong decision. Instead of going to help McClellan, he directed McDowell, along with Frémont, to go after Jackson.

Jackson had achieved his purpose. McDowell never carried out the one decisive, war-ending move he might have made. In the event, neither McDowell's lead division under James Shields nor Frémont got a barrier across the Valley Pike. Jackson easily slipped past, and marched south.

Once more, vastly superior Union forces converged on Jackson. Frémont pursued him along the Valley Pike, while Shields pressed along the South Fork of the Shenandoah River to the east. Jackson stopped at Port Republic on the South Fork, twelve miles southeast of Harrisonburg. Here he was once again in the central position, this time between Shields on the east bank of the river and Frémont, advancing on the west. On June 8, 1862, Jackson's division commander Richard Ewell stopped Frémont five miles northwest of Port Republic, and the next day Jackson threw back Shields at Port Republic. Unable to consolidate, both defeated Union forces retreated northward. Jackson—having freed the Shenandoah Valley, neutralized Frémont's and Banks's armies, and kept McDowell from joining McClellen—moved his entire army secretly to Richmond, where he assisted in fighting the battles of the Seven Days on June 26–July 2, 1862. In these battles, Robert E. Lee, who had taken command after Johnston was wounded, drove McClellen away from Richmond to a defensive position on the James River, which he abandoned in early August.

None of this would have been possible except for Jackson's masterful exploitation of the central position at Staunton and at Port Republic.

Napoleon: Champion of the Central Position

No great commander before Napoleon Bonaparte saw the central position as an axiom of war. Its potential was little recognized. Commanders occasionally *found* themselves in the central position tactically, and made the most of the opportunity. Frederick the Great, for example, successfully defended Prussia during the Seven Years War, 1756–63, by striking from the central position against his enemies separately before they could unite.

However, in the very first move of his very first campaign—in Italy, 1796–97—Bonaparte deliberately drove into the central position between the Austrians on the east and the Piedmontese on the west, and, by keeping them apart and striking first one, then the other, set up the conditions for the spectacular victories that followed. These victories defeated Austria, gave most of Italy to France, and guaranteed France's previous seizure of Belgium and the west bank of the Rhine River.[3]

The French government of the Directory did not expect much from the Italian campaign in 1796. The main effort of the French army at the time was aimed at Austria, then a large empire covering much of central Europe. The idea of sending Bonaparte to Italy was to divert attention from a major French advance on Austria through Germany. Bonaparte was to drive the Austrians out of Piedmont and Lombardy in northern Italy, thus opening the way for him to march to Austria through the Tyrol and join the French army, which would supposedly be moving on Austria through southern Germany.

In reality, there was little hope for such an ambitious plan. The offensives in northern Italy and Germany were too far apart to support one another, with the formidable Alps separating the French armies. If either campaign slowed, the Austrians could readily transfer troops to the other theater. Bonaparte, however, saw that a decisive victory could be achieved in Italy, and made plans accordingly.

In March 1796, Bonaparte's army of 24,000 was in two groups, one spread out along the Maritime Alps (separating southern France from Italy), and the other along the narrow coastal strip of the Italian Riviera from Genoa westward. In the Apennine Mountains, only a few miles to the north and west of the French troops along the coast, 25,000 Piedmontese troops stretched from the town of Ceva on the east to Cuneo on the west. Northeast of the Piedmontese, 31,000 Austrians were wintered in quarters in nearby towns, especially Alessandria. Other Austrians were occupying a thin outpost line in the Apennines from Carcare to the heights above Genoa, just north of the French troops on the coast.

Bonaparte assembled about half of his army around Savona, on the

Italian Campaign, 1796–1797

coast twenty-two miles west of Genoa, and planned to drive northwest through a pass in the Apennines to eliminate an Austrian outpost at Carcare. This would place him in the central position between the Austrians and the Piedmontese. He planned then to turn on the Piedmontese, and drive them out of the war, before moving east to deal with the main Austrian army.

Bonaparte sent 9,000 troops to Carcare, smashing a smaller Austrian detachment. He was now between the Piedmontese and the principal Austrian force.

Bonaparte ordered his general, André Masséna, to block the Austrians to the east, and turned the rest of his force against the Piedmontese fortress of Ceva, twelve miles west. Unfortunately the commander of that force dallied, while Masséna's troops disregarded orders and scattered to forage and plunder. They were attacked and routed by the Austrians.

Exasperated, Bonaparte canceled the attack on Ceva, and swiftly brought a strong force back to the east, driving the Austrians back. He was afraid the Austrians might counterattack, but in the event they kept their main forces twenty miles north, protecting the city of Alessandria and their main line of communications back to Austria.[4] This allowed Bonaparte to turn on Ceva with a much superior force. The Piedmontese withdrew to Mondovi, about ten miles west, hoping they could hold it, but Bonaparte drove them out by a sudden frontal assault before they could prepare defenses.

Bonaparte now ordered a march on the Piedmontese capital of Turin, forty-two miles north. The threat to their capital was too much for the Piedmontese, and they asked for an armistice. Bonaparte agreed on April 28, 1796, but demanded permission to cross the bridge over the Po River at Valenza, on the direct path to Bonaparte's next objective, Milan, capital of Lombardy, which Austria ruled, and the main base of the Austrian army.

The demand that he use the Valenza bridge was, however, a deception. It induced the Austrian commander, Baron Johann Peter Beaulieu, to believe Bonaparte would make his principal assault there, and he ordered his 25,000 troops to the north bank of the Po at Valenza to block it. But Bonaparte sent only a part of his army, now approaching 40,000 men, to threaten—not actually attempt—a crossing at Valenza. This smaller force held the Austrians in place, allowing Bonaparte to march the bulk of his army east down the undefended south bank of the Po to Piacenza, about forty miles southeast of Milan. Now, if Beaulieu remained at Valenza, Bonaparte could drive on Milan and cut him off from his line of communications to Vienna.

To prevent this, Beaulieu quickly abandoned Milan and all of Lombardy, and ordered full retreat northeast back into Austria. But some troops mistakenly closed into an Austrian fortress in eastern Lombardy, Mantua on the Mincio, a tributary of the Po. Over the next eight months the Austrians lost much of their army trying to relieve it. Mantua surrendered on February 2, 1797, and Bonaparte advanced into Austria, forcing the Austrians to sign a preliminary agreement at Loeben on April 18, 1797, formalized in the Peace of Camp Formio on October 17.

In this peace, Austria gave Belgium to France, and ceded Lombardy to a new French-dominated Cisapline Republic in northern Italy. Bonaparte, however, permitted Austria to annex the proud Venetian republic in compensation.

Bonaparte had broken the back of the Austrian position in Italy in his movement to the central position at the very start of the campaign. When this succeeded in dividing the two armies, the Piedmontese and the Austrians henceforth were in strategic retreat.

Waterloo: Failure of the Central Position

Several more times during the wars that engulfed Europe from 1800 till 1814, Napoleon exploited the central position, especially when his forces were weaker. After a long series of battles beginning with the French retreat from Moscow in 1812, and culminating in the occupation of Paris on March 31, 1814, Napoleon was forced to abdicate. As a sop, the allies gave him the little Italian island of Elba. Compared to the French Empire, Elba was a pitiful crumb, and, moreover, much too close to France. The temptation was too great, and Napoleon returned from Elba in March 1815, remounted the throne, and dared the allies to oust him.

France's military situation was decidedly inferior to that of the allies, principally the Austrians, Prussians, Russians, and British. Those countries had twice the forces Napoleon could raise, and their plan was to crush him by numbers. From Belgium, a British-Dutch army under the Duke of Wellington and a Prussian army under Marshal Gebhard Leberecht von Blücher would press south. From Germany, an Austrian army under Marshal Karl Philipp Schwarzenberg would advance west, with the Russians following.[5]

To prevent the junction of these enemy armies, Napoleon had to move fast, and he had to win decisively.

Napoleon knew Schwarzenberg, coming from Germany, would be slow. Thus he could ignore the Austrians for the moment. His greatest opportunity lay in Belgium. Wellington and Blücher would think he was going to defend, not attack, because French forces in the north amounted to only about 124,000 men, as opposed to 85,000 men in the

The Waterloo Campaign, June 15–19, 1815

British-Dutch army and 123,000 in the Prussian army. Napoleon thus could achieve strategic surprise. Moreover, the allied position in Belgium was in peril because the British and Prussian armies were not concentrated. Wellington had posted his army in the vicinity of Brussels, Blücher around Namur, thirty-five miles southeast.

Napoleon saw that a potentially fatal gap lay between the two armies. If he could advance into southern Belgium to the crossroads of Quatre Bras ("Four Corners"), sixteen miles southeast of Brussels, he would be in the central position between the British and the Prussian armies. From there he could beat in turn the British and the Prussians, then swing southeast to deal with the Austrians and Russians.

Early in June 1815, Napoleon ordered the five-corps Army of the North to concentrate in the vicinity of Avesnes, about forty miles south of Quatre Bras, and on June 12 he left Paris for Avesnes. The Prussians and British were oblivious of the French movements until the night of June 14, when Prussian outposts reported many bivouac fires. The sentries belonged to the 33,000-man 1st Corps of Hans Ernst von Ziethen, the most advanced allied force.

When Ziethen reported the French presence, the Prussian general Blücher ordered his three remaining corps to march to Sombreffe, only twenty-five miles north of the French-Belgian frontier. Around Sombreffe the three corps were to connect with 1st Corps. This was most foolhardy, for the move would place the Prussian army within easy reach of the French army. Napoleon might well be able to defeat the Prussians before the British could respond, and thereby push Blücher entirely out of the strategic picture.

This prospect was made all the more likely by the fact that the British commander, the Duke of Wellington, did not get word of Napoleon's movement until June 15. When he did, he assumed the French were going to advance south of Brussels toward the English Channel and try to cut off his communications with England.[6] Accordingly, he ordered his troops to be ready to march southward. What he should have done was to move to the southeast, that is, toward Quatre Bras, to support the Prussians around Sombreffe.

After issuing his orders, Wellington went to a ball being put on by the

Duchess of Richmond on the evening of June 15. During the party he got word that Napoleon had advanced his entire army on Charleroi, fifteen miles north of the frontier. Wellington and the Duke of Richmond went into the study to examine a map. Wellington at once recognized that Napoleon was threatening to place himself between the British and Prussian armies. "Napoleon has humbugged me, by God!" he shouted. "He has gained twenty-four hours march on me."

Wellington now redirected the British army to Quatre Bras. But many of the officers were at the duchess's ball or others, and the order was carried out in extreme confusion. It was late on the afternoon of June 16 before strong British forces reached Quatre Bras.

Meanwhile at Charleroi on June 15, Napoleon met Marshal Michel Ney, to whom he gave command of the left wing of his army, 1st and 2nd Corps and a cavalry division. He told Ney to sweep the enemy off the Charleroi-Brussels road, and to occupy Quatre Bras that very day. Napoleon called Ney "the bravest of the brave" for his courageous actions as rearguard commander retreating from Moscow in 1812, but unfortunately Ney profoundly lacked judgment and had learned little from the many battles he had fought. Napoleon had said, back in 1808, that Ney was as ignorant "as the last-joined drummer boy," but apparently selected him for this job because he had few other choices. Napoleon had left his best marshal, Louis-Nicolas Davout, as governor of Paris, because he could trust no one else to hold the capital. But Davout said, "If you are victor, Paris will be yours, and if you are beaten, neither I nor anyone else can do anything for you."[7]

When Marshal Emmanuel de Grouchy subsequently arrived at Charleroi, Napoleon gave him command of his right wing, 3rd and 4th Corps and two cavalry divisions, and told him to push the Prussian advance corps under Ziethen back toward Sombreffe, ten miles north of Charleroi. Grouchy was another bad choice. He was a skilled cavalry general, but had never commanded a corps, much less an army wing.

Grouchy was slow in pressing the Prussians, and Napoleon went forward himself and accelerated the attack, driving the corps back to a point just four miles southwest of Sombreffe.

Meanwhile, on the afternoon of June 15, Ney evicted a Prussian detachment from the village of Gossalies, just north of Charleroi, but then sent only his cavalry division on toward Quatre Bras, six and a half miles beyond. Halfway there the horsemen came under fire from the Dutch Nassau Brigade, which had taken up a position and which then withdrew to Quatre Bras. The French cavalry found Quatre Bras too strongly held, and withdrew.

Thus the first great blunder in the Waterloo campaign had been made: Ney did *not* press on to seize Quatre Bras on June 15. Napoleon had not interposed his army between the British and the Prussians. When Ney talked with Napoleon that night, the emperor, oddly tolerant, told him to occupy the crossroads the next day, June 16.

At 8:00 A.M. on June 16, Grouchy informed Napoleon that strong Prussian columns were approaching Sombreffe, indicating that most of Blücher's army was assembling there. Napoleon rode up and quickly realized that Blücher had placed three corps, 84,000 men, around the village of Ligny, just south of Sombreffe, and was so far forward that Napoleon could attack him before either Blücher's 4th Corps of 31,000 men or Wellington could possibly join him. He was giving Napoleon exactly what he had been seeking when he got into the central position—the opportunity to defeat one enemy before having to deal with the other.

Napoleon's plan in this battle was brilliant. Although he had just 77,000 men at Ligny, Napoleon evened the odds by sending only cavalry to contain a Prussian corps along Ligny Creek to the east, and ordered a frontal attack with his two infantry corps directly on Ligny. This would compel Blücher to exhaust all his reserves in stopping the assaults. The decisive blow would be delivered by Ney, who supposedly would already have captured Quatre Bras. Ney was to send back at least a corps to descend on the undefended right rear of the Prussians at Ligny. Meanwhile the Imperial Guard, a special force of veterans that Napoleon reserved for culminating attacks, would deliver the coup de grâce by smashing through the center at Ligny. Napoleon expected to destroy two-thirds of Blücher's army, and compel the remainder to fall back to the northeast.[8]

With Napoleon in charge at Ligny, the attack went well. But Ney waited till 11:00 A.M. to order the 2nd Corps to concentrate at Frasnes, and Jean-Baptiste Drouet d'Erlon's 1st Corps at Gossalies. Even when the 2nd Corps got to Quatre Bras, it advanced with extreme caution, although it comprised 19,000 infantry, 3,000 cavalry, and sixty guns, plenty of force to do the job, since only 7,800 infantry, fifty horsemen, and fourteen guns were defending Quatre Bras. If Ney had exhibited the slightest boldness, nothing could have stopped the French. But he did not, and by 3:00 P.M. strong British reinforcements came up, along with Wellington himself.

Ney hoped to use the 20,000-man corps of Drouet d'Erlon to break through the British, but as this force was marching toward the cross-roads, Napoleon sent a courier to turn it onto the Prussian rear at Ligny. Unfortunately the courier misunderstood the instructions, and ordered it to march on the *French* rear. Ney, hearing about the order, turned the corps around once again and directed it to Quatre Bras, where it arrived well after nightfall—having marched back and forth all day, accomplishing nothing.

Meanwhile, Étienne Maurice Gérard's corps stormed into Ligny. Blücher had to throw in all his reserves to contain the assault. The time was ripe for Drouet d'Erlon to strike the Prussian rear, but he was marching to Quatre Bras. The Imperial Guard swept the enemy out of Ligny with bayonets at 7:30 P.M.—in the midst of a huge thunderstorm. The Prussians withdrew, but were kept from disintegrating by the charge of all available Prussian cavalry, led by Blücher himself, whose horse was struck by a bullet and rolled over on the seventy-three-year-old marshal. His aide dragged him, dazed, to safety.

The 1st and 2nd Prussian Corps then fell back west of Sombreffe, just as Napoleon had expected. If Drouet d'Erlon had been on hand, they would have been destroyed. Even so, Ligny was a great French victory, costing the Prussians 25,000 men, and the French fewer than half as many.

At 9:00 P.M. the fight at Quatre Bras ended in a draw. Losses were 4,000 on each side. The British still held the field, but they would have to retreat the next day, because, with the Prussians defeated, the French could sweep around their rear and cut them off from Brussels.

Despite the errors of Ney, Napoleon had achieved the first half of his objective in the central position—he had driven Blücher from the field. He had every reason to believe the Prussians would retire on their supply bases to the northeast, and he could turn with impunity against Wellington. Indeed, first reports from cavalry patrols checking on Prussian movements indicated Napoleon was right. On the morning of June 17, 1815, Napoleon sent Grouchy with two corps (3rd, 4th) and cavalry to seek out the Prussians and report back. From this point on, it was not Napoleon's concept that was at fault, it was Grouchy's execution.

Napoleon told him to explore first toward Namur and Liège. Not until 10:00 P.M. that night, however, did Grouchy discover that the Prussians had retreated north to Wavre, from where they might move west and join Wellington at or near Brussels. The Prussian chief of staff had ordered the army to retire on Wavre, not with the idea of aiding the British, but because many of the troops had originally moved in that direction. When Blücher recovered, he decided to concentrate at Wavre, and go to the aid of the British if attacked.

Meanwhile, Wellington, still at Quatre Bras, learned on the morning of June 17 that the Prussians had retreated from Ligny. He was compelled to retreat back toward Brussels. But his troops were unmolested because Ney, despite Napoleon's orders to attack at first light, did nothing. Ney's troops were still in bivouac when Napoleon rode up at 1:00 P.M. Livid, he got the pursuit under way at 2:00 P.M. Hence the British had a good head start, their advantage increased by a huge thunderstorm that kept the French from advancing across country to cut them off and force them to stand.

Before nightfall the British had pulled up on the low ridge of Mont St. Jean, just south of the village of Waterloo, a few miles from Brussels. At 6:30 P.M., Napoleon's vanguard arrived at La Belle Alliance, on the next low ridge south, and, sending cavalry up, found Wellington's army.

Napoleon got a message from Grouchy at dawn the next day, June 18, that the Prussians were at Wavre, ten miles east of Waterloo. He replied, describing the situation at Waterloo, and telling Grouchy to head for Wavre, push the Prussians before him, and keep in touch. The order was not clearly written, for Napoleon meant Grouchy must keep his two corps *between* the Prussians and the British. But Napoleon probably assumed this was plain common sense—this was, after all, the reason Grouchy had been sent on his mission in the first place. Yet, incredibly, Grouchy could not see this logic. His idea was to press on the *rear* of the Prussian army with a small force.[9]

At 11:30 A.M. on June 18 at the town of Walhain, seven miles south of Wavre, Grouchy and Marshal Gérard heard the roar of gunfire in the direction of Mont St. Jean. This in fact was the opening round of the battle of Waterloo, and Gérard—responding in the way responsible officers have acted from the dawn of warfare—said, "I think we ought to march on the cannon," thus concentrating all possible forces on the battlefield.

But Grouchy refused, saying it was merely an action by the British rear guard to delay Napoleon's advance. To Gérard this could not be true because Napoleon had already told Grouchy the British were emplaced just south of Waterloo. Therefore the gunfire had to signal the start of the battle. Grouchy's two French corps, 33,000 men, had been detailed to keep the Prussians from joining the British. Surely, therefore, Gérard argued, they should be *between* the two hostile armies, not *behind* one of them, where they could be easily deflected by rearguard defenses, and where they could not possibly keep the Prussian army from moving wherever it wanted. But despite Gérard's protestations, Grouchy would not be moved.

If Grouchy had followed Gérard's recommendation, his two corps could have easily placed themselves on Blücher's left flank—and thereby prevented him from marching on Waterloo.[10]

Instead, in a single column, which greatly narrowed his strength, Grouchy continued to march on Wavre, where he launched timid attacks on the tail of the Prussian army and accomplished nothing. As J. F. C. Fuller writes, "With such subordinates as Grouchy and Ney, Michael and all his angels would have lost the campaign."[11]

By the morning of the battle of Waterloo, Napoleon had gained two tremendous advantages—he had moved expertly into the central position at Quatre Bras and had separated the two hostile armies, and he had soundly defeated one of these armies, the Prussian, and sent it fleeing. By any reasonable standard this would have been enough to ensure him victory, because, true to his doctrine, Napoleon had then turned with superior force, 72,000 men, on the remaining enemy force, the British army of 67,000 men under Wellington, lined up at Waterloo.

In other words, he was about to carry out the last element of the threefold premise upon which he had entered the campaign in Belgium. He had already separated the two hostile armies. He had already defeated one. And now he was poised to defeat the other. Unfortunately for Napoleon, achievement of this last element had been jeopardized by two decisions, a prescient one by Blücher and a muddleheaded one by Grouchy. Blücher, discovering that his chief of staff had concentrated to the north and not the northeast, realized his army had landed by happenstance where it could go to the assistance of the British, and he exploited that opportunity. Grouchy, defiantly obtuse in the face of gunfire from Waterloo and the pleadings of Gérard, eliminated his 33,000 men from the scales of the contest by remaining on the tail of the Prussian army, where it could achieve nothing.

The entire story of Waterloo can be explained by these two decisions. Because of them, Napoleon was unable to complete the three tasks mandatory for victory. Since the Prussians did not run away, but came to Wellington's aid, Napoleon could not drive the British back in defeat beyond Brussels or their supply base at Antwerp, and he could not prevent the junction of the two allied armies. Consequently his other achievements went for naught, and the whole campaign ended in disaster.

At the start of the battle, before he realized the Prussians were moving on his right, or eastern, flank, Napoleon hoped he could overpower the British and drive them off their positions centered on Mont St. Jean on the north-south Brussels-Charleroi highway, anchored on the right, or west, by the walled chateau, or farmstead, of Hougoumont, and stretching eastward for two miles on the ridgeline along which ran the road from Wavre.

Napoleon's aim was to break the British center and exploit the penetration. For this purpose he assembled a huge battery of eighty cannons at La Belle Alliance, on the ridgeline just south of the British position. He first sent in a diversionary attack on Hougoumont with a division commanded by his brother Jerome. Napoleon's intention was to draw in additional British troops to weaken the center. Instead, owing to the repeated unsuccessful attacks by Jerome against the solid walls of the farmstead, it drew in more French troops, not British, and contributed nothing to the battle.

Ney led several direct attacks against the center of the British line, which, though they weakened the British, failed to crack Wellington's position. Nevertheless, Napoleon believed he might still drive through the center with another concerted attack. Just prior to it, however, Napoleon, scanning the northeastern horizon, spotted a "dark cloud" emerging from woods about five miles away. He thought it might be Grouchy, but soon learned it was the advance guard of Frederick William von Bülow's Prussian 4th Corps, forcing Napoleon to divert a corps to try to stop it.

But Bülow's force was much too powerful, and around 4:00 P.M. his troops reached the village of Plancenoit, nearly in the rear of the French position. They were only kept from unhinging the entire French line by the swift intervention of troops from the Imperial Guard. But the Prussian pressure against Plancenoit continued to build.

Meanwhile, Ney made repeated direct attacks against the British. They all failed, with heavy losses, the most spectacular being a charge by 12,000 French cavalry who were unable to break the fourteen squares, each of about a thousand men, which the British and allied infantry regiments formed, the men in four ranks, the front rank kneeling, musket butts in the turf, bayonets sloping forward, the rear ranks firing volleys. These bristling formations turned back horse and man.

The denouement came at a little past 7:00 P.M. In desperation, Napoleon sent eight battalions of the Imperial Guard straight against the British. Despite heavy artillery fire, they got within range of the British, but, supported by only a few guns, against the superior British force they had no real chance. They received devastating fire and rushed back down the hill in confusion.

The battle had been lost. Wellington, seeing the enemy in chaos, spurred his horse to the forward edge of the ridgeline, took off his hat, and waved it in the air. Everyone recognized this as the signal for a general advance. The British army poured down the slope, the cavalry in the lead.

Napoleon saw the whole French front give way and fall back in rout. He managed to get away, protected by his Imperial Guard, but the French lost 25,000 men that day, and 8,000 more were captured. Wellington suffered 15,000 casualties, Blücher 7,000.

On July 15, 1815, Napoleon climbed on board the British warship *Bellerophon* in Rochefort harbor, and began his journey to exile on St. Helena, an island in the south Atlantic. The allies insisted that he be removed to a place where he no longer could pose a danger to the peace of Europe. He died on St. Helena in 1821. France, weary of defeat, accepted its restored Bourbon monarchy for a while, but an attempt by the monarchies of Europe to return to the reactionary days before the French Revolution was doomed. France soon ousted the Bourbons and later turned to Charles Louis Napoleon, the emperor's nephew, who became president of the Second Republic in 1848 and proclaimed himself emperor as Napoleon III in 1852. The "little Napoleon's" rule ended in the disastrous defeat of France in the Franco-Prussian War in 1871.

Kasserine Pass, Tunisia, 1943

With the exception of Stonewall Jackson's brilliant exploitation of the central position in the Shenandoah Valley campaign of 1862, the rule of the central position played no significant part in wars after Napoleon until another military genius, Erwin Rommel, reintroduced it in World War II. Indeed, the history of the central position is largely tied to its use by great generals. The reason for this is twofold.

In the first place, few commanders throughout history have been able to appreciate the potential of the central position. They sometimes shy away from it, seeing danger rather than opportunity, or more frequently they fail to think of it. We have mentioned the example of Abraham Lincoln, who sent Irwin McDowell's corps at Fredericksburg in the wrong direction in 1862, after Jackson in the valley, instead of against Johnston at Richmond. The very most that could have been achieved was the destruction of Jackson's little army, whereas McDowell's presence at Richmond would have had the potential of ending the Civil War with an overwhelming Union victory.

The other reason why the central position has been a province of great captains is that they have the courage of their convictions. Universal characteristics of great commanders are their ability to see a situation as a whole, confidence in their own judgment, and, above all, determination to exploit an advantage they have discerned. Looking back, the decision of Napoleon to drive directly between the British and Prussian armies in Belgium may seem to have been the obvious or logical choice. But it would have been a rare commander with the courage to commit his entire army and his own fate to such a move. To the fainthearted, the maneuver looked more like sticking one's head in the lion's mouth. Likewise, when Stonewall Jackson moved back to Port Republic in 1862, he seemed to the Union commanders to be trying to do what they would have done in like circumstances—get away from vastly superior strength. They had no idea Jackson was maneuvering into the central position between them, and were utterly confounded when, instead of fleeing over the Blue Ridge, he turned on each Union force and smashed it.

When the German dictator, Adolf Hitler, precipitated the Second World War on September 1, 1939, by attacking Poland, the element that mesmerized generals, soldiers, and public alike was *blitzkrieg*, or lightning warfare, carried out with fast-moving tanks accompanied by quick-striking Stuka dive-bombers that could hit battlefield targets with pinpoint accuracy. With these weapons the Germans achieved unparalleled victories in western Europe in 1940, defeating France and the Low Countries and throwing the British off the Continent in weeks.

Hitler could have established an invincible empire if he had moved with substantial force into North Africa, and seized the Suez Canal. This would have driven the British Royal Navy out of the Mediterranean, and allowed German panzer, or armored, columns to overrun the Middle East, gain an unlimited oil supply, and place German air and armored forces on the southern frontier of the Soviet Union within striking distance of the main Soviet oil fields in the Caucasus Mountains and along the shores of the Caspian Sea. This would have forced the Soviet dictator, Joseph Stalin, to do anything to prevent a German attack, while German possession of the Middle East, North Africa, and most of Europe would have given Hitler a virtually unassailable empire that, in time, could have matched the strength of the United States.

Hitler, however, was obsessed with a desire to destroy the Soviet Union and to turn large parts of it over to German settlers. Accordingly he ignored the strategic advantage of a drive into the Middle East, and attacked the Soviet Union frontally on June 22, 1941, a decision that ultimately brought on the defeat of Germany.

To North Africa, Hitler sent wholly inadequate forces, his aim being not victory, but to keep his Italian ally, Benito Mussolini, from seeking a separate peace. However, Hitler also sent Erwin Rommel to North Africa. Rommel was an infantry hero in the First World War, commanded Hitler's personal bodyguard in the Polish campaign, and from this position leveraged command of the 7th Panzer Division in the campaign in the west in 1940. Rommel's division smashed across the Meuse River at Dinant, Belgium, in the first days of the campaign, and moved with such speed and emerged at such unexpected places that the French called it the "ghost division."

Rommel was the only true military genius to emerge in World War II. Hitler didn't recognize his genius, however, and virtually ignored the victories he scored in the Desert War. In a spectacular campaign in the spring and summer of 1942, Rommel swept aside British forces and drove to El Alamein in Egypt, only sixty miles from Alexandria. But Hitler failed to send him the few additional forces he needed to drive on to the Suez Canal, leaving Rommel stalemated at El Alamein, and vulnerable to a buildup in enemy power undertaken by the British commander, Bernard Law Montgomery. He launched an attack on October 23, 1942.

Montgomery moved directly and with agonizing slowness, but Rommel's forces were too weak to stop him, and he withdrew along the coast of Egypt and Libya toward the Libyan capital of Tripoli. Meanwhile, American and British forces invaded Morocco and Algeria on November 8, 1942, and commenced a drive to capture Tunisia before the Axis could do so. They failed. German and Italian forces flown in

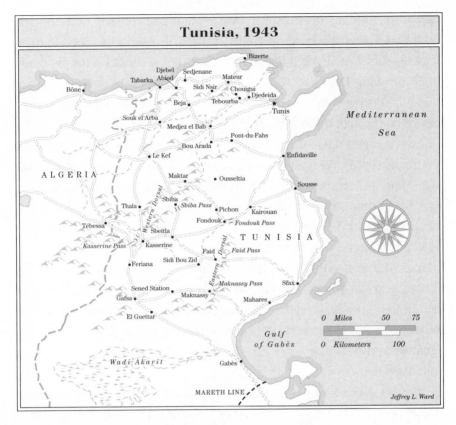

Tunisia, 1943

Bizerte

Djebel
Tabarka Abiod Sedjenane
Mateur
Sidi Nsir
Chouigui
Bône Djedeida
Beja Tebourba
Tunis
Souk el Arba
Medjez el Bab
Pont-du-Fahs
Bou Arada
Le Kef
Enfidaville
ALGERIA
Maktar Ousseltia
Sousse
Sbiba
Thala Sbiba Pass
Pichon Kairouan
Fondouk Fondouk Pass
Tébessa Sbeitla
TUNISIA
Kasserine Pass Kasserine
Faid Faid Pass
Feriana Sidi Bou Zid
Maknassy Pass Sfax
Sened Station
Gafsa Maknassy Mahares
El Guettar
Mediterranean Sea

Western Dorsal

Eastern Dorsal

0 Miles 50 75

Gulf of Gabès

0 Kilometers 100

Wadi Akarit Gabès

MARETH LINE

Jeffrey L. Ward

from Italy seized eastern Tunisia. Meanwhile, Rommel reached western Libya, and on January 23, 1943, he ordered evacuation of Tripoli, and withdrawal to the Mareth Line, about a hundred miles inside the Tunisian border, built before the war by the French.

When Rommel pulled his beaten panzer army into Tunisia, he realized he had landed in the central position between the Americans and British in Tunisia and Montgomery's British 8th Army in Libya. Montgomery was moving toward the Mareth Line at his usual snail-like pace. His army could be ignored for a couple of weeks. The Allies in Tunisia had been stopped by the rains of Mediterranean winter and were arrayed on a north-south line with the British in the north, the newly organized French 19th Corps in the center, and the U.S. 2nd Corps under Lloyd R. Fredendall in the south.

This presented an opportunity Rommel couldn't pass up, especially as he spotted an extreme weakness in the American and French positions:

they were holding the Eastern Dorsal mountain passes of Fondouk, Faid, and Gafsa far eastward into central Tunisia with only outpost detachments. Since this Allied line was a thin shell, Axis forces could crack through; Faid and Gafsa were especially poorly defended. They then could drive sixty to seventy miles to the west beyond Feriana and Kasserine through the passes in the Western Dorsals.

Once through these passes, the Axis troops would arrive at the huge American supply base and headquarters at Tebessa—well *west* of the Allied line in Tunisia and deep into the Allied communications zone. If Axis tanks then drove straight north to the sea a hundred miles away, they might cut off the entire Allied army in Tunisia, or force it to withdraw into Algeria, with devastating consequences.

Then Rommel could turn back, combining his forces with the 5th Panzer Army in Tunisia, and either destroy Montgomery's 8th Army or drive it into precipitate retreat. In other words, Rommel could execute a classic example of the central position. From the Mareth Line, Rommel could strike first at the Americans and British in Tunisia, then turn back on Montgomery coming up from Libya.

Rommel set about to eliminate the Allied forces shielding the Eastern Dorsal passes. The American corps commander, Fredendall, had played into his hand, having placed light forces at the passes, capable only of delaying tactics. He should have set up one or two strong mobile reserves behind this screen, capable of moving with great force and authority to any spot the Axis forces struck. This is what Dwight D. Eisenhower, the Allied top commander in North Africa, had recommended. Instead Fredendall scattered his reserves in bits and pieces all across his front, and immobilized his infantry by placing them on various hills along the line, where, if surrounded, they could not escape.

Days later, on February 1, 1943, the 21st Panzer Division, with ninety-one tanks, overwhelmed a poorly armed French garrison at Faid Pass. The Allied high command correctly concluded that Axis forces were planning an offensive. But no one suspected danger from Rommel, thinking he was too weak after retreating across Libya to make any move into Tunisia. The danger they saw was from Axis forces flown into northern Tunisia, and concluded the attack would come thirty miles farther north, at Fondouk Pass. British General Kenneth A. Anderson held back about half the strength of the U.S. 1st Armored Division in reserve behind Fondouk.

Rommel's principal aim was to seize Sbeitla, thirty-five miles west of Faid Pass. At Sbeitla two roads led through the Western Dorsal passes, one due north twenty miles to Sbiba, the other by way of Kasserine, twenty miles west, toward Tebessa. To assist in this drive, Rommel asked Hans-Jürgen von Arnim, 5th Panzer Army commander, to send down the 10th Panzer Division, with 110 tanks, plus a dozen of the new Tiger tanks with heavy armor and a powerful 88-mm gun.

But human envy is a tremendously eroding force, and Arnim was deeply resentful of Rommel's fame, and didn't want to assist him in gaining even more. Arnim provided only one tank battalion and four Tigers, and withdrew these shortly afterward for an attack he was planning farther north.

Behind the Mareth Line, around the town of Gabès, Rommel assembled a battle group with twenty-six tanks and two small infantry battalions from Africa Corps, along with twenty-three obsolete Italian tanks, and told its chief, Major General F. K. von Liebenstein, to seize Gafsa and keep moving.

Meanwhile the attack from Faid opened on February 14. One group from 21st Panzer made a wide sweep from the north around the U.S. 1st Armored Division's Combat Command A, and struck the Americans in the flank, while another went around the other flank and struck from the rear. At the same time two groups from 10th Panzer swept straight through Faid Pass and pinned down the Americans frontally. The Americans fled, leaving behind the guns of five artillery battalions, forty tanks, and sixty half-tracks (partially armored combat vehicles). Next morning the 1st Armored's Combat Command C counterattacked across thirteen miles of open plain, to be met by a storm of shells as it came within range. The shellfire stopped the charge, while German panzers swung on either flank. The whole U.S. command retreated in confusion, losing fifty-four tanks, fifty-seven half-tracks, and twenty-nine guns.

The Germans surrounded the numerous American detachments on hills around Faid, forcing their surrender, and closed off any chance of defense. The panzers then attacked Sbeitla on the morning of February 17. The Americans defended stubbornly till nightfall, then fell back. In three days the Americans had lost 150 tanks and had nearly 3,000 men captured, while German losses had been minuscule.

Meanwhile the battle group under Liebenstein occupied Gafsa, and on February 17 rushed on to seize Feriana, twenty miles southwest of Kasserine, an entry point to the passes of the Western Dorsals. Liebenstein's group destroyed a number of American armored personnel carriers (APCs) and guns, and seized the airfield at Thelepte, where the Americans destroyed thirty aircraft on the ground to keep them from falling into Axis hands.

As the crisis unfolded for the Allies, General Fredendall acted in panic. He pulled American forces back westward to Tebessa, and set fire to some of the supply dumps.

Rommel's plan was succeeding brilliantly. He now resolved to drive through Tebessa, then turn north to the sea. If the plan succeeded, the Allies would have to pull their forces out of Tunisia or face destruction. In a message to Arnim, Rommel made it plain the thrust north had to be well west of the Western Dorsals, because the Allies had many troops close to these mountains, but few to the west. If the German thrust was made close to the Western Dorsals, Allied reinforcements could block it easily. If it came to the west around Tebessa, nothing could stop it.

But Arnim balked, telling Rommel he could not see the possibilities of a strike from Tebessa to the Mediterranean. Yet they were obvious. The real reason Arnim refused was envy and a desire to gain fame himself. Rommel appealed to the Italian *Comando Supremo*, in charge of all operations in Tunisia, which agreed to the offensive but—showing utter ignorance of strategy—required that it go not by way of Tebessa, but immediately behind the Western Dorsals.

This was madness, for Allied reserves were close to the Western Dorsals, and they could swiftly close the passes in them, and prevent a quick sweep to the Mediterranean.

Exasperated but realizing there was no time for argument, Rommel put his Africa Corps on the road for Kasserine Pass with the aim of breaking through toward Thala, twenty-eight miles north of Kasserine, while directing 21st Panzer to strike from Sbeitla to Sbiba, about the same distance north. Rommel ordered Arnim's 10th Panzer Division to Sbeitla, where it could support Africa Corps or 21st Panzer, whichever needed help. But Arnim delayed, and the division was not on hand when the attacks opened.

The blows came where the Allies were expecting them. Anderson sent the British 6th Armored Division to Thala, and the 1st Guards Brigade to Sbiba. Just as Rommel had predicted, the strikes were so close to the Allied lines that reserves were getting into blocking positions quickly.

At Kasserine, German motorized infantry, used to the wide-open spaces of the desert, tried to rush the pass, ignoring the 5,000-foot mountains on either side, which the Americans held. Artillery forward observers there called down heavy mortar and artillery strikes, which stopped the German attack.

Meanwhile, the 21st Panzer Division was held up by water-soaked roads, a dense minefield, and the guards brigade at Sbiba. This division, too, made the mistake of attacking frontally in the valley, instead of first securing the hills on either side.

Rommel concluded that the Allies were weaker at Kasserine, and focused his attack there, ordering the 10th Panzer Division to come up. But when Rommel arrived on the morning of February 20, the division commander told him Arnim had held half the division in the north, including the Tigers, which Rommel was counting on.

Panzer grenadier infantry and Italian mountain troops now made flanking moves on both sides of the pass, ousting the American forward observers, while, for the first time in Africa, Rommel unleashed *Nebelwerfer* rocket launchers, modeled after the Russian Katyusha launcher, which threw out eighty-pound rockets four miles. The rockets were not accurate, but shook the Americans badly, and by 5:00 P.M. the pass was in German hands.

During the night, to confuse the Allies and force them to divide their forces, Rommel moved armor toward Thala to the north and Tebessa to the west. Fredendall brought a combat command of the 1st Armored Division to hold the Tebessa road, while the British 26th Armored Brigade Group at Thala moved south to a position ten miles north of Kasserine Pass.

On February 21, a battle group of 10th Panzer (thirty tanks, twenty self-propelled guns, two panzer grenadier battalions) pressed north against the 26th Brigade, repeatedly flanked its positions, destroyed forty tanks while losing a dozen, and forced the brigade back to Thala. There a string of German tanks, led by a captured British Valentine tank, followed on the 26th's tail, got into the brigade's assembly area, overran some infantry, shot up many vehicles, and captured 700 men.

Next day, February 22, Rommel learned from aerial reconnaissance that strong Allied reinforcements were approaching. This reduced his already thin hopes of breaking through to the sea. He concluded nothing more could be accomplished, and ordered withdrawal. Fredendall didn't see what was happening, so the Germans got away with no losses.

Rommel had proposed a move from his central position at the Mareth Line that could have thrown the Allies out of Tunisia. Afterward, the combined Axis armies in Tunisia could have turned against Montgomery, coming up from Libya, and driven him back. The two triumphs could have changed the whole complexion of the war. But the envy of General von Arnim and the inability of the *Comando Supremo* to see prevented this victory. Instead, Rommel achieved only a local success, 3,000 Americans killed and wounded and more than 4,000 prisoners taken, plus 200 destroyed tanks, against German losses of fewer than a thousand. The Axis now had no hope of stopping the Allies. The fall of Tunisia, the occupation of Sicily, and the invasion of Italy followed.

Implications for the Future

The two world wars and Korea were largely fought on long main lines of resistance (MLRs), where armies formed continuous fronts over extensive distances. In these circumstances the idea of the central position, never a prominent factor in military strategies, was disregarded. Significantly, it was used only by Erwin Rommel in Tunisia in 1943, where there was no MLR but only widely spaced outposts and strong points.

Wars no longer will be conducted along MLRs because weapons have become so accurate and deadly that soldiers cannot survive on them. This means forces now must be kept in small units, spread over wide areas, and hidden as much as possible from observation. New opportunities will therefore be presented to use the rule of the central position, since it flourishes in an arena where troops are not concentrated and where a resourceful commander can drive between two or more enemy elements.

With the elimination of MLRs, we can deposit forces anywhere they can disrupt the enemy, divide his forces, or cut off his lines of supply. The concept of the central position also can be expanded because we can move troops in and out of positions much more quickly than was possible in earlier wars.

Napoleon had to get into the central position by marching bodies of men, Rommel by driving tanks. Their movements could be spotted and countermeasures taken. Today we can drop troops by helicopters or V-22 Osprey vertical-lift transports at any spot tactically or strategically important to us. These troops can move out on raids in all directions, or, remaining where they can disrupt enemy movements, disable his operations.

In late October 2001, when we were not sure whether our air-attack program would bring about the collapse of the Taliban government, British military authorities urged the Pentagon to establish a large firebase (or defended position) inside Afghanistan. This would have been a new twist on the central position—depositing a force by air into the very midst of enemy territory. Such a force would have challenged the Taliban, in effect saying, "What are you going to do about it?"[12] With modern weapons, plus support by U.S. bombers and attack aircraft, a force in such a position would be virtually impossible to defeat, yet would disrupt the enemy's governmental, transportation, and military structure.

The Taliban government did disintegrate the second week of November 2001, and no major U.S. incursion was necessary. However, the idea points to future wars. It would be a modern application of the central position, and has many possible uses.

The British proposal was precipitated by a nighttime strike on October 20, 2001, on a complex outside Kandahar by U.S. Army Rangers and a Delta Force unit. The aim was to kill or capture Mullah Mohammed Omar, the Taliban leader, who had a house there. A simultaneous Rangers strike at an airbase sixty miles southwest of Kandahar was a decoy. The main strike did not find Omar, but did bring on a Taliban counterattack. The Americans suffered several men wounded as they withdrew. The operation generated criticism because it was not a sudden, unexpected blow by a small team, a Delta Force specialty, but was preceded by four AC-130 gunships that poured heavy fire into the surrounding area. This advertised the attack and, because it took a considerable length of time, allowed Taliban fighters to arrive and set up a strong defense.

The Kandahar strike resembled other assaults carried out by the American military over the years. In Vietnam, Americans often landed at a point to carry out a search-and-destroy mission. The Vietnamese fought long enough to extract American casualties, then withdrew. The Americans also withdrew, having accomplished little.

If, instead, a strong force were dropped into an enemy area, it could either remain in place and invite enemy attack, likely to fail, or it could move against important enemy centers—cities, airfields, major road intersections, or other objectives.

7

Employing a Superior Weapon

IT'S RARE FOR one side in any war to possess a superior weapon for long. Either the other side quickly copies the same weapon, or it develops an antidote. For this reason we speak of conventional war as being normally "symmetrical," or between sides using more or less the same weapons. But asymmetry of weaponry has, in fact, been a key factor of war through the ages.

A few countries, of course, possess the ultimate asymmetrical weapon, nuclear bombs. So devastating are nuclear weapons, however, that since their use in World War II, their role in warfare has been one of deterrence only. With the rise of international terrorism, the threat that a terrorist group might obtain a nuclear weapon has made the danger of a nuclear attack much more pressing. That demonstrates, in a terrifying way, the extraordinary potential power that a superior weapon can yield. In this case that power comes not only from the weapon, of course, but from the will to use it.

World War II was the last war in which true symmetry—that is, parity in weapons—came anywhere close to being the norm, and even in that war there was much asymmetry. Only the most important of many disparities were the Germans' panzer divisions, which had no match for well over two years, and the western Allies' sea and air power, which became so overwhelming by 1943 that Germany and Japan had no hope of countering them.

Since 1945, all wars have been distinguished by far greater asymmetry. In Korea the Americans endured inferiority to the North Koreans' Soviet-built T-34 tanks for less than two months, from June 25 to mid-August 1950. Thereafter, American weapons were so vastly superior that the North Koreans, and the Chinese who intervened in late October 1950, were forced to build camouflaged deep bunkers in the mountains to withstand American artillery and air strikes. Vietnam was marked by armies that fought completely different kinds of war using different weapons: the French and Americans conducted an orthodox conventional war, the Vietnamese Communists a guerrilla war. The Persian Gulf War of 1991 was a textbook case of asymmetry: the Iraqis possessed mainly weapons from the early 1970s, while the Americans fought with weapons nearly twenty years newer and many times more deadly. In the air attacks on the Taliban government of Afghanistan in the fall of 2001, American weapons were even more accurate than in the Gulf War, and, moreover, were directed against an enemy with no air power and no air-defense system.[1]

Many battles and campaigns have been won over the millennia by commanders who exercised the principle of employing a superior weapon against an enemy who was either unable to recognize that he faced a better weapon, or refused to take steps to counter it. Such failures are perplexing, given the powerful incentive armies have to match the weapons of their enemies. Yet the history of warfare is replete with cases of commanders who had every opportunity to appreciate the effects of a superior weapon, and for one reason or another did not adopt it, or develop a defense against it.

Adrianople, A.D. 378

The battle of Adrianople presents one of the most astonishing examples in history of both the employment of a superior weapon and the failure of the opposing commander to adjust to its use. The result was the virtual destruction of a Roman army.

This unprecedented defeat came about because the Roman military establishment had failed to address the challenge raised by a new type of warrior, the armored cavalryman mounted on a heavy horse and armed with the lance and sword. While living in the Ukraine, the Goths, a Teutonic people, had adopted this weapon from steppe tribesmen. Their skillful use of this formidable new type of soldier won this turning-point battle in 378.

This was the first overwhelming victory of a barbarian people over the Romans, and foreshadowed the ultimate disintegration of that empire. For centuries barbarian tribes sought to migrate into the empire, and claim territory for themselves. The victory of the Goths proved that the previously invincible Roman army could be beaten, and redoubled barbarian efforts to breach the Rhine and Danube frontiers.[2]

Until the battle of Adrianople, the Roman army relied primarily on its armored legionary, carrying his shield close to his left shoulder and cutting his way with his short two-edged sword through the thickest hedge of enemy pikes. The legionary had ruled virtually supreme in the Mediterranean world for half a millennium.

But on the steppes to the east, a different type of warfare had emerged, based on two weapons. One was armored cavalry, which gained its power by the shock effect of a strong horse and a long lance that could outreach swords. The other was the powerful but short (three-foot) compound bow, formed by combining wood, horn, and sinew.

The Goths were the first Teutonic people to place their main reliance on the horse. However, they adopted the heavy cavalryman armed with the lance, not the light horseman armed with the bow. The reason probably was that wielding the bow from horseback required great strength and far more skill than learning to ride a horse and charging with a lance. Only the Gothic infantry employed the bow, along with spears, javelins, and swords. Though some foot soldiers may have taken up the compound bow, they mostly used the much weaker and longer (five-foot) bow common to Europe, made wholly of wood and having a pull of fifty to sixty pounds at most.

The Goths also possessed a remarkable defensive apparatus: mobile wagon forts, or laagers, which the Roman writer Ammianus Marcellinus described as being formed in circles with their wagons as a rampart or fortification, "as if enclosed in a space between city walls."

The Romans were unprepared for the armored lancer because they had experienced only marginal contact with him, or with the compound bow. The Parthians, rulers of present-day Iran, used both weapons to stop Rome's eastward expansion, but did not themselves attempt to conquer the Roman Empire. The main danger along the frontiers of the empire for years had been from barbarian raiding parties bent on plunder, not settlement. For several centuries, therefore, the Romans faced no challenge from cavalry incursions. Though they used their own cavalry to hunt down and evict raiding parties, they continued to rely primarily on their infantry for major warfare.

All this changed when the entire Goth nation, men, women, and children, entered the empire, driven as fugitives into Dacia (present-day Romania) in 376 by the Huns, a fierce and savage people from the steppes.

After crossing the Danube into Thrace (the southeast Balkans) with consent of the Roman emperor Valens, the Goths were deceived and denied food by Roman officers. They rebelled, and, to their surprise, found that their lances and horses could carry them through the ranks of imperial infantry. Emboldened, they decided to conquer a place for themselves in the Balkans.

Their two main weapons—armored cavalry and a mobile defensive fort—afforded the Goths a distinct advantage in battles, and they ranged with impunity over Thrace and neighboring regions for two years, causing much disruption and damage. At last, in the summer of 378, a Roman commander, Sebastianus, decided to strike back. He took 2,000 men at night out of Adrianople, about 140 miles west of Constantinople, fell on a large band of marauding Goths on the nearby Maritza River, and, using the tactics of a surprise ambush, routed them. This success convinced Emperor Valens the time had come to attack the Goths. He formed a large army from all over the eastern parts of the empire, and marched to Adrianople. This was the first large Roman army that had been sent against the Goths. The Gothic chief Fridigern perceived an opportunity to defeat the Romans, and he began concentrating his forces.

The Gothic infantry moved to a hill about eight miles from Adrianople (present-day Edirne, Turkey), and there established their laager, which consisted of the Goths' wagons formed in a wide circle, chained together, with the infantry and their draft animals inside. Valens marched his army within arrow range of the fort on August 9, 378, and began to deploy his legions to attack the wagon fort.

Valens arrayed his army in the traditional Roman order—infantry in the center, with cavalry on each wing, whose main job was to protect the infantry, not win a decision on their own. Meanwhile the Goths, behind their wagon shield, unleashed storms of arrows at the Romans, greatly distracting them, but at the same time completely absorbing their attention.

The Romans were unaware that, out of sight, the Gothic commander Fridigern was assembling his superior weapon, his cavalry.

The Romans now attacked the wagon fort. But they were unable to crack through at once because the chained wagons constituted a formidable barrier, requiring the Romans to break up their close-ordered formation in order to get between the wagons and fight the Gothic infantrymen hand-to-hand as individuals.

As this indecisive battle was raging, the Gothic cavalry descended upon the Roman cavalry on the left "like a thunderbolt." The Roman horsemen were caught unawares, and the Goths' lance outdistanced the Romans' swords and short spears. Though the Goths rode some of the Romans down and trampled them, most of the Roman horsemen fled.

The Gothic cavalry now crashed against the Roman legions on the left wing, rolled them up, and drove them in on their own center, as well as into the reserves behind. The impact was so tremendous that the legionaries were pressed together in helpless confusion, most unable to raise their swords. In a few minutes the Roman left, center, and reserve were compressed into a single indistinguishable mass, incapable of maneuvering against the Goths.

Then, in the finishing blow, the Gothic infantry burst out of the wagon fort and charged the massed Roman infantry head-on. At the same moment the Roman cavalry on the right flank saw that the battle was lost, and fled, followed by as much of the infantry on that side of the field as could get away.

Now the abandoned Roman foot soldiers realized the horror of their position. They were beset flank and rear by horsemen, and on the front by Gothic infantry. Unable to deploy or fly, they had to stand and be cut down. Into this quivering mass the Gothic horses and men charged, driving lances and slashing swords. Finally, at nightfall, after two-thirds of the Roman infantry had been slain, some of the surviving legionaries took advantage of the dark to run away.

Emperor Valens, many Roman dignitaries, and 40,000 men fell at Adrianople that day. The Roman army of the east was virtually annihilated.

Despite their overwhelming victory, however, the Goths did not gain security. They tried to besiege Adrianople, but, unable to breach its walls, had to move on. They stopped before Constantinople and found that capital's walls even more formidable. Valens's successor, Emperor Theodosius (378–395), offered the Goths the devastated districts of Thrace on condition that they provide soldiers for the imperial army. An uneasy peace ensued, but the Balkans remained in chaos for many years.

Theodosius realized that Adrianople was a terrible turning point for Rome, and saw that cavalry must make up the most important part of Roman armies thereafter. He bribed every Teutonic chief he could find to enter Roman service. Soon infantry lost its central position in the Roman army in the east. But Roman commanders in the west, still fighting mainly barbarian raiding parties on foot, did not recognize soon enough the revolution that had taken place at Adrianople, and failed to create strong cavalry forces. The west of the empire was slowly overrun by barbarian invasions.

The Eastern Roman Empire, or Byzantium, survived in attenuated form because the Byzantine rulers created a new type of warrior, the cataphract, that armored soldier on a heavy warhorse bearing a lance and wielding the compound bow. Using this dual-purpose warrior as the basis of a defensive tactical system designed to retain territory they already held, not conquer new lands, the Byzantines were able to preserve their empire for many years.[3]

Hastings, 1066

While the Roman Empire in the east was slowly transformed into a new civilization, Byzantium, barbarian invasions destroyed the western Roman Empire. The new civilization that arose in western Europe was shaped in large measure by the failure of the people there to adopt the horse-archer, developed to such perfection on the steppes.

The horse-archer not only was fast, but could deliver arrow storms that could shatter almost any enemy force. And the horse-archer was inexpensive, requiring only what every tribesman of the steppes already possessed, horses and the compound bow.

Perhaps the reason he did not appear in Europe was that horsemanship and archery were tremendously demanding skills. Whereas the steppe tribesman *had* to master both to survive, these skills were rare in Europe. In time the Europeans developed their own style of horseman, the heavy cavalryman, and the development of this type of warrior led to many of the features of European feudal society.

The heavy cavalryman required expensive armor, a big horse, a good sword, and a strong lance, and he had to be highly trained in their use. He was a professional soldier, and the need to maintain such an expensive, elite warrior led directly to the feudal system. Rulers granted lands and farm workers to warriors so they could acquire the wealth to sustain themselves as fighters. Eventually the warriors became a privileged aristocracy of dukes, barons, counts, and knights. Thus most of the population was reduced to servitor status.

The feudal system developed at different rates in Europe, but had advanced to almost full stature in France by the middle of the eleventh century. Warfare there was conducted primarily by the knight on horseback, although foot archers, mainly peasants or town dwellers, wielding the traditional five-foot European bow, still served. Across the English Channel, however, the Anglo-Saxons and the Scandinavians, who had settled Britain in the centuries after the fall of Rome, continued to rely almost entirely on foot soldiers, who did not use bows but wielded swords, spears, and axes. They rode horses, but only to and from battles.

When William, duke of Normandy, decided to conquer England in 1066, he employed the knight on horseback and the bow and arrow, and therefore possessed weapons superior to those of the English. William combined these weapons with excellent generalship, but he prevailed primarily because the English had failed to keep pace with developments in warfare on the Continent.[4]

The English system of war had progressed little from that practiced by the old Teutonic tribes who had crossed the North Sea long before. Though the English wore some armor, their main defense was an iron-rimmed shield measuring thirty-six by fifteen inches made of linden wood, and their main weapon was a six-foot, iron-tipped wooden spear, though some also carried a short sword or dagger. For battle, one side climbed on a hill, lined up in a tight formation, a "shield wall," with the king in the center, and waited to be attacked. Then the two sides would hack and hew at each other till one side gave way.

The English later employed some housecarls, or paid professional men-at-arms, to stiffen the ranks of the national militia, called the *fyrd*, and adopted the Danish battle-ax and javelin. But they continued to disregard the bow and arrow. They also built only the most elementary fortifications. The art of castle-building with stone was far advanced in France, but most English castles in the eleventh century were wooden stockades set up on mounds.

William the Bastard, the son of Robert I of Normandy, was born in 1027 to a tanner's daughter at Falaise. When he was seven his father died on a pilgrimage to the Holy Land. William's life thereafter was surrounded by danger, but at age twenty he defeated rebel barons, demolished their castles, and took iron control of the Duchy of Normandy.

William now aimed at the crown of England, a realm far bigger and richer than his duchy, and claimed succession upon the death of Edward the Confessor. Another claimant was Harold Hardrada, king of Norway, who also threatened invasion. When Edward died on January 5, 1066, the English Witan, or council of notables, knowing the times demanded a strong king, elected Harold Godwineson Earl of Wessex, who had enjoyed great success in wars against the Welsh.[5]

William sent out calls for volunteers to build a substantial army. He attracted a large number of adventurous noblemen, mostly from France, hopeful of great spoils of war if he won. As he gathered his army at St. Valéry at the mouth of the Somme River in northern France, the Norwegians invaded England on the north. Harold Hardrada spread into Yorkshire in early September 1066 with a large force. He burned Scarborough, routed the earls of Northumbria and Mercia near York on September 20, and was pressing for the surrender of the city.

King Harold with his housecarls,[6] who had ridden forward on horses, surprised the Norwegians at Stamford Bridge, seven miles from York, on September 26, and all but annihilated them, killing Harold Hardrada. The battle was fought in the traditional way of both the English and Norwegians—on foot.

Meanwhile on September 28, only two days after Stamford Bridge, William of Normandy and his army of 5,000—2,000 knights and 3,000 infantry—landed at Pevensey, on the south coast of England. The next day he marched to Hastings, eleven miles east, terminus of the Roman road to London. Here William pitched his camp and built a small wooden castle, probably made of logs from trees in the vicinity.

Harold got word of William's landing on October 2 while still at York, and set out at once for London, 200 miles away, his men riding horses. He got to London on October 7 or 8, and spent several days gathering the militia from neighboring counties. On October 11 he marched forth to meet William, with an army probably no larger than William's. Harold's aim was simple: to surprise William's army by speed of advance just as he had surprised the Norwegians.

The better strategy would have been to remain in London until his whole army had been assembled, harry or despoil the country to the south to starve William's forces, and wait for William to approach him. If William had to march into the interior, he would face a long and dangerous campaign. His forces were insufficient to keep communications open with the south coast, and defeat in the interior would spell the annihilation of his army. But William knew Harold's personality. He was impetuous and bold, and anxious to preserve the villages and crops of southern England. Consequently, William began the systematic destruction of villages on the coast to lure Harold within striking distance. If so decoyed, Harold's army might be defeated before reinforcements could arrive.

On October 14, 1066, Harold took up an excellent position for his people's kind of fighting. His army drew together in one great solid mass, or shield wall, facing south along a convex open hill about eight miles north of Hastings on the road from London. The ridgeline was about 260 feet above sea level. It was 1,100 yards long and 150 wide. Deep woodland beginning a mile to the north stretched back into the Wealden Hills. At the hill's topmost point, 275 feet, Harold took his place and raised his standards. On the west, or right, flank was a deep marshy area (150 feet above sea level) drained by the Malfosse Stream (modern-day Manser's Shaw). On the east, or left, flank the road from Hastings rose in a long, slow ascent. In the center a steep rise led up from Ashten Brook (180 feet).

The English thus occupied a highly defensible bastion above the surrounding countryside, approachable only by climbing. The well-armed housecarls, perhaps 2,000 men, were grouped around the king, the militia ranged on either side. They covered the hilltop completely. Witnesses reported their spear shafts looked from below like a wood. Harold admonished his men not to break out from their wall to pursue the enemy. Their security, he emphasized, was in maintaining such a solid formation that the Normans could not penetrate it.

At daybreak William marched on the English host. His army was divided into three corps, each made up of three lines: archers in front, infantry armed with pike and sword, and finally the mailed knights. The left or western corps, which moved into the Malfosse Stream and upward, was composed of Bretons and men from western France. The right or eastern corps was made up of French and Flemings, and advanced up the London road. The center corps, which William himself commanded, was composed of Normans, and it pressed up from Asten Brook.

When the archers in all three lines got within about a hundred yards of the English line, the maximum effective range of their bows, they let fly their arrows. Since they were approaching from below and the arrows had to come at a low and predictable angle, however, the English were able to block most of the shafts with their shields. When the archers advanced farther up the slopes, they received a furious discharge of missiles—javelins, spears, axes, even rocks. They were swept back, but the heavily armed infantry pressed on and got into hand-to-hand fighting with the English. They could make no impression on the shield wall, however, and began to recoil. Then William called up his horsemen. As the foot soldiers dropped back, the knights rode, chanting their battle song, through terrain already strewn with wounded and dead, and dashed at the English line. There was a fearful crash of man and beast against pike and sword. The Normans knocked down the front rank, but could not crack the line. English axes cut through shield and mail, lopped off limbs, even felled horses.

The Bretons on the left wing retreated down the hill in wild disorder. A large mass of English militiamen disregarded their orders to remain in ranks, and rushed after them. Seeing this crowd flying into the stream bed, William wheeled the horsemen in his center and threw the knights upon the English flank. The rash peasants were ridden down and slaughtered in a matter of moments.

The great bulk of the English host had not chased the routed Bretons, however. All along the line, the Norman onslaught wavered, and the greater part of the army drew back. A rumor spread that William had been killed. He took off his helmet and rode in front of the men to quiet their fears.

Then he formed up his disordered units, and directed a second general attack. This time the Normans made a few temporary breaches in the English line, yet again failed. But then William had an inspiration. He called for a feigned retreat by some of his trusted knights. On his command, they wheeled about and fell back in seeming disorder. Once more a large number of English were deceived into thinking the enemy was fleeing, and they broke ranks and rushed after the knights. When the English were well down the slope, William repeated his former stratagem: the intact portion of his knights fell on the Englishmen's flank, while those who had simulated flight turned back and attacked. Once again many militiamen were hewn to pieces.

Harold's host was thinned and shaken, but they drew together and continued to fight. Until this time William's two superior weapons—his knights on horseback and his archers—had not proved decisive against the English shield wall. Realizing this, William focused his efforts on exploiting them to the full. He ordered numerous assaults by the mailed horsemen, all of which failed, but which broke shields and ripped mail. Between assaults, William directed his archers to pour high-angle volleys into the English wall. These arrows came down on the top of the English, and the ranks soon filled with wounded men. In time their supply of javelins and spears gave out, and they could only stand passively waiting for night and the exhaustion of William's forces.

So it was that the arrow and not the lance and sword settled the day. One of the arrows struck Harold a mortal blow in the eye. The continuing arrow showers, coupled with news of the king's fall, broke up the English host at last. A band of Norman knights burst into the mass, and cut Harold to pieces as he lay wounded. The English now retreated in disorder to the forest in the rear. Only a few of the English got away. Most died on the field or in flight.

The stationary tactics of men wielding axes, spears, and swords had failed before William's combination of archers and cavalry. Part of the reason was William's generalship. Without the bows, his knights might have surged endlessly against the shield wall, while the archers, if the knights had not been on hand to stop a general charge of Harold's men, could easily have been driven from the field.

A few days after the battle of Hastings, William occupied Dover, then Canterbury, and then marched westward and circled around London, approaching it from the north. At Little Berkhamstead, seventeen miles north of the city, the London magnates surrendered to him. He sent a body of men to build a fortress that later became the Tower of London. On Christmas Day, 1066, he was crowned in Westminster Abbey.

William had won the crown of England by bringing two superior weapons against the English. The English had lost because they failed to adapt to new developments. By William's success and the English warriors' failure, the world was changed. England was drawn away from its Scandinavian connection toward the richer world of western Europe, consolidating the West into a single great and increasingly dynamic culture.

Breitenfeld, 1631, and Lützen, 1632

For well over 400 years, from around 1000 to about 1450, the principal military problem in Europe was how to drive an enemy out of his fortifications. During this period the feudal system reached its apogee. Lords devoted much of their resources to creating stone castles with high walls, usually built on some eminence. Castles, as well as the walled cities that developed simultaneously throughout western Europe, were extremely difficult to reduce with the siege methods available—mainly starving the inhabitants, but also digging under walls to undermine them, flinging stones with catapults against walls, and rolling towers up to walls to form a platform from which to attack.

During the Hundred Years War (1337–1453), when the kings of England tried but failed to win the crown of France, there were occasional devastating victories by the English on the battlefield, at Crécy in 1346, Poitiers in 1356, and Agincourt in 1415. Although these were important in increasing English power and prestige, the essential fact of the Hundred Years War was that walled cities and castles could rarely be captured until the people in them began to starve.

In the second half of the fifteenth century, however, cannons became powerful enough to breach even the strongest stone walls.[7] But cannons cost lots of money, and only kings or rulers had enough of it to build and maintain them. Cannons thus gave rulers the means not only to knock down the walls of recalcitrant nobles, but they increasingly concentrated power in central kingdoms at the expense of the nobility, and gradually eliminated the purpose for which the aristocracy had been created in the first place—to fight wars.

Although the aristocrats held on to their privileges, cannons and the gunpowder that fired them led to totally different armies, composed primarily of infantry and artillery. The knight on horseback no longer could overwhelm an enemy by charging with his lance, and knights evolved into cavalry whose principal jobs were reconnaissance, screening advances and retreats, and breaking enemy formations that were inadequately protected or had been disrupted by infantry or artillery fire.

Because the first cannons were designed to knock down castle walls, they were heavy, clumsy, hard to move, and not important on the battlefield. The battlefield now had become the decisive arena, however, since castles and walled cities no longer were effective militarily. The weapon that initially became the key to the battlefield was not the cannon but the handheld matchlock musket. First appearing in 1521, it was six feet long, had a range of a hundred yards or less, weighed fifteen pounds, and was fired from a fork-shaped rest.[8] Firing and loading a matchlock took time, leaving musketeers vulnerable to cavalry charges. Also, until the middle of the seventeenth century, no one thought of putting a pike or bayonet on the end of the musket barrel. Accordingly, soldiers armed with pikes or long spears were needed to protect the musketeers.

In this period the Spanish led the way. They developed a military formation known as a *tercio*, or "battle," of 2,000 to 3,000 men, one-third musketeers and two-thirds pikemen. Originally the tercios were formed in rectangles thirty men deep. The deep formations were a direct copy of the ancient Greek phalanx. But the strength of the phalanx was its forward *thrust*, which a deep formation accentuated. The purpose of the tercio was firepower, and it's obvious that soldiers in the rear ranks could not fire their muskets. Therefore the only purpose the deep formation served was to intimidate the enemy.

By the beginning of the seventeenth century, artillery became somewhat lighter and somewhat more mobile. Whenever cannons were brought on the field, they could blow great holes in tercio formations. This led commanders facing artillery to reduce the tercio depth to ten men. But as it took a long time to load the heavy, single-shot musket, they felt they could not reduce the depth any more. This was because they needed ten ranks to keep fire going by means of a peculiar system known as the "snail," or caracole. The men in the front rank fired, then withdrew to the rear to reload, while the second rank stepped up, fired, and moved to the rear.

Strong blocks of pikemen and musketeers in this caracole formation were impossible for cavalry to break with swords or lances. Horsemen began to rely on the new wheel-lock pistol.[9] Cavalry in deep formations trotted up on the enemy tercios, stopped, and fired pistols rank by rank—in "snail," or caracole fashion—each rank retiring to the rear after it fired. Cavalry thereby not only lost the shock effect of galloping horse and leveled lance, but because pistols had extremely short ranges and horsemen were often exposed to musket fire, they were likely to be shot down before they could make much of an effect on a tercio formation, leading to a great decline in cavalry attacks.

Spanish tactics were slow, cumbersome, and methodical, but nevertheless nearly invincible because the Spaniards' opponents were less well trained and less reliable. The Spanish formed their tercios mostly of native Spaniards, whereas other armies were composed of ill-trained mercenaries hired for only a season. A condottiere, or professional soldier, signed a contract with a ruler, and recruited and paid his own men, who took oaths of allegiance to him, not the ruler. The mercenary bands were often little more than an armed rabble.

But the tercio was about to be ousted by King Gustavus Adolphus of Sweden (1594–1632). By improving both artillery and the musket, and by introducing new tactical concepts, he transformed warfare—and created the first truly modern army. A number of Gustavus's original improvements stemmed from two Dutch leaders, Prince Maurice of Orange and his cousin, Prince William Louis of Nassau. They realized that the hired bands they were using were never going to defeat the tercios, and in 1590 they embarked on a program to create an improved army.

The Spanish were their enemy, because they were trying to gain their freedom from the king of Spain, ruler of the Low Countries (present-day Holland, Belgium, and Luxembourg).

Relying primarily on a translation of the Byzantine emperor Leo the Wise's *Tactica*, issued around 900, they focused on two elements that had distinguished ancient armies, drill and discipline. They built flexible, maneuverable, but above all mobile units, which they made much smaller and shallower than the Spanish tercio, sometimes only five or six ranks deep. They also reversed the Spanish ratio of one musketeer to two pikemen, forming units composed two-thirds of musketeers—although they retained the awkward snail, or caracole, method of firing. To lead these new formations, Maurice and William Louis created the first officer corps in the modern sense—that is, professionals trained in one or more military specialties, specifically taught to lead men into battle, and directly responsible to the ruler, not some condottieri chieftain. With their new-model army, the Dutch princes gained many successes against the Spanish.

Gustavus adopted the Dutch drill, discipline, officer corps, and downgrading of pikemen. But Gustavus realized that the Spanish system, which nearly everyone except the Dutch had copied, was too slow and inflexible, and could be overthrown by two superior weapons. One, developed by others but adopted by him, was a lighter wheel-lock musket that no longer needed a crutch or rest. The other, developed by Gustavus himself, was lighter, more mobile artillery. Thus the revolution in warfare that Gustavus set in motion was based on the principle of employing superior weapons.

The wheel-lock musket was a vast improvement over the old heavy matchlock musket fired from a fork-rest. Now musketeers could aim, fire, and reload much faster. To gain maximum effects from this weapon, Gustavus created a new infantry formation and new tactics. He eliminated the snail, or caracole, forming his battalions instead in six ranks, directed, when they went into action, to spread out to three ranks. A thinner formation made his infantry less vulnerable to artillery. At most three men could be struck down by a single cannonball. In the deeper tercio an entire line of infantrymen, ten men, could be flattened. In addition, the battalions could unleash immensely heavier firepower than other armies. With their lighter weapons, all three ranks could fire at the same time—the first rank kneeling, the second rank leaning over, and the third rank standing.

However, the greatest change that Gustavus effected was in his artillery. To render his guns mobile, he shortened barrels, lightened carriages, and reduced his cannons to three sizes or calibers. He also created a wholly new kind of gun, a light, highly maneuverable, wide-muzzle, four-pounder cannon (firing four pounds of pellets and metal fragments—called canister). Using fixed ammunition in wooden cases, the gunners could fire eight shots in the time musketeers could fire six. Two four-pounders accompanied every regiment (two battalions, or about 1,100 men). These cannons pulled within close range, and sprayed canister into the massed tercios.

Finally, Gustavus realized that the caracole tactics of cavalry ignored cavalry's great strength—its shock value, or capability of disrupting and scattering an enemy formation. To restore shock, he formed his horsemen into three ranks, and ordered them to charge at a gallop instead of a trot, and to use the naked sword, reserving the pistol only for the melee when the enemy horse or infantry had been broken.

Lighter muskets and cannons and charging cavalry were tremendous innovations. But their impact was vastly multiplied by the fact that the tercio formation remained ten ranks or more deep—and thus was highly vulnerable at long range to solid shot of cannon, which could knock down a complete file of men, and at short range to canister, which sprayed out a deadly hail of metal balls and fragments directly into the massed bodies. At the same time, tercio firepower was limited because only musketeers in the front ranks could fire.

Gustavus tried out his new-model army and perfected his tactics in wars with Poland, but the Thirty Years War (1618–48) raging in Germany was increasingly threatening Sweden's interests. Gustavus sought control of the Baltic Sea because Sweden held Finland and was trying to annex territory in Poland and in the present-day Baltic states of Estonia, Latvia, and Lithuania.

The Thirty Years War had erupted as a religious dispute between Protestant and Catholic rulers in German states. Each side wished to advance its religion at the expense of the other. But the war soon lapsed into a political struggle in which Ferdinand II, the Hapsburg ruler of Austria, sought to transform the virtually impotent Holy Roman Empire (comprising Germany) of which he was emperor into a true German empire by reducing to obedience the many small independent states in Germany. By 1630 this effort was on the verge of succeeding, when his excellent general, Albrecht von Wallenstein, began to seize German territories along the Baltic coast.

Wallenstein was a capable general, with a great strategic sense. But he also was ambitious, and probably was maneuvering to gain a base of power in northern Germany and become the true ruler in Germany, downgrading or even removing Emperor Ferdinand. Seeing this danger as greater than any resurgence in opposition by Protestant states, Ferdinand ousted Wallenstein in August 1630. Leadership devolved upon Johan Tilly, seventy-two years old, who had little military ability compared to Wallenstein.

Just prior to this event, Gustavus decided to intervene in the war in Germany. On July 6, 1630, he landed a Swedish force on the Baltic coast of Germany, and planned to bring his army up to 40,000 men in order to challenge the Imperial host. Gustavus got little help from the Protestant princes of Germany. Elector, or ruler, John George of Saxony was a secret enemy, and Elector George William of Brandenburg offered no support.

Gustavus waited nearly nine months before undertaking any decisive advance, and then only after Tilly pressed the siege of the Protestant city of Magdeburg on the Elbe River in spring 1631. Gustavus made no move to stop this, and the troops of Tilly's lieutenant, Gottfried Heinrich Graf zu Pappenheim, stormed Magdeburg's ramparts on May 20, 1631, killed 25,000 of the 30,000 inhabitants, and burned the city to the ground.

At last Gustavus realized he must take action. He marched on Berlin and, at the mouths of his cannons, forced George William to renounce his neutrality. Tilly's army, now having eaten all the food in the vicinity of Madgeburg, invaded Saxony and compelled the surrender of Leipzig. This brought John George, the Saxon ruler, to Gustavus's side as well. On September 15, 1631, the Saxon army of 18,000 untried recruits joined Gustavus's 23,000 men, and they marched to relieve Leipzig.

Tilly's troops were in a highly undisciplined state, and his best course would have been to stand fast in Leipzig and await reinforcements. But Pappenheim wanted to fight, and, on a reconnaissance, sent back a message from Breitenfeld, five miles north, that he had sighted the enemy, and had to be supported. Tilly marched out, arrayed his army of perhaps

Gustavus Adolphus's Campaigns, 1631–1632

35,000 men on "a pleasant and fruitful plain," and waited for Gustavus on September 17, 1631.

Tilly was a master of the Spanish tactical system, and set up his seventeen tercios, each with 1,500 to 2,000 men, in a line, with heavy bodies of cavalry on each wing. But he had only twenty-six cannons, which he placed in front of the tercios to his center and right.

The Swedes had fifty-one heavier cannons and twenty-four of the highly mobile four-pounders attached to the regiments. Gustavus drew up the army facing south, with the Swedes on his right and the Saxons on his left, his heavier cannons in the center under his artillery chief, Lennart Torstensson. Of the Saxon formation nothing is known, but Gustavus, like Tilly, arrayed his cavalry on each of his wings. He also interspersed numerous fifty-man platoons of musketeers among his cavalry to protect against Imperial horsemen.

The battle opened with an artillery duel that lasted two and a half hours. The Swedes had the best of it, because their guns, being more numerous, fired three rounds to the Imperialists' one. Pappenheim, in charge of the 5,000 Imperial cavalry on the left, could stand the firing no longer. Without waiting for orders, he moved against the Swedish right-wing cavalry under Johan Baner. This was foolish, because the Imperialist cavalry's pistol caracole was no match for the platoons of musketeers, who poured salvo after salvo into the Imperial horsemen. Pappenheim charged the Swedish right seven times, and seven times he was repulsed with bloody losses. On the last occasion, the Swedish commander hurled his reserve horsemen against the Imperialists, and drove them in rout from the field.

Meanwhile, the Imperialist cavalry on Tilly's right, mistaking Pappenheim's move as a signal for a general advance, charged the Saxons in front of them. The Saxons apparently put up no resistance at all, and promptly fled the field. This exposed Gustavus's left flank. Tilly took immediate advantage, and ordered the tercios on his right wing to advance to the place where the Saxons had vacated, then wheel onto the Swedish flank. He thus accomplished a classic maneuver called a change of front, in which his right wing—which had been facing north—made a left turn, and advanced west against the Swedes' flank. At the same time he ordered the right-wing cavalry to attack the Swedish rear.

Any other army of that era would have collapsed, but Gustavus's army could maneuver twice as fast as the Imperialists. He ordered Gustav Horn, commanding the left-wing Swedish cavalry, to wheel to the left to meet Tilly's change of front, and two infantry brigades in the center (two regiments each, or about 2,200 men) to turn and reinforce Horn. The infantry stopped the Imperialists with four-pounder cannon and musket fire.

While this action was going on, Gustavus saw his chance to deliver a decisive blow. Since Pappenheim's cavalry had fled the field, Tilly's left flank was exposed, and Gustavus ordered a regiment of cavalry to strike this flank. As this charge went in at a gallop, Gustavus put himself at the head of four infantry regiments, and advanced directly on the center of Tilly's line, seized Tilly's artillery, which were still standing there, wheeled the guns around, and pounded the Imperial infantry behind with their own cannons and the regimental four-pounders. At the same time the Swedish infantry poured round after round of musket fire into the massed Imperial troops.

The casualties were far too much for the tercios to endure. They lost all cohesion and stampeded to the rear. With this the entire Imperial army disintegrated. Tilly lost 7,000 killed, 6,000 wounded and captured on the field, and another 3,000 captured by cavalry pursuit. The Imperialists surrendered all their artillery, and their entire supply train. Gustavus's dead and wounded did not exceed 3,000, most caused by cannon fire.

Gustavus achieved victory because his forces could deliver much more firepower than the enemy—the infantry in their extended formations using their superior muskets, and the superior Swedish light artillery moving forward with the infantry and delivering canister fire within yards of the enemy line. The seizure of Tilly's artillery and its use against the Imperialists was a fortuitous addition to Swedish firepower.

Tilly was left with no guns and only a third of his army, which fell behind the Saale River in Thuringia. Gustavus now possessed a great opportunity. The road to Bohemia and Austria was open. If he had struck at once for Vienna, the Hapsburg capital, Tilly would have been forced to challenge him—and almost surely would have been shattered. This would have allowed Gustavus to occupy most of the Hapsburg lands, oust Ferdinand as emperor, bring peace to Germany, and gain Sweden a solid strategic position in the Baltic.

But Gustavus considered a march on Vienna too risky. Instead he marched to the Rhineland, which gained him nothing but secure winter quarters. As a result, Tilly raised new forces, and a chastened Emperor Ferdinand hastily struck a deal with the ousted commander Wallenstein to form another army in Bohemia. By the spring of 1632 the empire was stronger than ever, and Gustavus had achieved little from his stunning victory at Breitenfeld.

Gustavus Adolphus is one of the most contradictory captains in history. He possessed an innovative mind that utterly transformed the battlefield, yet his strategic vision was so profoundly lacking that he could chart no way to achieve final victory or gain lasting benefits from his battlefield triumphs. His example shows that a superior weapon is useless unless the commander exploits it to achieve some goal or purpose.

On April 10, 1632, Gustavus stormed Donauwörth, the most westerly fortress of Bavaria on the Danube River, and five days later made a spectacular crossing of the Lech River. Tilly was mortally wounded, but the Imperial army merely retreated downstream to Ingolstadt, which Gustavus found too strong to take quickly.

Once again the road was open to Vienna, and once again Gustavus refused to take the risk. Instead he tried to draw Wallenstein into battle by devastating northern Bavaria. But Wallenstein would not take the bait, and joined up with Bavarian forces. When Gustavus built an entrenched camp near Nuremberg, Wallenstein set up a camp nearby, intending to wait out the Swedish king. With his men running out of food, Gustavus finally assaulted Wallenstein's camp on September 3–4, 1632, was severely repulsed, and now, at long last, moved toward Vienna, hoping to draw Wallenstein after him.

But Wallenstein turned away and marched straight to Saxony, seized Leipzig, and began despoiling the countryside. A great strategist would have ignored this attempt to draw him north. He would have abandoned his line of communications, and seized Vienna and the heart of the Hapsburg empire. Instead, Gustavus rushed headlong back to Saxony, where the perfidious elector, John George, withdrew his army to Torgau on the Elbe and refused to join him.

On November 16, 1632, unsupported by his Saxon allies, Gustavus fought his last battle at Lützen, a few miles southwest of Leipzig.

Wallenstein lined up his 25,000-man army—four great tercios in the center, cavalry on either flank, cannons on the right front—for two miles north of the east-west Lützen-Leipzig road, built on a raised causeway above a low, flat plain. He anchored his east on the Flossgraben, a small stream, and his west on Lützen.

Gustavus had only 18,000 men with him, and deployed his army much as at Breitenfeld—infantry in the center with forty four-pounder cannons, cavalry on the flanks, his twenty-six heavy cannons in front of the infantry. Once again Swedish mobility and superior weapons were transcendent. When a morning mist lifted for a while, Gustavus personally led his right-wing cavalry across the elevated road and, though wounded in the arm, drove back Wallenstein's left-flank horsemen. The fog settled again, and Gustavus blundered into a party of Imperial cavalry, who shot and killed him and two of his three companions. The third rode back to inform the Swedish army.

Instead of disheartening the Swedish soldiers, the news filled them with fury. They attacked the Imperial tercios headlong. Pappenheim, who arrived with 8,000 Imperial cavalry, pushed the right-wing Swedish cavalry back to its starting place, but the encounter degenerated into a wild melee in which Pappenheim was killed. Meanwhile the infantry fight in the center raged with extreme violence for a while, but Swedish firepower was much greater, and, as had happened at Breitenfeld, the Imperial tercios collapsed and the men fled.

There was no pursuit. Wallenstein lost about 4,000 killed, the Swedes about 1,500. Sweden gained little from Gustavus's campaigns, and Germany suffered greatly. The war went on another sixteen years till 1648, leaving a horribly shattered land. Eight million people died, whole regions were depopulated. In Bohemia, of 35,000 villages in 1618, only 6,000 remained. Because Germany was woefully weakened, France gained by far the most and, under the "Sun King" Louis XIV (1638–1715), embarked on a campaign of aggrandizement that disrupted Europe for the next sixty-five years.

Though Gustavus failed to achieve a lasting victory for Sweden, he left a remarkable legacy. It was manifested not in glory to Sweden, which soon sank back into obscurity, but in subsequent generals who adopted his use of lighter muskets and cannons, imitated his more-mobile formations, and consolidated his introduction of modern war to the world.

War in the Desert, 1941–1942

The opportunity to employ a superior weapon occurs in every era. Oftentimes the superior weapon is not exclusive to one side and could be adopted by both, yet some commanders are unable or unwilling to follow the rule. This was the case with the opponents of Gustavus. They saw the new musket, the new artillery, and the new formations that Gustavus had created. But they did not change—possibly because they did not comprehend the revolution, or found it too difficult to scrap the familiar system they knew. In any event, the revolution introduced by Gustavus was picked up not by his opponents, but by disciples who came later.

Occasionally the challenge is not to transform an entire military system, but to adapt to circumstances that require a new approach. The most indelible example of this in modern times is how the German general Erwin Rommel applied this remedy in Libya and Egypt in the years 1941–1942, and how the leadership of the British army misunderstood what was happening, and suffered enormous losses as a result.[10]

Adolf Hitler did not want to fight a campaign in Africa, and only sent Rommel and modest German forces to Libya primarily to keep his Italian ally, Benito Mussolini, in the war. Mussolini had done little to prepare Italy for the conflict. His armies were vastly inferior to the British, and atrociously armed. But he wanted to keep the Italian colony of Libya, and was happy to get German help.

Shortly after Rommel landed in Libya on February 11, 1941, he grasped the essential nature of desert warfare: everything depended upon mobility.

"In the North African desert," he wrote, "nonmotorized troops are of practically no value against a motorized enemy, since the enemy has the chance, in almost every position, of making the action fluid by a turning movement around the south."

Rommel discerned that desert warfare was strangely similar to war at sea. Motorized equipment could move at will over it and usually in any direction, much as ships could move over the ocean. Rommel described the similarity thus: "Whoever has the weapons with the greatest range has the longest arm, exactly as at sea. Whoever has the greater mobility can by swift action compel his opponent to act according to his wishes."

The key to victory in the desert was the tank, whose armor could withstand most enemy fire, and whose guns could shatter unarmored or lightly armored vehicles. The British had concluded from these two factors that armored warfare would consist primarily of tank-on-tank battles.

But since German and British tanks were more or less comparably armed and armored, each side on average would destroy about the same number of enemy tanks as it lost itself. In other words, stalemate would ensue unless the British deployed many more tanks than the Axis. This, in fact, was the British plan, and they brought far more tanks into the field than the Axis, aiming to gain victory by overwhelming numbers.

Rommel recognized the British theory was correct, if one accepted the premise that armored warfare would consist of tank-on-tank battles. But with Hitler uninterested in Africa, Rommel knew he had no chance of matching British tank numbers. He decided to fight the war differently than the British expected, resolving to withhold his relatively few tanks until the final push or drive to gain a decision—and to find another way to destroy British armor.

He and other German officers had already discovered a weapon eminently suited for this purpose—the 88-mm high-velocity antiaircraft gun. In the 1940 campaign in France, German commanders found that this gun, designed to shoot down high-flying aircraft, could blast through eighty-three millimeters of armor at 2,000 yards, making it by far the most formidable antitank weapon on either side.

The Germans also had another weapon, the 50-mm antitank gun, a light and nimble piece that could penetrate fifty millimeters of armor at 1,000 yards. The 50-mm gun could sometimes crack the thirty- and forty-millimeter armor of the fast British cruiser and Crusader tanks, but could break through the 70-millimeter frontal armor of the slow "infantry" Matilda tank only at point-blank range.

With these two weapons, which he used in new ways, Rommel created a tactical system—based on the concept of sending guns after tanks—that virtually nullified the vast British superiority in tank numbers. And since Rommel was extremely bold in his offensive movements, he used his fewer tanks to throw the British into precipitate retreat time after time.

For offensive moves, Rommel leapfrogged 50-mm antitank guns from one shielded vantage point to another, while keeping his tanks stationary and hidden, if possible, but giving protective fire to the guns as they advanced. Once the antitank guns were established, they in turn protected the tanks as they swept forward.

In defensive operations, Rommel tried to bait the British. His panzers, usually his faster, weakly armed light tanks, advanced to contact the enemy, then retired. The typical British response was to mount a "cavalry" charge, though visibility was obscured by dust and sand stirred up by the supposedly retreating enemy. Waiting in ambush in hollows and draws to the rear were 50-mm guns, while behind them was a "gun line" of 88s. The 50-mms picked off British tanks that got within range, while the 88s took on the advancing enemy armor at distances far beyond the capacity of the tanks' two-pounder (40-mm) guns to respond. The British contributed to the success of this tactical system by almost always dispersing their armor widely over the front. Since Rommel tried to concentrate his armor, he could be fairly confident that he could outnumber British tanks at whatever point he decided to strike. The British also committed their armor piecemeal, mostly in single units of squadrons or regiments, instead of full brigades, and never in massed brigades. This meant that even when they had more tanks, they usually didn't attack with superior numbers.[11]

As Rommel remarked to a captured British officer in November 1941, "What difference does it make if you have two tanks to my one, when you spread them out and let me smash them in detail?"[12]

The British took a long time to understand Rommel's tactics, and they never copied them. Yet they had a 3.7-inch high-velocity antiaircraft gun with penetrating power equal to the 88, but did not use it in an antitank role. Their original antitank gun was a relatively poor two-pounder (40-mm) piece, but in the spring of 1942 they introduced the six-pounder (57-mm) gun that had 30 percent greater penetration than the German 50-mm gun.

The British failure to respond to Rommel's innovations is all the more remarkable because of the tremendous losses they experienced. For example, on June 15, 1941, thirteen Matildas attacked Halfaya Pass on the Libya-Egypt border, guarded by four dug-in 88s, their barrels horizontal with little visible above ground. The British commander radioed back his last message: "They are tearing my tanks to bits." Only one of the thirteen Matildas survived the trap. The same day, a few miles southwest on Hafid Ridge, another German gun trap of four 88s and 50-mm guns stopped cold an attack of British cruiser tanks. By nightfall the British had lost more than half of their tank strength, while Rommel's tank numbers had not been reduced at all.

In the long run, Hitler's failure to supply the army in Africa was more important than Rommel's astonishing victories. In the summer of 1942, Rommel, with vastly inferior forces, drove the British into headlong retreat. He stopped at El Alamein, only sixty miles west of Alexandria, and then only because his army had dwindled to just a few tanks. Here the British at last were able to create a solid defensive line. From that point on, Rommel's army was doomed. The British built up overwhelming strength, and attacked in October 1942, joining with American and British forces who invaded Morocco and Algeria, and driving the Axis powers out of Africa in the spring of 1943.

Implications for the Future

We can draw two contradictory conclusions from the examples above: a superior weapon is extremely effective, and yet, even so, employing a superior weapon does not necessarily bring victory. Thus the real lesson these campaigns teach us is that *how* we use our weapons is far more important than *what* weapons we use.

For example, the German panzers (plus the first effective ground-attack or aerial-artillery weapon in war, the Stuka dive-bomber) could not be stopped by any existing Allied weapons from 1939 until the late fall of 1941. Adolf Hitler's fatal mistake was failure to exploit this superiority while he still had it. That is, after the defeat of France in 1940 he should have pressed on to gain an impregnable defensive position by seizing North Africa and the Middle East. He did not. When the Soviets began to deploy good tanks, but especially antitank guns, in late 1941, German superiority began to erode, and by the late fall of 1942 it had vanished.

Also, Saddam Hussein of Iraq should have recognized from the experience of the Germans in World War II—a prime example was the battle of Normandy, June–August 1944—that a power cannot hope to stand in a toe-to-toe battle against another power with better weapons. His weapons, in other words, were useful *only* against an enemy armed in a similarly antiquated manner, like Iran, or who had vastly inferior weapons, like the Kurds and other dissidents within Iraq.

Unfortunately for the world, leaders like Saddam Hussein have been common. They have brought on wars they had no chance of winning. Many were unable to evaluate their true situations, and walked straight into disasters.

Consequently this rule of war—to develop a new weapon, or to employ an existing weapon more effectively than one's opponent—can be extremely successful, but has limits. It can be decisive *only* against an enemy who cannot develop ways *around* the weapon or the use of it.

We faced a brilliant example of adaptation to superior power by the Chinese in the Korean War (1950–1953). Their weapons were far behind those of American forces, and to overcome the disparity, they devised clever methods that emphasized their strengths and exploited American weaknesses. They dug deep bunkers into the hillsides, and relied largely on small arms (machine guns, rifles, and grenades) and mortars. All of these could be moved by hand and foot, so the Chinese forces did not need trucks or roads. Thus American air interdiction against their supply lines was largely ineffective, while bunkers negated the effects of most American shells and bombs. Americans therefore were required to fight the kind of war dictated by the Chinese, not by themselves.

American bombs are much too powerful nowadays for another enemy to employ bunkers as a defense against us. But the different, innovative thinking that the Chinese employed may well be duplicated by our current and future opponents. For example, to avoid our weapons, our enemies might employ a semiguerrilla war strategy—hiding from our aircraft and heavy weapons, and striking from ambush, or from mountains, swamps, jungles, and forests. Surprise blows from unexpected places have the potential for neutralizing even the most powerful weapon, simply because a surprise blow might come too fast for it to be deployed.

Such unconventional adaptability is probably the single greatest challenge the United States and other advanced nations must meet in the future. For the vast technological superiority of the West can lead to the easy assumption that our weapons will always be better, and that our enemies will always be as easy to beat as Saddam Hussein, or the almost helpless Taliban. Our weapons probably *will* be better, but their very superiority will lead our opponents to devise new methods of overcoming us. The effective attacks on the World Trade Center and the Pentagon using our own commercial aircraft should warn us that we must be prepared for highly unconventional types of strikes, against which our vastly superior weapons may be all but useless.

8

Driving a Stake in the Enemy's Heart

ONE OF THE potentially most decisive rules of war is to press straight into an enemy's vitals, and destroy the means by which he can resist. This was the method we used to overturn the Taliban government of Afghanistan in a few weeks in the fall of 2001. Because of the immense capacity of American aircraft and airborne forces to strike at great distances, this rule will form the basis for many campaigns in the future.

If this maxim is applied correctly, it can strike at the very *will* of the enemy to resist. Wars ultimately are decided by the application of thought by the leaders of the opposing sides to devise effective strategies and maneuvers. The history of warfare is replete with examples of weak forces overcoming large forces, of small tribes or states destroying great empires. Therefore, power itself is no guarantee of victory, despite the fact that the relative strength of one side versus the other is one of the most important factors that determines the outcome of wars.

There is no arena in which this truth is more evident than in those campaigns in which one side invades the territory of another, and tries to eliminate resistance. A successful campaign of this kind depends on careful analysis, firm action, and the intelligent execution of valid plans. Success requires sufficient power, but ultimately depends more upon the resolve of the commander. The general who fails in the execution of this strategy usually finds himself cut off and isolated. But the commander who achieves victory with this strategy sometimes ascends to world fame.

Driving a stake in the enemy's heart aims at eradicating the power of an enemy to resist by inflicting an overwhelming blow to a country's vitals. The strategy is based on the principle that organized resistance is impossible if an enemy's civil and military administration, factories, distribution system, transportation grid, and communications are disrupted or seized.

The Allies achieved a victory by this means in the spring of 1945, when they overran Nazi Germany. Later that year, for the first time in history, the Americans achieved victory with air power alone when they shattered the centers of most Japanese cities in firebomb raids, culminating in the destruction of Hiroshima and Nagasaki with atomic bombs in August 1945. The air raids on Japan, though delivered from outside the country, so disrupted factory production, movement of goods, housing of people, and delivery of food that Japan was virtually immobilized, and would have been incapable of more than localized defense in the event of invasion.

An invasion into enemy territory can elicit all manner of responses from the defending population, many of them unpredictable. There are some cases, as for example the American incursion into Afghanistan in 2001, where the invaded people are so oppressed by their own government that they actually welcome intervention. In general, however, a commander can anticipate firm opposition from both the enemy military and the civilian population, and must examine carefully how to meet various kinds of opposition.

A brilliant case in point is that of Alexander the Great when he set out to conquer the Persian Empire in 334 B.C. He faced a daunting task. His country was modest in size compared with the empire, which was enormous, stretching from Egypt in the west to the Indus River in the east. The actual heart or center of power of the empire lay deep in the interior, around Babylon, in Mesopotamia, and Susa and Persepolis, in present-day Iran. Alexander could not march on this heartland until he had gained a position of strength inside the empire, and until his rear was secure. Otherwise his army might be cut off from Macedonia and Greece and, without supplies and reinforcements, would perish.

Alexander's first and most crucial task was to defeat the Persian army that met him more or less on the doorstep when he entered Asia Minor. This victory came at the Granicus River in May 334 B.C., and ensured him control of western Anatolia. However, the Persian (mostly Phoenician) fleet dominated the Aegean and eastern Mediterranean seas, and, if left undisturbed, might block his supply line back to Macedonia and foment uprisings in Greece. Alexander knew he had to figure a way to eliminate this threat before invading Persia's heartland. He decided to march down the coast of the Levant to Egypt, occupying all the bases of the Persian fleet, and thereby eliminating the naval threat. His rear was now secure, and he was in possession of several bases that guaranteed his supplies.

Having protected his position, Alexander then advanced into Meso-potamia. There he destroyed Darius's army at Arbela in 331 B.C. This bat-tle, fought near Babylon, secured him the heart of the Persian Empire, and thereby destroyed Darius's legitimacy as ruler. Alexander became his successor.

Alexander marched from one secure point to the next, which gave him the chance to drive the stake into the heart of the Persian Empire at Arbela. But another great captain, the Carthaginian general Hannibal, was unable to drive a stake in the heart of the Roman republic during the Second Punic War, 219–202 B.C., because he failed to secure a base in Italy. His failure was due to the defensive genius of the Roman com-mander, Quintus Fabius Maximus.

Carthage, a great commercial state located near present-day Tunis, was seeking revenge for losses it suffered in the First Punic War against Rome, 264–241 B.C. Hannibal had defeated two Roman armies in Italy, due to his incomparable cavalry, and was trying to destroy Rome itself.

Fabius, knowing he could not challenge Hannibal's horsemen, resorted to an indirect approach. A vital element in his strategy was pre-venting Hannibal from gaining the support of the numerous semi-independent cities in southern Italy that were allied to Rome. If Hannibal achieved a certain amount of success, he might readily win support from these cities. If he was kept on the defensive somehow, the cities would be reluctant to go over to him. Fabius's solution was to fight the Carthaginians in small-scale "Fabian" guerrilla actions, only in the hills where his forces could withdraw into places inaccessible to Hannibal's cavalry.

Because of Fabius's small-scale, but almost constant, attacks, Hannibal was obligated to stay on the defensive, and was unable to establish alliances with cities where he could be sure of procuring food and other supplies, and from which he could launch attacks against Rome and retire his troops at the end of campaigns. At last, after sixteen years of inconsequential operations in Italy, Hannibal was called back to confront an invasion of Carthage in 202 B.C. by the Roman commander Scipio Africanus, who had created a powerful cavalry, and was threatening the city of Carthage. Scipio defeated Hannibal at the battle of Zama in present-day Tunisia, and ended the war.

One of the most notorious later examples of a flawed execution of driving a stake in the enemy's heart was Napoleon's invasion of Russia in 1812. Napoleon aimed to capture Moscow, disrupting the empire's administration, and dictating peace. But the czar and his generals— calling on the populace to fight to the death—successfully marshaled tenacious resistance. Unlike previous operations in which Napoleon dueled with opposing generals on the battlefield, in the Russian campaign his primary adversary was the stubborn Russian people.[1]

Rather than provide the French with shelter and supplies, the Russians even burned Moscow, and destroyed vast quantities of food that might have fallen into French hands. Facing the grueling Russian winter with no secure base and no means of supply, Napoleon was forced to order a devastating retreat.

There are two crucial factors determining the success or failure of a campaign to overrun a state. One is a clear understanding of where the state's heart lies, along with a firm plan for reaching that heart. The other is the resolve on the part of the leader to carry the campaign to its conclusion. Without this resolve, no plan can succeed, because all great invasions present immense challenges, distractions, and difficulties that can divert a leader to lesser objectives or cause him to give up entirely. In the examples below, the resolve of the leaders, or the lack of it, made all the difference.

The American March to Mexico City, 1847

In 1846 the United States and Mexico went to war primarily because many Americans believed that the country had a "manifest destiny" to expand all the way to the Pacific Ocean. The United States sought to acquire a huge region Mexico possessed, all the territory from Texas west to California.

The key campaign in the war, General Winfield Scott's drive to seize Mexico City in 1847, was one of the most successful invasions ever undertaken. The campaign resulted in the cession of all the territory that now makes up the southwestern corner of the United States.[2] The march to Mexico City is a textbook case of driving a stake in an enemy's heart. Scott understood that the Mexicans perceived Mexico City as the center or core of their country, and that they would grant huge territorial concessions in order to regain the city.

With a tiny army, Scott made an amphibious landing on the east coast of Mexico, at Veracruz. He then marched 270 miles across the high mountains in the center of Mexico, broke through numerous barriers, and overwhelmed fiercely contested fortresses at the gates of Mexico City. Nowhere was he defeated, or even severely checked. On the last stage of his drive against the capital, he had with him fewer than a third of the number of Mexican troops arrayed against him. The brilliant campaign beautifully illustrates how an invader should conduct a drive deep into enemy country, and how a defender should *not* respond.

However well an offensive drive is conducted, it can still fail if the resisting army undertakes a strong, determined, and imaginative defense. Scott's dedication to his goal was the primary reason for the campaign's success. Yet a factor that contributed vastly to the victory was the bad leadership and poor judgment exhibited by the Mexican commander and president, Antonio López de Santa Anna.

Despite failing to organize adequate defenses at any point, Santa Anna remained in power because the government of Mexico was distracted by numerous rival contenders for the presidency. The constant turmoil that ensued created instability and irresolution, and prevented another, more competent, leader from taking command and creating a well-led, well-trained, well-disciplined army. Scott, on the other hand, possessed an army with all of these merits, though it was small.

The Americans decided to invade Mexico at Veracruz because they could achieve nothing decisive by driving into northern Mexico from Texas. In 1846 an American army under Zachary Taylor advanced to Saltillo, 150 miles south of the Texas-Mexican border, but could not cross the forbidding desert that stretched 250 miles to San Luis Potosí. Because Mexico possessed no navy, however, a good alternative was to seize the port city of Veracruz, and march over the national highway from there to the capital.

The Mexicans were well aware that the Americans intended to land at Veracruz, but they nevertheless failed to reinforce the garrison there of 4,400 men. Furthermore, the commander, Juan Morales, showed no willingness to challenge the Americans. Thus 10,000 Americans came ashore on March 9, 1847, about three miles south of the city, against no opposition. Cannons hidden behind the landing site could have been rolled forward by the Mexicans, and used to blast the Americans' wooden flatboats out of the water. Instead, Morales kept his troops behind the city walls, and waited till American artillery came ashore and began bombardment. The city and its forts surrendered on March 29.

Scott quickly gathered supplies and moved out toward Mexico City on April 8. He was spurred to leave because of fear of yellow fever, which was endemic in the low country of Mexico. Scott hoped to get quickly to fever-free Jalapa, 4,700 feet high in the Sierra Madre mountains and seventy-four road miles inland.

Santa Anna tried to stop Scott at the pass of Cerro Gordo (Fat Mountain), ten miles east of Jalapa, a move that would keep the

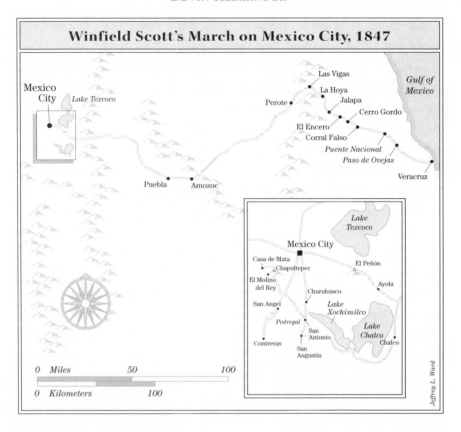

Winfield Scott's March on Mexico City, 1847

Mexico City
Lake Texcoco

Las Vigas
La Hoya
Perote •
Jalapa
Cerro Gordo
El Encero
Corral Falso
Puente Nacional
Paso de Ovejas
Gulf of Mexico
Veracruz

Puebla • Amozoc

Lake Texcoco
Mexico City
Casa de Mata
Chapultepec
El Peñón
El Molino del Rey
Ayola
Churubusco
San Angel
Lake Xochimilco
Pedregal
San Antonio
Lake Chalco
Contreras
San Augustín
Chalco

0 Miles   50   100
0 Kilometers   100

Jeffrey L. Ward

Americans in the lowlands and the region of fever. He assembled 12,000 troops, but placed most of them at the western end of the pass. The Americans swept around the hills above the pass, and came out on the rear of the Mexicans. Santa Anna inexplicably had prepared for only a direct advance along the roadway by the Americans, and had made no provisions to guard against an envelopment. Thus the Mexicans were completely surprised, and fled in panic. The Mexican army disintegrated, and did not re-form.

Having suffered few losses, Scott's army marched on to Jalapa, where it found plenty of food and fodder. Scott then sent one division thirty-five miles farther west, where food was also abundant. Dividing the small American army in two looked from the outside like an extremely hazardous act. But the Mexican army had ceased to exist after one abortive battle, and Scott was not worried about an attack. His main concern was about guerrillas—bandits mostly—who preyed on his supply columns coming up from the coast. Protecting this supply line took too many men, especially considering that 3,000 volunteers were due to be discharged soon because their one-year enlistments would be expiring.

President James K. Polk and Secretary of War William L. Marcy were creating new regiments to replace the volunteers, but they would take time to arrive. Meanwhile, Scott sent the 3,000 volunteers home. He was left with an army of just over 7,000 men, which he marched to Puebla, only eighty miles by road east of Mexico City. All the while, guerrilla attacks continued.

While he waited for enough men to join him to allow him to commence the last leg of his march, Scott made a profound decision. The guerrillas were making it too dangerous to dispatch convoys to and from Veracruz without strong escorts. On June 4, 1847, Scott abandoned all stations between Veracruz and Puebla, in effect cutting his army off from the coast. With no supply line, his army would have to live off the land.

Scott's army was small, but the Mexicans were making no attempt to besiege it at Puebla, or even to inhibit collection of food and fodder. Every Mexican leader understood that the United States would be able to dictate terms of peace if Scott seized the capital, and still the Mexicans failed to strike. If the Mexicans had attacked Scott's army every step of the way, the Americans could have been so weakened that the campaign might have faltered or even failed. The passivity of Mexican leaders in face of the peril their country faced is almost inconceivable, though the failure should be attributed to the chaotic, disorganized government in Mexico City, as well as to Santa Anna's lack of military acumen. He never appreciated the opportunity to make repeated strikes against Scott's force while it was stymied at Puebla.

On July 8, Scott finally received 4,500 troops, and on August 6 got 2,400 more. The next day Scott's leading division marched out of Puebla toward the capital. The army, 11,000 men, was marching, Scott announced, "with naked blade in hand."[3]

In the meantime Santa Anna had formed a new army, of 36,000 men, but no better trained or led than the army that had bolted at Cerro Gordo. He intended to remain on the defensive, relying on the fact that Mexico City was built on a former island in a once-huge lake that was slowly drying. The basin's floor contained six lakes, extensive marshes, and low-lying fields. Mexico City could be approached only along elevated roads and causeways. Santa Anna figured that his troops, posted along the narrow elevated avenues, could stop any American advance.

Sure that the Americans would approach along the national highway from the east, Santa Anna accordingly posted thirty cannons and 7,000 troops atop El Peñón, a 450-foot hill just south of the highway, and about eight miles east of the capital.

When the American advance guard arrived eight miles east of El Peñón on August 12, engineer captain Robert E. Lee, later of Civil War fame, rode ahead to confirm that the Mexicans were in force there and that seizing the position would be costly, since the only approach was a mile-long causeway over a wet marsh. Lee searched for a better route. He found it in a road that led around the southern shore of Lakes Chalco and Xochimilco, and then on to Mexico City.

Scott ordered the army to move along this twenty-five-mile route. The Americans emerged on August 18 at San Augustín, nine miles due south of Mexico City, and just southeast of an egg-shaped lava field, the Pedregal, about two and a half miles wide and a couple miles deep— reputed to be impassable by man or beast.

Santa Anna assembled more than 20,000 men, twice Scott's entire army, in four concentrations along a four-mile arc just above the Pedregal. His major position was the village of San Antonio, a couple miles north of San Augustín on one of the causeways leading into the city. San Antonio was protected by the Pedregal to the west and soft, marshy ground next to Lake Xochimilco on the east.

When American cavalry rode up to San Antonio they were met by heavy cannon fire, causing Scott to question whether he could get around the Pedregal on the west. He turned to Captain Lee, who found a rough trail on the southern edge of the lava field that connected with a north-south road west of the Pedregal. Scott ordered three of his divisions to advance along the trail on August 19.

Just west of the lava field, the Americans encountered the division of General Gabriel Valencia, a political rival of Santa Anna, who had shifted his 5,000 men from a position north of the lava field to a point a couple of miles south. This move was in direct disobedience to orders from Santa Anna, since it split the Mexican forces. But Valencia thought he might gain glory by defeating the Yankees.

In the early afternoon of August 19, three American brigades, 4,500 men, moved a couple of miles north of Valencia's force and cut him off from the rest of the Mexican army.

Now a large part of the American army was between Santa Anna's main elements to the north and Valencia's division to the south. If the two Mexican forces attacked together, they might rout or destroy the whole American force. Santa Anna recognized the opportunity, but for unknown reasons he did nothing. It was an incredible failure of command.

That night Santa Anna sent Valencia an order to slip his men northward in the darkness past the Americans. But Valencia refused. On the morrow, he replied, he would "mop up" the Americans.

Meanwhile, American engineers had found a path by which to pass around Valencia's force to the west and rear. The Americans moved in stealth during the night and, at dawn on August 20, struck Valencia on three sides. In minutes Valencia's entire division broke and ran.

Santa Anna fled northward, ordering the force at San Antonio, on the east side of the Pedregal, to withdraw as well. To cover his retreat, he directed 1,500 men to hold the Franciscan convent of San Mateo at Churubusco, just north of San Antonio, and a regiment to guard a fortified bridgehead on the south bank of the Churubusco River, 300 yards away. The remainder of the army formed north of the river.

For the first time the Americans encountered inspired defense from Mexicans. The soldiers at the convent beat off every rush of the Americans, while cannons posted there did heavy execution. The Mexican regiment at the bridgehead threw back two charges by American infantry, but at last succumbed in hand-to-hand fighting, while the troops guarding the convent finally surrendered after an American scaling party breached the walls.

The Mexicans were in chaos, the city of Mexico virtually defenseless, and the Americans surging forward in the flush of victory. But General

Scott now made a grave error. Santa Anna proposed a truce, and Scott fell for the ploy. From August 25 to September 6, 1847, while an American State Department representative got nowhere negotiating terms of peace, Santa Anna resurrected a defense of the city. The American soldiers, in frustration and mounting anger, sat on their hands. At last Scott, realizing he'd been duped, resumed hostilities.

On September 8, 1847, Scott's forces seized El Molino del Rey (King's Mill) and a huge stone building, Casa de Mata, a thousand yards west of the castle of Chapultepec, located a couple of miles west of the city of Mexico. The castle, on a 200-foot hill, was the former residence of the Spanish viceroys and was now the site of the Mexican military college. Chapultepec guarded access to both routes leading to the city from the west. On September 12, American soldiers surged over the parapets of Chapultepec, shot or brushed aside Mexican defenders, and swept through the buildings. Six young cadets died in the melee, to be venerated in Mexican history as *Los Niños Heroicos*. The Americans now rushed down the two causeways to the city itself.

Santa Anna withdrew to Guadalupe Hidalgo, a few miles north, and the city fathers surrendered to Scott.

With Scott occupying their capital, the Mexicans had little leverage, and, at the Treaty of Guadalupe Hidalgo on February 2, 1848, gave the United States exactly what it wanted, the territory that became the states of California, Arizona, Nevada, Utah, and parts of New Mexico, Colorado, and Wyoming.

Sherman's March, 1864–1865

In the American Civil War, the Union general William Tecumseh Sherman conducted a campaign as sharply focused as General Scott's in Mexico, and drove a stake into the heart of the Confederacy. This campaign, not Ulysses S. Grant's battles against Robert E. Lee in Virginia, actually won the Civil War.

When his army captured Atlanta on September 2, 1864, Sherman virtually split the Confederacy in two. Atlanta was far more important militarily than the Confederate capital, Richmond, because it was the South's railroad hub. Psychologically the loss of the city was even more significant, for the capture demonstrated that the Confederate government was incapable of keeping invaders from even the deepest reaches of the South.

When Sherman later marched into Savannah, Georgia, on December 20, 1864, a deep cloud of gloom and defeatism settled over the South. From that point on, no sensible Confederate believed victory was possible. Sherman's march into the Carolinas in early 1865 was the final act that led to the surrender of Lee's army at Appomattox on April 9. How did Sherman achieve his objective?

By 1864 the North had gained mastery of the Mississippi River and sealed off the states west of the river (Texas, Arkansas, and Louisiana) from the rest of the Confederacy. It had also occupied Tennessee and parts of Mississippi. But the Confederacy still possessed a powerful bastion: Virginia, the Carolinas, Georgia, and Alabama. Moreover, Lee's army in Virginia continued to bar the way to Richmond, and the Northern people were getting exasperated by the inability of Abraham Lincoln's government to end the war and stop the terrible bloodshed. Lincoln knew he had to achieve a great victory in 1864 or he was certain to be defeated in the November presidential elections by George B. McClellan, who was calling for peace with the South.

In March 1864, Lincoln placed Grant in command of all Union armies, with instructions to defeat Lee's army and drive the Confederate government out of Richmond. This, he thought, would be the key to victory.

Grant put Sherman in command of the Federal armies in the west, but he anticipated no great decisions there. He instructed Sherman to break up the Confederate army of Joseph E. Johnston, just south of Chattanooga, Tennessee, advance from there into the Confederate interior, and do as much damage as possible.

Sherman, an 1840 West Point graduate who gained no active service in the Mexican War, had earned a growing reputation conducting long operations in the west during the Civil War, but had given no hint he was capable of the decisive campaign he was about unleash. Sherman saw what neither Lincoln nor Grant did—that the South could be defeated by striking into its heart, and the heart of the South was Georgia. This he resolved to do.

Sherman's army of 100,000 was bigger than Johnston's army of 60,000, but—in order to bring up food and other supplies—Sherman was compelled to march along the single railroad line that ran from Chattanooga to Atlanta through the rough, heavily forested, almost foodless mountains of north Georgia.

With Sherman limited to a single line of approach, Johnston seemed to be at a tremendous advantage. Johnston believed he could simply build a powerful entrenched barrier anywhere along the rail line, and shatter any Federal attack. By this time in the war, the lesson had been learned by both sides that, given the newer weaponry both had, any frontal attack on a barricaded position was a recipe for defeat. Behind these barricades, soldiers fired Minié-ball rifles with a range of 400 yards, and they brought up light cannons armed with canister. Sherman, therefore, had no chance of overcoming such a defense.

Johnston accordingly built strong entrenchments across the railway line at Dalton, twenty-five miles south of Chattanooga. Apparently failing to heed the lessons against attacking such a position, Sherman sent 74,000 of his men against Dalton on May 4, 1864. But he ordered them only to create a distraction, not actually attack. Meanwhile he marched a 24,000-man force around the west of Dalton through the forests, and arrived on Johnston's rear. Johnston was forced to evacuate his powerful position and retreat southward.

Sherman repeated this maneuver all the way to Atlanta, time after time swinging around Johnston's flank and evicting his troops from their entrenchments without a battle. Only once, at Kennesaw Mountain, near Marietta on June 27, did Sherman strike directly at Confederate positions, and he stopped this attack as soon as he realized it would fail.

Johnston could think of no way of stopping Sherman, and continued to fall back. What he should have done was to split up his army into small, independent detachments and set them to the task of breaking the railroad back to Chattanooga and beyond to Louisville, Kentucky, the rear base of Sherman's army. If Rebel troops had repeatedly stopped traffic on the railroad, even if only for a day or two at a time, the Union army would have begun to starve in the mountains of north Georgia, and would have been compelled to retreat. But Johnston was an extremely orthodox and unimaginative soldier, and never considered this strategy.

Confederate president Jefferson Davis removed Johnston on July 17, and replaced him with an even less suitable general, John Bell Hood, notorious as a "fighting soldier." Hood was a man of little intellect who had never grasped the profound change in warfare brought on by the Minié-ball rifle, field fortifications, and canister-filled cannons pulled up to the firing line. He proceeded to order a series of direct attacks around Atlanta that cost thousands of Confederate lives, failed miserably, and forced him to evacuate the city on September 2, 1864. Sherman tele-graphed Washington: "So Atlanta is ours and fairly won." This victory brought great enthusiasm in the North, ensured Lincoln's reelection in November, and guaranteed continued pursuit of the war.

Meanwhile Hood took his army west, hoping to draw Sherman's army after him. But Sherman would not be duped, and instead sent all his wounded and many of his other troops back north, and, with a stripped-down army of 60,000, struck out for the Atlantic coast. The Confederates could not tell whether he was aiming at Augusta to the east, Savannah to the southeast, or Macon to the southwest, and were compelled to use the few troops they had to guard all three places.

Thus, with little opposition, Sherman captured Savannah on December 20, 1864. The Confederacy now was mortally wounded. With the railroads broken in Georgia, Confederate commanders had extreme difficulty transferring troops from one region to another. But more than anything, Confederate morale collapsed. As Sherman marched into the Carolinas early in 1865, burning homes and barns, killing livestock, and seizing horses and mules, soldiers with Lee's army at Petersburg began to desert to go home to aid their families.

The surrender at Appomattox was only the final death throes of the Confederacy. The fatal blow had been delivered seven months previously, when Sherman captured Atlanta and drove a stake into the Confederacy's heart.[4]

Stalingrad, 1942

There can be no greater contrast in leadership to that shown by Scott on his march to Mexico City and Sherman on his march to Atlanta than the German dictator Adolf Hitler's campaigns in the southern Soviet Union in 1942.

In the spring of that year, Hitler set in motion a massive campaign to seize the oil fields in the Caucasus and along the shores of the Caspian Sea, and, by depriving the Soviet Union of its major sources of oil, drive a stake in the heart of his enemy. Since oil propelled armies, and since Germany itself was desperately short of oil, the drive for the Caucasus could have ruined the Soviet war effort, strengthened the German war effort, and might have led to a negotiated peace.

But Hitler coupled this project with another requirement—his soldiers *also* had to seize the city of Stalingrad on the Volga River, hundreds of miles in a different direction from the Caucasus. His stated aim was to interdict the flow of oil barges on the Volga, though capture of the Caucasus would have stopped this traffic just as readily.

While Scott and Sherman focused on their military objectives from first to last, Hitler could not make up his mind what his main target was, Stalingrad to the east or the oil of the Caucasus to the south. He divided his strength, failed to achieve either objective, and, because of the enormous losses he suffered at Stalingrad, was so weakened that Germany lost the war.[5]

By 1942, Germany was in a desperate situation militarily. The United States had entered the war, and was embarking on the vast expansion of its industry that was soon to provide the Allies with many times more weapons than Germany and Japan could produce. The strength of the Soviet army was growing daily. The *Ostheer*, or German army in the east, was down to 2,400,000 men, more than half a million fewer than when

Germany had invaded the Soviet Union half a year before. Tank production was one-third that of the Soviets, the German air force had lost half its aircraft, one-third of the remaining artillery consisted of old French pieces taken after the fall of France in 1940, and shortages of fuel and ammunition were great and growing.

Hitler no longer had any hope of victory. The Soviet Union, however, had already suffered enormous losses in the war. If Germany could stop Soviet offensives and cause even more losses, Joseph Stalin might agree to a negotiated peace. The United States and Britain might also tire of the war and allow Germany to keep some of its gains in Europe. Such a scenario was the only possible hope Hitler had remaining—and it was an extremely long shot.

Militarily, Germany had just two reasonable choices. It could husband its remaining resources, go over to the defensive in the east—as it had done successfully in World War I—and devote most of its efforts to building defenses against attacks in the west by Britain and the United States. Or Germany could drive into the Caucasus and seize the oil wells, giving it the single commodity it needed most and denying oil to the Soviet Union. Of the two, the latter would have been the better, because capturing the oil would cripple the Soviet Union's military effort, while seizure of the Caucasus would seal off the only route—through Iran—by which Britain and the United States could send substantial supplies to Russia.[6]

But Hitler refused to face reality. Although at first he mitigated the damage by sending only one army toward Stalingrad and four into the Caucasus, in less than a month after the two offensives started on June 28, 1942, he reversed his priorities and directed three armies against Stalingrad and only two into the Caucasus—though the Caucasus was clearly an objective of infinitely greater importance.

The result of this reduction of forces was that Army Group A, under Wilhelm List, could not drive the Russians out of the high passes of the Caucasus. Thus the cities of Batum, Tiflis, and Baku, which would have secured the oil and the region, remained in Russian hands.

Meanwhile, Friedrich Paulus's 6th Army swept down the right bank of the Don River, crossed the Don at Kalach, and pressed toward Stalingrad.

The 16th Panzer Division reached the Volga just north of Stalingrad on August 24, 1942.

Now the stated purpose of Hitler's offensive had been achieved—guns on the high bluffs above the Volga could interdict shipping on the river below. But Hitler insisted on seizing the entire city, which stretched for fifteen miles along the river and two to four miles back from it. Stalin had issued a *"Ni shagu nazad!"* ("Not a step back!") order on July 28, and Russian reinforcements were streaming into the city from the east.

The Germans therefore were thrown into a bitter street-by-street, even building-by-building, battle. Germans, backed by tanks, crashed against barricades that blocked nearly every avenue. Russians fought back from machine-gun nests within buildings and amid the rubble. Mortars hidden in holes and crevices dropped shells on advancing Germans. The Russians held obstinately in fortresslike factories and warehouses. The Germans were soon exhausted. Supplies were slow in arriving and insufficient, ammunition in short supply. Progress was only a step at a time, counterattacks were frequent, and losses were high.

This was precisely the wrong strategy for Germany. The 1942 campaign's purpose was to drive a stake into the Soviet Union's heart by depriving it of its oil. Now the primary aim had become the capture of Stalingrad, a city irrelevant to this purpose. The entire objective of the campaign had been perverted. What was worse, the effort emphasized German weakness and Soviet strength. One of the most experienced German panzer leaders, Friedrich-Wilhelm von Mellenthin, voiced the opinion of nearly all senior officers: "By concentrating his offensive on a great city and resorting to siege warfare, Hitler was playing into the hands of the Russian command. In street warfare the Germans forfeited all their advantages in mobile tactics, while the inadequately trained but supremely dogged Russian infantry were able to exact a heavy toll."[7]

Hitler had lost sight of his strategic aim—the oil of the Caucasus. Instead he focused his attention on keeping the German 6th Army at Stalingrad, and, despite the pleas of his generals, did nothing to prevent Soviet forces from sealing off the city in a giant encircling movement that commenced on November 19, 1942.

Hitler now made the worst in a long series of mistakes in this campaign: he refused to allow the army to break out. He was obsessed with keeping Stalingrad. The inevitable result was that the Soviet army tightened its grip on the city, an effort by Erich von Manstein to cut through to the city failed, and on February 2, 1943, the last German soldiers in Stalingrad surrendered. A quarter of a million German soldiers had been sacrificed to no purpose whatsoever.

The entire fault for the tragedy lay on the shoulders of Adolf Hitler. A campaign that had started with the logical purpose of capturing the oil of the Caucasus and crippling the war-making capacity of the Soviet Union had been diverted into a hopeless battle to hold a useless city far away from the oil fields.

By 1943 the incapacity of Hitler as a commander was evident to all. The Achilles' heel of dictatorship was revealed—when a tyrant cannot see reality, there is no way to remove him. At Stalingrad Hitler demonstrated that his judgment was so incredibly poor the Allies were certain to prevail.

The Drive to the Yalu in Korea, 1950

In October 1950, the United States decided to drive a stake in the heart of the Communist North Korean state by occupying the country and reuniting Korea under the right-wing government of South Korea. This decision was made by President Harry Truman after American forces landed at Inchon. It was seconded by Secretary of State Dean Acheson and by the Far East commander, Douglas MacArthur.

The North Koreans had penetrated deep into South Korea, but were stopped by American and South Korean forces at the "Pusan perimeter" around the southern port city of Pusan. The invasion of Inchon, far to the north of the perimeter, and the swift capture of Seoul, twenty miles away, severed the rail line supplying the North Koreans, and forced them into precipitate retreat back beyond the thirty-eighth parallel, the boundary between the two Koreas.

Communist China deeply opposed a forced reunion of the country, and warned the United States it would intervene if American forces entered North Korea. Yet President Truman believed the assurances of General MacArthur that the Chinese were only bluffing, and authorized the sweep of several columns toward the Yalu River. The Chinese did intervene, caused enormous American losses, and forced the Americans to retreat back into South Korea, abandoning their effort to destroy North Korea.

The American effort failed because the American leadership refused to face reality.

Upon the surrender of Japan in August 1945, Korea had been divided between American and Soviet occupiers. The Americans created a right-wing state in the south, the Soviet Union a Communist state in the north. North Korea had invaded the south on June 25, 1950, with the aim of forcibly reuniting the peninsula by destroying the South Korean government. Now the United States intended to do the same thing in reverse, destroying the North Korean state and reuniting it by force with the south.

But the goal flew in the face of Communist China's suspicion that the United States had a much deeper motivation—to place its army on the Yalu River in order to help its informal ally, Chiang Kai-shek, leader of the Chinese Nationalists, whom the Communists had only driven from the mainland to Taiwan the year before.

Believing that the Korean War represented the first stage of a Soviet effort to conquer the world, and that Communist China was only a satellite of the Soviet Union, the United States turned to anti-Communist Chiang shortly after the Korean War started. Communist China was *not* a tool of the Soviet Union, however, and its leaders feared the Americans would sponsor a Nationalist offensive across the Yalu in an attempt to reconquer China. That is why Beijing warned the United States that it would intervene if American forces crossed into North Korea.[8]

President Truman and Secretary of State Acheson discounted the danger, believing MacArthur, who said the Chinese threats were "diplomatic blackmail." Truman authorized MacArthur to advance into North Korea. The attack got under way on October 9, 1950.[9] When MacArthur met with President Truman at Wake Island in the Pacific on October 15, he downplayed any possibility that the Chinese would intervene, and, he said, if they did, they would be soundly defeated.

"If the Chinese tried to get down to Pyongyang [the North Korean capital] there would be the greatest slaughter," he told the president.[10]

Truman believed his senior military commander's assessment. As a result, American forces advanced into North Korea with no concept of the provocation they had aroused or the dangers they faced. Unlike General Scott in Mexico, who assessed all problems and created counters for all challenges, MacArthur decided the Chinese were bluffing, made no preparations to defend his forces, and sent all his troops in small, separate, unsupported columns driving deep into the interior of North Korea. Each column was isolated, and extremely vulnerable if it hit solid opposition.

On the west, 8th Army moved up to and beyond the Chongchon River, some sixty miles south of the Yalu. On the east the 1st Marine Division with some 7th Infantry Division elements advanced from Hungnam, on the sea, some sixty miles up a narrow mountain road to the Chosin (Changjin) Reservoir.

The Chinese Communist ruling Politburo made a brilliant decision on October 6. It decided to send "volunteers" to Korea. Although these men were in regular units of the People's Liberation Army (PLA), calling them volunteers kept the war limited to the Korean peninsula—and prevented the United States from having a cause to attack China directly. Later this suited the Truman administration as well, since it feared the Soviet Union might intervene if it felt Red China was directly threatened. As a result, the Politburo and the Truman administration, working toward the same end, preserved the Chinese "sanctuary," as MacArthur was to call it, and saved Chinese cities from bombardment.

In addition, the decision worked to the military advantage of the Chinese. By limiting the war to mountainous Korea, the Chinese were able to exploit their strengths—manpower, digging in, and light weapons—while partially neutralizing their glaring weakness—no motorized forces and scarcely any trucks to carry forward heavy weapons or supplies. By restricting the war to rough terrain, the Chinese also partially neutralized American superiority in heavy weapons, motorized equipment, and air power.

In a series of violent attacks beginning November 24, 1950, the Chinese surrounded most of the 1st Marine Division and elements of the 7th Infantry Division around Chosin Reservoir, and destroyed or drove back all the isolated columns of 8th Army on the Chongchon River on the west, causing the 2nd Infantry Division alone more than 5,000 casualties, and shattering the attached Turkish Brigade.

Forces of 8th Army retreated 120 miles, the longest retreat in American history, back below the thirty-eighth parallel. The marines and soldiers at the Chosin Reservoir suffered great privation and 6,000 casualties retreating to the sea along a single narrow mountain road.

By the beginning of 1951, all United States and allied forces were below the thirty-eighth parallel, and the Truman administration had given up its plan to drive a stake in the heart of North Korea by overrunning the country and joining it to South Korea. None of the American losses need have occurred. They came about because Truman, Acheson, and MacArthur did not examine the sincere objections that Red China had voiced so loudly, and they paid no heed to Beijing's threats.

MacArthur, by his refusal to prepare for any significant attack on his troops, violated all the rules for advancing into the heart of an enemy country. But President Truman and Dean Acheson share the guilt for failing to comprehend the concerns the Red Chinese conveyed so clearly, and for failing to find a different solution than destruction of the North Korean state. This case should remind us that any plan with such an ambitious, far-reaching goal must be examined carefully and realistically, and all possible perils ascertained if possible before it is placed in motion.

Implications for the Future

The days of massive movements of troops on the ground deep into enemy territory have passed. But the rule of occupying an enemy's heartland to subvert his capacity to resist is alive and well, as was demonstrated in the American campaign against the Taliban of Afghanistan in fall 2001. American leaders used few troops, but struck at Taliban centers of power by air, and pursued action on the ground through cooperation with the Northern Alliance, a rebellious group, and later with tribal leaders in other parts of the country.

Although today we can reach enemy centers of power by air, the necessity of troops actually occupying the ground and rooting out the enemy was shown graphically in Afghanistan. We cannot rely on air power alone to finish the job of destroying the enemy. Invasions in the future are likely to follow this scenario of leading with air strikes and then sending in troops. We will not always have accommodating allies to help us locally, as we did in Afghanistan, and in such cases we will likely have to drop ground forces at key locations by air. Only rarely will we march an army into foreign territory in the future. Rather we will send in small, select forces.

For example, one proposal advanced for defeating Saddam Hussein is to drive a stake into Iraq's heart by inserting a force into southern Iraq, seizing the country's oil fields, the source of Saddam's wealth and power. Denied oil, his regime would fail. Street-by-street fighting to occupy the Iraqi capital of Baghdad would not be mandatory.[11]

This sort of strategy can be used in other situations. For example, the trade of an enemy country could be interrupted by blocking its sea- and airports, or intercepting its ships at sea, or even, as was shown in the case of the Al Qaeda terrorist network, by closing its international financial and banking networks. In summary, raw military power, like that exerted by General Winfield Scott in his march to Mexico City, will not be practiced in the future. But the idea of such power striking at the heart of an enemy, exerted in modern and more sophisticated ways, still has great validity.

9

Blocking the Enemy's Retreat

ONE OF THE most powerful tools a commander can employ is the rule of cutting off the means of an enemy's withdrawal and supply. This can lead to the outright destruction of the enemy's force. One of the earliest records we have of the successful implementation of this rule is from 480 B.C., when the Persian king Xerxes maneuvered to the rear of a force under the Spartan king Leonidas guarding entry into Greece at the pass of Thermopylae. From that position Xerxes blocked the Greeks' line of supply and retreat. Though some allied Greeks surrendered, the Spartans fought to the death.

Although the rule can be applied by either an attacking or a defending force, it is most often seen in cases where a defender closes off the escape route of an attacker. The process usually takes the form of an ambush. The defenders create one or more powerful barriers blocking the enemy's retreat, which is almost always a decisive maneuver. When, despite all odds, an army that has been blocked is able to escape, its exploits ascend into legend.

One of the greatest adventure stories of all time is "the march of the ten thousand" Greek mercenaries under Xenophon from near Babylon to the Black Sea. In 401 B.C., Cyrus rebelled against his brother, Artaxerxes II, ruler of the Persian Empire, and recruited an army that included 10,000 Greeks. The two brothers met at Cunaxa, between the Tigris and Euphrates rivers. The Greeks threw the left wing of Artaxerxes' army into flight. But on the other side of the field Cyrus was killed, and his Persian adherents ran away. The revolt ended with the death of Cyrus, and the Greeks were obliged to make their way out of the country as best they could.

The Greek generals were treacherously murdered in a parlay under safe conduct with the enemy, and the remaining Greeks elected new commanders, including Xenophon, who, in his *Anabasis* ("The March Upcountry"), recorded the most famous retreat in world history, 2,000 miles up the Tigris River valley, over the hills of Kurdistan and Armenia, to the Black Sea in 400 B.C. With unimaginable courage, the Greeks fought their way on foot day by day for five months through open plains and high mountain passes, while hostile armies and tribesmen attacked them frequently at the front, sides, and rear. In *Anabasis*, some of the most effective rearguard defenses are recorded for the first time. One of many examples was the practice Xenophon followed when the army was entering a defile. He threw forward troops to seize the heights commanding the defile, thereby keeping the enemy from sending rocks and arrow storms down on the army as it filed through the defile below.

A more modern case of a blocked army escaping, and one of the supreme instances of heroism in history, was the "breakout to the coast" of the U.S. 1st Marine Division and elements of the 7th Infantry Division in the Korean War.[1] The marines and soldiers, who had been cut off and isolated by a surprise Chinese ambush at the Chosin (Changjin) Reservoir in North Korea, overcame numerous Chinese blocks along the narrow mountain road from the reservoir to the Sea of Japan in December 1950. Remarkably, the commander, marine general Oliver Smith, employed precisely the same tactic Xenophon used. He sent troops ahead to occupy the hills on either side of the road, and to evict Chinese forces trying to set up roadblocks and ambushes in passes and defiles.

Closing off an enemy's retreat is most effective when, as has happened countless times, commanders have ventured too far into dangerous situations, and thus allowed their forces to be surrounded and destroyed. Cases in point are those of first the French and then the Americans in the Vietnam War. The French and American forces were obliged to disperse their combat units at numerous outposts or fortified positions throughout the country, in order to prevent the Communist forces from seizing large areas. The Communists took brilliant strategic advantage of this overextension. They often surrounded an outpost, set up a roadblock, and then assaulted a force that had been sent to relieve the outpost. Even when the French or Americans could break through the barrier, they often suffered heavy losses.

Today helicopters and transport aircraft can supply or evacuate an isolated force more readily than was possible in earlier wars. But this remedy is applicable only to relatively small units. The way the rule will likely be used to best effect in the future is as an offensive tactic. Commanders will deploy forces by air either to block crucial lines of supply or to cut off the retreat of enemy forces. Several important examples of the use of the rule in the past reveal key dangers that commanders must be aware of in the future when they deploy troops deep within enemy territory.

Teutoburger Wald, A.D. 9

One of the most significant and far-reaching examples of the use of the rule of blocking an enemy's retreat occurred in Germany when native tribes closed in on a Roman army that had pushed far into German territory, and massacred it in A.D. 9. The destruction of this army led Rome to abandon its goal of conquering German territory up to the Elbe River, and the frontier of the empire was moved back to the Rhine River. This decision left a divided Europe, split between the Latin and Germanic cultures, with each struggling for supremacy from the day of that battle all the way to 1945, when Germany was at last shattered by the Allies. That defeat led ultimately to the formation of the European Union.[2]

The Romans had not originally set their sights on the territory between the Rhine and the Elbe. Caesar Augustus, also known as Octavian (63 B.C.–A.D. 14), considered the Roman Empire more or less complete with the seizure of Egypt and the advance of the empire's frontiers to the Rhine and Danube rivers, a process that was finished by 12 B.C. But he soon realized that the boundary formed by the Rhine and

Danube left a triangular stretch of non-Roman territory (present-day southwestern Germany) that cut into the empire. He perceived that this projection might serve as an avenue of invasion for barbarian peoples. If he pushed the empire's frontier to the Elbe, however, the eastern boundary would run in an approximate straight line from present-day Hamburg in the north to Vienna, and would be much more defensible.

In order to do so, the Romans would have to subdue the Germans, who were then a semisavage collection of Indo-European tribes that inhabited the raw, misty country east of the Rhine, mostly covered with mountains, forests, and swamps.

The Germans were "wagon folk," a seminomadic people little interested in agriculture, who moved with their herds of cattle and sheep from place to place as opportunities arose, forming ramparts of carts (wagon laagers) to fight from when danger appeared, and living mostly on milk, cheese, and meat. Population density was low, only eleven or twelve persons per square mile.[3] At the time, more and more German warrior bands were crossing the Rhine to raid and despoil the blossoming cities and countryside of the Roman provinces that constituted Gaul (present-day France).

In 12 B.C., Augustus assigned eight Roman legions to his stepson Drusus to subjugate Germany to the Elbe. By 9 B.C., after various victories against ill-organized German bands, Drusus reached the river. There he was thrown from a horse and died, and his brother, Tiberius, took over the campaign and brought the effort to a successful close by 7 B.C. But the Romans had only defeated the Germans in battle, and had not persuaded them to abide under Roman rule. Revolts erupted in A.D. 1, and accelerated thereafter. Tiberius returned in A.D. 4 and reconquered the region in a series of brilliant campaigns.[4]

The Romans set up a new province, Germania, in A.D. 5, but this province existed almost exclusively in name, for the Romans occupied only a few citadels in the territory. The region's continued existence as a Roman province depended on the loyalty of the native tribes, and in A.D. 6, Augustus made a great error. He appointed a new governor, Publius Quintilius Varus, the husband of his grandniece, who as governor of Syria had established a notorious reputation for avarice and stupidity.

The Roman writer Dio Cassius commented that while the Germans were slowly adapting to a new way of life, they still "could not forget the customs of their ancestors, their local habits, their uninhibited lifestyle, and their armed power." Varus wanted to change the Germans' culture too quickly, and exacted tribute from them as a subjugated people. "This the Germans did not like," Cassius wrote.[5]

Already smarting under the rule of Rome, the Germans were spurred into a conspiracy to revolt by the outrageous behavior of Varus. A remarkable leader emerged to take charge, Arminius, who was twenty-five years old. A German noble who had served in the Roman army, he had gained Roman citizenship. Arminius was an expert on Roman military tactics, and knew the Germans had no chance of defeating the Roman legion in open battle because of their discipline and skill at wielding their short sword in close combat.

As opposed to the Romans' tightly knit and highly flexible legion, the characteristic German fighting formation was a crude wedge of massed unarmored warriors, carrying short, sharp spears, headed at the wedge's point by the bravest warriors. The wedge's only tactical maneuver was to storm forward. Though excellent for bowling over a weaker or frightened foe, the wedge could seldom overcome a cohesive body of Roman legionaries. Once the wedge was driven back, it tended to break up in disorder.

Arminius foresaw another way to defeat the Romans, however, by luring them deep into the German interior with affirmations of friendship and cooperation. In forested regions far from the Rhine, the Roman legions would be unable to deploy in their usual open battle formations, and could be cut off by Germans emerging from the forest as the Romans marched through on narrow paths. This was a canny application of the rule of blocking an enemy's retreat.

Varus foolishly accepted the entreaties of friendship from the Germans, and in A.D. 9 he embarked with three legions on what he saw as a show of force through a province he believed at last had been subdued. He planned to march to the Weser River, which flowed north some seventy to eighty miles west of the Elbe, deep into the province. He expected to impress the tribes east of the Weser by displaying the power of his force at an advanced base, or summer camp.

Incredibly, Varus had been warned of the Germans' plan for ambush by an ally of Rome, Segestes, a German chieftain. Segestes had learned of Arminius's plans from other leaders, and wanted revenge on Arminius, because he had eloped with Segestes's daughter. Segestes told Varus of the plot and advised him to call off any advance. But Varus was so confident in the high striking power of his army that he disregarded the advice.

On its way to the Weser, the Roman army, accompanied by many women and children, pack animals, and supply carts, marched along a narrow, well-trodden forest path used since prehistoric times. A commander should always be certain of the loyalty of the inhabitants he will encounter before he marches unsupported into the interior of a country. This was especially the case with Varus, since the only way out was the way he went in, along that narrow trail through a deep forest, on which his troops would be vulnerable to attack out of the cover of the forest at any point.

Varus expected to leave the Weser in the fall, marching back west to either the main Roman base of Vetera on the Rhine, or possibly Haltern, an intermediate Roman camp on the Lippe River about twenty-five miles east of the Rhine. Not entirely devoid of caution, he believed that spending the winter on the Weser would be too dangerous.

Well before Varus's anticipated departure, the German conspiracy commenced. In a subterfuge engineered by Arminius, Varus received a report in September that a tribe somewhere in the vicinity of the town of Aliso, some miles southwest of the summer camp, had rebelled against Roman rule. Varus decided to deal with this supposed mutiny, and closed the camp a bit early. He commenced the march of his entire army, including women, children, and supply column, perhaps 30,000 people, back toward Aliso, from where he planned to dispatch forces to deal with the rebels, sending the remainder of his force on either to Haltern or Vetera.

The Romans had not marched more than a few miles from the summer camp when a cry rang out that the Germans were attacking. Emerging from the woods at numerous points on both sides, the Germans struck at the unsuspecting Romans, killing many. Chaos ensued, worsened by a huge storm that made the ground slippery and weapons hard to use.[6]

Varus found a relatively open spot, and quickly erected a fortified camp for protection that night—a practice the Romans had followed for centuries at the end of a day's march. Varus did not head back to the summer camp, as that way was no less dangerous than the way forward. Instead he ordered the army to burn all unnecessary baggage and wagons, and strike out again on the path toward Aliso.

On the second day, the Romans were able to advance because the German conspirators were still gathering, and their attack therefore was relatively weak. Also, part of the route ran through open terrain where the Germans were unable to approach close enough to inflict much damage. Although the Romans still suffered losses, the column remained intact. After a march of eight or nine miles that second day, however, heavy woods appeared at the northern entrance to a narrow gorge, the Dören defile of the Osning Mountains (Teutoburger Wald). Here the Romans found the passage blocked by Germans. Varus would only be able to drive through the defile by first organizing a flanking movement on the heights on either side, which would dislodge the Germans. It was too late in the day to undertake this operation, however, so Varus withdrew a short distance and built another fortified camp, intending to force his way through the defile the following day.

The next morning, in more heavy rain, the Romans took by storm the first sand dunes that marked the entrance to the defile. But behind these dunes lay more dunes extending for a mile deep into the gap. As the Romans advanced, flanking each dune on either side, the Germans put up a violent defense, moving back only slowly. At last the Romans stopped. They were exhausted, had suffered heavy casualties, and were facing even heavier resistance. The Romans moved back to their camp, as the Germans pressed after them.

Despite their best efforts, the Romans had been unable to break through the defile, and now they were hopelessly trapped because thousands of Germans now surrounded the camp. Small bodies of Roman cavalry rode away, hoping to cross the mountains at some other point. Varus and a number of higher officers committed suicide, and the rest of the army surrendered unconditionally. Years later the Roman commander Germanicus, sent by Augustus to seek revenge for this terrible defeat, found whitened bones, fragments of javelins, and skulls fixed on the trunks of trees. The Germans, in spite of the Romans' surrender, sacrificed many of the survivors to their gods, and made the rest slaves.

The catastrophic battle of Teutoburger Wald stopped the expansion of the Roman Empire. Germanicus made a number of spectacular campaigns in Germany, but in A.D. 14 Augustus died, and his successor, Tiberius—seeing the effort to conquer the Germans as hopeless—decided to pull back permanently to the Rhine, and go over to a defensive strategy. The province of Germania ceased to exist.

Saratoga, 1777

Immensely significant battles like that of the Teutoburger Wald are rare. Yet in the American Revolution a campaign ending at Saratoga, New York, in 1777 assured the independence of the American colonies from Britain and set the United States of America on its road toward world power. The campaign was won by blocking the enemy's retreat.

British general John Burgoyne conceived a brilliant plan to end the rebellion of the American colonies. Burgoyne had already seen much service in the Revolution when, on leave in England in late 1776, he wrote a proposal for a two-pronged attack on Albany from Canada by 8,000 British and German mercenary troops, plus several thousand Canadian volunteers and Indian warriors. The main drive was to go south along Lakes Champlain and George to the Hudson River at Fort Edward, capturing Fort Ticonderoga on Champlain en route, then continuing down the Hudson. Meanwhile a diversionary force was to march from Montreal to Oswego, on Lake Ontario in western New York, march east and seize Fort Stanwix on the eastward-flowing Mohawk River, then press down the Mohawk to the Hudson, joining with the main thrust to capture Albany. Crucial support would come from a large army then occupying New York City under the command of William Howe, which was to advance up the Hudson River to meet the drive from the north. New England would thus be cut off from the other colonies, and could be subdued by massive attacks. The British felt this would so demoralize the colonies to the south that they would give up in despair.[7]

If the British had carried out Burgoyne's original plan as he conceived it, they likely would have defeated the Americans. For the only rebel

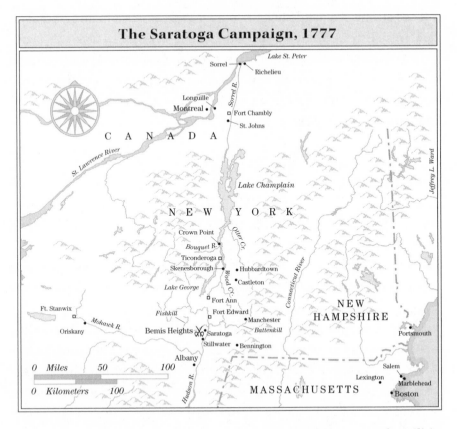

forces that could oppose them were ill-trained soldiers, mostly militias from New York and New England, whereas the British had seasoned regular armies in both Canada and in New York.

The ambitious plan failed because of the staggering incompetence of two men, Lord George Germain and General Howe. Burgoyne got no support from Howe, who went instead to Pennsylvania. Germain was the head of the War Office in London, and was one of the most underhanded and vicious men ever to hold high office in Britain. He had been cashiered from the army because of cowardice in the Seven Years War, and was ruthless in claiming full credit for achievements of subordinates. However, his conniving had won the support of the plodding prime minister, Lord North, and King George III. Burgoyne presented the plan to Lord Germain, who roundly snubbed him and ignored the plan, thinking, incorrectly, that it had been partially conceived by Sir Guy Carlton, governor-general of

Canada. Germain hated the governor-general because he believed, again incorrectly, that Carlton was seeking his job.

Realizing Germain was ignoring him, Burgoyne then turned to King George, whom he knew. While out riding, he gave the king a copy of his plan and persuaded him to read it. George endorsed the concept, and in January 1777 sent instructions to Germain and his other ministers to implement it.

Germain was furious, but he was forced to cooperate. Even so, he malingered till March 26, when he finally wrote Sir Guy informing him of the plan's adoption. Germain then drafted a letter to Sir William Howe in New York describing the plan, but, because he wanted to get away to the country for a holiday, refused to wait for the letter to be copied for him to sign. The letter was therefore never sent.[8] Since the entire British strategy was predicated on the union of two armies at Albany, it is almost beyond belief that Germain would fail to notify Howe of the plan, but that is precisely what happened.

Howe was almost as culpable as Germain, however. Word of the plan leaked out almost immediately. Germain sent details to managers of his large estates in Canada, who talked about it, and their revelations became common currency throughout North America. Even the American commander, George Washington, recognized what was afoot, and took what steps he could to deter Burgoyne. Howe must have been fully apprised, and in time Burgoyne informed Howe directly, by couriers, of the progress of his march. But Howe had other plans. He was fixated on the idea that if he captured the rebel capital, Philadelphia, he would end the war. This, of course, was nonsense. His real targets should have been Washington's Continental Army of 11,000 and the forces of the rebellious colonies.[9] Philadelphia, unlike Paris, Vienna, or Madrid, was not the administrative, political, and economic center of a nation state, whose capture would shatter resistance. It was only a town in a group of widely dispersed colonies, each of which had its own economy and political institutions. Nevertheless, Philadelphia was Howe's obsession, and rather than head to Albany to meet Burgoyne, Howe marched his troops to Philadelphia.

Howe's deputy commander in New York, Sir Henry Clinton, wrote

Howe several times after he had gone to Pennsylvania, suggesting that he return north to meet Burgoyne. But Howe brushed aside the suggestions.

Howe's incompetence in failing to recognize the danger in which he was putting Burgoyne, not to mention his inability to see the strategic brilliance of Burgoyne's plan, is staggering. Any competent corporal, much less a general, would have recognized that Burgoyne was isolated in a hostile, alien land, and, without help, could be rescued only by a miracle.

Burgoyne, unaware that Howe had no intention of joining him around Albany, commenced his march on June 1, 1777, from Montreal, and went south through rolling country toward Lakes Champlain and George. His army consisted of 8,000 men, almost half of them German mercenaries, the remainder British regulars. He also had a detachment of unenthusiastic Canadians, and some hired Indian warriors, who came and went as they pleased, were given to drunkenness and to violence against anyone they met, friend or foe, and whose use, insisted on by Burgoyne, aroused the bitter antagonism of the American settlers. Employing Indians guaranteed the mobilization of practically every American rifle and musket within range of the British army.

The British proceeded by water to Crown Point, at the northern extremity of the passage between Lake George and Lake Champlain, ten miles north of Fort Ticonderoga, an extensive wooden fort on the west bank of Lake Champlain. Ticonderoga was held by 2,000 Americans under Major General Arthur St. Clair. The fort was touted as being virtually impregnable, but it was nothing of the sort, especially since it was dominated by a mountain, Sugar Loaf Hill, 600 feet high, directly opposite the fort. The hill was unoccupied by the Americans because they thought it too steep.

When the British arrived on July 1, Burgoyne saw that the hill was key to the position. His artillery commander, Major General William Phillips, ordered his gunners to emplace cannons atop it, in the process uttering a comment that became a motto of British artillerymen from that day forward: "Where a goat can go, a man can go, and where a man can go he can haul up a gun."

On July 6, seeing that the British had cannons atop the hill, the American St. Clair immediately ordered the evacuation of Ticonderoga, and retreated southward. The British occupied the fort.

Burgoyne then *built* a road through a virtual wilderness from Skenesborough, twenty-two miles south of Ticonderoga, to Fort Edward on the Hudson, twenty miles south. After agonizing effort, the British cut their way through to Fort Edward, arriving on July 30.

Meanwhile the British expedition coming from the west along the Mohawk valley collided with American militia forces, and retreated back into Canada, the whole operation a total failure.

While this fiasco was being played out, Burgoyne was at Fort Edward, trying to assemble food, draft animals, carts, and other supplies to move forward. He sent an expedition for this purpose to Bennington, Vermont, about thirty-five miles southeast of Fort Edward, but that force was virtually eradicated in a battle at Bennington by Vermont and New Hampshire militiamen.

This victory had an electric effect on the Americans, who discovered they were capable of destroying a British force. Burgoyne, on the other hand, was dismayed because he knew the Americans would now cut his communications back to Canada, and he would have to secure food, wagons, and horses along the way if he was to continue on to Albany.[10] Doing so would incur further delay.

Meanwhile, on September 12, the American army of 12,000 men under a new commander, Horatio Gates, occupied a position known as Bemis Heights, a few miles south of the village of Saratoga on the western bank of the Hudson River, and about fifty-five miles south of Fort Edward. Gates fortified these heights and planned to stay behind them and await attack.

Burgoyne knew he was so deep into enemy-held territory that it was impossible at this point to retreat to Canada. Militia forces were on call in an instant to block his march at almost any point if he turned north. While he lingered at Fort Edward, the Americans reoccupied Ticonderoga. In doing so, the Americans carried out a textbook example of blocking the enemy's retreat. By wrongly putting his faith in Howe to march up from New York to his aid, Burgoyne now had only one hope if his army was to survive—to go *forward* and defeat the Americans on Bemis Heights.

Burgoyne crossed the Hudson, and on September 19, 1777, as he advanced, the Americans held tight behind their entrenchments. The battle was the biggest collision of the war, involving 16,000 men, with heavy fire of cannons and muskets. Fighting ended at nightfall with neither side having made headway or withdrawn. The British were astonished at the staying power of the Americans. They lost 600 men, twice as many as the Americans, very heavy casualties for so small an army.

That same day a courier from the British general Clinton got through to Burgoyne saying he was advancing up the Hudson with 2,000 men—all he could get together. Burgoyne was overjoyed, and decided to wait till Clinton arrived before attacking again. But Clinton's expedition was a will-o'-the-wisp. It was far too small, was operating in hostile country, encountered heavy opposition while attempting to seize two forts along the Hudson, and became vulnerable to being surrounded itself. Clinton pulled back to New York.

Fighting resumed at Bemis Heights, with skirmishes for many days. While more American reinforcements arrived nearly every day, the Indians and Canadians, who had been fighting along with the British, sensed defeat and began to melt into the forests. Food for the British was running short. Many men got sick. By the first of October they had only 5,000 men fit for combat.

Burgoyne realized his last hope was a bold stroke that might break through the American barrier. In a council of war on October 6, he decided to attack, but the effort came far too late. The Americans not only were strongly entrenched, but now numbered close to 20,000 men. On October 7, Burgoyne advanced, but the Americans drove the British back in a series of bitter engagements. In a last-ditch effort, Burgoyne withdrew northward, and on October 12 the Americans surrounded his army at Fishkill Creek. Five days later he surrendered.

The British had committed a classic blunder in sending an army deep into the heart of a hostile country without adequate support and without any means of extricating it, thus allowing the enemy to block its retreat. From 1777 onward there was virtually no chance of a British victory.

The effects of Saratoga were immediate. The American envoy in Paris, Benjamin Franklin, found that the previous indifference of the French to American requests for help vanished. In December the French agreed to a treaty, which they signed in February 1778, recognizing the United States of America as independent. This was tantamount to a declaration of war. France was eager to avenge itself against Britain, which had seized Canada and effectively driven France out of India in the Seven Years War, 1756–1763. In addition, France persuaded Spain and Holland to join in the alliance against Britain as well. As we will see next, a French naval squadron delivered the final stroke that caused Britain to give up the struggle and acknowledge American independence.

As the celebrated English historian Sir Edward Creasy wrote in 1850: "No military event can be said to have exercised more important influence on the future fortunes of mankind than the complete defeat of Burgoyne's expedition, a defeat which rescued the revolted colonists from certain subjection and which, by inducing the courts of France and Spain to attack England in their behalf [to get revenge for previous British victories at their expense], ensured the independence of the United States."[11]

Yorktown, 1781

In the spring of 1781, the principal bastion the British held to fight the rebellious American colonies was New York City, which they had occupied in September 1776 and held ever since. The Royal Navy kept open the supply and communications line from Britain to New York. But the British had little scope to launch a land campaign from the city because an army led by George Washington and the French commander in North America, the Comte de Rochambeau, kept British land forces bottled up in New York.

Because of this strategic impasse, thinking began to be directed to the numerous harbors of Virginia's Hampton Roads, at the southern end of the Chesapeake Bay, the largest estuary in North America, fed by most of the rivers of eastern Pennsylvania, Maryland, and Virginia.

If the Royal Navy occupied the bay and set up a naval and supply base at one of the Hampton Roads harbors—Old Point Comfort on the tip of the peninsula between the James and York rivers was the port most favorably located—then the British could guarantee their supply line back to Britain and might use the rivers emptying into the bay as avenues to drive deep into Virginia. Lord Cornwallis, the British commander in the south; Sir Henry Clinton, who was now the British commander in

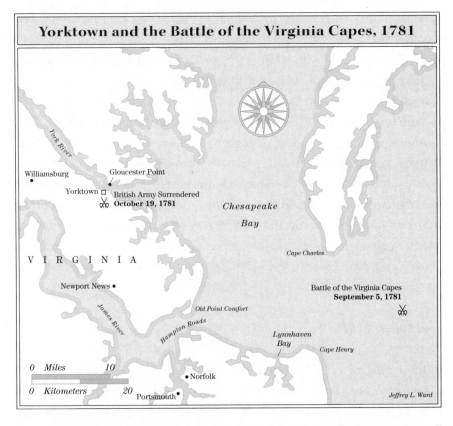

Yorktown and the Battle of the Virginia Capes, 1781

Williamsburg

Gloucester Point

Yorktown ☐ British Army Surrendered
October 19, 1781

York River

Chesapeake Bay

V I R G I N I A

Cape Charles

Newport News •

Battle of the Virginia Capes
September 5, 1781

James River

Old Point Comfort

Hampton Roads

Lynnhaven Bay

Cape Henry

0   Miles   10

0   Kilometers   20

• Norfolk

Portsmouth •

Jeffrey L. Ward

America; and Lord George Germain, chief of the War Office in London, all favored a campaign in Virginia.

Cornwallis wanted to go even further: evacuate New York, concentrate British power at Hampton Roads, and begin a campaign to conquer not only Virginia but also the other middle colonies. Once those colonies were returned to allegiance to the crown, the British could turn separately on the remaining rebels, first on the southern colonies of North and South Carolina and Georgia, and then on New England. But Germain was incapable of so resolute an action, and hoped in some vague and never articulated way to combine efforts in New York and Hampton Roads. Trying to combine the two was strategically dangerous, because all the territory between the Chesapeake and New York was held by the Americans, and the only way the two bases could keep in touch was by sea.[12]

On May 20, 1781, Cornwallis joined his army with a small British expeditionary force at Petersburg, Virginia, about eighty miles by road west of Hampton Roads. Cornwallis had moved up from Wilmington, North Carolina, giving up for the present a two-year effort to subdue the Carolinas. He tried to bring to battle a small American force in Virginia, but the rebels' commander, the French general the Marquis de Lafayette, avoided the British. In July 1781, Cornwallis moved toward Old Point Comfort.[13]

Hampton Roads presented a peculiar danger to the British: if Washington assembled a large army in Virginia *before* Cornwallis could be reinforced, and if French naval forces could block the narrow entrance to the Chesapeake, then Cornwallis would be isolated and compelled to surrender. The Americans would thereby exercise the rule of blocking the enemy's retreat, closing off any possibility of supply or retreat for Cornwallis's army.

General Washington fully appreciated the opportunity and, upon learning of Cornwallis's movement toward Hampton Roads, began to pressure the French to send a naval force to close off the narrow entrance into the Chesapeake (between Cape Charles on the north and Cape Henry on the south, also known as the Virginia Capes).

Control of the Chesapeake was an absolute prerequisite for the British to undertake a campaign in Virginia. Yet the British leaders were extremely slow in realizing this, even after March 8, 1781, when a squadron of eight French ships under Sochet Destouches departed Newport, Rhode Island, where it had been lying, to make a concerted effort to control the waters of Chesapeake Bay. Destouches also carried a detachment of French troops to reinforce Lafayette.

British lookouts spotted the departure of Destouches's ships. The only British ships available, a squadron of eight harbored at Gardiners Bay on the eastern end of Long Island, went in pursuit of the French. The two fleets collided just outside the Virginia Capes on March 16. Although the British came out of the engagement the worse for wear, Destouches abandoned his effort to sail into the Chesapeake, and returned to Newport.

The peril for the British being trapped in the Chesapeake remained. Not only was it imperative for the Royal Navy to guard the Virginia Capes, but it was incumbent upon Clinton and Germain to reinforce and resupply Cornwallis's 8,000-man army at once. Neither happened. Cornwallis in Virginia was being placed in precisely the same position that Burgoyne had been placed in New York—isolated deep within hostile territory with no means set in motion either to extricate him or to go to his assistance.

Instead, Clinton and Thomas Graves, the admiral commanding the British squadron that had returned to Long Island, got into a long-distance discussion by letter with Cornwallis as to *which* port at Hampton Roads he was to occupy and defend. Clinton and Graves wanted Cornwallis to fortify Old Point Comfort. But when one of Cornwallis's engineers examined the site, he thought it unsuitable (though in later years it became the site of Fort Monroe, a famous U.S. Army bastion). Cornwallis decided instead to fortify a nearby port, Yorktown. In mid-July he positioned troops at both the village of Yorktown and the village of Gloucester Point, across the York River from Yorktown. Although Clinton had 16,000 men at New York, he did not send reinforcements to Cornwallis, and Lord Germain and the British Admiralty disregarded any suggestion that the French could contest British supremacy at sea.

Accordingly they were unprepared for the challenge they were about to face. The French commander, the Comte de Grasse, set out from Brest, France, on March 22, 1781, with a large fleet and convoy of troop transports, bound for the West Indies. When General Washington and the French commander Rochambeau learned about de Grasse's expedition early in May, they wrote de Grasse asking him to seal off Chesapeake Bay.[14] The message left on May 21 by a fast frigate to Cap Français (present-day Cap-Haïtien) in Haiti, and was waiting for de Grasse when he put into the port on July 16. The French admiral acted with good judgment and vigor, and the same frigate that had brought the dispatches to de Grasse went back with his answer. By August 15, Washington and Rochambeau knew the French fleet was headed for the Chesapeake, along with 3,500 French soldiers de Grasse was bringing along to reinforce the Americans in Virginia.

De Grasse's message galvanized Washington and Rochambeau. Leaving 4,000 troops at West Point to watch Clinton's troops in New York, Washington and Rochambeau set out with 2,000 Americans and 4,000

French on August 20 on the 400-mile march to Virginia. On August 30 the forces marched into Philadelphia, where they were met by wildly cheering crowds, and on September 5 they reached Head of Elk (present-day Elkton, Maryland), on an inlet of Chesapeake Bay.

Meanwhile, de Grasse, to conceal his coming as long as possible, took the Old Bahama Channel, a little-frequented route, northward. Chasing de Grasse on a more direct route northward from the West Indies was the British admiral Sir Samuel Hood, with fourteen warships.[15]

On August 27 the French commander at Newport, de Barras, with eight battleships, four frigates, and eighteen transports—carrying all the French siege artillery—left to rendezvous with de Grasse, making a wide circuit out to sea to avoid the English.

The same day Admiral Hood, coming north, put into Chesapeake Bay, searching for de Grasse. Not finding him, he sailed on to New York to join Admiral Graves, who had five serviceable ships. Graves told him de Barras had departed Newport, thus pointing to a meeting at sea with de Grasse, then a move into the Chesapeake. At once the combined squadron of nineteen ships, with Graves in command because he was senior, set out to beat the French into the bay.

But de Grasse had already arrived. On August 30, three days after Hood had searched for him in vain in the Chesapeake, de Grasse's twenty-eight men-of-war dropped anchor in Lynnhaven Bay, just within the Virginia Capes. The 3,500 troops he brought with him joined Lafayette.

Graves, painfully surprised to find de Grasse inside the bay when he arrived on September 5, 1781, nevertheless prepared to attack. But he took so long forming his nineteen ships in the traditional line of battle (the ships in a row, one behind the other) that de Grasse had time to slip his cables, get into the Atlantic, and sail his twenty-four ships past the British line of battle, delivering heavier fire than the British could respond to. The British ships suffered great damage to their rigging and 336 casualties (to 221 French losses), which slowed the ships' movements, and made them vulnerable to another attack by the French. But de Grasse, instead of engaging in another head-to-head slugfest, held to his primary mission of preventing the British ships from getting into the bay and protecting Cornwallis's army. De Grasse repeatedly blocked the

Virginia Capes, remaining outside the bay for five days, and allowing de Barras to slip safely into the bay, carrying with him the French siege guns. Graves learned that de Barras had reached the Chesapeake, and since his eight warships could augment de Grasse's fleet, Graves decided to return to New York to repair his rigging. With him disappeared Cornwallis's last hope of succor.

De Grasse promptly returned to the Chesapeake, brought Washington, Rochambeau, and their men down by ship from Head of Elk, and agreed to Washington's plea to remain inside the bay till Yorktown had surrendered.

By September 27 the American-French army totaled 17,000 men, more than twice Cornwallis's. The British position was not favorable for defense without the cannons of warships, and was open to the French siege artillery, which began to bombard the British ramparts on October 9. On October 14, French and American detachments stormed two key redoubts, on which the French placed cannons that now raked the whole British position. Cornwallis's situation was impossible, and a desperate attempt to cross the York and escape through poorly guarded Gloucester Point failed because of a heavy storm.

On October 17, Cornwallis opened surrender negotiations, and on October 19 his 8,000 men marched out while a band played a tune titled "The World Turned Upside Down." With this capitulation the hope of subduing the colonies died in Britain. But the issue had actually been decided more than a month before, off the Virginia Capes—when de Grasse's squadron applied the rule of closing off the enemy's retreat, by sealing off Cornwallis's army. The naval engagement was a small affair, almost a draw, and yet it prevented vital relief from getting through to Yorktown. This is a classic example of a relatively minor sea battle profoundly influencing the course of history.

Chancellorsville, 1863

There was a moment on May 2, 1863, when the Confederates almost won the American Civil War. That moment occurred during the battle of

Chancellorsville, Virginia, when General Stonewall Jackson spotted the key to the complete destruction of the Union army: Joe Hooker, its commander, had placed the bulk of his forces, over 70,000 men, in a position with only a single way to retreat—United States Ford—over the Rappahannock River. If Jackson could move around Hooker and block passage over this ford, the Union army would be locked between Jackson's corps on the west and Robert E. Lee's two divisions on the east, and would be forced to surrender. Thereafter the two remaining corps of the Union army, isolated in front of Fredericksburg, could be encircled and forced to give up as well.[16] The brilliant maneuver only failed because Jackson was struck down only minutes after directing a subordinate commander to execute the move.

Jackson was able to march around the Union army, and his routing of its 11th Corps was one of the most spectacular flanking movements in military history. But the success of this maneuver, great as it was, was only the first act in Jackson's masterful plan to block the Union retreat. The last specific command he gave before a volley struck him down was to division commander A. P. Hill to execute what should have been the coup de grâce: "Press them. Cut them off from United States Ford, Hill. Press them."[17]

As Porter Alexander, the great artillery leader of the Army of Northern Virginia, noted, the Union army found itself in the potentially disastrous position at Chancellorsville because of "the perfect collapse of the moral courage of Hooker, as commander in chief, as soon as he found himself in the actual presence of Lee and Jackson."[18]

Hooker did not want to repeat the calamitous performance of his predecessor, Ambrose E. Burnside, four months earlier. Burnside, planning to force his way to the Confederate capital of Richmond, attacked the Confederate army headlong when it was lined up on the heights just west of Fredericksburg, on December 13, 1862. The assaults were complete failures, and cost the Union army 13,000 casualties.

Hooker came up with an alternative, indirect approach to weaken or destroy the Confederate army and open a way to Richmond that was the best strategic concept ever devised by a Union commander against Lee. The plan only failed because Hooker lacked the resolve to carry it off. At the time, Hooker's army remained stationed just east of Fredericksburg on the other side of the Rappahannock River from Lee's army, still holding the heights just west of the town.

Hooker launched 10,000 cavalry deep into the Confederate rear, hoping to close off the railroad line supplying Lee's army. At the same time he designed a twofold infantry strike: a frontal assault with 40,000 men to engage and hold Lee's 60,000-man army in place on the heights above Fredericksburg, and a wide, turning movement to the west with three corps totaling 42,000 men under Henry W. Slocum directly onto Lee's left flank, a move that, if successful, would have shattered the Rebel army.

On April 29, 1863, the frontal assault on Lee's army on the heights began. Two corps under John Sedgwick, shielded by heavy fog, crossed the Rappahannock about three miles below Fredericksburg, opposite Stonewall Jackson's corps on Prospect Hill. Sedgwick made no attempt to storm Jackson's position, however, and Hooker did not order him to do so. This was a terrible error because Sedgwick's entire job was to force the Confederates to fight where they were, and thus prevent them from moving west, where the decisive strike would be launched by Slocum.

While Sedgwick's move was getting under way, Hooker commenced Slocum's wide flanking movement on April 27. The purpose of this movement was disguised by Slocum marching far to the northwest, along the banks of the Rappahannock. Lee assumed Slocum's troops were headed for the Shenandoah Valley, and could be dealt with later.

Ahead of Slocum moved 10,000 cavalry under George Stoneman, striking for Gordonsville, about thirty-five miles southwest, where they would then turn east and try to cut the main Confederate supply line, the Richmond, Fredericksburg & Potomac Railroad (RF&P), just north of Richmond. Hooker believed that depriving Lee's army of food and ammunition, combined with the move on his western flank, would cause Lee to "ingloriously fly" back toward Richmond. Lee's army, so Hooker thought, would be destroyed between the main Union army advancing down from the north, and the cavalry, which would then be holding north of Richmond.

Lee, however, had no intention of flying, ingloriously or otherwise, though he soon realized he faced an immediate threat from Slocum's

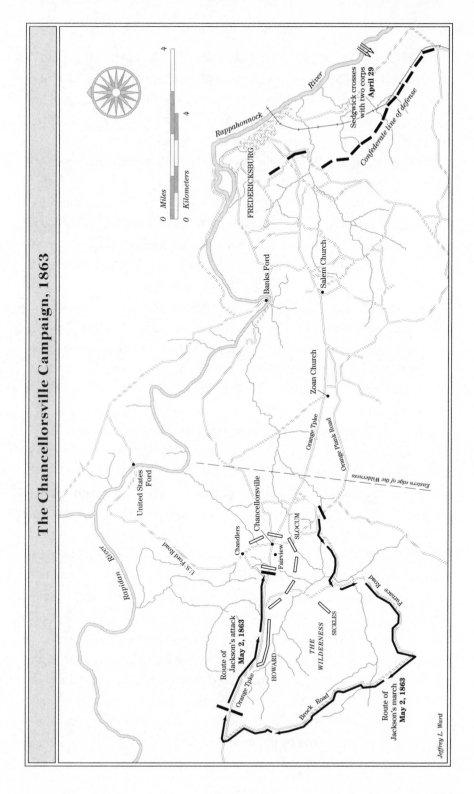

The Chancellorsville Campaign, 1863

Rappahonnock River

Rapidan River

FREDERICKSBURG

Sedgwick crosses
with two corps
April 29

Confederate line of defense

Banks Ford

Salem Church

Zoan Church

Orange Tyke

Orange Plank Road

Eastern edge of the Wilderness

United States Ford

U.S. Ford Road

Chandlers

Chancellorsville

Fairview

SLOCUM

THE WILDERNESS

SICKLES

HOWARD

Furnace Road

Orange Tyke

Brock Road

Route of
Jackson's attack
May 2, 1863

Route of
Jackson's march
May 2, 1863

0 Miles 4

0 Kilometers 4

Jeffrey L. Ward

flanking force. His cavalry chief, Jeb Stuart, reported that Slocum's infantry had crossed to the south bank of the Rappahannock at Kelly's Ford, twenty-three air-line miles upstream from Fredericksburg, and had turned back east. Stuart underestimated the size of the Federal force, however, believing it was only one-third its actual strength.

Lee dispatched a division under Richard H. Anderson to the crossroads of Chancellorsville, about nine miles west of Fredericksburg, to form a barrier to slow the Union advance. By the morning of April 30, Stuart had picked up stragglers from the three corps under Slocum. He and Lee now knew 42,000 men were marching directly on the Rebel left, or west. Anderson had no hope of holding such a force, and Lee ordered him to pull back to a strong position and dig in. Anderson withdrew to Zoan Church, four and a half miles east, and began to build entrenchments.

The next day, April 30, 1863, Slocum's three corps reached Chancellorsville. Hooker commenced marching 30,000 more Union troops, who had been held in reserve on the other side of the Rappahannock from Fredericksburg, across United States Ford, about five miles north of Chancellorsville. Once the forces were combined, they were to drive a few miles eastward into open country to meet the Confederates. There the Union's vast superiority in numbers and in artillery, 438 cannons against Lee's 170, would be invincible.

The Union troops would have to get east of Chancellorsville quickly because their position there was highly dangerous. Chancellorsville was two miles inside the eastern edge of the Wilderness, a wild region that stretched another twelve miles west along the Rappahannock and eight to ten miles to the south. This land had been cleared in the previous half-century to supply charcoal for iron furnaces in the area, and a dense second growth of briars, underbrush, pine, cedar, and low-branched hardwood trees had now filled in. Only the roads and a few isolated places were cleared. This territory would be a labyrinth for any fighting force, and Hooker knew he had to get out of the Wilderness as fast as he could. His greatest strength, his artillery, would be useless in those dense thickets.

Stuart sent 1,000 Rebel cavalrymen after the Federal cavalry under Stoneman that was trying to move on the RF&P Railroad, and reserved the remainder, 3,300 men, to concentrate where they were most needed—at the front of Lee's army. Stoneman's cavalry broke rail lines in places. But, despite Hooker's belief that his cavalry could hold a position deep in the enemy rear, this was impossible to accomplish for any length of time. Once off their horses, troopers lost their mobility, and needed supplies to remain in place. In addition, the main Union cavalry weapon, the Sharps single-shot carbine, had a range of only 175 yards, compared to the Confederate rifle's 400 yards. Since the Confederates could send local militia to oust them, Union cavalry could only break a line and move on. Knowing the inherent weakness of cavalry operating in his rear, Lee ignored the breaks on the railway lines, and Stoneman's move degenerated into a giant, but useless, raid.

Meanwhile, Sedgwick remained inactive in front of Fredericksburg, keeping his troops tightly in place along the river, and posing no threat to the Confederates on the heights. Lee turned his attention to the much more dangerous threat on the western flank. He perceived that if Hooker advanced much farther east he would be free of the Wilderness, and would be within range of Banks Ford, five miles west of Fredericksburg. Banks Ford would give Hooker another avenue of reinforcement and retreat, if needed, and Lee determined he must stop the Union advance.

Accordingly, on April 30, Lee sent a division to aid Anderson at Zoan Church, and ordered Jackson to march three of his divisions at daylight the next morning, May 1, to the church, to take charge of the western flank, and "repulse the enemy." Lee thus boldly left only 10,000 Confederate troops at Fredericksburg, turning his back on the idle Sedgwick, and concentrating 47,000 men and 144 guns on the west to confront Hooker.

In the meantime Hooker directed his now-70,000-man force to move out of the Wilderness into open terrain, and to seize Banks Ford that same day, May 1.

Having moved with great dispatch, Jackson arrived at Zoan Church at 8:00 A.M. on May 1, and made one of the most masterful decisions ever conceived by a military leader—he told the Rebel troops to forget building defensive emplacements at the church, and instead *advance* directly against the Federal army. He knew that if he could push Hooker back into the Wilderness, the Union army would be thrown on the defensive and, moreover, would be deprived of its artillery. The heavy odds favoring the Union forces would be evened.

Jackson's advance stunned and apparently intimidated Hooker. Instead of using his immensely superior power to drive Jackson back, Hooker withdrew to Chancellorsville, forming defensive lines behind an arc of crude but strong earthworks just east and south of the crossroads.

Hooker either didn't recognize or refused to admit the danger in which he had placed the Union army. When General Darius N. Couch, the chief of 2nd Corps, reported on the night of May 1, Hooker said, "I have got Lee just where I want him. He must fight me on my own ground." Couch later wrote, "To hear from his own lips that the advantages gained by the successful marches of his lieutenants were to culminate in fighting a defensive battle in that nest of thickets was too much, and I retired from his presence with the belief that my commanding general was a whipped man."[19]

Lee arrived on the west during the afternoon of May 1 and, with Jackson, quickly determined that, because of the hastily built Union entrenchments, they stood no chance of assaulting the Union lines frontally.

As they were talking, Jeb Stuart rode up with the news that his scouts had found the Federal line was stretched out to the west from Chancellorsville along the east-west Plank Road through the Wilderness. Oliver O. Howard's Union 11th Corps on the extreme west of this line was "floating in the air," with no defenses on its western flank. Thus the entire Union position could be flanked by circling around the south, moving west, and then attacking Howard's western flank, driving directly east along the Plank Road. Jackson also perceived that the position of Hooker's army offered an opportunity for him to block Hooker from retreat and thereby destroy his entire army. If Jackson got on Hooker's rear, he could force the Federals away from his one avenue of retreat across the Rappahannock, United States Ford. Hooker then would have nowhere to turn, and would be compelled to surrender.

Early on May 2, Jackson awoke from a short sleep and found from his chaplain that a nearby resident, Charles C. Wellford, knew the region well. He sent his mapmaker, Jedediah Hotchkiss, to question Wellford. Hotchkiss returned a short time later with details of a route to go around the Union army on the south to reach Oliver's western flank. Wellford's young son, Charles, was to lead the way.

Jackson and Lee were conferring around a campfire. Hotchkiss traced the route recommended by Wellford. Lee said, "General Jackson, what do you propose to do?" Jackson replied, "Go around here," pointing to the line Hotchkiss had drawn. Lee: "What do you propose to make this movement with?" Jackson, without hesitation: "With my whole corps." Lee replied, "What will you leave me?" Jackson: "The divisions of Anderson and McLaws."

This was the moment of truth. Here was an opportunity that might never come again. Lee was astonished by Jackson's boldness. A simple flanking movement was being turned by Jackson into a stroke that could win the war. Recognizing the danger to the eastern wing of his army—he would be left with just two divisions, and Hooker might still decide to attack—Lee also recognized the opportunity. He answered calmly, "Well, go on."[20]

On the morning of May 2, 1863, Jackson's three divisions, led by Charles Wellford, hiked for twelve miles around the Union army, and at about 2:00 P.M. came up on the Plank Road west of Oliver's corps. Though Jackson would have preferred to move his corps immediately between Chancellorsville and United States Ford, he had seen he wouldn't be able to do that because there was no direct road. Therefore his plan was to attack eastward along the Plank Road. He would first roll up Howard's 11th Corps, and then drive into the rear of the three other Union corps around Chancellorsville. Once there, Jackson planned to turn northeast, cutting off Hooker's retreat by severing his connection with United States Ford.

Jackson lined up his men carefully. They understood the importance of their attack, and when Jackson released them at 5:15 P.M., the eager and excited Rebel soldiers burst forward against a wholly unprepared enemy. With little resistance, the Union 11th Corps collapsed, the men running pell-mell to the rear.

Hooker, in command at the Chancellor house at the crossroads, did not get the news of Jackson's attack till 6:30 P.M., when Captain Harry Russell, one of his aides, heard violent noise and, turning his glass westward, yelled, "My God, here they come!" Hooker nearly panicked, but was saved from immediate catastrophe because Robert E. Rodes, commander of the Rebel division leading the assault, stopped about a mile and a half west of the crossroads to get his troops in better order. Rodes called on A. P. Hill's division, following in reserve, to move up to take the lead. This took valuable time, and was in direct violation of Jackson's command to drive forward irrespective of order or confusion.

Accordingly, Hooker's staff had time to snare a few artillery batteries fleeing eastward, plus a few on hand, and deploy them at a stretch of cleared land just west of the crossroads, called Fairview. There Hooker also sent Hiram Berry's division, the only force nearby, to form a tentative line along a creek at the western edge of Fairview.

It was 8:45 P.M. before A. P. Hill was able to deploy his first brigade, North Carolinians under James Lane. The night was clear and there was a full moon, so, despite the late hour, the advance could continue. Jackson arrived at the front, and gave Lane his orders himself: "Push right ahead, Lane, right ahead."

When A. P. Hill arrived from the rear shortly afterward, Jackson issued his famous last command to Hill: "Press them. Cut them off from the United States Ford, Hill. Press them." Hill said he was unfamiliar with the route to the ford, and Jackson designated his engineer, J. Keith Boswell, well acquainted with the roads in the region, to guide him.

Jackson then went ahead of Lane's line along with Boswell, Hill, and his staff to scout out the terrain toward the ford. Only minutes before, Union cavalry general Alfred Pleasonton had ordered the 8th Pennsylvania Cavalry to attack Lane's North Carolina brigade. To send horsemen through thick woods and underbrush against infantry was a foolish move. The charge collapsed, but for some time horseless riders and riderless horses rushed about in the dark woods, creating chaos.

Lane's men were on the alert for the Union cavalry, and when Jackson's party moved onto a small road ahead of Lane's brigade, his men mistook Jackson and company for Federal cavalry. The order was given to fire, with Jackson's party not more than twenty paces away. Captain Boswell and an orderly fell dead, and three bullets struck Jackson.

A. P. Hill was hit by artillery fire shortly afterward, and command descended on Jeb Stuart. But Stuart was miles away and couldn't get to the front till after midnight. As a consequence, the strike for United States Ford was never undertaken. The opportunity to block the Union retreat was thereby wasted, and Hooker was so stunned by the Confederate attack that he withdrew as soon as possible across the ford.

In this fateful engagement, the South lost its greatest chance to destroy the Army of the Potomac, as well as its greatest general. As a result of his wounds, Jackson contracted pneumonia and died May 10, 1863.

Implications for the Future

Armed forces today cannot be massed in large bodies for fear of being easily detected and then destroyed by highly accurate fire. Instead, smaller forces will be transported to targeted destinations by air. Under some circumstances, substantial forces may reach their destinations by ground transportation. But the days of long, vulnerable columns of vehicles using established roads have passed, unless the enemy has few or no long-range weapons, and is too weak to organize an ambush. Forces sent in will be only of the size necessary to accomplish a *specific* task, and they will be sent only to carry out that task, and will be removed as soon as the task is completed. They will also be supplied in most cases by air.

A silhouette of this coming military structure could be seen in the special forces who operated in widely separated detachments, and U.S. Marines and later members of the 101st Airborne Division who formed a modest-sized but powerful base near Kandahar in Afghanistan in the autumn of 2001 and winter of 2002.

All this may seem to eliminate the danger of the practice of blocking retreat, but it does not. The precise peril Varus, Burgoyne, Cornwallis, and Hooker faced will challenge armies in the future in cases where a general places more forces on the ground than can be supplied or removed if the situation turns against him. Commanders may well be tempted to make this mistake.

The great danger in coming years will be from commanders who put *too much* reliance on technology and machines, and who assume they can go virtually anywhere because their aircraft can always get them out if the situation gets dicey. This was the presumption of French general Henri Navarre when he placed 13,000 troops at Dien Bien Phu, deep in the jungles and mountains of northwestern Vietnam in 1954. Navarre relied on transport aircraft, primarily American-built two-engine C-47s, to deliver supplies if the roads were blocked, and to evacuate the force if required. He did not anticipate the response of the Vietnamese Communists. After closing off all road approaches to the base, they ringed the bastion with cannons and antiaircraft guns, rendering Navarre's airstrips inoperable. As a consequence the French lost the entire force—*and* Indochina.

Navarre's blindness to possible enemy action was an extreme case. But he should be an object lesson to future commanders, especially in fluid situations where numbers of forces might be dropped at widely separated locations. If air resources are insufficient to withdraw *all* these forces simultaneously in case danger erupts, then one or more of the forces might be isolated and destroyed. In other words, reliance on the capacity of a distant air-transport authority to deliver precisely what is needed in *every* circumstance can lead to disaster.

That was the mistake of Adolf Hitler, who assumed he had enough Junkers Ju-52 transports to supply the German 6th Army surrounded at Stalingrad in November 1942–February 1943. Though his air-transport officers told him there were not sufficient aircraft, Hitler refused to listen, and heeded the false assurances of his air force chief, Hermann Göring. By placing an impossible burden on the air force to deliver adequate food, fuel, and ammunition to keep the 6th Army in operation, he brought about the destruction of the entire army, a quarter of a million men, and handed over the initiative to the Soviet army. The loss of Stalingrad was the precursor to the defeat of Germany.

The rule of blocking an enemy's retreat in the future will probably be applied to best effect in scenarios reminiscent of Navarre at Dien Bien Phu and Hitler at Stalingrad, where the *means* to supply an army or to get it out of harm's way are denied. These means can include fire that keeps aircraft from arriving or departing, and too few aircraft to support all the detachments at various locations. This inherent danger should put commanders on alert that they must land only as many forces inside enemy territory as available aircraft can readily supply and evacuate.

10

Landing an Overwhelming Blow

D URING THE FALL of 2001, television screens were full of pictures of American bombers demolishing positions in Afghanistan identified as Taliban strong points. It seemed a simple process: locate an enemy bastion, call up airplanes, and watch them blow it out of existence. The Americans were following the rule of landing an overwhelming blow: concentrate an irresistible force on one part of the enemy, deliver the strike, and, at the same time, prevent the remaining enemy from interfering.

Alas, following this rule is not usually as simple as it was in Afghanistan. There native opponents knew where Taliban strong points were located, and pointed them out to American spotters. The Taliban had no aircraft with which to contest the skies, and U.S. aircraft dropped inerrant "smart" bombs guided by the Global Positioning System (GPS) and by laser, infrared, and radar sensors. Despite a few desperate battles, such as the Anaconda operation near Gardez in eastern Afghanistan in February and March 2002, the Taliban and Al Qaeda were more suited to desultory sniping in the hills, trained in the tradition of their great-grandfathers who fought against the Bengal Lancers in the days of the British Raj. This was war between totally asymmetrical forces, and the Taliban were completely outclassed by American technology.

The challenge is usually vastly more complex than what the Americans encountered in Afghanistan. Ordinarily a general faces an enemy armed just as well as he is. In the strategy of landing an overwhelming blow, the first question is *where* can the general land the blow? That is, at what place will the enemy be hurt badly if struck? The second is *what* to do about the rest of the enemy force? This double-faceted problem has bedeviled commanders from the most ancient times, and it appears in a vast number of guises.

For example, Americans were baffled by the hedgerows of Normandy in June and July 1944 during World War II. The Americans had many more weapons and greater manpower than the enemy, but the Germans took brilliant advantage of the *bocage* of Normandy—a region cut into thousands of small fields, bordered by raised banks overgrown with dense shrubbery, brambles, hawthorn, and small trees. Each tiny field became a separate battlefield. Advancing American infantry and tanks were caught by fire from *Panzerfäuste,* or bazooka rocket tubes, and machine guns posted in the hedgerows. The Germans could remain hidden till a tank was within fifty yards, destroy all but the heaviest tank with one shot, and stop the advance of the infantry cold. Once the Germans had interrupted an attack in this way, they brought down pre-registered mortar rounds on the field. These mortars caused three-quarters of American casualties in Normandy.

How could the natural fortresses of the *bocage* be overcome? Where could the Americans land a crucial blow? How could other enemy forces be kept from interfering? Commanders tried a number of methods, but none worked well enough or fast enough. At last individual GIs came up with a solution: they welded bulldozer-like blades on the fronts of American tanks that could plow through the thickest hedgerow quickly. Just inside the hole broken in the hedgerow, offering only a small target for a *Panzerfaust,* the tank, with its cannon and machine gun, could cover the advance of infantry across the field. Enemy in the hedgerows were thereby neutralized, and the hedgerows themselves kept other enemy from coming to assistance. The solution was an excellent answer to a difficult problem, and illustrates how spontaneous thought on the battlefield is sometimes necessary to implement an ancient military maxim.

The most difficult part of applying the rule of landing an overwhelming blow is *not* the mandate to find a decisive point to attack; that point is often self-evident. The *real* challenge is to deliver a blow *without* being first thwarted or deflected by the enemy, who may recognize the decisive point targeted as quickly as the attacker. A commander's principal problem, therefore, is disguising his intention so as to keep his opponent from subverting his effort by some decisive action of his own.

This has never been easy, and sometimes the difficulty of doing so simply cannot be surmounted. There are myriad variations by which defending commanders may impede an attack. In local or small-unit actions, they may unleash diversionary efforts at various other places to distract the attacking commander from his main target. Or if a defender guesses correctly where a strike is coming, he may launch a spoiling attack to occupy or break up the landing site.

At the strategic level, defending commanders must look beyond the actual site of a strike to find places where one or more equally decisive counterstrokes can be delivered. A prime example is the strategy the Russians used in the Stalingrad campaign in the autumn of 1942. Instead of trying to drive the Germans by brute force back through the twisted ruins of the city, the Russians built up strong armies many miles away on both sides, and then struck—not at Stalingrad itself, but at the corridors that carried supplies to the enemy at Stalingrad. In other words, the Russians delivered a crippling, although indirect, blow at the German army in Stalingrad by attacking weak positions on either side of the city with overwhelming force, thereby isolating the city.

Leuctra, 371 B.C.

The first record we have of the successful use of the rule of the overwhelming blow—indeed it was the first great tactical innovation in history—was when the Theban commander Epaminondas applied the maxim against a superior Spartan army in ancient Greece. Ever since, the rule has been applied in a thousand different ways, but the original maneuver Epaminondas carried out remains the classic, clearest example, and a model for all others.[1]

The essence of Greek warfare, developed more than two centuries previously, was the phalanx, normally made up of one or more solid squares of armored infantry—ten or more men deep and at least ten wide—equipped with long spears. The success of the phalanx depended on an advance of these squares in perfect order, all the forward spears of the phalanx striking the enemy's front at the same time. Whichever phalanx proved the stronger prevailed, the loser breaking and running.

Phalanx warfare arose because the rough, mountainous geography of Greece created isolated localities in which small farming communities built independent walled cities for their defense. These cities were frequently at war to secure farmland, forests, streams, and other resources. A phalanx required little skill on the part of soldiers, and all the able-bodied men in these cities could serve in it. Hence, Greek warfare generally consisted of a violent collision of the phalanx of one city against the phalanx of another. Whichever side did the most damage won.

Since the military state of Sparta emphasized extreme discipline in its soldiers, Sparta's phalanxes generally prevailed against other Greek armies. But coupled with the Spartans' discipline was extreme conservatism—unwillingness to change their traditional shock tactics.

In 404 B.C. Sparta defeated Athens in the long Peloponnesian War, and assumed the dominant place among the Greek city-states. But Sparta's hand was heavy, and other cities chafed under Spartan oppression. By 376 B.C. Athens and the city of Thebes in Boeotia (northwest of Athens) had managed to expel the Spartans from central Greece and defeat them in a naval battle. But the Thebans and Athenians quarreled, and Sparta sponsored a conference in 371 B.C., proffering peace as a guise to divide the two allies and to force Thebes to give up its new role as leader of the cities of Boeotia. Thebes, however, refused, and left the conference. Not wanting to allow Thebes time to build up a strong defensive force, Sparta's King Cleombrotus launched a quick invasion. In July 371 B.C. he moved a Spartan army of 10,000 men to the open, treeless plain of Leuctra, about nine miles southwest of Thebes.

The Theban commander Epaminondas could muster only 6,000 infantry to meet the challenge, and in the ordinary shoving match of phalanx warfare he knew he was bound to lose. While the Theban line was about 1,350 feet long, the Spartan line was nearly twice that length, and divided into three detachments, each twelve men deep.

Epaminondas came up with the simplest of ideas, but it was something entirely new. Instead of forming the Thebans in lines parallel with the Spartan army, Epaminondas drew them up in "oblique" order, in three detachments. The one on the left advanced ahead of the second and third, which held back a few paces. Also, while the two right units were only about eight men deep, the left column was much stronger, fifty men deep and about seventy wide. Since this force was much larger than the Spartan right wing opposite, it could deliver a far superior thrust to the Spartan wing, and could then wrap around the wing and drive it into the center. The left-hand body was led by a specially trained and reliable force of 300 picked warriors, the Theban "Sacred Band," recruited from mutual friends.

Epaminondas gave the order to advance, instructing the right-wing elements to pace themselves behind the heavy left-hand force. This kept the right-hand units out of contact with the Spartan detachments opposite, but still close enough to threaten them, and to prevent them from moving. Epaminondas thus locked the entire Spartan line in place, thereby preventing an effective counterattack.

When the Spartan king, Cleombrotus, saw the left Theban wing drawing toward his right, he realized he was in danger of being outflanked, and tried to extend his line to prevent this—but he didn't have time to complete the maneuver before the Thebans were upon him. His effort, moreover, put the Spartan wing in some degree of disorder, and when the commander of the Theban Sacred Band saw this, he commanded the men to attack on the run. The Thebans wrapped around the Spartans' right wing, engaged them in bitter hand-to-hand fighting, mortally wounded Cleombrotus, drove the Spartans on the right toward the Spartans in the center, and caused them to break formation and run away.

The Spartans lost a thousand men, and fell back to their entrenched camp. The Thebans saw a chance to besiege this camp and destroy the entire Spartan army. Had they done so, their victory would have been decisive. But Athens and other Boeotian cities did not like the idea of Thebes gaining so much power, and they forced the Thebans to allow the surviving Spartans to march home. Even so, Thebes achieved dominance in Greece with the battle of Leuctra. Its position depended upon Epaminondas's leadership and battle skill, however, and when he was killed while using similar tactics in a victory over the Spartans at Mantinea in the Peloponnesus in 362 B.C., Theben hegemony ended.

Nevertheless, the lesson Epaminondas taught resounded through the ages—the decisive importance of concentrating superior force against a selected point of the enemy's front, while, at the same time, preventing other parts of the enemy's force from intervening.

Rossbach and Leuthen, 1757

Despite the acknowledged brilliance of Epaminondas's tactics at Leuctra, the attempt to concentrate overwhelming force on a portion of the enemy has probably been the single greatest cause of failure for commanders over the millennia. Confronted with the bristling weapons and overt challenge of an opponent directly in front of them, countless generals have ignored the possibility of indirect approaches that would pit their strength against enemy weakness, and have launched headlong assaults straight into the heart of enemy resistance, mistakenly believing they were delivering an overwhelming blow.

One of the most flagrant of these failures was the "Charge of the Light Brigade" on October 25, 1854, at Balaclava in the Crimean War. Lord Cardigan, commander of the British cavalry force, in an act of unbelievable stupidity, ordered the lightly armed cavalry to assault the front of Russian artillery batteries. Perhaps he thought the horsemen could ride down the gunners, but the force arrayed against them was far too great for the attack to have any possibility of success. Riding through a narrow, mile-long valley, exposed to fire from other Russian guns on the left and right flanks, the light brigade did manage to break through the batteries ahead, but, now isolated in the midst of the Russian army, was forced to turn and retreat back through "the valley of death," as Alfred Lord Tennyson wrote in his poem. In twenty minutes the brigade lost 247 of its 673 men, having achieved nothing.

Lord Cardigan violated the premise of the rule of landing an overwhelming blow because he used a small force to attack a much larger force, in direct contrast to Epaminondas, who sent a large force against a much smaller force. Cardigan also made no provision to prevent other parts of the Russian army from interfering.

Cardigan had no excuse for this pathetic misapplication of the rule because a century before Balaclava, Frederick the Great of Prussia, in two battles during the Seven Years War, had famously demonstrated both how the rule of the overwhelming blow should and should not be practiced. In doing so, he set clear standards that could be followed by any commander thereafter.[2]

In the Seven Years War (1756–1763), Prussia's only ally was Britain, which furnished money and little else, being occupied primarily at that moment with seizing France's colonial possessions, including Canada and India. By 1757, Prussia was in a perilous condition. France, Austria, Saxony, Russia, and Sweden, with populations totaling 70 million, had formed a coalition that intended to wipe Prussia, with just 4,500,000 people, off the map.

Frederick had gotten himself in this fix because of greed. In 1740, having just ascended the throne, he seized the rich province of Silesia (now part of Poland) from Austria. This territory was the size of Massachusetts, Connecticut, and Rhode Island combined, had a population of 1,500,000, and increased Frederick's revenues by a third. Maria Theresa, ruler of Austria, offered France the Austrian Netherlands (present-day Belgium) for help in getting Silesia back, while Russia wanted East Prussia, Sweden coveted Pomerania and other territory along the Baltic Sea, and Saxony sought Prussia's provinces in central Germany.

The armies of eighteenth-century Europe were largely mercenary, employed by kings who used military means and diplomacy to advance their own narrow dynastic interests, and who evoked few sentiments of nationalism or patriotism among their subjects. This was a cynical age, and the hired armies were the most cynical of all, composed of the dregs of society, subjected to ferocious discipline, and kept separate from the civilian population because they were so vicious. Officers were afraid to allow soldiers any freedom, lest they desert. As Frederick himself commented, "If my soldiers began to think, not one would remain in the ranks" because conditions were so bad. Frederick also asserted that a soldier "must be more afraid of his officers than of the dangers to which he is exposed."[3]

Such armies moved slowly because they were tied to the nearest magazine or supply base for food and other needs. And since such armies were expensive, kings hated to consume them too liberally in combat. Hence the zenith of generalship in this period was not battle, but being able to maneuver an enemy *away* from his supplies, thus forcing him to retreat. In this environment, armies kept close to their magazines, marched very short distances in a day, and paid only passing attention to what should have been the key to their fighting effectiveness, the rate of fire their soldiers could achieve with their muskets. Rate of fire was all-important in actual battle, and it depended upon how quickly soldiers could load, aim, and discharge their single-shot muskets.

Frederick understood this. His army already emphasized discipline to a greater degree than any other army in Europe, but he instituted three changes that turned it into a vastly superior force. He trained his soldiers to march faster and farther. He also trained them to fire their muskets at a higher rate than soldiers in other armies.[4] And he emphasized mobile artillery drawn by horses at a time when other armies paid mobility little heed. Thus in three ways—rate of march, rate of firing, and mobile field guns—Frederick's army was superior to the other armies of the period.

Although most generals sought only to maneuver on their enemy's rear and avoid battles, occasionally they decided to fight. Such battles were ordinarily head-on collisions because a general determined to confront his enemy usually had time to prevent him from maneuvering on his flank—since armies marched so slowly. That is, a general could normally block a turning movement by stepping directly into the enemy's path. These head-to-head battles were not usually decisive.

Frederick's three improvements to his army led him to devise a new method of combat, which turned orthodox practice on its head. Since Frederick's army marched faster than his enemies, he could move against one of his enemy's flanks, and attack it before his enemy could change front. This could bring total defeat rather than a drawn battle, as was so common. Other armies couldn't copy this tactic because they marched too slowly.

Frederick called his technique the "oblique order," and he explained it as follows: a commander should strengthen one wing of his army and employ it to attack the enemy flank, while holding back another, smaller wing to threaten the enemy's main force and keep it from changing position. Since the enemy army would already be deployed, it could not switch troops fast enough to the threatened flank before Frederick's columns struck. Frederick said an army of 30,000 could beat an army of 100,000 using this method.

The tactic was an adaptation of Epaminondas's simple technique at Leuctra, and this simple idea preserved Frederick's kingdom.

Frederick perceived the grave danger of the coalition gathering against him, and he tried to head it off by striking first in August 1756, invading Saxony and Bohemia, and defeating the Austrians at Lobositz in October. In response, the coalition determined to put armies totaling half a million men into the field to crush Frederick. Before the armies could move into place, however, Frederick struck again, defeating the Austrians at Prague on May 6, 1757. But then he recklessly attacked an Austrian army twice the size of his own at Kolin, Bohemia, on June 18, and lost 13,000 of his 33,000 men. This defeat forced him to withdraw into Saxony.[5]

As he withdrew, the allies closed in on him from all directions, though some of the forces were more formidable than others. A Russian army occupied East Prussia, and defeated a small part of Frederick's army that was blocking the road to Berlin to protect the Prussian capital from attack. The Russian force fairly quickly melted away, however, for lack of supplies. A small Austrian force followed the Russians and managed to occupy Berlin, but was then bought off by Frederick with a large ransom.

The more pressing danger came from a French army, with some German elements, of 60,000 men, led by Charles de Rohan, Prince of Soubise. The French enjoyed an awesome reputation in warfare, and

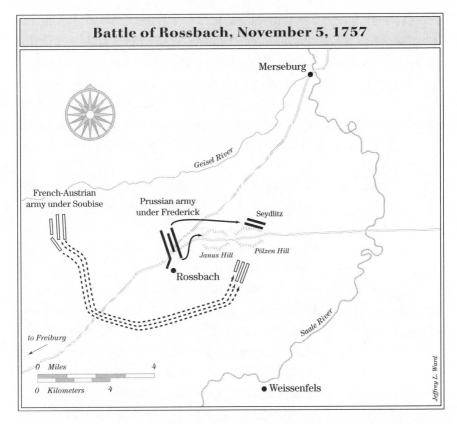

Battle of Rossbach, November 5, 1757

Merseburg

Geisel River

French-Austrian
army under Soubise

Prussian army
under Frederick

Seydlitz

Janus Hill   Pölzen Hill

Rossbach

Saale River

to Freiburg

0   Miles   4

0   Kilometers   4

Weissenfels

Jeffrey L. Ward

Frederick was justifiably anxious when, on October 27, 1757, Soubise reached Weissenfels in Saxony, on the Saale River about twenty miles southwest of Leipzig. Frederick had only 24,000 men in the vicinity of Leipzig. His other major force was opposing a large Austrian army under Prince Charles of Lorraine and Field Marshal Leopold Daun in Silesia. If Soubise continued to advance, he could push Frederick back toward Berlin, and, in concert with the Austrians, first destroy the Prussian army in Silesia, then turn on Frederick. Soubise encamped at the town of Mücheln, a few miles northwest of Weissenfels.

Hoping to stop Soubise, Frederick marched to Weissenfels, moved north across the Saale, and emplaced at Rossbach, about six miles east of Mücheln.

Pierre de Bourcet, an excellent French general on Soubise's staff, recognized that Frederick was in a precarious position. If Frederick could be held west of the Saale, and thus unable to fall back toward Berlin, the vastly superior allied forces might be able to surround and destroy his army. Bourcet urged Soubise to swing in a wide arc around to the southeast in an effort to block Frederick's line of withdrawal to Weissenfels and Merseburg, another nearby town on the Saale. Bourcet intended a maneuver on Frederick's line of communications. This would either lock Frederick in place or, if he saw the peril quickly enough, force him to retreat in haste.

But Soubise rejected Bourcet's advice, and resolved instead to copy Frederick's "oblique order" of attack by marching directly on the Prussian left flank, where Frederick was encamped at Rossbach. Since he had twice as many men as Frederick, Soubise believed victory would be his, once he struck Frederick's flank.

In making this move, Soubise demonstrated precisely how *not* to carry out an oblique order of attack. His first and greatest mistake was to march his army in clear view of the Prussians, since the terrain was a wide, open plain, without trees or hedges. This permitted Frederick to discern exactly what Soubise had in mind. As the Prussians could march much faster than the French and their German allies, Frederick was able to change his front in plenty of time to meet Soubise's challenge. Soubise's second blunder was *not* to deploy a large force directly against the main Prussian position at Rossbach in order to hold the Prussian army in place there. All he did was send a body of French cavalry to a village three miles west of Rossbach, to observe the Prussian camp and protect the left flank of his march.

On November 5, 1757, Soubise formed up his army into three columns and commenced marching east, while at the same time swinging around to the south so as to strike the left flank of Frederick's army, which was facing west. Soubise's army was led by French and Austrian cavalry, followed by infantry in marching order, not deployed for battle.

Frederick posted an officer on a roof in Rossbach to watch Soubise's movements, and also sent patrols into the now-abandoned French camp, where peasants said the allies had taken the Weissenfels road. But Frederick knew it was not likely Soubise would march to this town, because the bridge there remained broken.

At 2:00 P.M., Frederick learned from the outpost on the roof that the allied vanguard had reached a hamlet two miles south of the Prussian left flank, and was wheeling northeast toward the left rear of the Prussian army. Frederick climbed on the roof and saw for himself what Soubise was attempting to do.

He at once ordered his men to strike the Prussian camp, and directed his cavalry chief, Friedrich Wilhelm von Seydlitz, with 4,000 cavalry (thirty-eight squadrons)—followed by seven infantry battalions (about 3,500 men) and eighteen cannons—to move east down the Rossbach stream, which ran just north of the village, in the direction of Merseburg. Frederick ordered the move to interpose these Prussian detachments directly in the path of the French advance. The Prussian move was shielded from view of the enemy by two hills, Janus and Pölzen. Frederick placed his guns on the more westerly Janus, with the infantry adjacent to the hill facing south, while Seydlitz hid his horsemen just to the north of Pölzen, a mile and a half east of Janus.

As the French army continued to march on what Soubise thought was the rear of the Prussian army, Frederick was already moving a strong portion of his force east of its original position and turning it to face south, to confront the French head-on. Soubise's scouts caught indications of Frederick's rapid moves, but Soubise concluded the Prussians were in retreat, and all he had to do was to press on with his army, which was still in three long columns.

By assuming wrongly that Frederick was retreating, Soubise made no provision for a Prussian counterstroke. The prudent move would have been to deploy his army from its marching columns into a spread-out battle formation *before* he continued advancing. This would have allowed his infantry to discharge their muskets and his artillery to get in position to fire in the event they were attacked. Instead, Soubise kept his army in march formation.

Soubise's attacking force was somewhat stronger than Frederick's defending force, but because he had committed the unforgivable blunder of not deploying it for battle, it was effectively much *weaker* than the Prussian force. The Prussians were virtually assured of victory, provided only that they struck hard and resolutely.

Seydlitz, behind Pölzen Hill, watched the approaching heads of the allied columns. Without waiting for orders, he led his men forward at a trot, and signaled the start of the attack by throwing his tobacco pipe into the air. The Prussian cavalry galloped straight into the bunched Austrian and French cavalry in the lead, cutting and slashing through their mass, and driving them in panicked retreat westward over the horizon.

While this cavalry melee was under way, the eighteen cannons on Janus Hill opened on the allied infantry, still marching in columns. Under cover of this fire, Prince Henry advanced the seven battalions of Prussian infantry on the double to attack the enemy regiments. The artillery tore down whole files of allied infantry, while the muskets of the Prussian infantry found a target for nearly every one of their balls. In the chaos, the allied infantry, unable to deploy, fell back in panic. Seydlitz meanwhile had re-formed his cavalry in low ground south of the allied army. Seeing the total disorder of the enemy, he launched his whole command upon their rear. This drove the allied army in rout across the fields.

Soubise had done everything wrong. He had not actually made an oblique-order attack on the Prussian flank because he had failed to deploy another allied force to threaten the Prussian front and keep the enemy army in place. His movement was in plain view, and his army was so much slower than the Prussians that Frederick was able to draw up a solid defensive position on the two hills before the allies arrived. And Soubise's failure to deploy his army in battle formation was the final calamity that assured a Prussian victory.

The Prussians lost a little more than 500 men, whereas the allies lost 3,000 killed and wounded, and 3,000 made prisoner. The survivors had been reduced to a panic-stricken rabble. The victory at Rossbach had wide repercussions, reviving the fortunes of Frederick, and causing the English to increase their subsidy to Prussia nine times over. Europe also lost its fear of the French army.

Despite this crippling victory, Frederick's task was only half completed, for the large Austrian army under Prince Charles and Field Marshal Daun in Silesia might still march on Berlin.[6] Taking a week to refit at Leipzig, on November 13 Frederick commenced marching 170 miles eastward with 13,000 men to Silesia, occupying the town of Neumarkt on December 3. There Frederick learned that Prince Charles and Daun were at Leuthen, eleven miles to the east. Frederick's rapid march had surprised them, because they had assumed he would go into winter quarters after the battle of Rossbach.

Prince Charles and Daun drew up their 70,000-man army with 210 guns in a five-mile north-south defensive line from the village of Nippern on the north through Leuthen to Sagschütz on the south.

Frederick approached on the morning of December 5, 1757. He had only 36,000 men, comprising 24,000 infantry in 48 battalions and 12,000 cavalry in 128 squadrons. He also had 167 guns, of which 71 were heavy pieces.

When Frederick surveyed the Austrians' position, he saw that they were too far extended, over a five-mile-long front, which afforded the opportunity of carrying out an oblique-order attack on the southern Austrian flank at Sagschütz. The key advantage to a strike here was that his troops could march under the cover of a line of hills separating his army and the Austrian line of battle.

Frederick's complete plan was to feint that he was delivering his main stroke on the Austrians' right, or north, and then proceed to attack their southern flank at Sagschütz, and drive them off their line of communications.

In other words, Frederick intended to hold the whole Austrian line in place by a false move on the enemy north while moving the bulk of his army around to the south and striking an overwhelming blow on the Austrian left flank.

There were two vast differences between what Soubise attempted at Rossbach and what Frederick was planning at Leuthen. First, Soubise assumed the Prussians could not react in time to his move on their flank, yet the Prussian army was adept at changing its front quickly. More important, Soubise advanced against the Prussians in plain view across the open fields of Rossbach, thus signaling his action well in advance— while Frederick at Leuthen was making the most important part of his move in secret, behind a line of intervening hills.

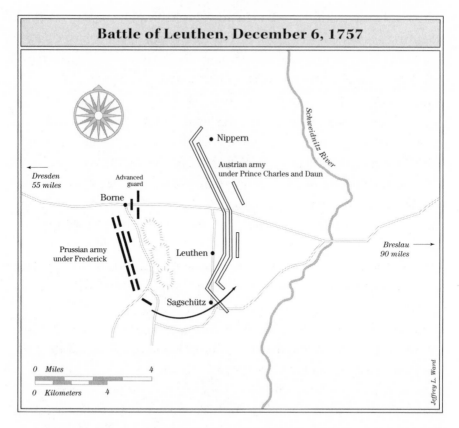

Battle of Leuthen, December 6, 1757

Nippern

Austrian army
under Prince Charles and Daun

Dresden
55 miles

Advanced
guard

Borne

Prussian army
under Frederick

Leuthen

Breslau
90 miles

Sagschütz

Schweidnitz River

0   Miles   4

0   Kilometers   4

Jeffrey L. Ward

As the Prussians advanced through heavy mist, an advance guard
encountered French cavalry outposts at Borne, a couple of miles from
Leuthen, and scattered them. Shortly afterward, the mist cleared and the
whole Austrian army could be seen stretched out along its five-mile front
so distinctly "that one could have counted it man by man."[7]

According to plan, Frederick sent his advance-guard cavalry toward the
enemy right wing, or northern flank, at Nippern. The Austrian commander
there was sure he was about to be attacked in force, and called so urgently
for aid that Marshal Daun sent him his reserve cavalry and part of the cavalry of the left, or southern, wing. Having successfully focused Austrian
attention on an expected attack at Nippern, holding the entire Austrian
army in place in anticipation of a major Prussian strike on the north,
Frederick now formed the main Prussian army into two columns at Borne,
and set it marching southward behind the protecting hills.

This was the crucial movement of the battle. As soon as Frederick marched his columns out of sight of the enemy, victory was his. Even if Prince Charles and Daun had recognized what Frederick was doing, they could not possibly have disengaged their army from its existing positions in time to get it to the south in time. In the event, Prince Charles and Marshal Daun were oblivious of the danger. Standing on a mill in the middle of the Austrian line, they watched the Prussian army turn southward and disappear behind the hills, and foolishly concluded that Frederick was in full retreat. "The Prussians are off," Daun said. "Don't disturb them."

Accordingly, Prince Charles and Daun were astonished a little after noon when they saw the head of the Prussian column reappear only a mile west of the Austrian southern flank, and then turn directly on it. The Austrian commander on this wing was horrified, and sent courier after courier begging Prince Charles for reinforcements. He was too late.

At about 1:00 P.M. the three-battalion Prussian advance guard stormed the defenses of Sagschütz. Within half an hour, aided by the highly mobile Prussian cannons, the whole Austrian left, or southern, wing was routed, and the entire area between Sagschütz and Leuthen was littered with Austrian fugitives, being pursued by Prussian cavalry. Now the Prussian infantry advanced in a double line directly on Leuthen and on the flank of the Austrian center.

At Leuthen a murderous conflict ensued, finally broken by a Prussian cavalry charge on the Austrian flank, causing the entire Austrian army to break and flee.

The struggle at Sagschütz and Leuthen cost the Prussian army 6,000 casualties, but the losses to the Austrians were annihilating, 10,000 killed and wounded, plus 21,000 prisoners. Frederick's oblique attack had worked perfectly. His much smaller army had concentrated overwhelming strength on the enemy's southern flank, and shattered the enemy army. The Austrians abandoned Silesia, and the effort to destroy Prussia in a concerted campaign collapsed. The war continued on till 1763, but Leuthen ensured further British financial support, and gave Frederick the strength to survive.

Trafalgar, 1805

In the half century between Frederick's victories and the height of the Napoleonic era in France, the concept of landing an overwhelming blow on one wing of an enemy faded from view. Napoleon employed different maxims to gain his victories. But in 1805, at Trafalgar, a British admiral, Horatio Nelson, adapted to naval warfare the techniques of Epaminondas and Frederick, and gained the most spectacular and decisive sea victory in history.[8]

By 1805 Napoleon, in his drive for world dominion, had achieved a dominant position on the European continent. He had annexed Belgium and the left, or western, bank of the Rhineland of Germany, occupied Holland and Switzerland, and conquered most of Italy. His last major obstacle was Britain, whose Royal Navy controlled the seas and prevented France from expanding its colonies and waterborne commerce, and, above all, deterred the French Grand Army massed at Boulogne from crossing the English Channel and occupying Britain. In order to gain control of the narrow seas between France and England, Napoleon built up the French navy and formed an alliance with Spain.

Napoleon was relying on the combined French and Spanish fleet to sweep the Royal Navy from the English Channel long enough for his Grand Army to cross over to England. However, before the allied commander, French admiral Pierre de Villeneuve, could get to the Channel, he was bottled up by Nelson's fleet at Cádiz, Spain. While trying to escape, Villeneuve was caught by Nelson and forced into battle off Cape Trafalgar, a few miles west of the southern coast of Spain on October 21, 1805.

Nelson's plan, conceived in detail before the battle, was based on the assumption that Villeneuve would arrange his larger thirty-three-ship fleet in the customary "line of battle" that all navies followed at the time. In this formation, warships sailed forward in a single line, one ship behind the other. Cannons were installed along both sides of warships so that ships could fire at any enemy on either side.

Nelson altered this orthodox tactical formation by dividing his smaller, twenty-seven-ship fleet into two separate detachments of unequal strength—a fifteen-battleship squadron under his subordinate

Cuthbert Collingwood, and a twelve-battleship squadron under Nelson himself. Instead of sailing alongside the enemy fleet and exchanging broadside artillery exchanges, as was the traditional method of carrying on a sea fight, Nelson ordered both of his squadrons to advance directly into the allied line of battle, at two different places.

Collingwood was to attack the head or leading ships of the twelve vessels of the allied rear, then sweep down with the overwhelming force of his fifteen ships on both sides, port and starboard, of the allied rear, dismantling each ship as they passed. Meanwhile, Nelson, with his smaller twelve-ship squadron, would attack the head of the allied center, not only holding it in place and making it unable to aid the rear being attacked by Collingwood, but also keeping the vanguard or front of the line out of the fight until it could turn about and sail back to the aid of the center. By the time this could happen, Nelson expected the center to be neutralized and the rear to be destroyed.

Nelson's plan was a brilliant application of the principle of landing an overwhelming blow—in this case by Collingwood on the rear of the allied fleet—while Nelson held the rest of the allied fleet in place by an attack on the center.

Villeneuve formed his fleet, as expected, in the customary line-of-battle formation and, at the time of engagement, was sailing northward a few miles west of the Strait of Gibraltar. The French-Spanish vanguard on the north of the line consisted of ten ships, and the center comprised seven ships. There was a gap between these two portions of the line and the rear, which consisted of a main body of twelve ships, followed by a reserve of five ships on the south. The reserve on the south would have difficulty sailing to aid the main body of the rear, because all ships were being driven by the same wind. Maneuvering in such fashion under wind power took considerable time.

The British fleet, already divided into its two squadrons, closed in from the west on the allied fleet. As Nelson's and Collingwood's two groups of ships were just on the verge of colliding with the French-Spanish fleet, Nelson's flagship, *Victory*, ran up the most famous signal in naval history: "England expects that every man will do his duty."

Nelson's method of holding the French-Spanish center and vanguard was to drive into the allied center of seven ships, separating them from the ten ships of the vanguard sailing ahead, and initially concentrating fire on the first three allied ships of the center. This was highly effective, shattering the ships. Just as Nelson had predicted, by the time the French-Spanish vanguard was able to turn about and return (and only five of them did so, the other five fleeing the fight), it was too late.

Meanwhile, Collingwood concentrated his superior strength on the leading ships of the allied rear. His ship, the *Royal Sovereign*, passed directly under the stern of the Spanish ship *Santa Ana*, fired a double-shotted broadside, and in an instant struck down 400 of the *Santa Ana*'s crew. The remaining ships of Collingwood's squadron came on and blasted the leading ships into hulks. Then his ships, now overwhelmingly superior, proceeded down the enemy line, enveloping the remaining ships of the allied rear and putting them out of action one by one. The five allied ships of the reserve never got into the fight until the end, and quickly fled the scene.

In the chaotic melee of the battle, Nelson exposed himself, refusing to remove from his chest the badges of honor bestowed on him by Britain. A sniper in the topmast of the French ship *Redoutable* fired a fatal shot at him. Nelson died several hours later, but not before he knew he had achieved victory.

Of the thirty-three ships in the French-Spanish fleet, only eleven returned to Cádiz.[9] No British ship was lost. In one great battle Nelson destroyed French naval power and established Britain as mistress of the seas.[10]

Implications for the Future

Carrying out the rule of the overwhelming blow will be one of the major aims in future warfare, especially by means of air power. Since the Persian Gulf War of 1991, the accuracy of bombs and missiles has increased immensely because of inerrant targeting using the Global Positioning System (GPS). Since nearly any target can be hit precisely, preemptive strikes against important enemy targets or installations will be a standard method of waging war. Such blows can be delivered at any level of intensity, from a mission to wipe out an enemy gun position all the way to missions to destroy an enemy's transportation network or electric grid.

For example, American air power eliminated Iraqi air defenses in the hours just prior to the active campaign against Iraq in the Persian Gulf War, while at the same time American air-superiority fighters drove the Iraqi air force from the skies. This action permitted American aircraft and cruise missiles to hit strategic targets in Iraq with impunity.

A decisive strike against an enemy army, such as Frederick achieved at Leuthen, no longer will be possible, however, because the accuracy of bombs and missiles will cause armies to disperse widely, leaving no large military concentration. Military forces will be in small, isolated units, and the characteristic strategy will be accurate missions against pinpoint targets, such as the American air force delivered in the battles against the Taliban and Al Qaeda in Afghanistan.

This same rule will be followed in ground fighting. Commanders will choose which ground targets they will assault, basing their decisions on the danger a particular enemy group or position poses. Thus a less dangerous target may be bypassed or relegated to a later operation. Most attacks will be carried out by dropping a superior force on an objective by helicopter or by the new V-22 Osprey vertical lift transport aircraft. In local operations, where enemy reaction is slow or nonexistent, land vehicles will continue to be used. But in every case the original idea of Epaminondas must be paramount: to bring overwhelming force to bear at some point, and to prevent this force being either deflected or nullified by an enemy counterstrike elsewhere.

11

Stroke at a Weak Spot

ONE OF THE most important rules of warfare is penetrating a weak point either discovered or created in the enemy's line or position. The idea is as old as warfare itself, since it emphasizes instinctive warrior virtues of bravery and bold action, and reflects the human urge to confront one's opponents directly. Among countless other examples, the battles of the American Civil War were largely based on this maxim. Most were frontal assaults seeking to drive a breach in the heart of the enemy position. Though in the Civil War the rule was often foolishly applied, it can be stunningly effective if employed with intelligence. The maxim will be important in future warfare, especially where an enemy force is dispersed and an attacker can strike into the enemy's center and disrupt his cohesion and equilibrium.

When executed properly, the rule offers a daring alternative to the orthodox or standard method of winning a battle or tactical engagement. This standard method, practiced since time immemorial in a variety of guises, is to hold the enemy in place in some fashion while sending a force around to his flanks or rear.

A modern incarnation of the standard method grew out of a specific problem on the western front in World War I. Murderous machine-gun, mortar, and artillery fire from trenches and fortifications virtually ruled out offensive movements. As mentioned in chapter 1, a German captain,

Willy Martin Rohr, devised a solution, "storm troop" tactics, in 1915. A small detachment, from the protection of a trench, would force the enemy in an opposing trench to keep under cover by laying down a "base of fire" with machine guns, mortars, and artillery. Meanwhile, under the protection of this fire, one or more small storm troop detachments would move inconspicuously over no-man's-land to the targeted trench, and "roll it up," primarily by the use of hand grenades.

Rohr's system developed thereafter into the standard tactics of conducting small-unit actions, called fire-and-maneuver by the U.S. and other armies. The Chinese Communists in the Korean War used the method when they crept up on an American unit or outpost at night and employed one small unit to lay heavy fire on the outpost, while other small units moved around to its flanks and rear, then attacked from all sides.

Breaking a hole in an enemy position is a good deal more difficult than fire-and-maneuver, for the obvious reason that an assault into the enemy's heart or center will generate the most intense and powerful reaction the enemy can muster. Applying the rule therefore requires immense foresight and planning. In fact, it is the most sophisticated method of winning a battle that has been devised. Of all the great commanders in history, only Alexander the Great and Napoleon employed the rule with great success and made it the centerpiece of their generalship.

Alexander used it in three of his four most decisive victories, and Napoleon employed it wherever conditions made it possible. Both leaders found or created weak places by deceiving or distracting enemy commanders in ways that caused them to make or expose a weak spot that could be exploited.[1]

While unimaginative commanders try to break into an enemy's position by sheer power, Alexander and Napoleon used little power and relied on subtlety. The sort of finesse they employed can be seen regularly in American football, for it's the more elegant way of pulling off a running play through the line. Such a play requires the offensive team to break a hole to allow the runner through. The offense can do this either by brute strength, pushing aside the opposing linemen, or by deception, perhaps faking a pass or an end run around the line, or some other ploy to pull men from the line. Brute strength is the solution of the straight-ahead warrior, deception the technique of the great general.

One of the best examples of using deception to create a hole in the enemy's line is Napoleon's "strategic battle," a type of approach he used numerous times. Applying this approach, Napoleon tried to rivet the enemy's attention with a strong frontal attack, drawing all enemy reserves into action. Previously he had assembled a large force, which he would then move on the enemy rear, threatening to block the enemy's line of retreat. The enemy commander could not accept having his avenue of withdrawal cut off, and was obliged to shift forces from his main position to counter the move on his rear. Such a move to guard the rear had to be made quickly, and the transfer of troops therefore almost always occurred at a point on the main line closest to where the rear attack was coming. Hence Napoleon knew in advance *where* the enemy would weaken his front. Once these troops had moved as expected, he launched an attack on this weakened spot with a previously drawn-up artillery-infantry-cavalry force, his *masse de rupture*, which crashed through, creating a gap for other troops to follow. This destroyed the balance and order of the enemy's position, and forced him to retreat or surrender.

Despite Napoleon's application of the "strategic battle," which brought him much success, the master who set down the rules of a stroke at a weak spot was Alexander of Macedon (356–323 B.C.).

The Granicus, Issus, and Arbela, 334–331 B.C.

Alexander became king of Macedonia in 336 B.C. after his famous father, Philip II, was assassinated by a disgruntled subject. Philip had created a powerful army, brought the tribes of the Balkans to heel, and pressured all the Greek city-states (except Sparta) into an alliance after the battle of Chaeronea in 338 B.C. Although Alexander had distinguished himself at this battle, and had been tutored for three or four years by the Greek philosopher Aristotle, no one expected him to survive the revolts and intrigues that erupted upon the death of his father.

Alexander, however, proved to be even more decisive and swift of action than Philip. In a series of lightning campaigns, he pacified the Balkan tribes that had risen on Philip's death, and, when Greece also tried to shake off Macedonia's yoke, eradicated the entire city of Thebes after it revolted and refused terms, an event that terrorized the other Greek cities, stopped all talk of resistance, and guaranteed a subservient hinterland.[2]

The army Philip had created was radically different from other armies. Whereas the Greeks relied for protection on large shields carried on their left arms, which kept their right arms free to wield an eight- or nine-foot-long spear, the Macedonians sacrificed an amount of shield protection in order to wield a longer, heavier, thirteen- to fourteen-foot spear, called the *sarissa*. This was a two-handed pike, and since the Macedonians needed both hands to wield it, they bore only a small round shield slung on the left shoulder. Because the Greeks carried such large shields, they could erect a formidable barrier that was difficult to penetrate, making the Greek phalanx as much a defensive formation as an offensive one. In contrast, the Macedonian phalanx was an almost totally offensive formation. Owing to its longer spears, the Macedonian phalanx could strike a Greek phalanx while still out of range of the Greek defenders, overpowering the Greek shield.

Not only was Philip's new phalanx thus superior to the Greek phalanx, but his even more important innovation was to turn his cavalry into the main fighting force of his army. Traditional Greek armies employed cavalry only on the wings, as protection. The decisive punching force of Greek warfare was the phalanx. Philip decided that main blows could be delivered by cavalry, equipped with metal-pointed wooden thrusting spears, making the horsemen on each of his flanks the fighting arms, especially the right flank, where he concentrated most of his strength. Thus the Macedonian army was transformed into a highly mobile force that could strike quickly and with great power.[3]

After his success in suppressing revolts, Alexander resolved to use the army his father had created to conquer the Persian Empire, the greatest kingdom on earth, stretching from the Aegean Sea and Egypt to the Indus River in present-day Pakistan.

Early in the year 334 B.C., when he was twenty-two years old, Alexander moved east across the Hellespont (or the Dardanelles, the strait connecting the Sea of Marmara and the Aegean), and marched into Anatolia, or Asia Minor, with an army of perhaps 30,000 men. His first aim upon doing so was to secure a base from which to operate. To do this he had to defeat a Persian army that had mobilized to drive him back into Europe. In May 334 B.C., the Persians drew up in a line along the north-flowing Granicus River, about forty miles east of the Hellespont.

The Persians had about 10,000 cavalry and 5,000 Greek mercenary infantrymen in a phalanx armed with the nine-foot Greek spear. Alexander did not have all of his army with him, but even so the Persian force was inferior in size. However, it occupied what the Persians considered to be a formidable defensive position on the high eastern bank of the Granicus. Foolishly, the Persian cavalry were arrayed along the river, where they were unable to charge, and could only defend. Furthermore,

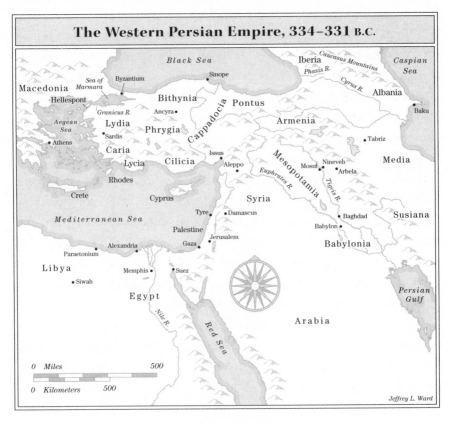

The Western Persian Empire, 334–331 B.C.

Jeffrey L. Ward

the Persians placed the Greek mercenaries *behind* the cavalry. Normally infantry occupied the front, but because the front was the place of honor, the Persian commanders didn't want to award it to mercenaries.

The greatest Persian weakness, however, was that their cavalry were armed primarily with javelins, probably two to a man, which were difficult to hurl with accuracy from a moving horse. The Persian cavalry therefore could neither charge an attacking force nor sustain a determined assault by the Macedonians.[4]

Facing the Persian line, Alexander decided to try to create a weak point on the enemy's front, then to penetrate this weak point and force the enemy to disintegrate under the blow. This is the first recorded example of the use of the rule of strike at a weak spot in an enemy position.

The Persian leaders recognized Alexander from the brightness of his armor, and from the aides and bodyguards who accompanied him closely. Since he had positioned himself on the right, they assumed he would strike their left. This Alexander had cleverly anticipated. When the battle started, he further encouraged the Persians' expectations by directing 3,000 light infantry and cavalry from his right center to advance *diagonally* and attack the extreme left of the Persian line. His object was to draw off some of their cavalry from the center.

The 3,000 Macedonians forged boldly into the Granicus River and tried to drive up the steep bank into the Persian left. A violent struggle broke out, with the Macedonians trying desperately to emerge from the river, the Persians fighting fiercely to prevent them. As Alexander watched, the Persians, just as he had hoped for, moved some of their center horsemen down to assist in the fight.

The Persian center was thereby weakened, and the moment to strike had arrived. Alexander at once launched all his remaining right-wing cavalry directly against the Persian center, followed by the right battalions of the phalanx. The elite cavalry, the Companions of Alexander, splashed through the water, and fought their way up the eastern bank. The battle became a melee, horse against horse, man against man. Alexander and his men got the best of it partly by force and discipline, but mainly because they were fighting with stout spears against short javelins.

Alexander had charged into the fray with his troops, and several Persian leaders rode forward to face him. As the Persian commanders approached, Alexander broke his spear and turned to his bodyguard for another. This also was broken. Demaratus the Corinthian then spurred up and gave Alexander his own. Alexander at once charged one of the attacking leaders, the son-in-law of the Persian king Darius, Mithridates, rolling him to the ground. As he did so, another Persian leader, Rhoesaces, struck Alexander with a battle-ax, and sheared off part of his helmet and two white plumes. Alexander whirled around, hurled Rhoesaces to the ground, and pierced him with his spear. Yet another Persian leader, Spithridates, then raised an ax to cut Alexander down, but the Macedonian known as Cleitus the Black severed the Persian's sword arm and saved Alexander's life. The sudden loss of three of their leaders greatly weakened the Persians' resolve—since in ancient times armies usually disintegrated when their leaders fell or fled.

Meanwhile squadron after squadron of Macedonian cavalry crossed the Granicus, along with the phalanx battalions, and joined in the fight. The Persian cavalry could put up only slight resistance to the thirteen-foot sarissas. Between the Macedonian cavalry and the phalanx, the Persian center caved in, the wings took flight, and the Macedonians shattered the Greek infantry, forcing the 2,000 survivors to surrender.

After his victory at the Granicus, Alexander freed the Greek cities along the Aegean coast that had been under Persian rule, and occupied key cities in western Anatolia. This guaranteed him a solid base. But Alexander did not move on immediately eastward into the heart of Persian power. Security was always Alexander's primary concern, and he was well aware that until the Persian fleets were removed from the Mediterranean and Aegean seas to his rear, he had no reliable passage back to Macedonia and Greece, which were his source of reinforcements and support. Most Persian ships were furnished by the maritime commercial city-states of Phoenicia in present-day Lebanon. Alexander resolved, therefore, to march down the eastern shore of the Mediterranean all the way to Egypt, and either force any city-state with a navy into an alliance, or reduce it by siege.

At the start of this campaign he achieved another great victory at Issus, at the northeastern corner of the Mediterranean, where he once again applied the rule of striking at a weak spot. The battle came shortly after he departed Anatolia in late October 333 B.C. Alexander had received reports that the Persian king Darius III, who had ascended the throne three years previously, was mobilizing a huge army about twenty miles into the interior of northern Syria. Alexander turned south down the coast, intending to march on Darius by way of the Syrian Gates (Beilan Pass) near Alexandretta. As this movement was under way, however, Darius unexpectedly marched around on the rear of Alexander's army and took up a position to his north.

When Macedonian scouts reported this movement, Alexander at once turned his army back to meet the challenge.

Alexander had 24,000 infantry and 5,000 cavalry. The Persian army was far larger, but the mass of the infantry were untrained tribal groups with little fighting quality. The Persians also had 10,000 Greek mercenaries and 60,000 light infantry called Cardaces, who carried javelins and small round shields. They possessed neither the solid discipline and hard fighting qualities nor the deadly sarissas of the Macedonian hoplites. Much of the Persian cavalry also were probably tribal bands, and not reliable, and the cavalry that were more disciplined were still armed with the inferior javelins.

Darius's force was lined up facing south along a small westward-flowing stream called the Pinarus, just before it debouched into the Mediterranean. As the Macedonians approached, Alexander turned his army out of its march order into its battle formation, his phalanx in the center and his cavalry on the wings. He took command of the right wing and entrusted the left, along the Mediterranean coast, to his general Parmenion. He told Parmenion to keep his left near the sea, so his outer flank couldn't be turned.

Darius meanwhile formed up his Greek mercenaries in the center of his line, with strong bodies of Cardaces, protected by archers, on each flank of the mercenaries. The remainder of his infantry, the tribal groups, he drew up in the rear of this battle front. Darius placed all but a fraction of his cavalry on his right, or western, wing, beside the coast, because the ground near the seashore was suitable for cavalry action. To protect his extreme left, or east, wing, he posted a force of light troops in the foothills in advance of his line of battle. Darius took his position in the center of the army alongside the Greeks.

Like other commanders, Darius failed to perceive that Alexander's power, as well as his striking arm, was in his cavalry. Darius thought his own cavalry could scatter the Macedonian horsemen on the western wing next to the sea, then turn on the rear of the Macedonian phalanx. The phalanx was indeed vulnerable to such an assault, since its strength was to the front, and required considerable time to turn in a new direction. Darius thus believed he might disrupt the phalanx's order, and drive the members in panic toward the mountains just to the east.

When Alexander got close to the Persians, he kept his Companion cavalry on the right, but—seeing that Darius had concentrated his cavalry close to the seashore—rushed most of his other cavalry to the left, or west, to reinforce Parmenion. Just before going into action, he also drove back into the foothills the detachment Darius had posted on the east.

As Alexander studied the Persian deployment, he worked out a brilliant plan of attack. The key was the Cardace infantry, whom he knew were a weak link. Darius had formed them up as infantry, but they had none of the defensive power of the Greek phalanx, and could be relatively easily ridden over by Alexander's cavalry.

As Alexander's right flank came opposite the Cardaces, he suddenly charged with his Companions, trusting more to speed than to force of arms to strike terror into the Cardaces. The Macedonians took the river at a gallop, yelling at the tops of their voices. The Persian archers, who were supposed to protect the Cardaces, fled, and in seconds the Companions were upon the Cardaces, causing them to take to their heels.

Darius saw his left collapsing. But instead of drawing the left of his Greek mercenaries back to form a defensive line, Darius turned his chariot about and fled the field.

The rest of the battle was an anticlimax. All the Persians on the field abandoned the battle when they learned that Darius had rushed away.[5]

Having dispensed with Darius, Alexander now marched down the coast. Cyprus and all the cities of Phoenicia submitted to him except Tyre, where he met fierce resistance. The siege of Tyre lasted a hard seven months, but Alexander prevailed and then, with no enemy navies to contest control of the sea, he marched on to Egypt. The Egyptians bitterly opposed Persian rule, and the people welcomed Alexander as a liberator. Alexander had himself crowned pharaoh, and having consolidated his control of the entire Aegean and eastern Mediterranean, returned to Tyre in the spring of 331 B.C., and set out to conquer the rest of the Persian Empire.

Alexander's final battle with Darius occurred on October 1, 331 B.C., at Gaugamela or Arbela in Mesopotamia, about fifty miles east of present-day Mosul on the Tigris River. Here again Alexander won by striking a weak spot in the Persian line—a weak place he himself created by causing a wild cavalry melee on his right flank, drawing off Persian cavalry, and thereby opening a hole in the center. Alexander penetrated this gap with his Companion cavalry. When Darius fled the battlefield once more, he lost all legitimacy as the Persian ruler and became a fugitive. Alexander was recognized as the rightful successor, and his succeeding campaigns into present-day Iran and beyond were designed to consolidate his power. Darius was eventually killed by his own bodyguards.

Alexander's advance came to a stop in the fall of 326 B.C., when, on the plains of northern India, his weary soldiers declined to go on. Alexander's eloquence to persuade them to continue failed. Knowing at last that he had reached the end of his empire, Alexander turned back. This was the greatest military campaign in history, and Alexander was the greatest conqueror of all time. He brought East and West together in a juncture that endured for a thousand years, and whose consequences abide with us today.

Austerlitz, 1805

Between Alexander and Napoleon (1769–1821) there are few recorded examples of commanders who consciously adopted the principle of striking at a weak spot. Perhaps Gustavus Adolphus came closest. His Swedish army broke through the center of German Imperial armies in 1631 and 1632, but Gustavus was able to do so because of his superior firepower, not because of special maneuvering.

Thus the accomplishments of Napoleon are all the more remarkable. He developed his methods sui generis, entirely on his own. Although he knew about Alexander's victories, the actual tactical methods Alexander employed were not appreciated until the twentieth century, when they were described by the English strategist J. F. C. Fuller.

Napoleon self-consciously developed what he came to call his concept of the "strategic battle." All the elements of this system can be found already in one of his earliest engagements, Castiglione in northern Italy on August 5, 1796.[6] He was aware at this date of what he was aiming for, and refined his technique in later battles. His great masterpiece was his victory over the Austrians and Russians at Austerlitz in Moravia on December 2, 1805. This battle matched the brilliance of anything achieved by Alexander. Indeed, Napoleon's method at Austerlitz was identical in concept to Alexander's method at the Granicus in 334 B.C. He deceived his enemy into moving troops away from the center of the line, and then struck a powerful blow into that gap.[7]

The Austerlitz campaign developed out of a coalition forged between Britain, Russia, and Austria, at that time a large central European empire. The aim was to recover the territories France had occupied since 1796 in Italy, the German Rhineland, and the Low Countries, and to push France back behind its old frontiers of 1789. Napoleon had been hoping to invade England with his Grand Army massed at Boulogne on the French coast, but he was unable to gain control of the English Channel, and decided to turn swiftly on Austria instead before substantial Russian forces could come to its aid.

Napoleon's Grand Army crossed the Rhine on September 26, 1805, on its way to Austria in a vast, sweeping movement across central Germany. It descended on the rear of a 57,000-man Austrian army under Karl Mack at Ulm in western Bavaria, forcing Mack to surrender on October 20. Napoleon then threatened a 50,000-man Russian army under Mikhail

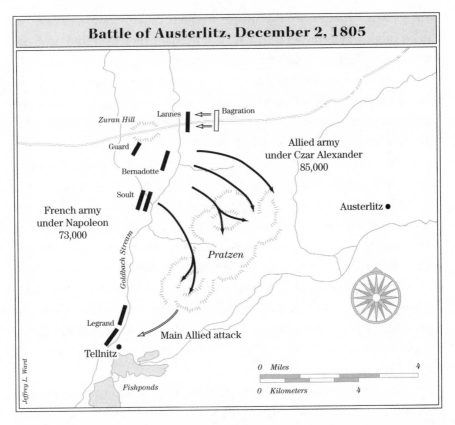

Battle of Austerlitz, December 2, 1805

Zuran Hill

Lannes

Bagration

Guard

Bernadotte

Soult

Allied army
under Czar Alexander
85,000

French army
under Napoleon
73,000

Austerlitz ●

Goldbach Stream

Pratzen

Legrand

Main Allied attack

Tellnitz

Fishponds

0   Miles   4

0   Kilometers   4

Jeffrey L. Ward

Kutuzov, which was advancing westward along the Danube, inducing him to withdraw northeast across the Danube. This allowed Napoleon's cavalry chief Joachim Murat to seize Vienna, cross the Danube, and drive Kutuzov all the way back to Olmütz (Olomouc) in Moravia, in close reach of the Russian frontier. There Kutuzov was joined by the Russian czar Alexander and the Austrian emperor Francis, along with Russian and a few Austrian reinforcements, which raised the allied army to more than 80,000 men. Napoleon did not want to press the allies any farther east. To do so would only consolidate their strength.

Instead of pursuing Kutuzov all the way to Olmütz, therefore, Napoleon stopped at the town of Brünn (Brno), forty miles west of Olmütz, on November 20. He had only 50,000 men, while Alexander and Francis at Olmütz, already with 80,000 men, would soon be reinforced by yet another Russian army. Napoleon was now in a dangerous situation. If he held back, the allies would soon overwhelm him by sheer numbers. If, on the other hand, he attacked with inferior forces on ground of the enemy's choosing, he was likely to be beaten.

His only hope was to entice the allies to attack him where and when he wanted before they had received more reinforcements. This was the course he set upon. Fortunately, Napoleon had three huge advantages: his extremely limber brain; the fact that there was a shortage of supplies in the region the allies were occupying, which gave them an incentive for quick action; and the overconfidence and lack of experience of the Russian czar.

Napoleon commenced a psychological campaign to make the Russians believe he was ripe for destruction. He kept 50,000 men at Brünn, pushed out only small, tentative detachments toward Olmütz, and, to give the impression he was frightened, opened peace overtures to Alexander and Francis. Meanwhile he roamed over the countryside between Brünn and Olmütz, searching for a location where he could fight a decisive battle under conditions of his own choosing. He found just such a site near the little town of Austerlitz, about ten miles east of Brünn, and moved his army there.

As Napoleon's precarious situation became more and more apparent, Czar Alexander, who was only twenty-eight years old and inexperienced in war, began to be convinced by a group of young courtiers around him, who urged him to take charge of military affairs. Kutuzov, a capable commander, lost authority, and Alexander began to exclude him from the decision-making process. Once when Kutuzov asked for Alexander's intentions, he was told tartly, "That is none of your business."[8]

Kutuzov had astutely urged caution and delay. He proposed that the allies withdraw back into the Carpathian Mountains. "The farther we entice Napoleon, the weaker he will become, and the greater will be the distance that separates him from his reserves," he said.[9] But Alexander wanted to test his presumed military skills against Napoleon. In the face of Alexander's foolishness, Kutuzov withdrew into himself, as did Emperor Francis, who possessed little influence in Alexander's court.[10]

Accordingly, on November 27, 1805, the allied army, now totaling 89,000 men, commenced its westward march from Olmütz to attack the

French. Napoleon sent hurried orders to Jean Bernadotte to bring his 1st Corps from its watch on the Bohemian border some fifty miles northwest, and to Louis-Nicolas Davout to come up with his 3rd Corps by forced marches from Vienna, both to join him at Austerlitz.

The key position on the field of Austerlitz was a three-mile-long ridgeline called the Pratzen, about a mile and a half east of a stream called the Goldbach. Napoleon had deliberately yielded the Pratzen heights, which seemed to be the best tactical position, and had formed his army instead mostly west of the Goldbach stream. He posted Nicolas Jean Soult's 24,000-man 4th Corps along four miles of the western bank of the Goldbach. Two of Soult's divisions were posted on the north, while only a single division, under Claude Juste Alexandre Legrand, occupied the lower two and a half miles of the stream down to Tellnitz, just above a group of shallow fish ponds.

The bait for the allies was the weakly held stretch manned by Legrand's division. Napoleon knew the allies would naturally take a route around his southern flank because they wanted to cut him off from Vienna. The weakness of the French on this flank would give them further incentive.

The reason Napoleon had left the Pratzen unoccupied was that he wanted the allies to climb onto it, see a seemingly weak French army ahead, and strike hard for its weakest position, Legrand's men on the southern flank. The brilliance of Napoleon's foresight was to appreciate that once the allied force departed the Pratzen in pursuit of the French southern flank, the Pratzen would of course be *vacated*. He could move troops onto it and from there mount a masterful counteroffensive.

While the main body of the allies pressed around the French southern flank, Napoleon knew the remainder of the allied force would move forward along an east-west-running highway about two and a half miles north of the Pratzen. These movements would *create* a hole in the allied center. Napoleon knew that he could win by striking directly into this hole with Soult's two divisions on the north, seizing the Pratzen, and then driving on what would now be the *rear* of the allied force on the southern flank.[11]

As the allied army approached just to the east of the Pratzen on November 30, 1805, the French corps coming from Bohemia arrived, while Napoleon learned that the leading division coming from Vienna would reach the field within twenty-four hours. Napoleon therefore knew that all of his forces would be in place in time for the battle.

The two divisions of Soult's corps that were to lead the assault on the Pratzen took their position on the northern portion of the Goldbach. Lannes's 5th Corps was deployed along the highway just to the north, and Bernadotte's corps was to move in just to the south of Lannes. The division that had come up from Vienna was to aid Legrand's troops around Tellnitz at the southern portion of the Goldbach line.

On the morning of December 1, allied forces began to climb the steepish slope to the extensive saddleback of the Pratzen. By the end of the day, Prince Bagration had deployed his 13,000-man corps along the highway a couple miles to the north, just as Napoleon had anticipated, and the 10,000-man Russian Imperial Guard was positioned about a mile south of the road in reserve. The remainder of the allied army was resting on the summit of the Pratzen and behind it.

About dawn on the morning of December 2, 1805, exactly as Napoleon had encouraged, Kutuzov ordered a movement of four columns, more than 55,000 men, southward over the Pratzen.[12] They were to cross the weakly held section of the Goldbach at and around Tellnitz, where the French line appeared weak. Once they had destroyed the French forces in the area, they were to turn north, to strike at the rear of Napoleon's forces positioned on the highway. During this turning movement, Bagration and the Imperial Guard were instructed to advance directly west along the highway in support.

On the Pratzen the air was clear, but as the allied soldiers descended from the heights they disappeared into thick fog. Marching almost blind, the first allied forces collided with Legrand's troops at 7:00 A.M. at Tellnitz. Within minutes the battle became general along the lower Goldbach in violent and chaotic fighting confused by the fog which drifted in and out. The allies slowly advanced and appeared about to debouch into the plain behind the French defenses.

While the allied movement proceeded, Napoleon talked with Soult on Zuran Hill, an elevation on the highway four miles northwest of the Pratzen.

"How long will it take you to move your divisions to the tops of Pratzen heights?" Napoleon asked.

"Less than twenty minutes, Sire," Soult replied. "For my troops are hidden at the foot of the valley, hidden by fog and campfire smoke."

"In that case," Napoleon responded, "we will wait for a further quarter of an hour."

His spyglass trained on Pratzen, Napoleon watched attentively as column after column of Russians and Austrians moved across the plateau. As he looked, the ridgeline became almost empty. With that, Napoleon gave the decisive order to Soult to advance. "One sharp blow and the war's over!" he shouted, as Soult mounted his horse and galloped away.

Within minutes, 17,000 French troops surged toward the Pratzen heights. Batteries of cannons followed closely behind.

One French division on the right surged up and drove away parts of the last Russian column on the Pratzen, which had not yet passed through. The other division on the left overran a few Russians in the valley, then struck and quickly routed five Russian battalions and artillery on the northern height of the Pratzen. The Russians of this column recoiled back into the valley to the east. With that, the heights of the Pratzen were in French hands. It had taken twenty minutes, just as Soult had promised.

Kutuzov was able to bring some Russian forces to contest the Pratzen, but canister from French guns threw back the attacks, and Napoleon, seeing that the decisive moment had come, committed reserve infantry and the Imperial Guard to secure the heights.

Napoleon reached the Pratzen just in time to witness the last throw of the allies—a counterstroke of the Russian Imperial Guard under Grand Duke Constantine at 1:00 P.M. The Guard made strong gains, but was stopped by the arrival of a brigade of French infantry. Finally a regiment of "Mamelukes," a cavalry force of Frenchmen Napoleon had raised in Egypt in 1798, charged the Russians, and drove them from the field.

Now Napoleon had to convert this capture of the center of the allied line into a full victory. He turned the Imperial Guard and Soult's two divisions directly southward on the rear of the allied forces still struggling with Legrand's troops at Tellnitz. Napoleon also detailed Bernadotte's corps to clear out any remaining pockets of resistance on the Pratzen.

When the Russians and Austrians realized that a large French force was descending on their rear, they made a frantic effort to flee. There were few passages through the chains of shallow fishponds at the southern end of the Goldbach. The ponds were frozen over, but many allied soldiers and horses plunged through the ice into the ponds as they tried to flee. Some drowned. Meanwhile, French artillery on the Pratzen pounded the allied columns. Recognizing defeat, thousands of allied soldiers surrendered. By 4:30 P.M., resistance had collapsed all over the field. Only fragments of the three allied columns that had crossed the Pratzen and pushed south had survived. Most were either dead or captured.

While the Pratzen battle was under way, Bagration's Russian corps had made a strong but expensive diversionary attack along the highway on the north. The attack was stopped by the French corps commanded by Lannes, and cost Bagration half of his 13,000 men. Bagration fell back on the town of Austerlitz, where the remaining allied survivors gathered, barely 33,000 of the original army of 89,000, with orders to retreat toward Hungary.

One great battle, as Napoleon had predicted, had decided the war. Two days later, Emperor Francis met in the open with Napoleon, and their conference resulted in an immediate armistice. France and Austria signed the Peace of Pressburg on December 27. In the agreement, Napoleon was awarded Austria's Tyrol and additional territories containing two and a half million of Austria's twenty-four million people.

Czar Alexander meanwhile was hurrying back to his homeland with the 26,000 Russians who had managed to survive the debacle. He signed no peace treaty, but sent a message to Davout, whose troops were monitoring the withdrawal: "Tell your master that I am going away. Tell him that he has performed miracles."

In England the news of Austerlitz proved the last blow for the great British prime minister William Pitt, who had struggled valiantly against Napoleon and was to die in January 1806. Shortly before the end, he told his niece, Hester Stanhope, "Roll up that map of Europe. It will not be wanted these ten years."[13] Napoleon was now on the way to becoming arbiter of Europe—a domination that only vanished in 1812 when he made the fatal mistake of invading Russia.

Implications for the Future

Since Napoleon numerous commanders have tried to break up enemy positions by driving into them, usually by finding a weak spot that already existed in the enemy line. In the future commanders may be able to locate such weak places more readily by using aerial or satellite surveillance. But the true teaching of Alexander and Napoleon is to maneuver or manipulate the enemy in order to *create* weak places that he otherwise would not allow.

As we have seen, making such weak points requires extraordinary planning and foresight. Therefore, the use of this rule in the future will depend, as in the past, upon imaginative minds that search for opportunities, and seize them when they manifest themselves. The fact that American football coaches employ the maxim routinely to develop strikes through opposing lines shows that the concept is widely known. It is much more difficult to carry out in the stress and confusion of battle, however. Nevertheless, the rule remains the gold standard of tactical operations. Commanders should always strive for it. Even if they do not find it, they may discover in their search imaginative ways to employ other principles of warfare.

12

Caldron Battles

A TACTIC OF WAR likely to be used frequently in future conflicts is that of the caldron battle. The rule behind this type of battle is to envelop the enemy on all sides, preventing his retreat, and then destroy him in place. This is the same fundamental method as that advocated in the new concept of swarming discussed in chapter 1, but it is also one of the most ancient forms of attack.

The anthropologist Lawrence H. Keeley, in his book *War Before Civilization*, states that the most common form of primitive warfare was raids and ambushes, in which the principal means of attack was surrounding an isolated group or a village, usually at night, and, on a signal, moving in from all sides.[1]

The all-around attack, or caldron, remained the preferred method in tribal warfare up to recent times, even when tribesmen were confronting Western military forces. Against fortifications, tribesmen almost always lost. In the open, however, they quite often won. Generations of boys in the first half of the twentieth century thrilled to the stout defense of Fort Zinderneuf in the Sahara Desert by a French Foreign Legion company against Taureg tribesmen, as depicted in Percival Christopher Wren's fictional but fact-based *Beau Geste*. Yet when Europeans met tribesmen in the open, they were often surrounded and slaughtered. Though armed with artillery, 150 French soldiers behind a stockade of thorn bushes were destroyed by an equal number of Tauregs at Goundam, Algeria, in 1890. In 1904–1907, in German Southwest Africa (present-day Namibia), Herero tribesmen failed against machine guns behind stone walls, but succeeded against Germans caught in the open.[2]

The rule of attacking from all sides has been decisive in many historic encounters, including the greatest battle of annihilation in history, at Cannae in 216 B.C. The Germans' failure to carry it out properly in France in 1914 led to their defeat four years later, and was the foundation of the most successful German campaign on the eastern front in World War II.

Although in pure theory caldron battles aim at the total destruction of the enemy, in fact outright annihilation is seldom the aim of the attacking force. Though surrounding an enemy and closing in on him from all directions theoretically leaves no avenue of escape, in most cases quite a few soldiers are able to get out of even the tightest ring. This does not invalidate the effectiveness of caldron battles, however, because in many cases the attacker is not actually seeking total destruction, but rather is merely trying to induce an enemy to withdraw and abandon his aggressions or intentions. An effective alternative to the true caldron approach, therefore, is *not* to close the ring—that is, to leave the enemy a route of escape in order to *prevent* a fight to the finish. This tactic usually works because most human beings, given the choice of fighting to the death or running away, will choose the latter. The technique has been practiced by wise commanders from ancient times forward.

The nonlinear battlefield and highly mobile forces create conditions that give the rule special relevance today. In future wars, in which separate small units are likely to be spread far over the landscape, caldron battles may be more effective if they are limited to strikes against only a couple of enemy elements, on the premise that the violent destruction of one or two units may induce the others to depart. As the Chinese Communist leader Mao Zedong said, "Injuring all of a man's fingers is not as effective as chopping off one of them."

Whether on this smaller scale or in the traditional full form, caldron battles will remain important in warfare, and they require a fundamental understanding of how military operations are carried out.

Cannae, 216 B.C.

The most famous caldron battle ever fought, and the model that commanders have tried to copy ever since, was conducted in the Second Punic War by the Carthaginian commander Hannibal Barca, against a Roman army at Cannae, on the Aufidus (Ofanto) River in southern Italy in 216 B.C.[3]

Hannibal (247–183 B.C.) was, of course, one of the greatest captains of all time. The system he carried out at Cannae was foolproof and has never been improved upon. Yet this victory, like most other victories in warfare, came about not just because of the genius of a commander, but also because the opposing general was unable or refused to examine the situation *before* he stepped into it. For if the Roman commander, Terentius Varro, had listened to wiser voices urging him to avoid a frontal clash, or if he had comprehended the Carthaginian dispositions and pulled back, his army of 80,000 men would not have been destroyed.

The Second Punic War (219–202 B.C.) was started by the Carthaginians to exact revenge for their defeat by Rome twenty-two years before in the First Punic War (264–241 B.C.). Carthage was a great commercial state founded by the Phoenicians, and located near present-day Tunis in north Africa. After the first war, Hannibal's father, Hamilcar, compensated for Carthage's losses of Sicily, Sardinia, Corsica, and other islands in the Mediterranean by subduing the tribes of Spain and creating a new empire there.

Hannibal launched his invasion of Rome from Spain, marching overland through Gaul (present-day France), across the Alps, and into northern Italy in 218 B.C. The great strength of Hannibal's army was in cavalry, which were much superior to Roman horsemen. The Romans emphasized foot soldiers, and generally used cavalry sparingly, mostly to shield the flanks of their legions. The Carthaginians, on the other hand, recruited north African tribesmen with long experience in using horses to manage their herds, and who possessed skill from much practice in wielding long pikes and swords while riding.

With his cavalry, Hannibal routed a Roman force on the Ticunus (Ticino) River, in northern Italy, in November, and a large Roman army on the Trebia (Trebbia) River, south of Milan, near present-day Piacenza, in December. In the spring of 217 B.C. he advanced *through* the supposedly impassable swamps of the Arnus (Arno) River, and emerged south of a Roman army guarding the main road at Arretium (Arezzo) in the mountains of eastern Tuscany. When this army chased after the Carthaginians, Hannibal ambushed and virtually destroyed it at Lake Trasimene (Trasimeno).

With little difficulty, Hannibal moved on into southern Italy. He did not besiege Rome because doing so would have required a larger army than he commanded, and because he would also have had to organize supply lines that the Romans could have attacked with their greater manpower. Instead, Hannibal chose a strategy that emphasized his great strengths— the ability to move his army fast, superior cavalry, and his supreme generalship. With these he sought to break Rome's bonds with its Italian allies, and thereby weaken the city.

The Roman leader at the time, Quintus Fabius Maximus, appointed dictator for six months by the Roman senate, realized the Roman army could not hope to defeat Hannibal in open battle, because of the superiority of the Carthaginian cavalry. But he also realized that if Hannibal was able to pull the cities of southern Italy away from their alliance with Rome, he could establish a secure base from which to conquer Rome itself. The primary strategic necessity for Rome, therefore, was to prevent the defection of the southern Italian cities.

To achieve this, Fabius launched a guerrilla war in the hills, which did not directly challenge Hannibal's horsemen but weakened him and kept the Italian cities from going over to him. Despite its success, Fabius's strategy aroused great opposition within Rome because the Romans had long thrived on a tradition of offensive warfare. The senate therefore refused to renew Fabius's dictatorship, and, resolving that the army should give battle, named two consuls, or commanders, the ignorant and impetuous Terentius Varro and the more cautious Aemilius Paulus.

Rome assembled the greatest army it had ever placed in the field, comprising 80,000 infantry and 7,000 cavalry. In July 216 B.C. this army marched off to confront Hannibal, the two consuls alternating command each day. As the Roman force approached Hannibal, who was located at Cannae on the Aufidus River, about 200 miles southeast of Rome, Paulus sought to maneuver and wait for a favorable opportunity. Varro, however, wanted to give battle at once, and, using his day of command, advanced directly on Hannibal's 40,000 infantry and 10,000 cavalry.

On August 2, 216 B.C., Hannibal crossed to the west side of the Aufidus to meet the Roman force, and lined up his army within an arc of the river so that the river secured both of his flanks. Although the water level in the river was low at this time of the year, it nevertheless formed a barrier behind the Carthaginians that would slow retreat in the event they had to withdraw. Hannibal therefore had moved to what seemed to the Romans a precarious position.

Each army placed its infantry in the center and its cavalry on the wings, as was customary in ancient warfare. But Hannibal arrayed his infantry in a most unusual way. In the very center he pushed ahead his *least dependable* troops, Gauls and Spanish soldiers, keeping back the best troops, his African foot soldiers, on either side. Thus the Carthaginian infantry protruded *forward* in a convex line toward the Romans.

Varro foolishly made no analysis of the unorthodox Carthaginian formation, and simply perceived the infantry out front as a weak point his men could attack. This they did with their whole force, handily driving the Gauls and Spaniards back, just as Hannibal had intended. The convex line sagged ominously inward, becoming concave, and the Roman legionaries, believing they were on the verge of a great breakthrough and victory, crowded into this withdrawing center.

At this moment Hannibal gave the signal and the African infantry suddenly wheeled inward from both sides, striking the Romans in flank and enveloping them into a tightly packed mass. Meanwhile, Hannibal's heavy cavalry on his left wing had broken through the weaker Roman cavalry on that side, and had swept around the Roman rear to drive away the cavalry on the Roman left flank. Leaving the lighter Numidian (Algerian) cavalry on the right wing to pursue the Roman horsemen, Hannibal's heavy cavalry delivered the final blow by bursting onto the rear of the Roman legions, already enveloped on three sides by infantry and so compressed that they were unable to offer effective resistance.

The battle now turned into a massacre. Only about 6,000 Romans were able to break out and get away. More than 70,000 died. Varro ironically was one of the survivors, while Paulus fell in battle. Hannibal lost around 6,000 men.

Cannae was the perfect caldron battle. The Romans were pressed into an immovable mass in the center by Carthaginian forces that ranged on all sides. Hannibal brought this about not only by drawing the Romans inward, but by swinging both his flanks around them in a double envelopment. The final blow was to seal off any avenue of retreat by closing with his cavalry on the Roman rear.

Most of Rome's men of military age perished on the field that day. But the Romans did not give up. The senate mobilized young boys and old men and immediately marched two legions south to encourage Rome's allies. A few cities went over to Carthage, but most remained loyal. Rome reverted to the strategy of Fabius, declining battle, and keeping to the hills to avoid Hannibal's cavalry, seeking small gains in minor encounters, but slowly squeezing Hannibal into a narrow region in the south. The Romans couldn't oust him, but Hannibal couldn't advance and conquer the whole peninsula, either.

Stalemate ensued for nearly fourteen years. It was broken not by a direct attack on Hannibal in Italy, but by an indirect blow at Carthage itself, engineered by Publius Cornelius Scipio, known to history as Scipio Africanus. Scipio built up a cavalry force on Sicily that finally was able to match blows with Hannibal's horsemen, invaded north Africa, and so threatened Carthage that the rulers recalled Hannibal. In 202 B.C., on the field of Zama in present-day central Tunisia, Scipio met and defeated Hannibal's army in a battle that marked the downfall of Carthage and the ascendence of Rome.

The Schlieffen Plan, 1914

In succeeding centuries, Cannae took on an almost mystical significance, becoming a sort of military Holy Grail, the highest and purest form of intellectual perfection in warfare. But it was difficult to duplicate what Hannibal achieved, especially wrapping both flanks around an enemy at the same time he was held in place on the front and attacked on the rear. Only an extremely obtuse commander could be induced to advance directly into a trap such as Terentius Varro entered at Cannae. Against a less gullible enemy, the more reliable method was to attack his front to hold him in place, and then move on just one of his flanks, as Frederick the Great did at Leuthen in 1757.

By the last decades of the nineteenth century, the lesson of Cannae was directed most often not at attaining victory in one local tactical decision, but rather was used in planning strategic campaigns to achieve total victory. Planners realized that a great envelopment was less likely to be perceived by the enemy—and therefore more likely to be successful—if it took place across large stretches of landscape. Space could create obscurity, and veil intent.

The German general staff was especially active along this line, notably under Count Alfred von Schlieffen, chief of the staff from 1891 to 1905. He sought to achieve modern Cannaes in *Vernichtungskriege*, or "wars of annihilation." The aim was to avoid frontal attacks by deep concentric encircling movements around enemy flanks with infantry armies in order to drive enemy forces into pockets where they either had to surrender or be annihilated.

Plans incorporating this strategy led to both one of Germany's greatest victories, at Tannenberg in East Prussia, and one of its greatest defeats, on the Marne River in France, within just days of each other in the opening stages of World War I. The defeat ironically came in an operation that had been planned meticulously for a long time, whereas the victory resulted from an opportunistic application of the strategy with ad-hoc forces.[4]

The defeat on the Marne was the outcome of the German commander, Helmuth von Moltke, giving only lip service to the strategy while actually undermining it. Moltke was chief of the general staff, succeeding Schlieffen, and through his inept generalship he ruined a brilliant plan that had been developed by his predecessor. Since the "Schlieffen Plan" was later advertised as the strategy that failed against France and Britain in the opening campaign of the war, many people assumed the plan was at fault, but it was actually Moltke's implementation of the plan that brought disaster to Germany. This defeat ended the war of movement in the west, setting in place the trench warfare that ruled until the end of the war, and thereby directly causing Germany's defeat. If Moltke had carried out the plan as Schlieffen wrote it, Germany very likely would have defeated the French and British armies in a matter of weeks.

World War I came about, as President Woodrow Wilson asserted in 1919 after its end, because of industrial and commercial rivalry, especially between Germany and Britain. "This war," Wilson said, "was a commercial and industrial war. It was not a political war." About the same time, the English economist John Maynard Keynes wrote that, in the war, Britain had destroyed a trade rival.[5]

Germany's economy and population mushroomed between 1871, when it united, and 1914, when World War I started. It passed Britain, the previous world leader in industrialization, before the turn of the century, and thereafter the economic rivalry between the two countries became more and more acute.

France signed a defensive alliance with Russia in 1893, but so long as Britain was not a party, this would not have threatened the peace of Europe. In 1898, however, the German Reichstag, or parliament, passed a bill to expand the German navy. This precipitated a vast increase in naval construction in Britain, far outclassing the German effort. By 1909 Britain had four times the navy of Germany, and the disparity was growing, not shrinking. Despite that naval superiority, fear of Germany's economic growth caused Britain to sign a series of agreements with France in 1904, which grew into a secret military alliance.

This Anglo-French entente altered the whole political balance. As Arthur Balfour, British prime minister from 1902 to 1905, told an American diplomat in 1907, "We are probably fools not to find a reason for declaring war on Germany before she builds too many ships and takes away our trade."[6]

All that was needed now was a spark to set off the conflagration. It came when a group of Serbians bent on creating a "greater Serbia"—the same motivation that led to "ethnic cleansing" murders of non-Serbs in Yugoslavia eight decades later—shot down the Austrian archduke Franz Ferdinand and his wife on a street in Sarajevo, Bosnia, on June 28, 1914.

Austria-Hungary blamed Serbia, and handed it an ultimatum. The Serbs, supported by Russia, which wanted to expand its influence into the Balkans, refused to back down. After a month of intense negotiations, Austria-Hungary declared war on Serbia, Russia mobilized, and Germany, which had an alliance with Austria-Hungary, declared war on Russia on August 1. Within three days Britain, France, and Russia were at war with Germany and Austria-Hungary.

Germany thus faced France and Britain on the west, and Russia on the east. The German general staff, anticipating such a two-front dilemma, had wrestled with a solution for years. Schlieffen's plan, adopted in 1905, was designed specifically to permit Germany to win a war on two fronts.

Because the French army was expected to mobilize first, and because the heart of German industry was in the Ruhr region, just east of Holland, the danger of an enemy advance on the west was greater than from Russia on the east. Moreover, Russia's armies were notoriously slow in mobilizing, and might be disregarded for a few weeks—especially as Germany expected Austria-Hungary to absorb the initial Russian blow.

Nevertheless, victory over France had to come fast, because once Russia did mobilize, its armies would be twice the size of Germany's. In considering these factors, Schlieffen called for an extremely rapid "Cannae-like" victory over the French, after which the German army could be transferred east to take care of the Russian threat.

The Schlieffen Plan prescribed a gigantic enveloping movement, concentrating the vast preponderance of German strength on a right, or western, wing, that would wheel through the plains of Belgium and northern France, cross the Seine River near Rouen, circle around south of Paris, and turn back northward to press the rear of the French armies, which would be pinned down by much smaller German forces along the frontier in Lorraine.

The greatness of the plan rested on Schlieffen's distribution of force. Of the seventy-two German divisions expected to be available, fifty-three were to be allocated to the wheeling movement, ten to form a pivot facing Verdun, and only nine to be held on the left, or eastern, wing along the French frontier. The object was to keep the German left wing so weak that the French would be encouraged to attack into

Lorraine and press the Germans back toward the Rhine. The farther the French drove forward, the more difficult it would be to extricate themselves when the German pincer movement swept around onto their rear.

Schlieffen's plan was not a true Cannae, in that he prescribed a turn around just one flank. The effect would have been the same, however, because this great sweep would extend all the way to the rear, and then push the French armies back northward against German forces in Lorraine, who would act as a holding force, completing the encirclement and creating a caldron.

Moreover, if the French, as expected, took the offensive against the Germans in Lorraine, the effect would be, as the English military strategist Basil H. Liddell Hart wrote, "like a revolving door, the more heavily the Frenchman pressed on one side, the more forcefully would the other side swing around behind him."[7]

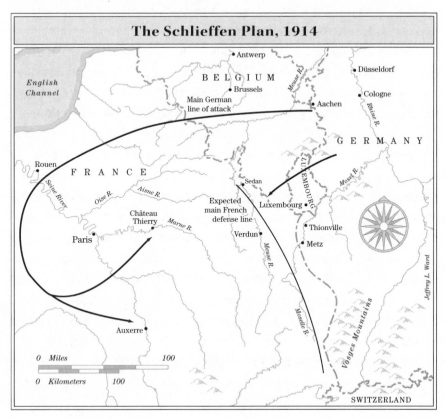

The Schlieffen Plan, 1914

The French war plan played perfectly into Schlieffen's hand. A new school of theorists, led by Ferdinand Foch, was fascinated with the idea of the offensive, and believed that if the French attacked forcefully they were bound to win. French fixation on this *offensive à outrance* ignored the experience of the American Civil War, which showed that defensive weapons fired behind fortifications or solid parapets could stop practically any attack, and also ignored the development of defensive weapons after the Civil War. The most important of these were the magazine bolt-action rifle, with an effective range of a thousand yards; the machine gun, perfected by Hiram Maxim in 1884; much more powerful explosives than gunpowder, beginning with Alfred Nobel's dynamite, invented in 1866; and quick-firing artillery, which could launch shells with accuracy miles from the front lines.

Even before the war opened, Moltke had altered Schlieffen's plan substantially. Of nine new divisions that became available after 1905, he allocated eight to the left wing, and only one to the right. As he put the plan into effect, he altered it even more.

The Germans sent forward thirty-four divisions in three armies (1st, 2nd, and 3rd) through Belgium to commence the wide arcing advance. Against them on the extreme left, or west, the French had only ten divisions in the 5th Army, plus the small four-division British Expeditionary Force. The German advance should have progressed with little trouble, but almost immediately Moltke began making profound blunders. He diverted seven divisions from the western wing to stand guard over Antwerp, Belgium, and Givet and Maubeuge, France, which had not surrendered, and sent another four divisions to East Prussia, to aid in stopping the Russians, though these were not needed, and not called for.

As the Germans advanced into Belgium, the French launched an offensive into Lorraine on August 14, 1914, with nineteen divisions, just as Schlieffen had anticipated. Departing radically from Schlieffen's plan, Moltke diverted six newly formed divisions to this wing, which should have gone to strengthen the western wing. He also allowed the commander on the eastern wing, Prince Rupprecht of Bavaria, to go over to the attack himself—thereby violating the entire premise upon which the

Schlieffen Plan was based, namely that the eastern wing at first should *withdraw* to lure the French into advancing.

The French forces were overwhelmed by August 20, and thrown back on their fortified barrier in the Vosges Mountains. In these positions, they easily repelled Prince Rupprecht's further attacks, and were able to send troops to reinforce the French western flank.

Now Moltke made the fatal mistake that destroyed any hope of carrying out the Schlieffen Plan. The Germans' flanking western wing was beginning to encounter substantial resistance from the British and French as it moved through northern France, and Moltke's mind-set suddenly changed completely. On August 28, 1914, he stated that the objective of the campaign "must be to advance as rapidly as possible on Paris, not to give the French army time to recover, to prevent it from forming fresh units, and to take from France as many of her means of defense as possible."[8] That is to say, Moltke at this point outlined a strategy of direct attack that was utterly at odds with the Schlieffen Plan, which was to go *around* any resistance that materialized.

He directed the 1st Army to continue to move in a southwesterly direction on a path that would lead about twenty-five miles west of Paris, but ordered the 2nd and 3rd Armies to turn southeast to the Marne River *east* of Paris. These orders alone constituted a radical departure from the plan, but Moltke foreshadowed his real intent by adding that it might be necessary to abandon the flanking maneuver altogether and wheel the 1st Army directly south if the enemy put up strong resistance on the Marne. In other words, instead of sweeping southwest of Paris and turning back, Moltke was thinking of turning the main thrust of the German army into a direct attack *east* of Paris. This would mean the French no longer would be enclosed in a trap.

Why did he do this? The answer must be that Moltke did not truly understand Schlieffen's plan. In the western sweep, as soon as he began to encounter heavy resistance from the British and French armies, he turned directly on them. What he should have done was to slip around the western flank of the British and French, and continue on southward. He forgot that the *real* aim of the Schlieffen Plan was to *avoid* battle wherever possible. Only when the Germans were on the rear of the British and French armies were they to turn back north, and drive them into a Cannae-like sack against the Franco-German frontier.

The commander of the 1st Army, General Alexander von Kluck, quickly forced the Germans into complete abandonment of the plan. Kluck had no comprehension of the true purpose of the plan, and when the commander of the 2nd Army, which was marching east of Paris, asked for assistance to help push back the French, Kluck at once complied, turning eastward on August 31. Moltke agreed to this move, and the result was that Kluck, in turning east, exposed his army's right flank. When Kluck reached the town of Meux on the Marne, twenty-five miles east of Paris, the French 6th Army attacked, on September 5. This opened the battle of the Marne, which raged for seven days, and which stopped the German advance in its tracks.

Thereafter ensued the "race to the sea" as each side tried to go around the other's western flank, finally ending on the English Channel at Nieuport, Belgium, a few miles east of the French port of Dunkirk. At the same time the defensive line extended eastward as well—becoming a continuous line of entrenchments from Switzerland to Belgium, and ending mobility on the western front. This front soon solidified into a rigid, almost impenetrable line of field fortifications backed by machine guns and massed artillery. Neither side thereafter could open enough space to reinstitute a war of movement.

Tannenberg, 1914

The Germans had committed the great bulk of their army to the western front, and had deliberately limited the forces available to oppose any Russian advance to a single army, the 8th, with 160,000 men in one cavalry and ten infantry divisions. This army, under Max von Prittwitz und Gaffron, was detailed to defend East Prussia, which extended along the Baltic Sea, bounded on two sides by Russian-held territory, Poland on the south and Lithuania on the east. The Germans very much wanted to hold East Prussia, because it occupied a special place in their history. Teutonic

Knights had conquered the region in the thirteenth century and colonized it with German settlers, and it was the site of many of the small ancestral estates of the Junkers, aristocrats whose sons had furnished the Prussian army with most of its officers for more than two centuries.

From the first days of the war, the French bombarded the Russian high command with demands that it do something quickly to relieve German pressure on the French. The Russians obligingly launched a two-pronged offensive into East Prussia on August 17, 1914, one from the east and the other from the south.

The plan was for the 200,000-man Russian 1st Army, under Pavel Rennenkampf, to advance into East Prussia on its northeastern border, drawing to it the German defending forces. Meanwhile the 250,000-man 2nd Army, under Alexander Samsonov, was to advance from the southern frontier and close upon the Germans' rear, cutting them off from retreat to the west.

This was a sensible and predictable plan that took advantage of the long German border projecting into Russian-held lands. But it suffered from two disadvantages. One was that the Russian armies were separated by the fifty-mile chain of the Masurian Lakes in the southeastern corner of East Prussia, which prevented coordination of efforts between the two armies. The other problem was that the avenue of approach from the east was limited to just forty miles, between the fortified region around the East Prussian capital of Königsberg on the north and the lakes to the south.

Along the Polish frontier to the south, there was one smaller problem: prior to the war, Russia had systematically prevented construction of adequate roads and railways close to the frontier, to form a barrier against a German invasion. These precautions now worked to the disadvantage of the Russians, whose troops had to advance through depopulated areas in deep tracks of sand.

When Rennenkampf crossed into Germany on the eastern frontier on August 17 with six infantry and five cavalry divisions, the German commander Prittwitz put into motion a defensive plan worked out by Count von Schlieffen years previously. Schlieffen had anticipated that any Russian attack on East Prussia would come from both the east and south. His plan was to strike hard with full strength at whichever

Battle of Tannenberg, August 26–31, 1914

Baltic Sea

Königsberg

Russian 1st Army
Rennenkampf

Gumbinnen

E A S T   P R U S S I A

Marienburg

German 8th Army
Prittwitz
(later Hindenburg)

Allenstein

Masurian Lakes

Tannenberg

Soldau

Russian 2nd Army
Samsonov

P O L A N D

Vistula R.

0   Miles   50

0   Kilometers   100

Warsaw

Jeffrey L. Ward

Russian army advanced first, then to turn against the other. In other words, Schlieffen was willing to commit virtually his entire strength to deliver a decisive, numbing blow against one enemy force, thus rendering it hors de combat, or out of action, so he could then turn his full attention to the other Russian force. His logic was based on experience with Russian forces, which usually moved slowly. Thus a force ignored for a few days was unlikely to cause irretrievable damage.

But Prittwitz did not possess either the imagination or the audacity of Schlieffen, and insisted on leaving a two-division corps, the 20th, on the south to guard against Samsonov. Accordingly, Prittwitz was unable to marshal sufficient strength against Rennenkampf to stop him in his tracks. Moreover, instead of scouting out the exact location of the Russian forces, and delivering a slanting blow to Rennenkampf's flanks, Prittwitz launched a headlong, frontal attack at Gumbinnen, about fifteen miles west of the frontier, on August 20. In this first major engagement of the

First World War in the east, the terrible trinity of machine guns, entrench-ments, and artillery stopped the assaulting German infantry dead—as it was subsequently to halt all other soldiers subjected to similarly insane orders from their superiors. German soldiers broke and ran to the rear.

The news from Gumbinnen set off a panic in 8th Army headquarters, particularly as Samsonov's advance guard crossed the southern frontier the same day. Prittwitz directed the entire army to retire all the way back behind the Vistula River, 160 miles west of Gumbinnen. This was a ridiculous order, and Chief of Staff Moltke realized that Prittwitz's nerve had failed him, and began searching for a replacement. He also detailed four divisions on the western wing in France to move to East Prussia—which arrived too late to be of assistance.

At least one German officer kept his wits about him. Lieutenant Colonel Max Hoffman, Prittwitz's brilliant and innovative staff officer, did not believe the situation was nearly as dire as Prittwitz pictured it. As a young captain, he had been an observer in the Russo-Japanese War of 1904–1905, and had seen the Russian generals Rennenkampf and Samsonov engage in a loud dispute on the railway platform at Mukden, Manchuria. This altercation had degenerated into actual fisticuffs, and Hoffmann was confident Rennenkampf would be in no hurry to come to the assistance of Samsonov by pressing on from Gumbinnen.

Before the troops around Gumbinnen had actually begun to move, Hoffman convinced Prittwitz to take bolder measures. One three-division corps at Gumbinnen (the 1st under Hermann K. von François) should be moved at once by railroad to the southern flank, Hoffman said, and, with the two divisions of 20th Corps already there, should attack Samsonov's left, or western, flank. Meanwhile the other two corps at Gumbinnen should march southwest by road to assist—essentially turning their back on Rennenkampf's Russian army at Gumbinnen. Prittwitz agreed, and talked no more about retreating.

On August 22, Moltke, five days after the Russian advance, wired Paul von Hindenburg, sixty-seven years old, a retired general who had fought in both the Austro-Prussian and Franco-Prussian Wars, asking whether he would take over command of 8th Army in East Prussia. The reply came: "I am ready." Hindenburg was known for steadiness of character, not brilliance of mind, and Moltke therefore hunted for a chief of staff for Hindenburg who was both brilliant and could take charge if need be. The German army put great reliance in its staff officers, who were expected to devise and, if necessary, carry out operations. He found the man he was hunting for in General Erich Ludendorff (1865–1937), who had shown great leadership and imagination in leading the successful attack on the Belgian fortress of Liège in the first days of the war.

Ludendorff drove to Koblenz, learned the situation in East Prussia from Moltke, and came to virtually the same conclusion Colonel Hoffman had reached.

Ludendorff hurried to Hanover, where he met Hindenburg, and together they traveled by special train to 8th Army headquarters at Marienburg, arriving on August 23. From the first, Ludendorff made most of the decisions, which Hindenburg ratified. At Marienburg, Ludendorff found that the movements already in progress, as formulated by Colonel Hoffman, fitted well with his own plans.

Next day it became apparent that Rennenkampf was not—as Hoffman had predicted—pursuing the retreating German forces with any urgency, and Ludendorff directed Fritz von Below's 1st Reserve Corps to accelerate its march southwest and to aim toward the right flank of Samsonov's Russian army, which was now stretched out along nearly sixty miles. By August 25, Ludendorff decided he could also use August von Mackensen's 17th Corps in this same role on the Russian right flank, leaving only a cavalry screen to watch Rennenkampf's movements.[9]

It's not clear that Ludendorff saw this yet, but the outline of a giant double envelopment of the Russian 2nd Army was emerging. It was not yet a Cannae, but if exploited, it would bring together the elements of a true caldron battle. The commander of the entire Russian northwest region, Yakov Grigorievich Jilinsky, believed the Germans actually were retreating, and demanded that Samsonov press forward rapidly so he could cut them off. But since the Germans had stopped retreating, the farther north Samsonov advanced, the deeper into a potential trap he drove his own army.

Samsonov now advanced northward two and a half corps in the center of his line. The German 20th Corps, facing them, gave way. Meanwhile, Samsonov's left wing on the west, the Russian 1st Corps and two cavalry divisions, also began moving northward. Ludendorff directed François's 1st Corps to attack this wing frontally on August 26. This straight-ahead approach casts doubt on whether Ludendorff had yet formulated the idea of an envelopment of the Russian army, and indicates rather that he was simply trying to push it back.

The order aroused the ire of François, who did not want to repeat the disastrous losses suffered at Gumbinnen. He complained that most of his artillery had not arrived, and anyway the attack should go around the *flank* of the left wing, not head-on. Ludendorff rejected his complaints, but François resisted passively by merely capturing an outlying ridge, and not committing his troops to a direct attack.

On the same day, more than fifty miles to the east, the right wing of the Russian army collided with Below's and Mackensen's corps moving southwest. The Russian right wing was able to withdraw southward.

Now the Germans were in position to execute a double envelopment. And on August 27, General von François, not Ludendorff, set it in motion. His artillery finally in place, François opened a fierce bombardment of the Russian left wing. Heavy shelling was new to soldiers in these first weeks of the war, and the Russians broke without waiting to be attacked by German infantry. At daybreak on August 28, François discovered that the entire Russian left wing had retreated back into Poland, across the southern frontier.

An astonishing opportunity now opened for the Germans. Both the Russian left and right wings had retreated, the left wing having vanished southward completely out of the fight, and the right wing having withdrawn under pressure from Below's and Mackensen's corps. Yet Samsonov ignored both these facts, and ordered the Russian center to continue advancing northward. In other words, Samsonov was paying no attention to the danger to his flanks and was making precisely the same precipitous, fatal plunge into the center of the enemy position as Terentius Varro had made at Cannae.

With the Russian left wing gone, François now had an open road to the rear of the Russian center, which he promptly took, moving to block all avenues of retreat by the Russian center. Meanwhile the Russian center made several attacks on the north but got nowhere against the defending German 20th Corps. Nevertheless, Ludendorff lost his nerve, and ordered François to press toward the immediate rear of the Russian center. Such an attack would have led through thick forests, and would have broken the iron band François was creating across the rear. Again François disregarded his orders and continued closing off the Russians' retreat roads.

Around midday, Ludendorff realized that the Russian attacks on 20th Corps had failed, and the Russians were on the verge of retreating, and told François to continue as he was already doing. By the evening of August 29, François's troops held a chain of entrenched posts at every crossroad all the way across the Russian line of retreat.

The Russians now were streaming back, becoming mixed in the forest maze that François had avoided. With the rear closed and the roads clogged with soldiers unable to get through, the Russian center dissolved into a mob of hungry, exhausted, confused men. A few beat feebly against François's barricades, but most surrendered. Samsonov realized belatedly what he had done. Instead of turning like a tiger on the danger from François advancing on his rear, and with every soldier he could find holding open the gates southward so his troops could extricate themselves, he had turned his back on the peril, and ordered most of his army to continue northward—into certain disaster. Somewhere in the forest, Samsonov separated himself a short distance from his staff, and fired a revolver shot into his head.[10]

Meanwhile the two German corps on the east—Below's and Mackensen's—failed to complete a true double envelopment of the Russian army because of mixed signals and faulty cooperation between the two. As a result, many of the Russian troops on the east escaped. Even so, 92,000 Russians surrendered, and possibly 50,000 died or were wounded. It was a brilliant victory. The battle got its name, on the suggestion of Colonel Hoffman, from the nearby village of Tannenberg, which had played no role in the battle, but was where the German Teutonic Knights had suffered a historic rout at the hands of Poles and Lithuanians in 1410. Calling it thus wiped out in German minds the stain of that earlier defeat.

Ludendorff immediately turned against Rennenkampf and forced him to retreat back into Lithuania. These victories set conditions for a later German advance into Russia. The battle of Tannenberg had not been conceived in advance and executed by deft hands. Instead, it had been constructed day by day, almost minute by minute, and relied for its tremendous success, in the end, on the failure of perception of the Russian commander. Even so, it is one of the great examples in history of a caldron battle.

Attack on the Soviet Union, 1941

Except in Germany, the idea of caldron battles fell out of favor after World War I. To most observers the Tannenberg campaign seemed an aberration, due more to poor Russian leadership and ill-trained troops than to a spectacular German double envelopment. Likewise, most non-German leaders believed the Schlieffen Plan had failed because the concept was unworkable. Few understood that Helmuth von Moltke had fatally undermined it.

By the end of the first year of World War II, the idea of caldron battles seemed to be completely passé because the Germans won the first two campaigns, against Poland in 1939 and the West in 1940, by means of *blitzkrieg*, or "lightning war." Its essence was a new element in warfare, panzer, or armored divisions, and its process was to concentrate panzers at one point, force a breakthrough, roll up and secure the flanks on either side, and then penetrate like lightning far into the enemy rear before he had time to react. Since *blitzkrieg*'s principal element was a deep penetration through a narrow gap punched into the enemy's line, its aim was to paralyze the enemy's ability to respond and to gain decisive objectives far inside the enemy's rear.

For many military leaders, the great armored breakthroughs, and the fluid war of movement which panzers made possible, seemed to usher in a new way of winning wars. Nothing apparently was able to stop tanks. Yet while British, American, and Soviet armies attempted to copy the

German panzer divisions, astute German leaders knew armored divisions were only a tool, and *blitzkrieg* only a method.

None of the Germans' stunning actions in Poland or in the West truly invalidated any of the rules of war. The senior German generals knew their country could not rely on tanks alone to win. Indeed, when Adolf Hitler insisted on invading the Soviet Union with 3 million men and 3,350 tanks on June 22, 1941 (Operation Barbarossa), the command planned not *blitzkrieg*, but a series of *Kesselschlachten*, or caldron battles, to defeat the Soviet army, which was one and a half times larger than the German forces.[11]

Their reasoning was that, in the vast spaces of the Soviet Union, caldron battles had the potential of achieving a decision, whereas a panzer breakthrough alone might penetrate for hundreds of miles, strike no hard enemy resistance, and be nothing but a modern-day cavalry raid, spectacular but serving no purpose. On the other hand, if the tanks in cooperation with mobile infantry encircled and destroyed a large concentration of enemy troops, on the order of Tannenberg, enemy strength would be drastically reduced. After one caldron was eliminated, the Germans could move on to encircle another concentration. This could continue, in theory, until the entire Soviet army was encircled and destroyed, one caldron at a time.

The potential for caldron-battle victories was greatly enhanced by the fact that the Soviet dictator, Joseph Stalin, lined up practically the entire Soviet army along the western frontier, leaving few reserves back in the rear that could strike at any German penetrations.

Hitler, however, demanded that his army advance in three widely different directions in the first weeks of the campaign—toward Leningrad on the north, Moscow in the center, and the Ukraine in the south. Once the drive toward Moscow had reached Smolensk, about 230 miles west of Moscow, Hitler called for a shift of the armor north to capture Leningrad, then a return of the armor to press on Moscow, while Army Group South continued to drive into Ukraine, over 700 miles from the German-Soviet frontier.

Hitler came up with this bizarre plan because he realized Germany did not have the strength to conquer the Soviet Union all at once. He hoped to solve the problem by committing two of his panzer groups, under Heinz Guderian and Hermann Hoth, to Army Group Center, commanded by Fedor von Bock, to destroy Red Army forces in front of Moscow. Army Group Center was to attack just north of the Pripet Marshes, a huge swampy region 220 miles wide and 120 miles deep, beginning about 170 miles east of Warsaw, that effectively divided the front in half. Led by panzers, Bock's armies were to advance from East Prussia and the German-Russian frontier along the Bug River to Smolensk, 400 miles into the Soviet Union.

Meanwhile, Army Group North under Wilhelm von Leeb, with one panzer group under Erich Hoepner, was to drive from East Prussia through the Baltic states toward Leningrad (St. Petersburg). Gerd von Rundstedt's Army Group South, with the last panzer group, under Ewald von Kleist, was to thrust south of the Pripet Marshes toward the Ukrainian capital of Kiev, 300 air-line miles from the starting points along and below the Bug, then drive on to the Donetz River basin, a huge industrial region 430 miles southeast of Kiev.

The first great encirclement was to be in Army Group Center around Bialystok, about sixty miles east of the German-Soviet boundary in Poland, the second around Minsk, 180 miles farther east. The two panzer groups were then to press on to Smolensk, 200 miles beyond Minsk, and there bring about a third *Kesselschlacht*. After that, Hitler planned to shift the two panzer groups north to help capture Leningrad. Only after Leningrad was seized, according to Hitler's directive, were the panzer groups to come back to the center and drive on Moscow. While all this was going on, Rundstedt's Army Group South was supposedly driving for the Donetz basin.

This was an impossible task. Hitler expected to conquer a million square miles of the Soviet Union in the first year. That's a region as large as the United States east of the Mississippi. The Russian invasion was completely out of scale with the war in the west in 1940, yet Hitler had no more troops and no more tanks. In the west the campaign had been fought in an area of 50,000 square miles, roughly the size of North Carolina or New York State. Thus the ratio of space to men was twenty times greater in the east than in the west.

German Attack on the Soviet Union, 1941

SWEDEN

FINLAND

Lake Onega

Finnish advance

Finnish advance

Helsinki ★

Aaland Islands

Baltic Sea

Gulf of Finland

Lake Lagoda

Svir R.

Volkhov ●

Tikvin ●

Leningrad

Volkhov R.

Tallinn ●

ESTONIA

Lake Peipus

Novgorod ●

Lake Ilmen

Northwest Front

Tartu ●

Pskov ●

Staraya-Russa ●

Sea of Moscow (reservoir)

Moscow-Volga Canal

Ventspils ●

Velikaya R.

Ostrov ●

Kholm ●

Loval R.

Ostashkov ●

Kalinin ●

Volga R.

Dmitrov ●

Liepaja ●

★ Riga

Dvina R.

LATVIA

Velikiye Luki ●

Krasnaya Polyana ●

ARMY GROUP NORTH (LEEB)

Siauliai ●

LITHUANIA

Polotsk ●

Velizh ●

Rzhev

Borodino ●

Mozhaisk ●

● **Moscow**

18th Army

Vilna ★

Vitebsk ●

Yartsevo ●

Vyazma ●

Yukhnov ●

Kashira

16TH ARMY Panzer Group 4

Barisov ●

Smolensk ●

Kaluga ●

West Front

9TH ARMY Panzer Group 3

Minsk

Mogilev ●

Klintsy ●

Roslavl ●

Tula ●

EAST PRUSSIA

Bialystok ●

Bobyrusk ●

Berezina R.

Novozybkov ●

Dnieper R.

Bryansk ●

ARMY GROUP CENTER (BOCK)

Gomel ●

Orel ●

4TH ARMY Panzer Group 2

● Pinsk

Pripet R.

Rechitsa ●

Starodub ●

Warsaw ★

Brest-Litovsk ●

Novgorod Severskiy ●

Sostka ●

Southwest Front

Kovel ●

Pripet Marshes

Desna R.

POLAND

Rovno ●

Zhitomir ●

Kiev ●

Lebedin ●

6TH ARMY Panzer Group 1

Ostrog ●

Berdichev ●

Poltava ●

Kharkov ●

17th Army

● Lvov

Ternopol ●

Vinnitsa ●

Cherkassy ●

Kremenchug ●

Donetz R.

SLOVAKIA

Chernigov ●

Karmenets-Podolskiy ●

Uman ●

Dnieper R.

Dnepropetrovsk ●

ARMY GROUP SOUTH (RUNDSTEDT)

HUNGARIAN CORPS

ROMANIAN 3RD ARMY

Pervomaysk ●

17TH ARMY

Zaporozhye ●

HUNGARY

11TH ARMY

Pruth R.

11TH ARMY

Nikolayev ●

ROMANIAN 4TH ARMY

Odessa

October 16, 1941

Sea of Azov

Danube R.

ROMANIA

CRIMEA

Sevastopol ●

Black Sea

Jeffrey L. Ward

– –	Positions on June 21, 1941
- - -	German advance to September 30, 1941
- - - -	German front of December 31, 1941
······	German front of January 31, 1942
◯	Caldron battles

0   Miles   200

0   Kilometers   200   400

Nevertheless, the German invasion of the Soviet Union was the greatest offensive campaign in world history. And it achieved astonishing early victories almost *entirely* because the German military leadership had decided to seek caldron battles. Indeed, the caldron battles in Russia in the summer and fall of 1941 gained the largest haul of prisoners of any encirclements ever achieved in any war.

On June 22, 1941, German panzers broke across the frontier and drove deep into the interior. They achieved almost immediate success everywhere except in the south, where German infantry struck strong defenses west of Lvov (Lemberg) and on the Styr River.

Stalin had erroneously calculated that the Germans would make their major bid into the Ukraine, and had concentrated his largest forces there, including most of his new T-34 tanks. This vehicle was the most successful armored weapon to appear in World War II. It had thicker armor than the German main battle tanks, slightly higher speed, and a better gun, a 76-mm high-velocity piece. Russians mounted strong armored strikes out of the Pripet Marshes on the north, but could not connect with other Russians on the open steppe to the south. The fight in the south was rough, but the two arms of the Soviet pincers never met, and Kleist's panzer group drove on to seize Lvov on June 30, and from there swept past Rovno and Ostrog through the "Zhitomir corridor" toward Kiev.

But in the center the German advances were spectacular. Guderian's Panzer Group 2 plunged across the Bug River at Brest-Litovsk, and Hoth's Panzer Group 3 drove out of East Prussia toward Minsk, 215 miles northeast of Brest-Litovsk. As the panzers moved east, they enveloped both sides of the Russian forces around Bialystok. Field Marshal von Bock ordered his infantry 4th and 9th Armies to encircle these bypassed Russians (twelve divisions) east of Bialystok. The first great *Kesselschlacht* began to develop.

By June 28, Guderian's panzers had reached Bobruysk on the Beresina River, 170 miles northeast of Brest-Litovsk, while Hoth's tanks had seized Minsk, eighty miles northeast of Bobruysk, thereby nearly closing off fifteen Russian divisions in another caldron west of Minsk.

The Germans learned they could outmaneuver the Russians with their *Schnellentruppen*, or fast troops, as they called their panzers and the motorized infantry divisions that followed close behind the tanks. But the Russians resisted stoutly everywhere. In the caldron battles at Bialystok and Minsk the Russians took advantage of the fact that the German panzers had moved on, and German infantry had to close the circles. In the chaos that ensued, many Russians were able to escape in small groups, while those who remained fought doggedly on, though without making strong efforts to break out. This was in part because the Germans finally threw strong rings of infantry and artillery around them. The Russians had few vehicles and thus few means of escape, and the Soviet commanders, fearful they would be shot as traitors if they ordered withdrawal, demanded fights to the finish.

Battles to the bitter end seldom occurred, however. Most of the Russians caught up in caldrons surrendered when they realized they could not get out, assuming they would be treated as ordinary prisoners of war. This accounts for the enormous numbers of Soviet troops captured in the first months of the war. The Soviets did not know at this time that Hitler had specifically ordered German soldiers to treat all the Soviet people with extreme brutality and inhumanity. Prior to the invasion, Hitler issued the notorious "commissar order," which called for immediate shooting of Communist party agents in the Red Army. He also limited courts-martial against German soldiers for violence they perpetrated against Russian civilians or soldiers. Since any Russian could be labeled a "commissar" or a "partisan," or guerrilla, German soldiers had virtually free rein to shoot anyone they pleased—and did so in great numbers.

In addition, Hitler sent in *Einsatzgruppen*, or extermination detachments, just behind the field armies, to hunt down and murder Jews. Finally he resolved to deport millions of Slavs or allow them to starve in order to empty the land for German settlers. These monstrous acts became generally known only afterward. Many millions of Soviet troops who surrendered in the first months of the war subsequently died from murder, starvation, or exposure.

In the caldron battles around Bialystok and Minsk, the Germans captured 233,000 Soviet troops, while Guderian's and Hoth's panzer groups rushed on 200 miles beyond Minsk for the third great series of encirclements near Smolensk. Since Army Group Center's infantry divisions were still miles behind the panzers, Guderian and Hoth wrapped their tanks and motorized divisions around three separate caldrons, two smaller ones east of Mogilev and west of Nevel, a greater one between Orscha and Smolensk. After grim resistance, the Germans shattered three Soviet armies, and by August 6 had taken 310,000 POWs. Nevertheless, about 200,000 Russians escaped to fall back and continue to block the road to Moscow.

In the other two army groups, advances had been astonishing as well. In Army Group South, Kleist's Panzer Group 1, with the help of 17th Army and a Hungarian corps, encircled two Russian groups around Uman, 120 miles south of Kiev, capturing 103,000 troops. In Army Group North, the Soviet troops withdrew northward toward Leningrad and avoided any great encirclement, but Leeb's army group seized the Baltic states, and threatened Leningrad.

Because Stalin had made the colossal error of lining most of his forces directly along the frontier, where they were largely overrun or captured in encirclements, the Germans were within sight of victory—despite the immensely overambitious objectives that Hitler had given them.

On the road to Moscow, especially, a stunning opportunity had materialized. Guderian's and Hoth's tanks had advanced 440 miles in six weeks, and were only 220 miles from Moscow. Dry weather was certain to continue till autumn. Although tank strength had fallen to half that at the start, there was every reason to believe the remaining German armor could reach the capital, the heart of the Soviet state.

Since Moscow was European Russia's railroad hub, possession of it could separate the Soviets on the north, near Leningrad, from those in the south, in the Ukraine and the Caucasus, the location of most of the Soviet oil fields. From this central position the Germans could turn to destroy troops in one sector, then in the other. It was a recipe for victory, and strategically was the one move that offered the possibility of success in 1941. It could negate Hitler's original mistake in trying to seize all of western Russia in a single year's campaigning.

But Adolf Hitler did not think in logical terms, and did not possess even the most elementary concept of strategy. He decided on a course of action that was ruinous to his interests and brought about his own destruction.

On July 19, 1941, less than a month after the start of the invasion, Hitler turned the campaign in a completely different direction, and thereby lost the one chance that the caldron battles had given him to seize Moscow. Ignoring the virtually open road to the capital, Hitler issued a directive ordering Hoth's panzer group to turn north to assist Leeb's advance on Leningrad, and Guderian's panzer group to turn south and help Rundstedt's army group bring about another caldron battle east of Kiev.

Army commander Walter von Brauchitsch, army chief of staff Franz Halder, and Guderian all were horrified at Hitler's directive, and managed to delay it until a conference with him on August 4. They told Hitler that continuing the advance on Moscow was vital. But he paid no attention. He was obsessed with seizing Leningrad, because this was the birthplace of Russian Communism, and he wanted the food and raw materials of the Ukraine. Yet the generals knew it was manifestly impossible to achieve all these goals in 1941 because the effort would divide Germany's limited resources in three separate directions. Their pleas made no impression on Hitler, who could conceive of no great strategic plan, and, once embroiled in a campaign, was ready to toss aside his earlier intentions to seize an opportunity that appeared.

The diversion of Hoth's panzer group to the north was foolish, for Leningrad strategically was of little importance. Hoth was unable to break through a steel band the Russians forged around the city, but wasted a month in the effort.

The attack on Kiev was a far worse blunder. It is one of the great examples in history of how a commander can be deceived by a short-term gain into abandoning a course of action that could bring victory. Kiev offered a tempting target. When Army Group South seized Dnepropetrovsk on the bend of the Dnieper River, 250 miles southeast of Kiev, Stalin ordered defense of Kiev at all costs, and sent three additional armies to reinforce the Southwestern Front under General Mikhail Kirponos and Marshal Seymon Budenny.

The situation was now set for a giant envelopment, for Guderian's panzer group was at Starodub, far to the east and north of Kiev. If Kleist's panzer group at the Dnieper bend advanced north, while

Guderian drove south, they could close off the region around Kiev. This was the opportunity that Hitler had seen, and this prospect pulled him away from the attack on Moscow.

On August 25, Guderian's panzers struck south from Starodub, and seized a bridge over the Desna River, sixty miles south, before the Russians could destroy it. But the Soviets resisted heavily along the river for a week before he at last broke out and continued onward. Meanwhile, Kleist's Panzer Group 1 moved from Dnepropetrovsk to the more westerly crossing of the Dnieper at Kremenchug, and launched his arm of the pincers on September 12.

By this time the Soviets were beginning to realize their danger. But they could do little to stop either panzer drive. Budenny sent a general to Moscow, asking permission to retreat. But Stalin told him to hold at any price, and replaced Budenny with Semen Timoshenko. The Southwestern Front therefore was left in a hopeless position. On September 14–15 the points of the German panzer columns came together at Lokhvitsa, 125 miles east of Kiev. The caldron was closed.

When Timoshenko arrived, he recognized the terrible danger the Russians faced, and ordered withdrawal on his own on September 16. But Kirponos, the tactical chief, could not bring himself to defy Stalin, and spent two days in a futile effort to get approval. By then the Germans had formed a powerful ring around the Russian armies, and tore them apart as they tried to break out. Kirponos died in the fighting. By September 19, when the Germans seized the city of Kiev itself, Russian resistance had virtually ended. More than 665,000 Russians went into German POW cages, the largest single military success in history and the largest haul of prisoners ever attained in a single battle.

But this seeming great victory was only an illusion, for, in achieving it, Hitler had lost his chance to capture Moscow, and win the war. By the time Guderian's and Hoth's panzer forces got back on the road to Moscow, supported by most of Hoepner's panzer group, the autumn rainy season had arrived, a period of mud called *Rasputitsa* (literally "time without roads"), which would slow or stop vehicles and the advance. After that would come the Russian winter.

Hitler ordered a new attack on Moscow on September 30. It succeeded well for the first month. Guderian advanced to Orel, only eighty miles south of Moscow, arriving so rapidly the streetcars were still running, and evacuations of factories were still under way. Once more the Russian habit of lining up troops against the Germans permitted panzers to break through at selected points and surround great bodies of troops. Guderian turned on Bryansk, 250 miles southwest of Moscow, and, with the help of Hoepner's Panzer Group 4 on the north, trapped thousands of Russians in yet another caldron. The German 4th and 9th Armies and Hoth's panzer group formed an additional caldron west of Vyazma, only 135 miles west of Moscow. By October 20, resistance in both caldrons ceased. The Germans counted 650,000 prisoners altogether, almost as many as were taken in the Kiev caldron.

But now atrocious weather descended on the battlefront. Heavy rains fell. As Guderian wrote, "The roads rapidly became nothing but canals of bottomless mud, along which our vehicles could advance at a snail's pace and with great wear to the engines."[12]

Despite the enormous losses the Soviets had suffered, Joseph Stalin found enough manpower to assemble more huge forces to stop the Germans. His spy in Tokyo, Richard Sorge, informed him on October 5 that Japan would soon attack the United States. This meant there was no chance the Japanese would drive into Siberia, and the large forces there no longer were needed. Stalin ordered twelve divisions with 1,700 tanks and 1,500 aircraft (altogether 250,000 men) to come west to the defense of Moscow.

Weather began to improve on November 2, 1941, when a frost hardened the mud. The Germans launched their final offensive on November 15. It has gone down in the annals of the German army as *"die Flucht nach vorn"* or "the flight to the front," the frantic attempt to get to shelter in Moscow before the onset of winter.

Panzer units gained a bridgehead across a canal at Dmitrov, about twenty-five miles north of Moscow, and one division came within eighteen miles of the city at Krasnaya Polyana. Guderian went around toughly defended Tula and approached Kashira, about fifty miles south of

Moscow. A legend endures that an advanced German patrol saw the towers of the Kremlin. If so, a view was all they got. Strong Soviet resistance and bitter cold halted the German offensive. Temperatures fell to minus 20 degrees Celsius, then further. The Germans had no winter clothing (fur caps, parkas, felt boots, snow hoods). The number of frostbite cases rose to 228,000. Tanks, machine weapons, and radios failed. Locomotive boilers burst.

Over the next fourteen days the offensive collapsed. The new commander defending Moscow, Georgy Zhukov, went over to the offensive on December 5, using three new armies that had been forming east of the Volga, as well as the troops arriving from Siberia. The Germans were at the end of their tether, and they recoiled backward. In horrible weather around Christmas 1941 and the early days of 1942, they finally stopped the Soviet offensive, both sides collapsing in exhaustion. By spring 1942 the Germans were about 150 miles west of Moscow, and never made another effort to seize the city.

The great caldron battles of 1941 had achieved tremendous successes. But Barbarossa had failed because Hitler tried to do too much with too few resources. It's ironic that the greatest caldron battle victory of all time, at Kiev, did more than any other thing to bring about Hitler's defeat. If the strength diverted to this battle had been expended on a drive to Moscow instead, the Soviet capital almost certainly would have been captured before the onset of winter.

Because of his failures, Hitler had lost the war. There was now no hope for anything better than a negotiated peace. And this Hitler refused to consider.

Implications for the Future

Vast sweeps of mechanized armies forming huge caldrons containing hundreds of thousands of men, as occurred in Russia in the summer and fall of 1941, have passed into history. But the ancient, original, small-scale version of caldron battles, encircling an enemy village or an isolated detachment and destroying it, offers tremendous scope for future war.

This was primarily how Taliban and Al Qaeda forces were destroyed in Afghanistan in the fall of 2001: American special forces teams allied with friendly local Afghan elements surrounded a Taliban or Al Qaeda strong point or cave complex, cut off avenues of retreat, and methodically reduced the position by air strikes, followed, in some cases, by ground action. This scenario was repeated all across Afghanistan, and shows how the concept of swarming, or all-around assault on an enemy element, can be implemented.

In the future it's likely—since main lines of resistance no longer will exist, nor large bodies of troops be deployed—that the primary job of reconnaissance, whether by satellites, unmanned aerial vehicles (UAVs), helicopters, or on the ground, will be to locate individual enemy elements. Once a particular element is pinpointed, it can be eliminated by the quickest and least expensive method. Sometimes this will be done by air strikes alone, or, as was necessary with the Taliban and Al Qaeda holed up in cave complexes, by a combination of air and ground action.

This kind of operation employs the caldron rule and is a modern version of guerrilla tactics. For the essential nature of guerrilla warfare is to locate and isolate an enemy element and then to destroy it with overwhelming strength. Guerrillas may be vastly weaker overall, but they can be extremely effective if—by good reconnaissance and wise deployment—they can concentrate a locally superior force against a locally weaker enemy.

13

Uproar East, Attack West

THE SENTENCE THAT best epitomizes the teachings of Sun Tzu, the great Chinese strategist from the fifth century B.C., is his admonition to "make an uproar in the east, but attack in the west." This prescription succinctly states another rule of warfare: induce the enemy to believe a blow is coming at one place, but actually deliver it at another.

This advice may seem self-evident. Surely any commander knows that all warfare is based on deception, and would never strike where the enemy expects. Yet the history of warfare shows that this simple rule has been followed a good deal less often than it should be. As we have seen in previous accounts, commanders over the centuries have frequently been mesmerized by the apparent vulnerability, or at least the accessibility, of an enemy directly in front of them, and have ordered frontal attacks, usually resulting in defeat and sometimes disaster.

The American Civil War is replete with cases of commanders doing just that, despite growing experience that frontal attacks were ineffective. In fact, five out of six direct attacks in the war failed. Commanders knew what the results of their frontal attacks were going to be, but few could think of alternatives. The most notorious example, of course, is Robert E. Lee's insistence on Pickett's Charge, in which 13,500 Confederates attacked directly into the massed rifles and guns of Union forces on Cemetery Ridge on the third day of the battle of Gettysburg in

July 1863. This attack killed or wounded nearly half the attackers in half an hour. But there were hundreds of other examples by commanders on both sides.

Hopeless frontal assaults into impregnable defenses reached their ultimate madness in World War I, in the opening stages of which the French, adhering to their misguided concept of *offensive à outrance*, or all-out attack, shattered nineteen divisions in direct assaults against machine guns and rapid-firing cannons, weapons vastly more deadly than those in the Civil War. But the worst and most flagrant case of official blindness occurred on the Somme River. There the British lost 60,000 men, 19,000 of them dead, in a single day of frontal attacks on July 1, 1916. Even these appalling losses did not stop the British generals. They continued hopeless assaults across no-man's-land until November 13, 1916. By that time the British had lost 420,000 men. All they gained was eight miles of shattered landscape. They made no breakthrough, and changed neither the strategic nor the tactical situation one iota.

The behavior of commanders in the American Civil War and the First World War was extreme, but not unique. Their failure emphasizes the need for armies and nations to find creative approaches to battle situations. The rule of uproar east, attack west is one of the best a commander facing the terrible prospect of a frontal assault has in his arsenal. The rule prescribes a solid, coherent, understandable doctrine to avoid maximum danger. This maxim will have much utility in future warfare. It is a method to reduce the effect of the extreme lethality of modern weapons, because an enemy expecting an attack at one place will concentrate his arms there, not where the blow actually is delivered.

Hydaspes River, 326 B.C.

Alexander the Great used the rule in a campaign he carried out along the Hydaspes (Jhelum) River in the Punjab region of present-day Pakistan. This remains one of the most brilliant military operations in world history. After invading the Persian Empire with his Macedonian army,

Alexander won three great victories over his opponents: at Granicus in 334 B.C., at Issus in 333 B.C., and at Arbela in 331 B.C.

The last of these victories, over the Persian king Darius in Mesopotamia, delivered most of the empire to Alexander, but he spent the next four years winning the untamed and often lawless regions to the east in present-day Afghanistan and along the Oxus (Amu Darya) and Jaxartes (Syr Darya) rivers, east of the Aral Sea. The battles Alexander fought there had a bizarre resemblance to the battles Americans fought in the same part of the world in 2001 and 2002 against the Taliban and Al Qaeda terrorists. In both cases they were waged against forces who drew themselves up into out-of-the-way, more defendable places, struck guerrilla-like blows from ambush, and usually had to be rooted out one small group at a time.

Finally, in 326 B.C., Alexander advanced into India. His army marched steadily past Kabul and Jalalabad, through the Khyber Pass, into and out of Peshawar and Attock on the Indus River, and arrived at Taxila, about twenty miles west of present-day Islamabad. At Taxila he stopped to survey the territory. Like the other ancients, Alexander believed the only land on earth consisted of Europe, Africa to Ethiopia, and Asia to India, which he thought was a small peninsula. Around all this land the Ocean Stream flowed. Thus Alexander expected, once he reached the ocean lapping the last projection of India, he would have conquered all the inhabited parts of the world. Then, and only then, Alexander reasoned, would he come to the end of his empire.

At Taxila, Alexander learned that an Indian kingdom ruled by a king named Porus existed in the northern Punjab between the Hydaspes River on the west and the Acesines River on the east (both upper branches of the Indus River system), and that Porus had massed an army at Haranpur on the Hydaspes, about 110 miles southeast of Taxila, to oppose Alexander's passage.

Alexander marched for Haranpur to challenge Porus. When he reached the city, he encountered a broad river about half a mile wide, with Porus's army drawn up on the eastern bank. Porus had about 5,600 cavalry, 40,000 infantry, 300 chariots, and 200 elephants. Chariots, drawn by horses, were an obsolete weapon because cavalry could ride around them and foot soldiers could strike at horse and driver with javelins. Elephants were another matter, because horses were terrified of their trumpeting and they could trample infantry if driven into them. Alexander's army was no larger than Porus's, since he had to leave large garrisons in his rear. He had no chariots or elephants, but he did have more cavalry.

Alexander found that all the fords of the river were covered by pickets or sentries with elephants. He knew his horses could neither be swum nor rafted across, because the elephants would make them frantic and uncontrollable, so he had to devise another way of getting across the river, and began constructing a series of strategems to achieve his aim.

First he divided his army into a number of columns, marching them up and down the river, hoping to find an unguarded ford. But Porus marched his elephants to keep up with the columns and block any attempted crossing. The elephants tired of the exertion, however, and Porus pulled them back, posting sentries along the river to report any enemy movement.

Next, because the summer monsoon was now commencing, Alexander ordered grain brought in from all quarters to his camp so that Porus would believe Alexander had resolved to wait for dry weather. Meanwhile he reconnoitered the river to find a suitable crossing place beyond the range of Porus and his elephants. He found it at the settlement of Jalalpur, about seventeen miles upstream (east-northeast) where a headland, or promontory, rose about 1,100 feet above the river opposite a thickly wooded, six-mile-long island. Here he could assemble troops out of view of sentries across the river, and could cross before they could bring reinforcements.

Now Alexander put in motion the "uproar" part of his strategy, in order to focus Porus's attention on the place he was *not* going to strike. He ordered sentries all along the stream to raise a din and keep fires burning, indicating a possible river assault at a number of different places. He left his general Craterus at Haranpur with 3,000 cavalry and 8,000 infantry, and directed him to make dangerous-looking preparations to cross. Sure enough, all these actions caused Porus to believe an attack was coming at or near Haranpur, and he kept his army massed there.

Meanwhile, staying away from the river so as not to be observed, Alexander marched part of his striking force, 5,000 cavalry and 10,000 infantry, to Jalalpur. He posted a second part of the striking force, 500 cavalry and 5,000 infantry, about halfway between Haranpur and Jalalpur. Marching the whole force to Jalalpur would have made it easier to detect, while posting the smaller force nearer Haranpur kept Porus's attention focused there. Alexander's aim was to cross the river at Jalalpur and descend on Porus's right, or northern, flank.

At Jalalpur, in a violent rainstorm, with the infantry in boats, and the cavalry on rafts drawing the horses on lines in the water behind,[1] the first of Alexander's striking force set out to cross the river. The Indian scouts spotted the fleet, and galloped off to alert Porus. The first striking force reached the eastern shore against no opposition, and marched south toward Porus's flank, dislodging the Indian sentries along the bank, and opening a way for the second striking force to cross over and join the first force.

As soon as Porus learned from the scouts of Alexander's move, he realized he was in a perilous position. If he kept his army at Haranpur, Alexander could attack his northern flank or his rear. If he moved against Alexander with his whole force, Craterus could cross the river at Haranpur and attack his rear. If he divided his force, one part to challenge Alexander, the other to defend against Craterus, he would not be strong enough against either to be likely to win.

Perhaps hoping that Alexander's force was merely a small raiding party, Porus sent forward only 2,000 cavalry and 120 chariots, commanded by one of his sons. When this force came up, Alexander scattered it easily, killing 400 horsemen, including Porus's son, and driving the chariots into clay along the river, immobilizing them.

When Porus got news of the disaster, he knew he faced his most formidable challenge to the north. Leaving a fraction of his army at Haranpur, he marched to meet Alexander with the remainder of his cavalry, 3,600 men, 30,000 infantry, and 200 elephants.

But Porus now was in a hopeless position. By focusing Porus's attention with an uproar at Haranpur, Alexander had nullified Porus's tactical advantages of a easily defended stream and elephants who could stop horses with their trumpeting. Furthermore, Alexander was now descending on Porus's flank with a major force, which Porus was compelled to challenge, and which required him to weaken his defenses at Haranpur, thereby opening a way for Craterus to force passage across the river at Haranpur. This Craterus promptly did.

Porus's effort to stop Alexander was a desperate and fruitless attempt to remedy a strategic dislocation that had already left him defeated. By good generalship, Alexander won the tactical engagement against Porus, sent the Indian army into panicked retreat, and captured Porus. But even if Alexander had not won this battle, Porus would still have lost, for Craterus was coming up on his rear. Between Craterus and Alexander, Porus would surely have been crushed.

Alexander went on into India for some distance after the battle of the Hydaspes, but not for long. His soldiers, exhausted after having marched halfway through Asia for eight years—and after finding no ocean as they trudged across the great dusty Ganges plain of northern India—at last called a halt. They wanted to see their families again. Alexander turned back, conquered not by distance or by enemy armies, but by the longing for home.

Quebec, 1759

The battle of the Hydaspes represents a perfect execution of the rule of uproar east, attack west. Another creative use of the rule was in 1759 in the French and Indian War, when a thirty-two-year-old English major general, James Wolfe, applied the Hydaspes model at Quebec. Though he died in the battle that culminated the campaign, he evicted France from Canada, and secured Britain's undisputed control of North America. Wolfe's capture of Quebec produced the political circumstances in which the United States of America emerged and the Dominion of Canada was formed, and was therefore one of the most momentous battles in world history.

All the evidence handed down to us about Alexander indicates that at the Hydapses he conceived on the spot and apparently without great reflection his brilliant application of the rule. While Alexander's mind saw the solution at once, Wolfe by contrast devised his plan over time. The course of Wolfe's thinking as his plan evolved can be reconstructed, and offers an excellent view of how a momentous military decision is made.

The French and Indian War was the American part of the Seven Years War (1756–1763), which broke out in Europe primarily as an attempt by Austria to regain Silesia, an Austrian province that Frederick the Great of Prussia had seized and held on to doggedly through the War of the Austrian Succession (1740–1748). In 1756, launching a war against Prussia, Austria sought military help from France, and promised to give France the Austrian Netherlands (Belgium) plus other territories in Germany in return. Such extensive transfer of territory would have greatly upset the balance of power in Europe, however, and Britain therefore determined to give financial aid to Prussia. Britain also embarked on a maritime campaign to deprive France of its most important overseas colonies, especially those in Canada and India.[2]

Britain had already clashed with France in North America before the war started, trying to drive the French out of the Ohio River valley by seizing Fort Duquesne (the site of present-day Pittsburgh) in 1755. The effort failed when a party of French and their Indian allies massacred most of a small British army and killed its commander, Edward Braddock, on the Monongahela River. George Washington helped to lead the remnants of the British force back to Virginia. Another British expedition, under John Forbes, assisted by a Virginia regiment commanded by Washington, advanced on Fort Duquesne in 1758. Rather than allow the fort to be captured, the French blew it up and withdrew from the Ohio valley.

The same year a British expedition seized the large French fortress and naval base of Louisbourg on Cape Breton Island, north of Nova Scotia. In the fighting a young brigadier general, James Wolfe, distinguished himself.

The remaining major French positions in North America were Fort Ticonderoga, on Lake Champlain, and the city and fortress of Quebec, on the St. Lawrence River. A combined British and colonial force under Jeffrey Amherst captured Ticonderoga in July 1759, and in June 1759 an 8,500-man expedition in 170 ships under James Wolfe departed Louisbourg to attack Quebec.

This almost impregnable fortress—located on a high, rocky headland above the tidal estuary of the St. Lawrence River on the south and the St. Charles River on the east—was by far the most important French position in North America. It barred access to the upper St. Lawrence and gave the French control of the Great Lakes and the vast hinterland beyond. The fortress was defended by 14,000 French troops and some Indians, under Marquis Louis-Joseph de Montcalm. Strengthening this French force were three French frigates and fifteen supply ships that hurried up the St. Lawrence to Quebec ahead of the British. With them was Louis-Antoine de Bougainville, an aide to Montcalm,[3] who brought an intercepted letter from the British general Amherst that outlined the whole British plan.

Montcalm knew he occupied an extremely strong position, and also knew the British could remain only until October at the latest, when gales and fog would compel the fleet to withdraw, and with it Wolfe's army. Accordingly, he sent his ships upstream to be out of harm's way, and decided to stay on the defensive, and wait out the British.

On June 26, 1759, the British expedition arrived and the next day occupied the Isle of Orleans, four miles downstream from Quebec. As he reconnoitered, Wolfe discovered the formidable task the fortress presented. Along the most accessible avenues of attack, for eight miles on the north bank of the St. Lawrence from the St. Charles to the Montmorency rivers, Montcalm had posted most of his army behind well-built entrenchments. To attack here would be deadly. To the west, or upstream, for miles Wolfe could discern no clear place to attack because high cliffs rose straight from the water's edge.

Wolfe decided his best bet was to lure Montcalm out of his defenses. He was confident his troops, which were far superior to the French in discipline and training, would win in a head-to-head encounter. Hoping for a quick engagement, Wolfe seized Point Lévis on the south bank of the river opposite Quebec, unloaded cannons, and began a systematic bombardment of the city. Although most of the lower town was destroyed, Montcalm would not be drawn out.

Still hoping to induce him to attack, Wolfe landed about two-thirds of his army on the north shore of the St. Lawrence just east of the city. But

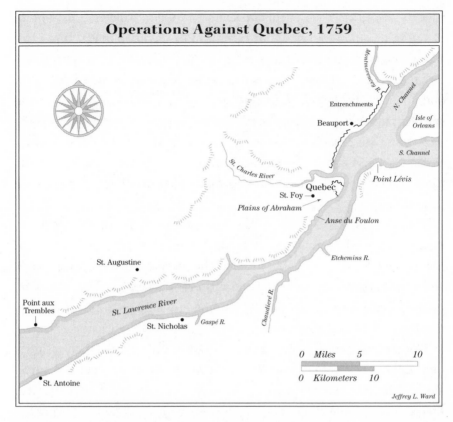

Operations Against Quebec, 1759

again Montcalm declined to move, and Wolfe turned to yet another ploy. On the night of July 18 he slipped a frigate and some smaller vessels past the guns of Quebec under cover of a bombardment from the cannons at Point Lévis, and anchored them upstream from the city.

This at last forced Montcalm to detach 600 men to guard the few foot-paths up the cliffs west of the city. But again Wolfe was foiled. All the paths up from the river were guarded by sentries, who could summon strong forces to block any attempt by Wolfe to scale the cliffs and attack. He could not embark even farther upriver, because that would allow Montcalm time to occupy fresh lines of entrenchments, and—most important—Wolfe's army then would be separated from the main part of his fleet and his base at the Isle of Orleans. His line of supply and communications could be cut with ease by Montcalm.

Exasperated, Wolfe at last decided to attack along the Montmorency

River, east of the city. But this presented a tough challenge. Just before it enters the St. Lawrence, the river tumbles over falls 250 feet high. Above the falls, the river flows for many miles swift and deep, offering no practicable ford. But below the falls the river runs broad and shallow, and could be waded close to its mouth. Here, Wolfe decided, was the ford his troops could cross.

To draw the French, Wolfe ordered a strong force to land just below a French redoubt about a mile west of the ford, and to seize it. Meanwhile the rest of his army massed at the ford, ready to attack French reinforcements.

Though this was a clever plan, when a group of British grenadiers landed, they rushed impetuously on the redoubt before the main body of British had formed up behind them. The grenadiers were swept back easily by French fire. Then a huge rainstorm descended. The rain made muskets unfireable, and Wolfe realized he now had no hope of winning, and broke off the engagement.

Wolfe then spent a month trying a new tactic; he attempted to interdict supplies to Quebec being floated down the St. Lawrence. Though he slowed the flow, some boats got through at night, and this tactic also failed. At this point Wolfe determined that he had no hope of overcoming the French entrenchments east of the city, and his only possibility was to find some vulnerable spot to the west, or upstream, from Quebec. On September 3 he evacuated his camp east of the Montmorency, and withdrew his army to the south bank.

From a boat in the river, Wolfe surveyed the north shore with a telescope. At last he observed a winding path up the cliffs at the cove called Anse du Foulon, just a mile and a half upstream from Quebec. He noticed only a dozen tents were pitched at the top. Because the French considered this spot almost inaccessible, they had posted merely a small picket.

Wolfe now set in motion a plan of attack based on the rule of uproar east, attack west. For his uproar, he directed his senior naval officer, Admiral Charles Saunders, to draw the main British fleet to a position opposite Montcalm's main entrenchment east of the city, between the St. Charles and Montmorency rivers. Saunders was to lower boats in order to suggest that a landing was about to get under way. Wolfe also

instructed him to open a violent bombardment of the French entrenchments on September 12. The ruse served its purpose admirably.
Montcalm concentrated his troops across from the British fleet, and kept
them under arms all night.

Meanwhile, Wolfe set up his main attack. During the night a single
lantern rose to the maintop of the *Sutherland*, Wolfe's flagship, and 1,600
troops embarked upstream from the Anse du Foulon on flatboats. As
soon as the tide began to ebb at about 2:00 A.M. on September 13, 1759,
the signal of two lanterns being raised was given, and the whole flotilla
of flatboats dropped silently downstream.

As the leading boats neared the cove, a challenge from on shore broke
the silence. A Scottish captain answered back in French that the boats
were from one of Bougainville's regiments. This satisfied the sentry and
the boats drifted on.

As the leading British detachment made a safe landing at Foulon Cove,
Wolfe, on a boat just behind, recited the lines of Thomas Grey's elegy—
"The paths of glory lead but to the grave"—and told those who could hear
him, "I would sooner have written that poem than take Quebec."

A band of eager volunteers, who had agreed to lead the way, swarmed
up the steep face of the cliff. They overpowered the French picket at the
top, and then covered the landing of the main body of British troops.
Before dawn, the British army was moving toward Quebec. Wolfe found
the open battlefield he longed for, the Plains of Abraham, just west of
Quebec. The plains, a tract of grassland named after Abraham Martin, a
French river pilot who had once owned it, stretched from the cliffs north
to the St. Foy Road, which ran parallel to the river.

With Wolfe's troops in such a threatening position, Montcalm was at
last forced to give battle. He had only two days' supplies in the city, and
Wolfe could now cut off further deliveries. Also, Wolfe could pull up cannons on the Plains of Abraham and batter down the rotten walls of
Quebec in only a few hours. Like the brave soldier he was, Montcalm
chose to fight, and began hastily to move troops over to the heights.

Meanwhile, Wolfe formed his army facing Quebec in a single line, two
men deep, enabling all soldiers to fire at the same time, since the second
rank could shoot past the ears of the soldiers in the front rank. At about

10:00 A.M. on September 13 the French main body advanced against the British. At 200 paces' distance the French opened fire—much too great a range for muskets to be accurate. During this action Wolfe received his first wound, in the wrist. He wrapped a handkerchief around it, and took no further notice.

The French redressed their line, and moved forward once again, cheering and with loud shouts, while the British stood silent. Wolfe had explicitly told his soldiers not to fire until ordered, and they obeyed. Finally, when the French line was only forty yards away, the command came. As the British historian J. W. Fortescue wrote: "With one deafening crash the most perfect volley ever fired on a battlefield burst forth as if from a single monstrous weapon, from end to end of the British line."[4]

A dense cloud of gun smoke drifted over the field. Under cover of the smoke the British reloaded, stepped forward, and fired again, and continued to do so for several minutes. As the British now advanced, the French were disintegrating, falling back in disorder into the town. Walking at the head of a grenadier force, Wolfe was an easy target. A bullet struck him in the groin, and a second in his lungs. While he was being carried to the rear, he realized his wounds were mortal, and asked to be laid down. A few minutes later he died. His final words, when told the enemy were on the run, were "Now God be praised, I die happy."

Montcalm was also mortally wounded, and he died in the town that night. Quebec surrendered just four days later.

The Defeat of France, 1940

By far the most successful example of uproar east, attack west in the twentieth century, and one of the most spectacular in world history, occurred in 1940 when the Germans overran the Low Countries and conquered France in six weeks. Britain and France had declared war on Germany on September 3, 1939, after Adolf Hitler invaded Poland, finally proving that the "appeasement" of Hitler was a failure, and that he was bent on conquering Europe and possibly the world.[5]

The German campaign in the west followed precisely Sun Tzu's admonition. The author of this strategy was *not* the German general staff, which was charged with developing war plans. In fact, the general staff (now joined with the army commander in the army command, *der Oberkommando des Heeres*, or OKH) came up with a plan that did not even anticipate defeating France, but only hoped to drive back the Allied armies to gain territories in Holland, Belgium, and northern France from which to pursue air and sea operations against Britain.

While the OKH's plan assigned an important role to two exceptional new weapons that had been developed after Adolf Hitler came to power in 1933—"fast-runner" tanks formed into powerful panzer divisions, and Stuka dive-bombers—the true power of these weapons had not been fully appreciated. They had no counter on the Allied side, and the chief of staff of Army Group A, Erich von Manstein, was appalled when he saw the OKH did not plan to exploit them fully.

"The offensive capacity of the German army was our trump card," Manstein wrote, "and to fritter it away on half-measures was inadmissible."[6]

Manstein proposed an alternative strategy: make a strong movement into northern Belgium and Holland to convince the Allies the main German blow was coming there and draw their forces in that direction, then use the mass of the panzer divisions to strike fast through the Ardennes, cross the Meuse River at Sedan in northern France before the Allies had time to react, then turn west and strike direct for the English Channel, thereby isolating all Allied forces in Belgium.

The OKH didn't like their plan being tossed out so peremptorily, and—since they were extremely orthodox soldiers—didn't have the faith in the panzers and the Stukas that Manstein and other, more imaginative, German generals possessed. Crossing a major stream like the Meuse at Sedan in their eyes required moving up infantry and artillery, and a carefully worked out, coordinated assault. This would take time, and while it was being mounted the French could build a strong defensive line along the Meuse.

Manstein didn't think so. He and the father of the German armored force, Heinz Guderian, were confident the Meuse could be breached quickly with only panzer divisions and German air force (Luftwaffe) bombers, especially Stukas, which could drop bombs with pinpoint accuracy on battlefield targets. The Stukas functioned as aerial artillery,

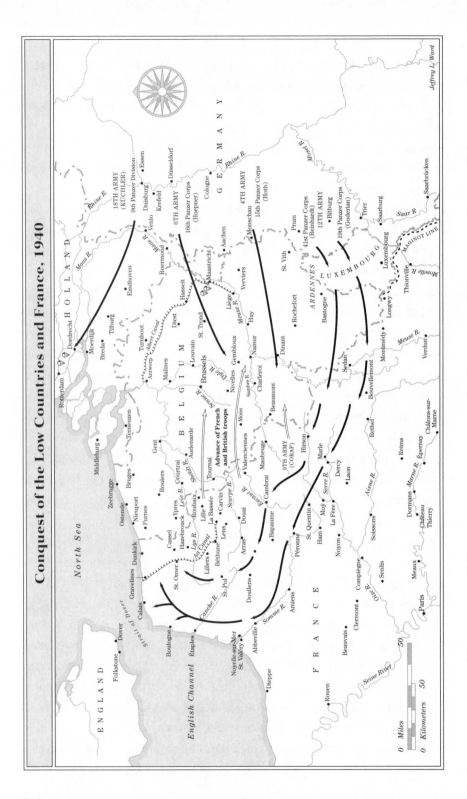

Conquest of the Low Countries and France, 1940

North Sea

English Channel

Strait of Dover

ENGLAND

Folkstone
Dover

HOLLAND

Rotterdam
Dordrecht
Moerdijk
Breda
Tilburg
Middleburg
Eindhoven
Venlo
Roermond
Duisburg
Essen
Krefeld
Düsseldorf

18TH ARMY
(KÜCHLER)
9th Panzer Division

Rhine R.
Maas R.

GERMANY

Cologne
Aachen

6TH ARMY
16th Panzer Corps
(Hoepner)

4TH ARMY
15th Panzer Corps
(Hoth)

Monschau
Verviers
Liège
Huy

41st Panzer Corps
(Reinhardt)
12TH ARMY
19th Panzer Corps
(Guderian)

Prum
Bitburg
Trier
Saarburg
Saarbrücken

Saar R.
Mosel R.

Luxembourg
MAGINOT LINE

LUXEMBOURG
Longwy
Thionville
Moselle R.
Verdun
Meuse R.

ARDENNES
St. Vith
Rochefort
Bastogne
Bouvellemont
Montmédy
Rethel

Sedan
Dinant
Namur
Beaumont
Hirson
Marle
Dercy
Laon
La Fère
St. Quentin
Ham
Moy
Noyon

9TH ARMY
(CORAP)

**Advance of French
and British troops**

BELGIUM

Antwerp
Malines
Brussels
Nivelles
Gembloux
Charleroi
Mons
Valenciennes
Maubeuge
Cambrai
Péronne

Diest
Hasselt
St. Trond
Louvain
Turnhout
Gent
Roulers
Courtrai
Audenarde
Tournai
Bapaume
Amiens

Maas R.
Maastricht
Albert Canal
Dyle R.
Senne R.
Sambre R.
Meuse R.
Escaut R.
Scarpe R.
Somme R.

Zeebrugge
Bruges
Ostende
Nieuport
Furnes
Terneuzen
Cassel
Ypres
Hazebrouck
Roubaix
Lille
La Bassee
Carvin
Douai
Arras
Doullens

Leie R.
La Lys R.
La Canche R.

Dunkirk
Gravelines
Calais
Boulogne
Étaples
Noyelle-sur-Mer
St. Valéry
Abbeville
Dieppe

St. Omer
Lillers
Béthune
St. Pol
Lens

FRANCE

Reims
Soissons
Compiègne
Senlis
Clermont
Beauvais
Rouen

Dormans
Château
Thierry
Chalons-sur-Marne
Épernay
Meaux
Paris

Marne R.
Aisne R.
Serre R.
Oise R.
Seine River

Rouen

0 Miles 50
0 Kilometers 50

the first such weapon ever developed. Manstein and Guderian believed the speed of the German advance would guarantee that the French would not have time to bring up enough troops to stop them. Speed also would ensure that few enemy units would be in place to block the panzers as they drove across France to the Channel.

The OKH stonewalled about approving Manstein's alternative and, exasperated by his efforts, used the excuse that he was overdue for promotion to assign him to command an infantry corps, with only a walk-on role in the upcoming campaign. The OKH hoped Manstein would conveniently disappear, but he took advantage of a luncheon Hitler held for new corps commanders to get a private audience with the Fuehrer, and, in the space of a few minutes, convinced him the plan would work. The next day Hitler ordered the OKH to adopt Manstein's proposal.

Accordingly, on May 10, 1940, the Germans delivered their first blows in Holland and northern Belgium. They were so sensational and convincing that they drew the Allied armies northward like a magnet. In the first great airborne assault in history, 4,000 German paratroops descended into the heart of the Dutch defensive system, at The Hague, Rotterdam, and Utrecht. The Dutch had expected to hold this region for a couple of weeks, long enough for the French to join them and hold it indefinitely. But the German paratroops quickly seized four airports, and a 12,000-man-strong air-landing division quickly arrived by transport. With these forces the Germans grabbed key bridges and held them till the 9th Panzer Division broke through the frontier and rushed to the bridges on May 13, eliminating all possibility of resistance.

Meanwhile other paratroops seized bridges over the Maas River and the Albert Canal at Maastricht, Holland, and captured the Belgian fortress of Eben Emael nearby by dropping paratroops on its undefended roof, sealing its gun ports, and forcing the garrisons to surrender.

Now Erich Hoepner's two-division 16th Panzer Corps burst across the Maas deep into Belgium and opened a broad path for Walther von Reichenau's following 6th Army.

The Allies had long anticipated that the Germans might strike through Belgium, and the Allied commander, General Maurice Gustave Gamelin, ordered the main force on the west wing, the 1st Group of Armies, including the eight-division British Expeditionary Force, to rush to the Dyle River, about fifteen miles east of Brussels.

Meanwhile the actual *Schwerpunkt*, or center of gravity, of the German offensive plunged almost unnoticed through the Ardennes toward the weakest point of the French line, sixty miles west. Well behind the panzers plodded the German infantry divisions on foot.

The leading element was the three-division 19th Panzer Corps under Guderian. His tanks were targeted at Sedan, on the Meuse five miles south of the Franco-Belgian border. Just to the north was Georg Hans Reinhardt's two-division 41st Panzer Corps aimed at Monthermé, about fifteen miles northwest of Sedan. About twenty-five miles north of Reinhardt was Hermann Hoth's 15th Panzer Corps with two divisions, the 5th and 7th (under Erwin Rommel, soon to be famous). This corps's job was to get across the Meuse and keep the Allies in Belgium from interfering with Guderian and Reinhardt in their thrust westward.

Chief of both Guderian's and Reinhardt's corps was Ewald von Kleist, who had never commanded armor before. Guderian had worked out a doctrine before the war stating that the speed of panzer advance alone would prevent the enemy from mounting any serious challenges to the flanks of the armored penetration, thus the flanks could be ignored. Kleist, less convinced about their invulnerability, became extremely fearful that the French would mount an attack on the flank. He could not believe Guderian's prediction that the enemy would take days to figure out the Germans' plan, more days to mount a counterstroke, and by then it would be too late.

During the night of May 11–12, two days after the invasion commenced, Kleist received reports that French cavalry were advancing from Longwy, about forty miles east of Sedan. He at once ordered one of Guderian's units, the 10th Panzer Division, to change direction and drive on Longwy. This would seriously upset Guderian's advance, and Guderian argued that the movement was unnecessary. Many of the French cavalry were still riding horses, while their lightly armored mechanized elements were no match for German tanks. Let them come,

Guderian told Kleist; they will be smashed. Kleist, after some hesitation, agreed. The French cavalry wisely decided not to advance.

Guderian's panzers captured Sedan and occupied the north bank of the Meuse on May 12. Under ordinary circumstances, German artillery should have been in place to suppress French artillery on the south bank of the Meuse that otherwise could disrupt any German infantry assault across the river. But German guns were still miles in the rear, tied up in the massive traffic jam of German infantry divisions marching to the front. On May 13, Guderian substituted Luftwaffe bombers for German artillery and instructed them to make both actual and fake bombing and strafing raids on the French defenders on the other side of the river. These repeated moves forced the French to keep their heads down, prevented French artillery from firing, and allowed German infantry that were a part of each panzer division to get across the river on rubber boats with scarcely any losses.

Meanwhile engineers hastily constructed a pontoon bridge over the Meuse, and the next day tanks began to cross. Reinhardt secured a narrow foothold across the river at Monthermé, but the terrain was extremely steep, and he had difficulty holding on under strong French pressure. Rommel's 7th Panzer Division, however, forced a huge breach on the river at nearby Dinant.

By the evening of May 14, elements of Guderian's corps had reached the town of Singly, more than twenty miles west of Sedan. That night André Corap, commanding the French 9th Army, the only Allied force now blocking Guderian's and Reinhardt's panzers along the Meuse, made a fatal mistake and ordered his army to withdraw to a new line fifteen to twenty miles to the west. He made this decision not only because the breakthrough at Sedan threatened his defensive line along the Meuse, but also because of the crossing at Dinant. Corap was responding to wild reports that "thousands" of German tanks were pouring through the breach made by Rommel (though Hoth's total corps strength was only 542 tanks).

When the French arrived at the new line, Guderian's panzers were already in possession of some of the positions the French 9th Army was supposed to occupy, while withdrawal from the Meuse removed the block holding Reinhardt. His tanks now burst out and drove westward along an unobstructed path. Guderian and Reinhardt had split the 9th Army in two, blowing open a sixty-mile-wide hole through which the panzers poured.

Kleist's tanks were now rolling through what resembled a long corridor, clogged with fugitives who created chaos, while the armor at the spear point had to be nourished with ammunition, fuel, and food. The Germans sought to build defensive walls along either side of this corridor, but the only troops they had were in Gustav von Wietersheim's 14th Motorized Corps of four divisions, which were almost as fast as the panzer divisions. They formed as many blocking positions as possible, but their numbers were too small and the distances too great. Solid lines could only be built by infantry, and most of it was far behind.

Though Gerd von Rundstedt, the commander of Army Group A, in charge of the offensive, was doing everything he could to bring up infantry, the pace was slow, and gaps were everywhere. To the orthodox soldiers who made up the German senior command, perils lurked at every crossroad. The generals were as stunned as the Allies at the speed of the panzers' advance, and Hitler himself got "monstrously nervous" and went to see Rundstedt at Charleroi on May 15. Rundstedt also was worried, and ordered Kleist to stop to allow the infantry time to catch up. Kleist told Guderian nothing of the anxieties at headquarters, and merely informed him to halt his tanks.

Guderian, along with the other panzer leaders, saw that a gigantic victory was within their grasp, but it could only be assured if they continued to drive west at maximum speed and not give the distracted Allies a chance to organize a powerful strike on the flank. Guderian extracted from Kleist the authority to advance for another twenty-four hours under the pretext of acquiring "sufficient space" for the infantry corps following.

Armed with this permission to "enlarge the bridgehead," Guderian drove to the village of Bouvellemont, twenty-four miles west of Sedan. This was the farthest projection of the 1st Panzer Division. In the burning village, a French blocking force held the last barrier stopping the panzers from sweeping unopposed across northern France. At the edge of the village, Guderian found exhausted German infantry. They had had no real rest since May 9, and were falling asleep in their slit trenches. Guderian explained to Lieutenant Colonel Hermann Balck, chief of the infantry, that his men had to crack the barrier and open a way for the tanks.

Balck went to his officers, who argued against an attack with worn-out troops. "In that case," Balck told them, "I'll take the place on my own." As he moved off to do so, his embarrassed soldiers followed and seized the village.

This was the last French point of resistance, and the Germans now rushed out into the open plains north of the Somme River with virtually nothing ahead to stop them. By nightfall on May 16, Guderian's spearheads were at the towns of Marle and Darcy, fifty-five miles west of Sedan.

This had been a glittering advance, and Guderian assumed its success had quieted the fears in headquarters. But when he informed Kleist that he intended to continue on at full pace the next day, Kleist flew into his airstrip and berated him for disobeying orders. Guderian at once asked to be relieved of his command. Following a day of tense disputes and negotiations, the commander of 12th Army, Wilhelm List, who had been called in to smooth ruffled feathers and find a solution, gave Guderian authority to make a "reconnaissance in force," a subterfuge that did not defy Rundstedt's command to halt, but slipped around it.

As Guderian unleashed his panzers, Rundstedt's command belatedly called off its stop order. Within two days, Guderian's tanks reached St. Quentin, eighty miles west of Sedan, and on May 19, 1st Panzer Division forced a bridgehead over the Somme near Péronne, almost twenty miles west of St. Quentin.

Just as Guderian had expected, the Allies had been stunned by the velocity of the panzer advance, and could not get together forces for a counterstroke. Only the newly formed French 4th Armored Division under Charles de Gaulle attacked with a few tanks at Laon, southeast of St. Quentin on the southern flank of the German advance. But he was severely repulsed. Despite the fact that the Allies had more tanks than the Germans, they continually failed to mass them in sufficient numbers. In most cases the Allies distributed tanks in small packets to the infantry divisions. Even when they met a concerted attack, the Allied tanks were too few to stop the panzers. More often they were not even on the scene when a German panzer column came through.

Only in Belgium, where the Allies were rapidly retreating because of the catastrophe building to their south, did a short Allied armored clash produce any effects. At Gembloux, twenty miles southeast of Brussels, a few French tanks were assembled, and briefly held up the advance of the panzers. But when the Germans brought up more armor, the French failed to do likewise, and the panzers burst through and continued onward.

At last the British organized a tank counterattack southward at Arras on May 21, with the aim of breaking through the German corridor and opening a path for the Allies in Belgium to withdraw into France. But the British attack was too small—fifty-eight slow Matilda "infantry" tanks and two battalions of infantry—to make a decision, although it did huge damage to Erwin Rommel's 7th Panzer Division.

Rommel's panzer regiment had moved northwest from Arras on the morning of May 21, with the division's infantry regiment and artillery to follow. Before the infantry and guns could get away, however, the British struck them. The Matildas were designed to work with infantry and could travel at only about the speed a soldier could walk. Thus they were not well suited for mobile armored operations—and reflected the ambivalence of the British, who built both "infantry" tanks and "cruiser," or faster, more mobile tanks comparable to the "fast-runner" German tanks that could travel about twenty-five miles an hour. Even so, the Matildas had seventy-five millimeters of armor, and were difficult to stop with anything smaller than large-caliber cannons.

As the Matildas bore down on them, the Germans saw the shells of their 37-mm antitank (AT) guns bouncing off the British tanks. The Matildas penetrated the enemy position, killed most of the AT crews and many of the infantry, and were only stopped by a frantic effort, undertaken by Rommel himself, to form a "gun line" of field artillery, especially high-velocity 88-mm antiaircraft guns, which materialized as the best antitank gun in the German arsenal. The artillery and the 88s destroyed thirty-six Matildas, and broke the back of the attack. Later the panzer regiment came back on radioed orders from Rommel, and struck the British on the rear. In a bitter tank-on-tank clash, the panzers destroyed seven Matildas and six antitank guns, but lost nine of their own medium tanks, and a number of light tanks.

The British fell back, and attempted no further attack. The Allied effort had been too weak and isolated. Yet it showed what might have been done if the Allied commanders had made a concerted effort. Rommel's division lost 387 men, four times the number it had lost in the campaign thus far. The attack also stunned Rundstedt. His anxiety fed Hitler's similar fears, and led to a momentous decision in a few days.

Meanwhile, on the afternoon of May 20, the 2nd Panzer Division reached Abbéville, on the lower Somme River, and that evening a battalion passed through Noyelles, fifteen miles away, and became the first German unit to reach the coast. In only ten days after the start of the offensive, the Allied armies had been cut in two.

On May 22, Guderian wheeled north from Abbéville, aiming at the Channel ports and the rear of the British, French, and Belgian armies, which were still facing eastward. Reinhardt's panzers kept pace on the east. By May 23, Guderian's tanks had isolated Boulogne and Calais, and come up to Gravelines, barely ten miles from Dunkirk, the last port from which the Allies in Belgium could evacuate.

Reinhardt had also arrived twenty miles from Dunkirk on the Aa (or Bassée) Canal, which ran westward past Douai, La Bassée, and St. Omer to Gravelines. The panzers were now nearer Dunkirk than were most of the Allies.

While part of the British Expeditionary Force (BEF) withdrew to La Bassée on May 23 under pressure from Rommel moving northward from Arras toward Lille, the bulk of the British moved farther north. Here King Leopold of the Belgians ordered his army to surrender the next day.

Despite these amazing gains, Rundstedt was shaken by the British tank attack at Arras, and gave Hitler a gloomy report on May 24, saying he feared other Allied attacks from north and south. All this reinforced Hitler's own anxieties. Although he had accepted Manstein's strategy to strike through the Ardennes, as the campaign went on Hitler failed to understand its capacity for complete victory, and did not comprehend that Guderian's brilliant exploitation was bringing about the most overwhelming military decision in modern history. The Germans had been out of danger from the first day, but to Hitler and to most of the senior German generals, that result was too good to be true.

Hitler now made a decision that was bewildering when it happened and remains bewildering to this day. He ordered Walther von Brauchitsch, the army commander, to halt the panzers along the line of the Bassée Canal.

There were virtually no Allied troops in front of the panzers. Guderian and Reinhardt were about to seize Dunkirk and close off the last possible port from which the enemy could embark. This would force the surrender of the entire BEF and the French 1st Group of Armies, more than 400,000 men.

Rundstedt had been worried, but not enough to stop the advance, and *this* command was madness! He protested, but received only the curt telegram: "The armored divisions are to remain at medium artillery range from Dunkirk [eight or nine miles]. Permission is only granted for reconnaissance and protective movements."[7]

Kleist thought the order foolish, and went ahead and pushed his tanks across the canal, but then received emphatic orders to withdraw behind the canal. There the panzers stayed for three days, while the BEF and remnants of the French armies streamed back to Dunkirk. There the Allies built a strong defensive position, while the British hastily improvised a sea lift.

The British used every vessel they could find, from civilian yachts to ferryboats and small coasters. In a magnificent display of dedication and resolve, they sent over 860 vessels and, between May 26 and June 4, brought back to England 338,000 troops, including 120,000 French, though they had to leave all their weapons on the beach. Only a few thousand members of the French rear guard were captured.

No one knows why Hitler stopped the panzers at Gravelines. One fairly plausible answer is that Hermann Göring, a Nazi crony of his, and chief of the Luftwaffe, assured Hitler his Stukas and other bombers could prevent the Allies from evacuating. The other is that Hitler did not want to destroy the BEF because he desired a settlement with Britain, and thought that allowing the troops to get back home would encourage the British to sign a peace treaty.

The Luftwaffe did a poor job. Göring didn't get the aerial campaign going until May 29. The Royal Air Force valiantly tried to stop the bombing runs, and were in part successful, while the soft sand on the beach absorbed much of the bomb blasts. The Luftwaffe did most of its damage at sea, sinking six destroyers, eight transports, and more than 200 small craft.

The "Miracle of Dunkirk" had precisely the opposite effect from what Hitler may have intended. It aroused the determination of the British to continue the war, and its memory bolstered and encouraged them until they won victory at the end.

With the evacuation of Dunkirk, the first stage of the campaign in the west ended. In three weeks the Germans had captured more than a million prisoners, while suffering 60,000 casualties. The Dutch and Belgian armies had been eliminated, the French had lost thirty divisions, nearly a third of their total strength, and these the most modern and mobile forces in the army. They had also lost the aid of eight British divisions now back in Britain. Only one British division remained in France south of the Somme.

The French still had sixty-six divisions, but the Germans employed panzer advances all across the front, beginning on June 5. The French armies disintegrated quickly. On June 22 the French accepted German terms, and on June 25 both sides ceased fire. The greatest military victory in modern times had been achieved in six weeks.

Its success can be attributed to the distraction that Manstein was able to create, by focusing Allied attention on a noisy "uproar" in Holland and northern Belgium, while the real attack came silently, almost unnoticed, far away through the Ardennes. Manstein's achievement ranks on a par with Alexander's magnificent campaign along the Hydaspes.

Implications for the Future

The deception contained in the rule of uproar east, attack west is of fundamental importance in every military operation, and is more significant than ever today because satellite, aerial, and ground reconnaissance is far better and more precise than before. Hence the enemy is likely to know where opposing forces are located, and be able to make plans to account for them. It will be more difficult for a commander to *hide* his forces, and therefore deceive the enemy by springing a hidden or unobserved threat on him—as, for example, Frederick the Great did on the flank of the Austrians at Leuthen in 1757.

Since the enemy is likely in the future to be able to determine with fair accuracy the locations and strengths of the forces opposing him, deception must rely, in most cases, on confusing or blocking an enemy's *perception* of what is happening. In this context, the strategy of Manstein in 1940 was perfect, because he arranged for German forces to deploy and then seemingly strike their hardest blow where the Allies *expected* it—in the north—thus missing where it was actually coming—to the south.

There are many ways in which a commander can make an enemy believe a strike is coming at a particular place, when it's actually a decoy. For example, a commander will normally expect an enemy to aim for a key communications center, whether it be a city or, in a tactical operation, a crossroads or an airfield. Thus the enemy will concentrate his forces to protect an obvious target. The opposing commander may exploit this enemy perception by striking at *another* city, crossroads, or airfield where the enemy is not expecting a blow. The alternative target may be some distance away, but mobility of forces today will permit a descent there as readily as one closer.

A movement against a country like Iraq could pose a good opportunity for the deception of uproar east, attack west. A strong threat might be mounted against the Iraqi metropolis and capital, Baghdad, drawing Iraqi attention and troops to this obvious target. Meanwhile the actual strike might be made either on the Iraqi oil fields in the south or to occupy regions in the north of the country, where Kurdish insurgents could become allies in ousting the government of Saddam Hussein.

The mobility of modern armies now gives a commander more possibilities than ever before to practice Sun Tzu's classic admonition to make noise in one place and to deliver the stroke at another.

14

Maneuvers on the Rear

MOVING TO STRIKE the enemy an unexpected blow on his rear has been the most successful means of attack since the earliest days of warfare. But normally this strategy has been carried out on a limited scale, in small tactical engagements or on the battlefield, such as, for example, Frederick the Great's strike at the Austrian flank and rear at Leuthen in 1757.

A rarely employed and much more sweeping version of the strategy can, however, achieve war-winning results. According to this strategy, a massive descent is made with one's entire army, or a large part of it, on the enemy's rear, thereby blocking the enemy's lines of communications or avenues of retreat. This is far different from the rule of blocking an enemy's retreat, as discussed in chapter 9. That method is essentially an ambush of a force isolated deep within enemy territory. A maneuver on the rear is a powerful, unexpected strike delivered from a long distance at some point far back on an enemy's already established line of supply and communications.

The most famous exponent of this method was Napoleon Bonaparte, and we use his term for it, *la manoeuvre sur les derrières*, to summarize this rule. The maxim is actually of ancient origin, however, for it was applied with tremendous success by Scipio Africanus against the Carthaginians in Spain in 209 B.C., and by Genghis Khan against the Khwarezmian Empire along the Jaxartes (Syr Darya) River in 1220.

Scipio led a Roman army attempting to cut off supply and reinforcements from Spain to the Carthaginian general Hannibal. Scipio's base in Spain was at Tarraco (Tarragona) on the northeastern coast. While the Carthaginian capital in Spain, the treasury, and the only port fit for a fleet was at New Carthage (Cartagena), the Carthaginian armies were widely separated, one at Gibraltar, another on the Tagus River, near present-day Lisbon, and a third near modern Madrid. Scipio ignored the enemy field armies and, with his whole army and fleet, moved on the Carthaginian rear to seize New Carthage. This deprived the Carthaginians of their gold and their sea connection to Carthage, in north Africa, thereby throwing them on the strategic defensive from which they never recovered. Scipio went on to conquer all of Spain for Rome.

The Mongol leader Genghis Khan wanted to conquer the Khwarezmian Empire, under Shah Mohammed, consisting of modern Iran, Afghanistan, and Transoxiana between the Oxus (Amu Darya) and Jaxartes rivers. He deceived Mohammed into thinking an attack was coming from the east by sending two 10,000-man divisions (tumens) over the 13,000-foot Terek Pass in the Pamir Mountains, down the Fergana Valley, toward Kokand, the eastern anchor of Mohammed's defensive line along the Jaxartes. Shortly after, Genghis crossed a wide desert on the north with six divisions and debouched at Otrar, on the lower Jaxartes, 400 miles northwest of Kokand. Three of these divisions attacked southeastward along the Jaxartes, while the Mongols at Kokand moved toward them along the river. This accomplished Genghis's aim of keeping the attention of Mohammed and his army focused along the river. Meanwhile, Genghis—having found a guide who knew the locations of the few watering holes in the desert—took a powerful force, comprising his remaining three tumens, across the desert and seized the strategically located city of Bokhara, 400 miles south, which blocked reinforcements and supplies from Iran, and also isolated Mohammed's capital of Samarkand, about 150 miles to the east. Samarkand quickly fell, Mohammed's armies evaporated, and Mohammed ended his life as a fugitive.

Though devastatingly effective, using the principle of maneuvering on the enemy's rear requires tremendous moral courage and confidence on the part of commanders. Lack of both prevented the Western Allied commanders from achieving a virtually bloodless conquest of Sicily in World War II. After the Americans and British captured Tunisia in May 1943 and drove the Germans and Italians out of north Africa, the Allied command decided to seize Sicily, and was contemplating an invasion of Italy. The Germans had few troops in Italy because Hitler had refused to allow the Axis armies in north Africa to evacuate. As a result, about 160,000 German and Italian soldiers had surrendered. They might instead have been moved to defend Italy.

The Allied command, under the American general Dwight Eisenhower, knew the Italians were reeling and the Germans possessed only a few formations, which they posted in Sicily. Allied intelligence further determined that the Germans had virtually no troops on the toe (Calabria) and heel (Apulia) of the Italian boot. Several Allied officers proposed that—since the Allies had complete control of the sea—they should ignore Sicily, and instead land in Calabria and possibly Apulia, which would have been a brilliant maneuver on the rear. The Allies would cut off all the German and Italian combat formations in Sicily, and force them to surrender without a fight.

But Eisenhower and the other senior officers in the Allied command were unwilling to undertake any operation that was not conservative, sure, direct, and under the protection of overwhelming sea and air cover. Accordingly the invasion of Sicily (Operation Husky) was a headlong frontal advance from the sea. Although they did not expect much opposition, the commanders earmarked ten divisions for Husky (July 10–August 17, 1943), more than they were able to get on the beaches of Normandy a year later. The Italians surrendered at every opportunity, but the four German divisions put up a powerful defense—which cost the British 13,000 casualties and the Americans 10,000. They were also able to evacuate most of their force, including their equipment, back to Italy across the narrow Strait of Messina. All of these casualties could have been avoided and the Germans decisively routed if the Allied command had struck Calabria instead of Sicily.

The Germans were now so certain Eisenhower and his generals were unwilling to take any chances, that they concluded the Allied invasion of the boot of Italy would *not* take place anywhere farther than the 200-mile range of Allied fighter aircraft, now based in Sicily. Hence the Germans were able to pinpoint correctly the invasion at Salerno, south of Naples, the only feasible landing site within reach of the airfields in northeast Sicily. The Germans concentrated virtually all their troops at Salerno, and though far weaker than the Allies, they inflicted enormous casualties.

It's ironic that the Germans did *not* use the knowledge they had gained in the Mediterranean concerning Allied insistence on air cover to figure out beforehand where the 1944 invasion was going to come in France. The Allies were certain to invade at a point within the 200-mile range of fighter bases in southeastern England. Only three such appropriate places existed—the Pas de Calais, the Normandy beaches, and Cherbourg and the Cotentin peninsula. If the Germans had concentrated three or four panzer divisions behind each of these beaches, they very likely could have smashed any invasion in the first hours.

Instead, the two top German armored leaders, Erwin Rommel and Heinz Guderian, disputed *how* the panzer divisions were to be deployed. Rommel wanted to push them right against the beaches. But since he thought the invasion was coming at the Pas de Calais, he argued to concentrate the tanks there. Guderian wanted to keep the panzers back from the coast and strike only after the Allies landed and moved inland. Because of this dispute, no one considered the fighter-range rule, and panzer divisions were not close enough and primed on June 6 to overrun the Normandy beaches.

Timidity, confusion, and disagreement are frequent intruders into the thinking of commanders in every war, not just the Allied officers in Sicily and Italy and the German officers in northern France in World War II. The rule of maneuver on the rear can offer a way to quick, decisive victory—but it must be pursued boldly, with resolute conviction. No officer ever followed these mandates more successfully and more surely than Napoleon Bonaparte.

Marengo, 1800

Napoleon Bonaparte's military genius burst on the world like a meteor. He was only twenty-five years old and inexperienced in war when he mounted cannons at the harbor mouth of the great French naval base of Toulon in 1793. By threatening to bottle up British warships in the harbor, he forced the British to abandon their occupation of the base. His action now looks like an obvious solution. Yet others at the time had not seen it. While all great ideas are simple, the gift of Napoleon and other military geniuses is to see the obvious when others do not.[1]

Bonaparte unveiled his first *manoeuvre sur les derrières* only three years later, in the opening stages of the Italian campaign of 1796–1797. In this operation against the Piedmontese and the Austrians, who were in alliance, Bonaparte turned first on the war-weary Piedmontese and drove them out of the war, then deceived the Austrians into believing he was going to attack them directly by way of Valenza on the Po River. Bonaparte's deception caused the Austrian commander to concentrate his army at Valenza.

Bonaparte then sent only part of his army to demonstrate against the Austrians at Valenza, and marched the bulk of it east to Piacenza, about forty miles southeast of Milan, in a bold move on the Austrian rear. He intended to cross the Po River there and drive toward Milan; this would block the Austrian line of communications and supply back to Vienna. The Austrian commander, sensing his peril, instead abandoned Milan and all of Lombardy, and rushed back in defeat toward Austria. Thus, Bonaparte's first maneuver on the rear did not destroy the Austrian army, but gained him most of northern Italy.

Bonaparte's ambitions to rule France burgeoned after he won the Italian campaign in the spring of 1797. He saw the time was not ripe, however, and turned his attention to engineering a campaign in Egypt beginning July 1, 1798. Although Egypt was nominally under the rule of the Turkish sultan, Bonaparte's aim was to weaken British control of India, although just how he thought possession of Egypt would bring this about was never clear. His military actions were successful, but the

Marengo Campaign, 1800

operation ultimately came to grief because Royal Navy admiral Horatio Nelson destroyed the French fleet at Aboukir Bay, east of Alexandria, on August 2, 1798, isolating the French.

Meanwhile, popular support for the French government in Paris eroded drastically. It had failed to set up an effective system of taxation, and financed its operations with virtually worthless printed money. Also a coalition of Britain, Austria, and Russia drove the French out of Italy and Germany. Bonaparte, seeing an opportunity to gain political power, returned to France on October 9, 1799. He was received with wild enthusiasm by the populace, who saw in him a way to restore French glory and regain lost territories. A month later he carried out a coup d'etat that ousted the government. Soon thereafter Bonaparte became First Consul, in effect dictator of France.

Bonaparte's first job was to defeat his closest enemy, the Austrians, who had two armies threatening to invade France: a 120,000-man force in southern Germany under the command of Paul Kray von Krajowa, and another force of about 80,000 men in northern Italy under Michael Melas.

Opposing Kray was a slightly smaller French army under Jean Victor Moreau along the Rhine River, the border with Germany, and opposing Melas was a 40,000-man French army under André Masséna around Genoa and the Italian Riviera.

Bonaparte saw a great opportunity to strike killing blows against both Austrian armies. His was a plan for two *manoeuvres sur les derrières*. For the first of these he proposed that the French commander Moreau hold Kray immobile in southern Germany by a feint attack with one corps across the Rhine into the Black Forest. Meanwhile, three of Moreau's corps would march through Switzerland, cross the Rhine at Schaffhausen, and sweep up onto Kray's rear. Kray's army would be caught front and rear, and forced to surrender.

Napoleon believed three of Moreau's four corps could finish the job against Kray's army, which meant he could release one corps, commanded by Count Claude Lecourbe, to move back south into Switzerland, and join a new Army of the Reserve that Bonaparte was forming. This combined army would seal off the Alpine passes back to Austria and Germany, thereby isolating Melas's Austrian army in Italy.

If Melas refused to surrender, the Army of the Reserve could proceed into Italy and join with Masséna, in the region north of Genoa, to consummate victory.

This brilliant plan was stillborn, however, because of the hesitation of Moreau. He considered himself a military rival of Bonaparte, and was reluctant to follow his lead. Moreau was also too cautious to undertake such a sweeping operation. He therefore contended that crossing the Rhine at Schaffhausen was dangerous, and because Moreau had the backing of many partisans in the army, Bonaparte was obliged to acquiesce.[2]

Bonaparte designed a new plan in two weeks, one that relegated Moreau to a secondary role, and that Moreau was willing to accept. According to this plan, Moreau was to launch a direct offensive and drive Kray back to Ulm, on the western Bavarian frontier. Half the Army of the Reserve would occupy Switzerland, while the other half would make for Italy through the Simplon or St. Gotthard passes in the Alps.

Lecourbe's corps would march south from the Rhine into Switzerland and pass into Italy, also through the Simplon and St. Gotthard passes, to help the reserve army cut off Melas from Austria.

The key difference in Bonaparte's new plan was that the reserve army and Lecourbe would be making a movement on the rear. They would come out of the passes to the northeast of Melas's army and easily be able to take possession of his main base at Milan, which lay directly south of the passes. Bonaparte also intended to establish a barrage, or military barrier, at the Stradella defile, about thirty miles south of Milan on Melas's main supply line back to Vienna. At Stradella, the gap between the Po River on one side and the Apennine Mountains on the other shrinks to just twelve miles, and here a few French could stop the whole Austrian army.

Before this new plan could go into operation, however, the Austrians reinforced Melas's army, bringing it to 100,000 men, and launched a surprise offensive to clear Masséna out of Italy, invade southern France, and capture Toulon. The attack, beginning April 6, 1800, actually drove Masséna into Genoa with 12,000 men, and pressed the remainder of his army, under Louis Gabriel Suchet, beyond Nice, into the valley of the Var River. By the third week of April, a 24,000-man corps under Karl Ott formed a tight ring around Genoa, while the British Royal Navy blockaded from the sea.

Although Bonaparte sent messages into Genoa telling Masséna to hold out for as long as possible, time now was of the essence. To provide assistance quickly, he directed his chief of staff to march the reserve army through the Alpine passes, Little St. Bernard and Great St. Bernard, that were farther west than the Simplon and St. Gotthard passes, and therefore would bring the French army closer to Melas's army, arriving on its northern flank. But this position was less advantageous strategically than the position Bonaparte had planned to take on Melas's rear.

In order to deceive Melas about where the reserve army was headed, Bonaparte also directed a small French division to demonstrate noisily against the Simplon Pass, as if planning to drive through there.

This improvised plan depended upon Melas *not* responding strongly or fast to the French movement, and was daring because if Melas did react swiftly, he could slow French movement through the passes with relatively few troops. Even if some columns broke through, Melas could maneuver his main force to destroy each column as it debouched from the Alps. Bonaparte had judged Melas correctly, however. The siege of Genoa distracted his attention, and Melas was convinced the primary French aim would be to defend southern France (Provence) against invasion. All the noise along the Alpine passes appeared to him to be merely a diversion, and he did not turn his army in that direction.

Melas therefore made an utterly typical response to what was in fact an unexpected move. The anticipation of such responses is the key to great generals accomplishing their victories. Extraordinary commanders like Bonaparte look for different, unusual, or unorthodox solutions to military problems, while ordinary commanders look for expected, usual, or orthodox solutions. Melas calculated that the enemy would respond as he himself would have responded in like circumstances. He, like most generals, would have met the direct challenge for France—the obvious danger posed by the invasion of Provence. It did not occur to him that Bonaparte would ignore this danger, and strike instead at the *heart* of Melas's strength, his line of supply and communications back to Austria.

Meanwhile, General Moreau, after much prodding, commenced his part of the plan, which was to neutralize and possibly defeat Kray's army in southern Germany. Moreau opened his offensive on April 25, 1800, and achieved considerable success. He had decided it would be safe to cross the Rhine at Schaffhausen after all, and sent Lecourbe's corps, which pressed behind the Austrians and forced Kray to retreat toward Ulm. Moreau then slackened his pressure, and though now he was supposed to allow Lecourbe's corps to turn south into Italy, he declined to release it.[3]

A smuggled letter from Masséna, which Bonaparte received in Paris on May 5, said rations were so low his army could not hold out more than fifteen days. Bonaparte sent word to be secreted in to Masséna that he had to hold out till June 4, and he started at once to join the reserve army, now marching for the St. Bernard passes.

The advance guard of 8,000 men under Jean Lannes marched up the Great St. Bernard Pass on May 14, with orders to occupy Aosta on the Italian side by May 16 at all costs. Bonaparte hoped for the bulk of the army to reach Ivrea, fifty miles south of Great St. Bernard, by May 18. The journey up was difficult. The top was 8,120 feet above sea level, and the way was covered with deep snow. The gunners were able to move their cannons only by dragging them through the snow in hollowed-out tree trunks.

Despite the problems, Lannes reached Aosta on May 16, as ordered, and captured the town after a brief skirmish. But the real challenge was posed as Lannes pushed farther south to a fort at the village of Bard, twenty-two miles from Aosta, at a narrow point between the mountains on one side and the chasm of the Dora Baltea River on the other. Held by 400 Austrian soldiers mounting twenty-six cannons, the fort blocked passage of French artillery and cavalry. But foot soldiers could walk on mule paths through the mountains, and Lannes bypassed Bard with his infantry, and pressed on to Ivrea, which he occupied on May 22, driving out 3,000 Austrians.

But the only way to pass cannons through Bard was by the one road through the village. On the nights of May 24 and 25, French gunners wrapped the wheels of guns and caissons with cloths and spread straw on the road. They pulled through six cannons quietly right under the noses of the Austrians. A single division was left to finish the job of reducing the fort, while the rest of the infantry hurried on.

When Bonaparte reached Ivrea, he had to choose among three directions in which to advance. One was to move southwest to Turin, and appear to be aiming at the rear of the Austrian forces attacking into Provence. He could also move more directly south, to Genoa, to relieve Masséna's army. Or, in a move that would allow him to accomplish his original goal of a move on Melas's rear, he could march due east sixty-five miles to Milan. This position would cut off Melas's line of supply along the north bank of the Po River to the Austrian army in Provence, and would also gain quick access to the Stradella defile, which would block Melas's main line of supply and retreat back to Austria.

Capture of Milan was by far the best choice, and, to an orthodox general like Melas, would be the least expected. In addition to the strategic advantages that seizure of Milan would give Bonaparte, the depots there held large quantities of food and weapons, which the French needed badly—since their supply line was still being blocked at Fort Bard.

To deceive Melas about his true intentions, Bonaparte sent Lannes with his 8,000 men toward Turin, attacking Chivasso on the Po River, twenty miles south of Ivrea. Lannes entered Chivasso on May 28, and convinced the Austrians the French thrust was toward Turin. Meanwhile the main French army pressed eastward against minuscule resistance and seized Milan, which Bonaparte entered in triumph on June 2.

In response, Melas had three choices. He could attempt escape through the Stradella defile back to Vienna. Or he could march north by way of Valenza on the Po River, and from there launch a breakout and thrust to Milan that might sever the French lines of supply. Finally, an escape route had opened to the south when Masséna surrendered on June 5, offering Melas the opportunity to move his base to Genoa. This port could serve as his refuge and terminus of a new avenue of supply, now by sea, protected by the Royal Navy. Thus in theory Melas could ignore the severing of his supply lines at Stradella and Milan.

Bonaparte perceived all three options, and sent a division to Valenza as a guard, while moving most of the remainder of his army across the Po to Stradella. But he recognized that the surrender of Genoa had introduced a wild card. He had no idea whether Melas would seize the chance to move there, or would mass his army to challenge the French army directly.

To prevent Melas from choosing the Genoa option, Bonaparte decided to advance on Melas, hoping to provoke him to fight. He sent Lannes forward with his 8,000 men from Stradella toward Melas at Alessandria, with Claude P. Victor's corps coming along behind. On June 9, Lannes collided with the 18,000-man corps of Karl Ott at Montebello, twelve miles west of Stradella, and rashly attacked it. He was saved from disaster by the timely arrival of Victor with 5,000 men, who struck Ott's flank, forcing Ott to retire in confusion on Alessandria, twenty-two miles west.

The presence on the north of Ott, who had besieged Masséna at Genoa, revealed that Melas was concentrating his army at Alessandria, and thus far was *not* pulling back to Genoa. For the next four days Melas did nothing while his army consolidated.

Bonaparte knew time was vital, and on June 13 sent a strong force toward Alessandria. He also started a corps under Louis C. A. Desaix marching toward Rivalta and Novi, thirty miles southwest, to cut the main Alessandria-Genoa road, in the event Melas decided to retreat to the port city. At the same time he alerted the division of J. F. Lapoype to be ready to march at a moment's notice to Valenza, in case Melas broke out in that direction.

The French advance passed over the plain of the Scrivia River, halfway to Alessandria, but encountered no Austrians, even though the enemy cavalry were far superior to Bonaparte's and the plain was one of the few places in Italy where cavalry could charge at full speed. Bonaparte concluded that if Melas intended to fight, he would have done so on the plain. Accordingly he decided that Melas, despite having massed his army at Alessandria, had decided to escape back to Genoa after all. This conclusion was reinforced by the quick withdrawal of 4,000 Austrians from the village of Marengo when the French advance guard came up on June 13. Marengo was two and a half miles east of Alessandria, just across the Bormida River.

In fact, Bonaparte was wrong. Melas, against all odds, had resolved to fight. He had never seriously considered withdrawing to Genoa, and also believed incorrectly that another French army was advancing on him from the west, coming from Provence. Melas decided to attack the French headlong at Marengo the next day, in order to reopen his line of communications with Austria.

Bonaparte no longer was expecting such an attack, and when 31,000 Austrians assaulted Victor's corps frontally at Marengo, Bonaparte insisted the attack was only a feint to shield Melas's withdrawal toward Genoa, or possibly to veil an attempt to sweep around the French army, cross the Po at Valenza, and drive on Milan.

Bonaparte, therefore, did not keep all his forces together to meet a major attack. Desaix's corps continued marching to block the Alessandria-Genoa road, and at 9:00 A.M. Bonaparte sent Lapoype's division on the march to Valenza as a precaution.

By 11:00 A.M., however, Bonaparte arrived on the battlefield, realized Melas was making his main attack at Marengo, and sent aides spurring furiously toward Desaix and Lapoype with orders of urgent recall. By 3:00 P.M. the French army was reeling back from Marengo in seeming defeat. Melas, thinking he had won, stopped the attack, formed the Austrian forces into a column of march, and sent it forward, assuming the French would withdraw from the field.

At about the same time a mud-spattered Desaix arrived at Bonaparte's headquarters and announced that one of his divisions was close behind.[4] The French artillery chief, A. F. L. V. de Marmont, massed eighteen cannons in front of the advancing Austrians and opened fire, which blew great gaps in the Austrian columns. Meanwhile, Desaix's division moved forward, preceded by four light cannons that poured salvos of canister into the head of the Austrians. The French infantry then advanced, while a 400-man cavalry force under François E. Kellermann made a spontaneous charge into the flank of the stunned Austrians. The Austrian army collapsed, lost 8,000 captives, and the survivors fled back into Alessandria.

A shaken Melas asked for an armistice. Negotiations for peace continued for most of the summer, but William Pitt offered the Austrians a subsidy to keep them in the war, and hostilities resumed in November. On December 3, 1800, General Moreau defeated Kray at Hohenlinden in Bavaria. That persuaded the Austrians to give in, and they signed the Peace of Lunéville on February 8, 1801, giving Italy largely to France, and confirming French possession of Germany west of the Rhine River. Britain held out for more than a year, but finally signed the Peace of Amiens on March 27, 1802.

The war had been won when Bonaparte improvised a descent on Melas's rear at Milan after he learned that Masséna had been bottled up at Genoa. This unexpected move, plus the strategic barrage he established at Stradella, severed Melas's lines of communication. In response, Melas made all the wrong decisions. He should have withdrawn into Genoa and gained his supplies by sea. But Melas, distracted and looking to Vienna for succor, not to the Royal Navy, decided to fight. Then, instead of swinging around to Valenza and getting on the flank and rear of the French as he should have done, he attacked the French frontally at Marengo.

Marengo illustrates a peculiar fact about great generals. Since they usually see all the problems associated with a given military situation, they occasionally assume that their opponents see them as well. For this reason, they sometimes *overestimate* the perception of their opponents, and take precautions that are not really necessary. If Bonaparte had not already been countering the two really dangerous moves Melas could have made—to Genoa or Valenza—the French would not have been inferior in numbers at Marengo. His retrieval of Desaix in time saved the day. Yet even if Bonaparte had been defeated at Marengo, he could have withdrawn to Stradella, blocked Melas's line of supply—and *still* won the campaign.

Island-Hopping in the Pacific, 1943–1944

One of the greatest factors contributing to the Allied defeat of the Japanese in World War II was the decision of American commanders to bypass huge Japanese garrisons on islands in the South Pacific, and to move on westward with air and sea forces to seize islands ever closer to the home islands of Japan.[5]

By this means, American forces hopscotched from one island to the other, well over 2,000 miles from the Solomon Islands, east of New Guinea, in 1943 to the Mariana Islands in June 1944. From Saipan, Tinian, and Guam in the Marianas, only 1,400 miles from Japan, new American long-range B-29 bombers commenced massive raids that virtually eliminated Japanese shipping between the Asian mainland and Japan, and eventually destroyed the central parts of most Japanese cities. Japan was reeling from these blows when the Americans, flying from the Marianas, dropped atomic bombs that destroyed Hiroshima and Nagasaki in early August 1945, and caused the Japanese emperor to sue for peace.

The U.S. Navy's thrust across the central Pacific and Douglas MacArthur's drive from New Guinea to the Philippines isolated nearly 2 million Japanese troops on bypassed islands and in southeast Asia and southern China.[6] These were troops the Americans and their allies did *not* have to fight.

The American decision to ignore Japanese garrisons on hundreds of islands, and then to gain new bases on islands beyond, was a perfect example of maneuvers on the enemy's rear. This was because—once

338

American ships and aircraft were positioned *between* the Japanese-occupied islands and Japan—the isolated garrisons were cut off from succor except by occasional submarines. More important strategically, they were unable to *do* anything militarily, because they could not get off the islands. In other words, the Americans *imprisoned* the Japanese on the islands they supposedly were defending. Indeed, the islands were, in effect, Allied prisoner-of-war camps, in which the inmates were obliged to support themselves.

In the aftermath of the Japanese attack on Pearl Harbor on December 7, 1941, Japanese forces occupied all of southeast Asia—Burma, Thailand, French Indochina, Malaya, and the Philippines—and spread over all the islands of the South Pacific from the Dutch East Indies (Indonesia) and northern New Guinea to the Solomons, some 500 miles to the east.

Since the United States devoted most of its strength to defeating Germany, much stronger and more dangerous than Japan, Allied forces in the South Pacific were extremely limited. The first significant Allied counterthrust against the Japanese occurred only after the drawn naval battle of the Coral Sea on May 7–8, 1942, and the great American victory in the battle of Midway on June 4–6, 1942.

In the months following, the Allies stopped the forward advance of the Japanese toward Australia and beyond the Solomons. Australian and American forces turned back a Japanese attack on Port Moresby, on the south shore of New Guinea, in September 1942, and American marines landed on the island of Guadalcanal in the southern Solomons in August 1942, and, after gruesome fighting under terrible jungle conditions, secured the island and its airfield by February 1943.

These repulses cost the Japanese four fleet carriers at Midway, two battleships and many smaller craft at Guadalcanal, plus hundreds of aircraft at both locations. Most especially the Japanese suffered extremely heavy casualties among their trained carrier pilots. Japan now had to go over to the defensive, hoping to retain the lands they had occupied, and to keep the Allies from breaking through the barrier they had erected from Burma around to the Solomons and across the central Pacific west of Hawaii.

The main avenues of advance open to the Allies were from New

Guinea to the Philippines under General Douglas MacArthur, or through the central Pacific under Admiral Chester W. Nimitz, the Pacific Fleet commander. American and British leaders at the Trident Conference in Washington in April 1943 decided to advance along both routes. The Philippines was the original target, not the Marianas. MacArthur had been ousted from this American possession in the first days of the war, and wanted to return. Its possession also could block Japanese shipping of oil and other vital materials from the East Indies to Japan.

The Marianas did not emerge at once as the logical base for B-29s to attack Japan. The first idea was to base them in China. But since the land route to China was blocked by the Japanese occupation of Burma, the difficulty of getting supplies by air transport over the Himalayas proved insuperable, although a few B-29 raids originating in India and refueling in China were carried out. However, the importance of the Marianas grew steadily in the minds of Allied planners, and at the Quadrant Conference at Quebec in August 1943 they became Nimitz's objective.

The principal strategic challenge in the southwest Pacific was the huge Japanese base at Rabaul on the northern end of New Britain Island in the Bismarck Archipelago, northeast of New Guinea. From this base, Japanese aircraft and ships could attack movements along the north coast of New Guinea or through the Pacific to the east and north. A major Allied priority, therefore, was the capture or neutralization of Rabaul. This required an advance on both sides of New Britain—along the north coast of New Guinea to the west and along the northern Solomons to the east.

The principal challenge in the vast watery reaches of the central Pacific was the lack of air bases from which to stage advances westward. The only candidates were tiny coral atolls, all of which bristled with heavy Japanese garrisons.

Guarding both avenues of approach was the large Japanese naval base at Truk in the Caroline Islands, halfway between Rabaul and the Marianas.

The concept of island-hopping was slow to develop, and came only after heavy fighting. Thus the Americans seized the Russell Islands between Guadalcanal and the next major island to the north, New Georgia, in February 1943. On June 30, 1943, they landed on the island of Rendova, just across a narrow strait from the Japanese air base of Munda on New Georgia. Three days later American troops attacked New Georgia, where they faced bitter resistance. The Japanese tried to run in reinforcements by light cruisers and destroyers. Air and sea battles raged throughout July 1943. Though the Allies lost one destroyer and one light cruiser, they sank several Japanese ships, and American pilots shot down many Japanese planes, flown by new and ill-trained pilots. Ground fighting was intense and, since virtually no Japanese soldiers willingly surrendered, required the killing of most of the 9,000-man garrison.

The fight for New Georgia was shorter than the battle for Guadalcanal, but almost as bitter. If the Allies had to attack each island in turn, the cost in lives, treasure, and time was going to be enormous, perhaps prohibitive. That is what the Japanese were counting on. As the next island to the north was Kolombangara, and as it was even more heavily garrisoned than New Georgia, an idea began to germinate.

The American commander on the spot, Admiral William Halsey, made the decision: he bypassed Kolombangara and achieved an almost unopposed landing on the next island to the north, Vella Lavella, on August 15, 1943. The 10,000-man Japanese garrison on Kolombangara was left to sit out the war.

But the *next* island, Bougainville, could not be bypassed. It was just east of New Britain. Together with the huge Japanese base at nearby Rabaul, Bougainville constituted a solid barrier to any further American advance into the central Pacific. If captured, however, the way would be opened to the Americans, while at the same time Rabaul would become relatively isolated—since American aircraft on Bougainville could attack Rabaul. Therefore, Bougainville had to be captured. The Japanese knew this, and placed 35,000 troops on the island. To throw off the Japanese, Halsey launched heavy air and naval strikes at both the northern and southern ends of the island, then invaded with the 3rd Marine Division in the center at Empress Augusta Bay on November 1, 1943, a move that totally surprised the Japanese.

To prevent the Japanese from sending heavy reinforcements from Rabaul, Halsey risked his two fleet aircraft carriers, *Saratoga* and *Independence*, in a heavy raid on the Japanese base, supported by land-based aircraft from New Guinea. The strike destroyed most of the car-

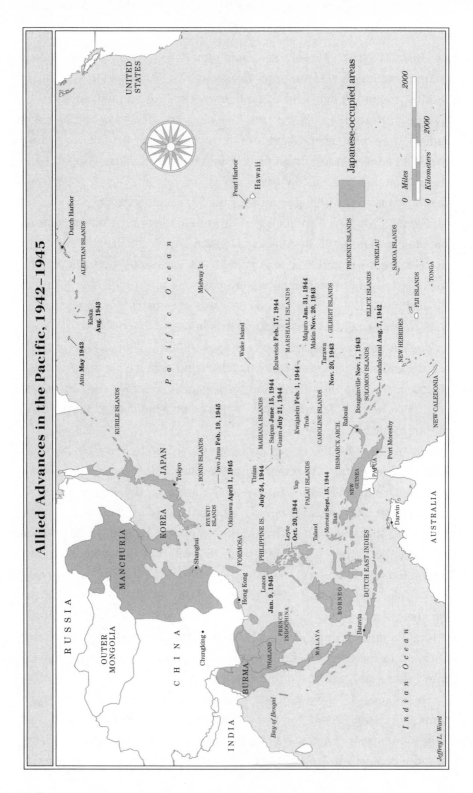

Allied Advances in the Pacific, 1942–1945

RUSSIA

OUTER MONGOLIA

MANCHURIA

KOREA

JAPAN

Tokyo

CHINA

Chungking

Shanghai

Hong Kong

KURILE ISLANDS

BONIN ISLANDS

Iwo Jima **Feb. 19, 1945**

RYUKYU ISLANDS

Okinawa **April 1, 1945**

FORMOSA

Tinian

July 24, 1944

Leyte

Oct. 20, 1944

Luzon

Jan. 9, 1945

PHILIPPINE IS.

Yap

PALAU ISLANDS

FRENCH INDOCHINA

THAILAND

BURMA

MALAYA

Batavia

BORNEO

DUTCH EAST INDIES

Talaud

Morotai **Sept. 15, 1944**

Biak

NEW GUINEA

PAPUA

Port Moresby

Darwin

AUSTRALIA

NEW CALEDONIA

INDIA

Bay of Bengal

Indian Ocean

Pacific Ocean

Dutch Harbor

Attu **May 1943**

ALEUTIAN ISLANDS

Kiska **Aug. 1943**

Midway Is.

Wake Island

MARIANA ISLANDS

Saipan **June 15, 1944**

Guam **July 21, 1944**

Eniwetok **Feb. 17, 1944**

MARSHALL ISLANDS

Kwajalein **Feb. 1, 1944**

Truk

CAROLINE ISLANDS

Majuro **Jan. 31, 1944**

Makin **Nov. 20, 1943**

GILBERT ISLANDS

Tarawa

Nov. 20, 1943

BISMARCK ARCH.

Rabaul

Bougainville **Nov. 1, 1943**

SOLOMON ISLANDS

Guadalcanal **Aug. 7, 1942**

NEW HEBRIDES

Pearl Harbor

Hawaii

PHOENIX ISLANDS

TOKELAU

ELLICE ISLANDS

SAMOA ISLANDS

FIJI ISLANDS

TONGA

UNITED STATES

Japanese-occupied areas

| 0 | | Miles | | 2000 |

| 0 | | Kilometers | | 2000 |

Jeffrey L. Ward

rier planes that had been sent to Rabaul, damaged six cruisers, and bluffed the Japanese navy out of the harbor, because the commander, Admiral Mineichi Koga, refused to believe Halsey would send in his carriers without a massive fleet of supporting warships (which he in fact did not have).

In the perimeter around Empress Augusta Bay, construction crews built a major air base, while the marines, joined by the army's 37th Infantry Division, slowly stifled Japanese resistance. The Japanese survivors withdrew into the interior, and became bystanders in the war.

While Americans and New Zealanders were moving up the Solomons, Americans and Australians advanced along the northern coast of New Guinea, a campaign culminating in the seizure of Finschhafen on the Huon Peninsula, directly west of New Britain, by the Australian 9th Division in late September and early October 1943. Many Japanese soldiers fell back into the jungle, where they posed a decreasing danger.

Rabaul was now isolated, deserted by the Japanese navy. At the Quadrant Conference, the American and British leaders elected to bypass the bastion. The 100,000-man Japanese garrison on New Britain and nearby New Ireland sat out the remainder of the war, totally useless.[7]

The problem in the central Pacific was entirely different from that in the Solomons and New Guinea. On these huge islands defeated Japanese could withdraw into mountains and jungles. The central Pacific, on the other hand, consisted of vast stretches of ocean and tiny islands. Air cover had to be by carriers, and all operations had to depend on floating bases—that is, supply ships that came along with the attacking fleet. There was no land on which to plant a base.[8] Japanese resistance would be bloody and brief, for there was nowhere to retreat. With American carriers and aircraft covering the region, there was no hope of evacuation. Consequently the Japanese would fight to the end, and sell their lives dearly.

The first targets were the coral atolls of Tarawa and Makin in the Gilbert Islands, 2,200 miles southwest of Honolulu, and 1,400 miles northeast of Bougainville. By now American industry was making giant strides in ship production, and the invasion fleet under Admiral Raymond A. Spruance was immense—six fast fleet carriers, five light carriers, six new battleships, as well as numerous other warships, and 850 carrier-based aircraft. The northern attack force, to strike Makin, consisted of 7,000 men of the army's 27th Infantry Division in six transports; the southern force, to hit Tarawa, counted sixteen transports carrying 18,000 men of the 2nd Marine Division.

After heavy bombardment, the attack began on November 20, 1943. Makin had only an 800-man garrison, but it held out for four days against the army division, which was hampered by inexperience. The greatest loss in the Makin operation was the sinking of the escort carrier *Lipscombe Bay* by a Japanese submarine, at a cost of 600 lives.

The garrison on Tarawa totaled 4,500 men, and the island was much more strongly fortified than Makin. Although naval guns bombarded the island for two and a half hours, and aircraft bombed it from end to end, one-third of the 5,000 marines who landed on the first day were killed or wounded crossing the 600-yard strip between the coral reef and the beaches. But the survivors forced the remaining Japanese to withdraw to two interior strong points, allowing the marines to spread over the whole island and hem in the strong points.

On the night of November 22, the Japanese solved the difficult problem of how to reduce the positions by switching over to repeated "banzai" counterattacks, in which the entire Japanese garrison was wiped out. In the fighting, 1,300 marines died and 2,000 were wounded. The losses shocked the American people, but the operation taught many valuable technical lessons, which were applied to later landings. These lessons included the length and nature of preliminary bombardments that were needed, the angle of fire of cannons, and details as to equipment and small-unit tactics in close-in fights.

The next step was the Marshall Islands, the chain just to the north, and the main intermediate objective on the way to the Marianas. But the sobering experience of Tarawa, combined with the success of Halsey's and MacArthur's bypassing of Japanese garrisons in the southwest Pacific, caused Admiral Nimitz to insist that instead of a direct attack on the nearest, most easterly of the Marshalls, all were to be bypassed, and the next strike was to be on Kwajalein Atoll, 400 miles farther on. Nimitz also ruled that if all went well, Spruance's reserve would be sent at once to Eniwetok Atoll, at the far northern end of the 700-mile chain of islands. The Japanese played into the hands of this strategy by sending what reinforcements they could to the easterly Marshalls, assuming they would be the next hit.

By now American naval power was greatly superior to Japan's. Moreover, Nimitz, since he was picking targets, could assemble American ships where needed, whereas the Japanese, not knowing where the next attack would come, had to keep their naval power far to the rear—mainly at the huge naval base at Truk in the Carolines, 1,100 miles west of Kwajalein.

Nimitz assembled two fresh divisions for the assault on the Marshalls, 54,000 combat troops. He also gathered twelve fast fleet carriers and eight battleships (which had now taken on a new role, that of bombarding enemy-held islands). Aircraft and gunboats were equipped with rockets. Preparatory bombardment was to be four times as great as the attack on Tarawa.

The fast carrier forces arrived in the Marshalls in January 1944, and launched 6,000 sorties that paralyzed Japanese air and sea movements throughout the Marshalls, and destroyed 150 Japanese aircraft.

On January 31, forces seized undefended Majuro, in the easterly Marshalls, which provided good anchorage for the navy's supporting Service Force. The main attack (7th Infantry Division) against Kwajalein came on February 1. Once again the Japanese garrison of 8,000, finding nowhere to go, assisted in their own destruction by numerous suicidal banzai charges straight into American guns. As a result, only 370 Americans were killed in gaining Kwajalein.

As the expedition's reserve of 10,000 men had not been called upon, Spruance sent it at once against Eniwetok, 700 miles from Truk. As a flank safeguard, a task force under Marc Mitscher launched a strike with nine fast carriers against Truk the same day (February 17, 1944) that the landings took place on Eniwetok. Mitscher sent in a second strike that night, assisted by radar to identify targets, and a third the next morning. Out of precaution, Admiral Koga had already withdrawn most of the

Japanese fleet to the Palau Islands, 1,200 miles west, but the American air strikes sank two cruisers, four destroyers, and twenty-six tankers and freighters in the Truk harbor. In addition the Japanese lost 250 aircraft, for an American loss of twenty-five—attributable primarily to the poor training of Japanese pilots compared to American.

The triple blow proved that American carrier forces could cripple a major enemy base without occupying it. Thus, not only did the strikes force the Japanese fleet back another 1,200 miles to the west, but all of the garrisons in the Carolines likewise could be ignored and bypassed.

With no help from Truk, the Eniwetok garrison could do little, and less than half of the 27th Infantry Division's strength was needed to overcome resistance in three days. The building of new airfields in the Marshalls now proceeded apace. The Marianas lay a thousand miles ahead.

The strikes against Truk had the additional benefit of causing the Japanese to withdraw all their aircraft from the Bismarcks, since these islands were now much too far from the Palaus to be sustained. Rabaul was thus totally helpless.

The Japanese still had not focused on the fact that the central Pacific offensive was aimed at the Marianas. They thought the Allies would continue hopscotching across the northern coast of New Guinea, while the American navy would head from the Marshalls to the Palaus, en route to the Philippines. Accordingly they focused on a move to stop MacArthur's advance on the Vogelkop ("Bird's Head") Peninsula of western New Guinea.

They had to change plans abruptly when word arrived that Marc Mitscher's carriers had commenced massive bombing of the Marianas on June 11, 1944, followed by massive bombardment of Saipan and Tinian by U.S. battleships on June 13, preparatory to the landing of 20,000 marines on Saipan on June 15.

The pre-invasion bombardment damaged the defenses of Saipan and Tinian, while attacks on air bases virtually eliminated Japanese air support. But the assaulting marines were slowed by the fierce resistance of the 32,000-man Japanese garrison, assisted by the fact that Saipan was not a coral atoll, but a good-sized island with mountains and jungles.

But on the morning of June 15, American submarines spotted the Japanese fleet steaming into the Philippine Sea, heading toward the Marianas. Spruance canceled intended landings on Guam, put his reserve, the army's 27th Infantry Division, ashore on Saipan to speed up its capture, and cleared the transports away to safer waters. The 5th Fleet assembled 180 miles west of Tinian, and waited for the Japanese.

Admiral Jisaburo Ozawa, in command of the Japanese fleet, had three large and six smaller carriers (500 aircraft), whereas Spruance's 5th Fleet had seven fast fleet carriers and eight escort carriers (956 aircraft), plus seven battleships, twenty-one cruisers, and sixty-nine destroyers.

Ozawa had hoped to use land-based aircraft on the Marianas as part of a "pincers" to destroy the American carrier aircraft. But Mitscher's planes had virtually destroyed the Japanese planes on the airfields, and Ozawa had only his carrier-based aircraft, which he sent in early on June 19. The flights were detected by American radar, however, and hundreds of American fighters climbed off the decks to meet them, while Mitscher's carrier-borne bombers once more attacked the Marianas airfields.

The outcome of this tremendous aerial battle was the massacre that became known as "The Great Marianas Turkey Shoot." American pilots were vastly superior to the raw and poorly trained Japanese pilots. The Americans brought down 218 Japanese aircraft, while the Japanese shot down just twenty-nine American planes. Worse, American submarines torpedoed and sank two of the Japanese fleet carriers, the *Shokaku* and the *Taisho*, both containing many more aircraft.

Ozawa thought most of his planes had landed on Guam, and, instead of getting away, hung around, hoping to retrieve them. American reconnaissance aircraft spotted his fleet the next afternoon. It was a wonderful bonanza, and Mitscher launched 216 carrier aircraft, knowing the recovery of the planes would have to come after dark. The American aircraft sank one fleet carrier and damaged two more, plus two light carriers, a battleship, and a heavy cruiser. In addition, they shot down sixty-five Japanese planes. The Americans lost twenty aircraft in action, but a further eighty were lost or crashed on the long night return flight. Many of the crews were saved, however.

On Saipan, the Americans drove the Japanese back in bloody fighting, capturing the commanding height of Mount Tapotchau on June 25. On July 7 the surviving 3,000 Japanese troops virtually committed suicide in colossal headlong charges into American guns, while many Japanese civilians killed themselves by jumping off high cliffs. American losses were 3,500 dead and 13,000 wounded.

On July 23, marines landed on Tinian, and seized the island in a week. Meanwhile army troops landed on July 20 on Guam, where the Japanese garrison of 18,000, helped by an intricate network of cave defenses, put up fierce resistance. The Americans cleared the island by August 12, 1944.

The battle of the Philippine Sea opened the way to invade the island of Leyte in the Philippines, which soon followed, while capture of the Marianas permitted the launching of massive and ultimately desolating B-29 raids against the home islands of Japan. By June 1945 the Americans had liberated the Philippines and seized the island of Okinawa, the final stepping-stone to the invasion of Japan. By this stage, even before B-29s dropped atomic bombs on Hiroshima on August 6, and on Nagasaki on August 9, 1945, at last bringing the war to a close, the Japanese had been hopelessly shattered by the island-hopping strategy of the Americans.

Not only were all of the garrisons on the Pacific islands neutralized, but the advance to the Philippines had closed off any movement or action by Japanese troops in the East Indies, in southeast Asia, and in southern China. While nearly 2 million soldiers had been bypassed, the Japanese were able to assemble only 1.8 million troops on the home islands to defend against invasion. The maneuvers on the rear in the Pacific in World War II were among the most successful and brilliant in world history.

The Inchon Invasion, 1950

On September 15, 1950, only three months into the Korean War (1950–1953), the American commander Douglas MacArthur carried out one of the most spectacular and successful maneuvers on the rear that has ever been accomplished. By means of a sudden and unexpected invasion of Inchon, the port city of the South Korean capital of Seoul, he isolated the invading North Korean army far to the south and caused its virtual destruction without a shot being fired.[9]

In the first weeks after the North Koreans invaded South Korea, aided by Soviet-made T-34 tanks, they knocked aside most resistance, pressing the South Koreans and their American allies into the small "Pusan perimeter" around the southern port city of Pusan. The North Koreans launched major offensives against the perimeter, hoping to drive the Americans into the sea and reunite Korea by force.

The Americans and South Koreans, supported by the United Nations and joined in late August by a small British brigade, were able to contain the attacks, and they hoped that, as more American weapons arrived, they would be able to go over to the offensive. But they faced the prospect of a slow, grinding, costly campaign to push the fiercely resisting North Koreans back beyond the thirty-eighth parallel, the dividing line between the American and Soviet sectors agreed to at the time of the Japanese surrender in August 1945. This line hardened into the boundary between two competing Korean states, a Soviet-sponsored Communist regime to the north and an American-sponsored right-wing regime under Syngman Rhee to the south.

MacArthur, the Far East commander, came up with a way to destroy North Korea's military quickly and without having to challenge it step by step back into North Korea. He proposed, only days after the war started, that the Americans and their allies deliver a maneuver on the North Korean rear by invading at Inchon, on the west coast well north of where the North Korean forces had moved, and driving swiftly from Inchon to Seoul, twenty miles away. This would eliminate the North Korean army just as thoroughly as Japanese garrisons were immobilized in the island-hopping campaigns in the Pacific in World War II.

The North Koreans would be defeated because there was only a single double-tracked railway line in Korea, which ran through Seoul, and the North Koreans depended upon this railroad to deliver supplies to their army. If this line were cut, the North Koreans would be as thoroughly immobilized as any Japanese garrison on a bypassed island in the Pacific. They would have to abandon most of their weapons and retreat on foot back into North Korea.

MacArthur saw what the North Koreans did not see—that the United States had complete control of the sea, and, since Korea was a peninsula, the U.S. Navy could approach any point it wished along the coast and there land an invading force. In fact, Korea could be seen as a *sack*. The farther North Korean troops advanced southward, the deeper into the sack they fell. And the American navy could close the sack *anywhere* it wanted to on the north, sealing off the North Korean soldiers from succor and reinforcement.

MacArthur's idea was a precise application of the principle of maneuver on the rear, and his selection of Inchon was masterful, because it

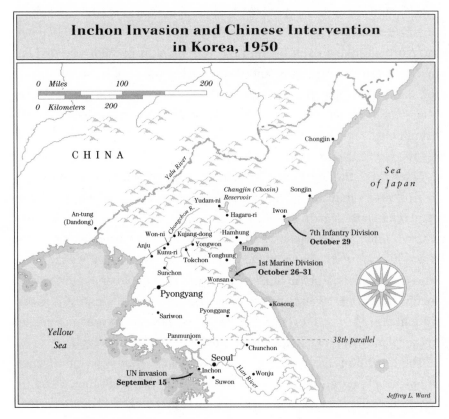

Inchon Invasion and Chinese Intervention in Korea, 1950

Jeffrey L. Ward

was the closest port to the all-important double-tracked railroad, and, moreover, was a port that, because of its excessively high tides, no one would consider a candidate for an invasion. In addition, Seoul was the capital of South Korea, and its recapture would constitute a strong psychological advantage as well.

Given all these factors, it's astonishing that the American Joint Chiefs of Staff (JCS), the body charged with directing U.S. military operations, balked at the idea of Inchon, and fought the concept almost to the last minute. The result—since MacArthur achieved a stunning and almost immediate victory—was that the JCS suffered immense loss in prestige, and MacArthur was elevated in the public mind into a military genius with infallible judgment.

This led in only a few weeks to one of the most stunning military reverses in American history. MacArthur turned out to be a military Dr. Jekyll and Mr. Hyde, capable of both brilliant ideas and devastatingly wrong judgments. For, after pushing for an American invasion and conquest of North Korea, he led the American army into an ambush laid by the Chinese Communists in the mountains close to the Chinese frontier. The Chinese violently opposed an American advance to the Yalu River, the frontier between China and Korea, because they feared a U.S.-sponsored invasion by the Chinese Nationalists, who had been driven to the island of Taiwan in 1949, and sought to reconquer the mainland with American help. The Chinese ambush shattered one American division, caused huge casualties, and forced all United Nations forces to flee back into South Korea.

The dispute over the invasion of Inchon constitutes one of the most revealing cases in modern history of how, in a given situation, one military leader sees opportunity when other military leaders see peril. While MacArthur looked at the *result* of an invasion of Inchon—the total loss of the means of supply and reinforcement of the North Korean army to the south—the JCS recoiled at the *danger* of what might happen if things went wrong.

MacArthur stated plainly that the North Koreans would not oppose an invasion at Inchon with any strength because they would not expect an invasion there and because the vast bulk of their military strength was being exerted against the Pusan perimeter. Thus there was no possibility of effective resistance.

The army chief of staff, J. Lawton Collins, took precisely the opposite view. He expressed fear that the American forces in the perimeter (8th Army) would be unable to make a junction with the invading force at Inchon (10th Corps). "Failure to make this junction might result in disaster to the 10th Corps," he wrote.[10] In other words, Collins saw 10th Corps as being in jeopardy, and talked about an "overwhelming force" concentrating against it before 8th Army could come up from the Pusan perimeter to relieve it. But where was this "overwhelming force" to come from? The American and allied armada numbered nearly 70,000 combat troops, almost ten times the North Koreans that might feasibly be able to get to Inchon. Meanwhile the American naval forces were totally overwhelming, amounting to 230 vessels, including four aircraft carriers that could provide as many aircraft as the space over the invasion site would allow.[11]

The chief technical objection the JCS raised was the site of the invasion, Inchon itself. The port experienced high tides and possessed extensive mudflats produced by waters funneling through the narrow Yellow Sea between the Korean peninsula on the east and the Chinese Shandong peninsula on the west. The situation is much like that in Canada's Bay of Fundy, closed in by New Brunswick and Nova Scotia.

Naval experts believed small landing craft would need twenty-three-foot minimum tides to operate safely over the mudflats and a twenty-nine-foot tide before Landing Ships, Tank (LSTs) could come in. Thus the navy could land men and equipment only from the time the incoming tide reached twenty-three feet until the outgoing tide dropped to twenty-three feet, about three hours. Troops ashore would be stranded till the next tide, about twelve hours later. The tide tables dictated September 15 as the earliest date the tide surges would be high enough. To wait longer would invite bad weather, and indefinite postponement of the invasion.

Given these constraints, and the fear of being isolated, as enunciated by General Collins, the Joint Chiefs advocated an invasion at Kunsan, a small port about a hundred miles south of Inchon, and only seventy miles west of the Pusan perimeter.

A landing at Kunsan might be safer from Collins's point of view, as being closer to 8th Army, but it would *not* be a descent on the enemy rear and would *not* establish a strategic barrage, or barrier, across his line of communications. Rather, the invasion would be on the flank of the North Korean line around the perimeter, and would require the North Koreans only to extend their line across the whole width of the peninsula, incorporating the invaders at Kunsan with the defenders of the perimeter. Any UN attack thereafter would have to be a direct assault against defended emplacements, driving the North Koreans back *on* their reserves and supplies, not severing the army *from* them.

MacArthur met in Tokyo on July 13, 1950, with Collins and Hoyt S. Vandenberg, air force chief of staff. When Collins presented MacArthur's arguments to Omar Bradley, the chief of staff, back at the Pentagon, Bradley called it a "blue-sky" scheme and said "Inchon was probably the worst possible place ever selected for an amphibious landing."[12]

MacArthur made a formal presentation in Tokyo on August 23 to General Collins, Admiral Forrest P. Sherman, the chief of naval operations, and other high officers. The Joint Chiefs inclined toward postponing Inchon until they were sure American forces in the perimeter could hold. But President Harry Truman, Secretary of Defense Louis Johnson, and Truman's roving ambassador W. Averell Harriman were enthusiastic. Truman called it a daring strategic conception. Thus civilians backed MacArthur, while the top military men hesitated.

At this moment the North Koreans launched a last, desperate attempt to drive the Americans and South Koreans into the sea. They had assembled about 98,000 men, one-third of which were South Korean civilians picked up on the streets and rushed into battle without training. The UN command had brought together 120,000 combat troops, plus 60,000 support personnel, while UN firepower had grown to several times that of the Communists. Thus the enemy assaults, though carried out with great effort, failed everywhere, and the North Korean army suffered 28,000 casualties within a couple of weeks.

The Joint Chiefs were frightened by the North Korean offensive, and implied in a message to MacArthur on September 7 that the invasion might best be postponed. MacArthur replied that the invasion represented "the only hope of wresting the initiative from the enemy and thereby presenting an opportunity for a decisive blow." The envelopment at Inchon, he stressed, "will instantly relieve pressure on the south perimeter." He also said the seizure of "the enemy distributing system" at Seoul would dislocate logistical supply, and result in the disintegration of the enemy.[13]

On September 8 the JCS informed Truman that they endorsed the invasion, but their approval remained grudging to the last. General Bradley wrote, "It was really too late in the game for the JCS to formally disapprove Inchon."[14]

The key to the assault on Inchon was the neutralization of a tiny island, Wolmi-do, just off Inchon. It contained 75-mm cannons inside deep revetments, which could sink marine landing craft. This the U.S. Navy accomplished by bombardment on September 13. The invasion was accomplished on September 15, 1950, by the 1st Marine Division with great speed, efficiency, and few losses. There were minuscule North Korean forces in the city, and they put up only fleeting resistance.

The marines, followed by the army's 7th Infantry Division, quickly moved on toward Seoul, which they captured in a series of fierce battles that ended on September 25 with the withdrawal northward of most North Korean forces, followed by a nasty series of fights in the streets of the city, where last-ditch defenders erected barricades that had to be broken down one at a time.

The North Korean command did not tell their soldiers around the Pusan perimeter that they had been cut off on their rear. But after a week, news filtered through, and the army disintegrated. Only about 30,000 of the 70,000 soldiers facing 8th Army eventually got back to North Korea, most of them walking through the mountains and nearly all leaving their weapons behind. There had been no chance for the North Koreans to retrieve the situation, because MacArthur had placed the North Koreans in an impossible position. Their defeat was inevitable, and their only hope for survival was to withdraw back into North Korea. The UN victory was due entirely to the application of the rule of maneuvering on the enemy rear.

The next stage of the Korean War grew out of the decision of the American leadership to pursue an objective endorsed by MacArthur and others to conquer North Korea and force it into union with Syngman Rhee's right-wing government in South Korea.

The Chinese Communists in Beijing warned the United States that they would intervene if Americans crossed the thirty-eighth parallel, though not if South Koreans did so. Truman ignored the warning, and sent MacArthur forward. He refused to believe the Chinese would enter the war, and allowed the UN forces to be extremely spread out and disconnected when the Chinese struck first in late October and then solidly in late November 1950. The result was the defeat of the UN forces, withdrawal back to South Korea, and, after a series of indecisive offensives on both sides, a bloody, battle-stained stalemate that lasted from the summer of 1951 to the summer of 1953, when President Dwight Eisenhower concluded a cease-fire with the Communists.

Implications for the Future

The concept of depositing a force on the enemy rear with sufficient power to disrupt his communications, supply, and means of operation has even greater significance today than in the past—because such movements now can be made much more swiftly and decisively by air. A hint of the possible future application of the rule was shown in the fall of 2001 when a large U.S. Marine Corps force dropped near Kandahar, Afghanistan, and at once disrupted Taliban and Al Qaeda communications and connections in the region of the Taliban's greatest strength.

Another possible application could be against a state that possesses large forces but whose weapons and technology are inadequate to meet a modern army in open combat. Such a defender may try to draw forces into a nasty urban battle, where, in the confines of a tightly built-up city, even heavy modern tanks are no proof against handheld weapons wielded at close range. We saw an elementary example of this strategy in Mogadishu, Somalia, in October 1993, when mobs attacked U.S. Rangers trying to rescue a downed helicopter crew. This kind of defense could be countered in many cases by deliberately avoiding closely built urban areas, and dropping a powerful force at a critical point that interrupts some of the country's lines of *economic* communication, like railroads, ports, air terminals, or oil refineries.

Another possible use of the rule would be to strike with so-called standoff weapons. For example, the threat to international peace posed by North Korea lies primarily in its sales of missiles and other weapons to rogue nations like Iraq and Iran, and its threat to build nuclear weapons. Perhaps diplomatic and economic negotiations will turn the rulers of North Korea in peaceful directions. But if negotiations fail, one possible scenario to stop North Korea's dangerous activities would be to deliver a modern-day maneuver on its rear—by imposing an iron block-ade of its seaports and airports, and by destroying with preemptive air strikes the physical infrastructure or plants necessary to build a nuclear bomb.[15] The threat of a possible North Korean retaliatory attack into South Korea need not be seen as a potential disaster. Against a waiting and heavily armed South Korean army, aided by American forces, espe-cially air power, North Korea's army would be shattered.

In chapter 13 we discussed how the United States might use the rule of uproar east, attack west to deceive a country such as Iraq into defending its capital while the real blow is struck elsewhere. We can likewise apply the rule of maneuvers on the rear to overcome a country such as Iraq.

For example, if the United States decided to eliminate the hostile activ-ities of Iraq without a full-scale invasion, it might deposit a force that would block the Iraqi leaders' access to the oil fields (and the source of their wealth) in the south, and from which air, rail, and road traffic going into and out of Baghdad could be interdicted by attack helicopters, gun-ships, and bombers. This would effectively shut down the Iraqi economy, avoid a dangerous battle through the streets of Baghdad, and force the Iraqi army either to come out and fight and be defeated, or remain in Baghdad and still be defeated. With such superior weapons, American forces could stop any attack, with minimum casualties to American forces.

Notes

Introduction: The New Kind of War

1. (In the notes in this book, single names refer to authors whose volumes are cited in full in the Selected Bibliography. Other sources are given in full in the notes. Numbers refer to pages.) The terrorists who attacked on September 11, 2001, were part of an organized crime syndicate or criminal insurrection group. The hatred they directed against the United States was irrational. In 1998, Osama bin Laden and fellow members of his World Islamic Front for Jihad Against the Jews and Crusaders issued a bizarre declaration against the United States for its "occupation" of the holy land of Arabia, its "aggression" against Iraq, and its support of "the petty state of the Jews." The declaration concluded: "To kill Americans and their allies, both civil and military, is an individual duty of every Muslim who is able, in any country, where this is possible, until the Aqsa Mosque [in Jerusalem] and the Haram Mosque [in Mecca] are freed from their grip and until their armies, shattered and broken-winged, depart from all the lands of Islam." See *The Economist*, October 6–12, 2001, 19, and "The Trap," by Hendrik Hertzberg and David Remnick in *The New Yorker* magazine, October 1, 2001, 37–39. See also Bergen, 18–23, for a summary of an April 1997 CNN interview with Osama bin Laden by Peter Arnett and Peter Bergen, which contained a number of similar complaints against the United States.
2. Clausewitz, 119, 406.
3. No responsible leader of a state will ever use nuclear weapons, because their employment would invite counterstrikes that would destroy his own people. But a terrorist group like Al Qaeda almost certainly would use a nuclear device if it could acquire one. This is the great danger the world now faces. Graham Allison, assistant secretary of defense in the first Clinton administration, wrote in the November 3, 2001, issue of *The Economist* that a primary objective of the United States must be to get at the source of the greatest danger today—the nearly 100 percent of the world's nuclear, biological, and chemical weapons of mass destruction stored in the United States and Russia. "The surest way to prevent nuclear assaults on Russia, America, and the world is to prevent terrorists from gaining control of these weapons or materials to make them," he wrote. The aim would be to make all nuclear weapons and material as secure as technically possible, as fast as possible. Recommendations for such controls were presented in

January 2001 by a task force chaired by Howard Baker and Lloyd Cutler (www.hr.doe.gov/seab/rusrpt.pdf).

4. China, although a great power, has never fielded an army with anything approaching the high technology of the United States or the Soviet Union. Its strength has always been its enormous potential manpower and its highly sophisticated tactical or small-unit operations. These strengths are most effective in defensive operations, and Communist China has never entertained aggressive ideas beyond the historic territory of China, including Taiwan and Tibet. Its intervention in the Korean War, 1950–1953, was to prevent an American or an American-assisted Chinese Nationalist incursion into mainland China.

5. The killings so soured American opinion that, after forcing the Somalis to release a wounded American pilot they had captured, the United States pulled out of Somalia. On July 20, 1950, American forces were able to approach undetected within a few yards of several North Korean T-34 tanks in the closely built streets of Taejon, Korea, and destroy them with new 3.5-inch "super bazooka" rocket launchers. See Alexander, *Korea*, 92–107.

6. I'm indebted to my former editor, Jonathan Slonim, for this brilliant suggestion. It is a much clearer method than the traditional chronological approach.

7. For a fascinating analysis of the development of the alphabet and writing, see Burke and Ornstein, 36–87. Although the characters of Chinese writing are often identified as pictographic or ideographic, they are actually logographic, or a system using symbols representing entire words. Characters only represent a specific word of the Chinese language. As examples, the character for "to love" depicts a woman and child, while the character for "peace" consists of the elements for roof, heart, and wine cup. See Sino-Tibetan languages, *Encyclopaedia Britannica*, 15th edition, vol. 16, 804.

8. Fuller, *The Conduct of War, 1789–1961*, 50–51.

Chapter 1. The Revolution in Warfare

1. For example, the one-man Javelin infrared-directed, fire-and-forget system weighs forty-nine pounds and fires a missile that is lethal against all tanks out to 2,500 meters. It has a day-and-night sight, and can strike targets either directly or on tanks' weakly armored tops. Gunners can lock onto a target before launch, fire, and then immediately take cover.

2. In October each year, *Army* magazine produces in its Green Book descriptions, with pictures, of all major ground weapons either in use in the U.S. Army or projected. *Army* is published by the Association of the United States Army, 2425 Wilson Boulevard, Arlington, Virginia 22201-3326, 703-841-4300, armymag@ausa.org.

3. There has been a radical increase in the past decade in the capacity of the United States military to deliver bombs precisely on target. For example, in the fall 2001 air war against the Taliban and Al Qaeda, American special forces units on the ground in Afghanistan spotted, or "painted," enemy targets using binoculars

equipped with laser rangefinders. They relayed coordinates by satellite phones on laptop computers to American aircraft circling high overhead, which then dropped bombs on the targets. Pilotless aircraft—the air force's long-range Predator and Global Hawk, and the army's short-range Hunter (the brigade-level Shadow was in development in 2001)—also provided sharp video images of moving targets within milliseconds to command centers nearby or thousands of miles away. In Afghanistan, Predator video cameras were linked to the cockpits of AC-130 gunships, allowing pilots to locate moving targets on the ground. The eye-in-the-sky Predator can also be used as a strike weapon, delivering Hellfire missiles directly onto targets. The Global Hawk unmanned reconnaissance aircraft flies higher (65,000 feet) and faster than the Predator and is less likely to be shot down. It takes close-up photographs. The air force links its aircraft together, allowing Predators, Global Hawks, RC-135 Rivet Joints, U-2 reconnaissance planes, and E-8C Joint Stars radar planes to share information, guide one another to uncovered areas, or focus on specific targets. Other means of locating targets include Boeing 707s carrying ground-target radars, and reconnaissance satellites high above the earth. The Pentagon's weapon of choice in Afghanistan was the joint direct-attack munition (JDAM), a $21,000 device attached to the tail of a simple gravity bomb that enables it to be guided by the Global Positioning System to fall within thirty feet of the target. Only four of 4,000 JDAMs dropped in Afghanistan went off target, but the misses did cause friendly deaths and injuries. The bomb also can be guided by lasers. Pilots of B-1, B-2, and B-52 bombers were able to support troops on the ground—guiding bombs to specific targets using off-the-shelf laptop computers. See James Dao, "New Technology Is Shielding Pilots," *New York Times*, November 29, 2001, and "Satellites and Horsemen," *The Economist*, March 9, 2002, 27.

4. See James Dao and Andrew C. Revkin, "A Revolution in Warfare," *New York Times, Science Times*, April 16, 2002.

5. Critics have decried the reluctance of Pentagon planners to recognize fast enough the need to reform the military radically. They cited as evidence the Pentagon's decision on October 25, 2001, to award to Lockheed Martin the first contract for a new supersonic joint strike fighter (JSF), to be used by all the services in a number of roles. The JSF is expected to be the biggest conventional weapons program in history. The air force plans to buy 1,763 JSFs, the navy 480, the marines 609, and Britain's Royal Navy 150. The fighter's key characteristic is its capacity for STOVL—short takeoff and vertical landing. This feature (shared by the subsonic Harrier jet used for years by the marines and Britain) will make the JSF far more versatile than any other fighter, because it will need little deck space on aircraft carriers to take off and land, and can use tiny fields to give close support to ground forces. The marine and Royal Navy version will be fitted for STOVL, the air force version for conventional takeoff and landing (CTOL), and the navy version CTOL modified for aircraft carrier use. Therefore, the JSF will be both a conventional fighter and a highly flexible aircraft that needs neither large air bases nor huge aircraft carriers. It will fly 600 nautical miles and carry 13,000 pounds of payload in the marine, Royal Navy, and air force versions,

17,000 pounds in the navy version. In any event the JSF is likely to be the last manned fighter. Unmanned aircraft most probably will be the aerial strike weapon of the future. These UAVs (unmanned aerial vehicles) are guided by on-board television cameras that beam pictures back to controllers in the rear, and use TV, infrared, radar, and laser homing devices to launch rockets and gunfire against targets.

6. Networks, whether connected by the Internet, wire, radio, or television, have three main forms: chain or line, where members are linked in a row and data must flow through an adjacent actor to get to the next; hub or star, where members are tied to a central node and must go through it to communicate with one another; and all-channel or full-matrix, where everyone is connected to and can communicate with everyone else. See David Ronfeldt and John Arquilla, "Networks, Netwars and the Fight for the Future," *First Monday, Peer-Reviewed Journal on the Internet,* October 2001, firstmonday.org.

7. The military calls its integrated information system C^{4}ISR, for "command, control, communications, computers, intelligence, surveillance, and reconnaissance." This system may generate so much information that it may have to find new ways to segregate the individual unit's need for immediate target or other data from the higher command's need for an overall picture, or, as the military calls it, "topsight." See Arquilla and Ronfeldt, 46. The biggest problem that a system with such immense amounts of information faces is how to winnow the important from the nonessential.

8. Arquilla and Ronfeldt, 46.

9. The Stinger is a "fire-and-forget" infrared-guided missile system. The operator can fire at his target, then immediately leave or take cover. The missile homes in on the heat emitted by either jet- or propeller-driven fixed-wing aircraft or helicopters. It can fly an intercept course to the target. Once the missile has traveled a safe distance from the gunner, its engine ignites and propels it to the target. TOW stands for "tube-launched, optically tracked, wire-guided" missile. It can stop any tank out to a range of 3,750 meters.

10. Coroalles, 62–72; Colonel Harry E. Rothmann, "The Air Assault Division and Brigade Operations Manual," 101st Airborne Division (Air Assault), Fort Campbell, Kentucky, August 1, 1988.

11. The U.S. Army possesses a formidable arsenal of attack and troop-carrying helicopters. The best attack helicopters in the world are the AH-64A Apache and AH-64D Apache Longbow. Both use a sight that acquires and designates targets and a night-vision sensor that permits the two-man crew to navigate and attack in darkness and adverse weather. The Apache's principal mission is to destroy high-value targets with the laser-guided Hellfire missile, which can destroy tanks at ranges of 6,500 meters. It also mounts a 30-mm automatic cannon and Hydra 70 rockets that are lethal against vehicles, ground objects, and personnel. The Longbow can conduct deep precision strikes, and provide armed reconnaissance and security. It has a millimeter-wave radar air-ground targeting system that can be used in all weathers, day and night. The Apache Longbow can hand over targets to other commands to execute, and itself can strike sixteen separate targets

in one minute. The army's transport helicopters include the CH-47D Chinook, which can carry weapons, ammunition, equipment, troops, and other cargo, and the UH-60 Black Hawk air assault helicopter, which can carry an entire fully equipped eleven-man infantry squad. It also can move a 105-mm howitzer, its crew of six, and thirty rounds of ammunition in a single lift.

12. The V-22 Osprey has two engines that can tilt vertically and horizontally, allowing it to fly both as a helicopter and an airplane. The Osprey can carry twenty-four fully equipped soldiers or 15,000 pounds of equipment more than 1,100 miles at a speed of about 240 miles an hour. That is twice the speed and range of most helicopters. The Osprey has had large development problems, but in 2001 Pentagon plans were to build 360 for the U.S. Marine Corps, fifty for the air force, and forty-eight for the navy. The marines see the Osprey as central to projecting power from ships at sea for vertical assault and envelopment and special operations missions.

13. The standard method of air assault into an enemy-held area is to form a "500-yard box" or ring—a secured sector 250 yards in all directions from a point of landing. Normally, army Apache or marine Cobra attack helicopters or AC-130 gunships would come in ahead and "pepper" a region about to be assaulted with machine-gun, rocket, or cannon fire to keep enemy forces in their holes or defenses. Then a UH-60 Black Hawk air assault helicopter would drop into the zone with a full squad of heavily armed infantry who would immediately spread out 250 yards from the landing point, firing as they went, to secure the 500-yard box or ring. Black Hawks are designed for quick exit by troops, unlike CH-47D Chinook transport helicopters or V-22 Ospreys, which are large carriers, designed for delivering reinforcements and equipment, not fast tactical deployment under battle conditions. Once a 500-yard perimeter is secured, however, Chinooks and Ospreys can drop in safely because most enemy fire will have to come from beyond the perimeter.

14. So long as weapons were not strong or accurate enough to prevent movements of large armies in the field or to prohibit defended main lines of resistance, the traditional organization of armies into corps, divisions, regiments, and battalions was the most effective structure, since it permitted commanders to apply the most force at the most crucial point in the shortest time. It should be obvious, however, that with the development of super-accurate weapons such concentrations of troops now are impossible. This has altered the military situation fundamentally.

15. See Bruce Gudmundsson, *Stormtroop Tactics* (Westport, Conn.: Praeger, 1989). Captain Rohr completely abandoned military formations, and put full responsibility on the commander of each small team for carrying out its mission. Initiative and flexibility increased greatly, and teams could concentrate on gaining their objectives without waiting for approval from higher command, and could use whatever opportunities or routes materialized. The system did not win the war, however, because advances still were made on foot. It was extremely successful in capturing small objectives, and, when a number of teams working together seized a number of interconnected points, occasionally made large

breaks in the enemy line. But Allied reinforcements coming up on railways could always close a gap before German infantry could move deep and wide enough to create a strategic breakthrough. The system required one additional element: fast-moving tanks or motorized forces that could exploit a breach faster than reinforcements could seal it, and thereby reinstitute a war of movement. This element came in World War II.

16. Alexander, *How Hitler Could Have Won*, 37–44.
17. Alexander, *Korea*, 302–3.

Chapter 2. Striking at Enemy Weakness

1. The goal is unattainable because it is always directed against a much stronger state using strikes that kill or wound only a small fraction of the state's population. The effect is to marshal the resources and resolve of the attacked state to defend itself. Therefore the attacks do not bring about submission to the terrorists, but the contrary.

2. Miller writes: "There is no more an Islamic world than there is an Arab world or a Christian world. . . . There will not be a single, unified Islamic *umma*, or community, any more than there is a single Arab nation, even in the unlikely event that Islamic radicals topple every quasi-secular government in the Middle East." See Miller, *God Has Ninety-nine Names*, 14.

3. As Jessica Stern points out in *The Ultimate Terrorists*, human beings may have a genetic fear of poisons (and, by implication, potentially lethal bacteria or other infectious diseases like anthrax and tularemia), and they fear catastrophic risks of exposure to such agents far more than ordinary or more usual dangers in society. See Stern, 35. This inherent aversion gives terrorists more impact than they otherwise would achieve. This was demonstrated in the enormous fear generated by a few cases of anthrax caused by letters containing the bacteria sent through the U.S. mails in September and October 2001.

4. There could be no more graphic an example of this than the worldwide revulsion that resulted from the kidnaping and brutal murder of *Wall Street Journal* correspondent Daniel Pearl by Moslem extremists in Karachi, Pakistan, in January 2002. The fact that the terrorists videotaped the murder of Pearl demonstrated a level of wanton savagery and evil that eliminated any possibility their political aims could receive a hearing. The response of the civilized world is to treat the perpetrators as mad dogs, and bring them to justice. Such actions are entirely counterproductive, and raise the question whether the terrorists who murdered Pearl have any coherent program at all.

5. A computerized national registration system of all citizens would permit law-enforcement agencies to identify unregistered persons, and seize some terrorists before they could act. But such a system has immense civil-rights implications, and would not be foolproof. Genuine registration cards might be stolen or fake ones created, while a system, to be really effective, would require an immense and virtually ubiquitous police presence.

6. Mao Zedong, 93. Mao actually likened the people to "water," but lake or sea provides a clearer metaphor in English.

7. Keeley, 8, 18–19, 37.

8. For a full exposition of this encounter, see Fuller, *Generalship of Alexander*, 234–45.

9. In 1937 Japanese aggression against China caused the Communists and Nationalists to patch up a truce of sorts. The same year, to advise the Chinese on fighting the Japanese, Mao Zedong published *Guerrilla Warfare*, the first systematic study of the subject. It summarized the lessons Mao had learned in his war of insurgency against the Nationalists, and showed how the same techniques could be used against a foreign aggressor. Samuel B. Griffith translated Mao's work in 1940. Praeger Publishers, New York, published it in 1961, with an introduction by Griffith.

10. Nigel de Lee in Pimlott, 46–48; Mao Zedong, 20–22, 47–48. In the long run Mao expected his tactics to lead the enemy to decline so far that leaders could introduce regular military forces, not guerrillas, to challenge the enemy and destroy him. This actually came about in the late stages of both the Chinese civil war in 1949 and the Vietnam War in 1975.

11. Mao Zedong, 97.

12. Giap, 105.

13. Krepinevich, 57.

14. American leaders were unable to see that the conflict in Vietnam not only was a war of liberation against imperial powers but was a civil war between the vast majority of the population, which was poor, and a small, elite class that had sided with the French and that possessed most of the land and wealth. The key to defeating the Vietcong was not battle at all, but removing abuses of power by the elites and ending their exploitation of the common people. But neither Diem nor any of the successive military governments in South Vietnam were willing to do this. Diem, for example, protected the holdings of the large landlords and required peasants to pay for land previously given them by the Communists.

15. Kolko, 179.

16. Karnow, 259–62.

17. Kolko, 166.

18. Details of operations around Pleiku and Chu Pong in July–November 1965 are drawn from Coleman and Moore and Galloway.

19. Alexander, *Great Generals*, 45.

20. Oman, *Middle Ages*, vol. 2, 99.

21. Besieging a walled city or castle could take months before the era of powerful cannons, and even then an army could gain only that single place. The plunder would not pay the cost of investing it.

22. Oman, *Middle Ages*, vol. 2, 196–201.

23. Oman, *Peninsular War*, vol. 3, 492. Other citations on the Spanish guerrilla war in Oman are vol. 1, 57–67; vol. 3, 83, 115–16, 488–92; vol. 4, 206–11, 463–64, 472; vol. 6, 189–90, 257–65. See also Read, 169–81.

24. For an analysis of the Boer War, see Alexander, *Future of Warfare*, 86–116.

25. The basic source for Lawrence's Arabian campaign is his *Seven Pillars of Wisdom*, listed in the Selected Bibliography (cited in the note following as Lawrence), and his condensation of the work, *Revolt in the Desert* (London: Jonathan Cape, 1927); (New York: George H. Doran, 1927). Works about him

include David Garrett, ed., *The Letters of T. E. Lawrence* (London: Jonathan Cape, 1938); Robert Graves, *Lawrence and the Arabs* (London: Jonathan Cape, 1927); Basil H. Liddell Hart, *T. E. Lawrence* (London: Jonathan Cape, 1934); Anthony Nutting, *Lawrence of Arabia* (London: Hollis & Carter, 1961); Robert Payne, *Lawrence of Arabia—A Triumph* (New York: Pyramid Books, 1963).

26. Lawrence, 192.

Chapter 3. Defend, Then Attack

1. Thompson, 78–81.
2. Totila could never overcome Byzantine arrows, but he gained many small victories by resorting to guerrilla tactics—surprise attacks at night, ambushes, and blows with overwhelming manpower against isolated enemy detachments. Totila made no attempt to copy the compound bow, however, because mastering it would require more skill and determination than his men possessed. He did recognize his inability to besiege walled cities, and tried to level the walls of every city he captured. Beginning in December 546, when Totila gained Rome, his men (and conscripted Romans) tore down one-third of the twelve-mile circuit of the walls of Aurelian (212–275).
3. Fuller, *Western World*, vol. 1, 323–29; Oman, *Middle Ages*, vol. 1, 23–36; Delbrück, vol. 2, 339–61, 375–83.
4. Oman, *Middle Ages*, vol. 2, 59–60. Details of the Crécy campaign are drawn from ibid., 111–58; Fuller, *Western World*, vol. 1, 437–68; Delbrück, vol. 3, 453–72.
5. Sir Charles Oman gives the best account. See Oman, *Middle Ages*, vol. 2, 101–8. The *Tactica* of the Byzantine emperor Leo the Wise, written around A.D. 900, advised use of infantry alone in hilly country, passes, or ground unsuitable for horsemen. In such cases he called for heavy infantry to occupy the center, and light infantry armed with bows and javelins to move forward on either flank, in a crescent formation. See ibid., vol. 1, 195–96.
6. If the French chivalry had learned archery and emulated the Byzantine cataphracts, horsemen who carried both lance and bow, they might have scattered longbowmen, shot them down from their saddles, and changed the battle equation. But the French *noblesse* considered bows and arrows inferior peasant weapons, and, as Sir Charles Oman writes, "the French knight believed that, since he was infinitely superior to any peasant on the social scale, he must consequently excel him to the same extent in military value." See ibid., 112. The Byzantine compound bow, unlike the longbow, could be wielded from horseback, because it was short and strong. It was virtually unknown in the West, however, and the knights' only choice would have been the much less powerful short bow, such as the Normans used at the Battle of Hastings in 1066.
7. The Minié bullet, or Minié ball, invented in 1849 by a French army officer, Claude-Étienne Minié, was effective to 400 yards and lethal and somewhat controllable out to a thousand yards. Rifles had been around for centuries, but had not become standard military weapons because the rifling in the barrel quickly became fouled by gunpowder combustion. Minié produced a bullet with a hollow

base. When fired, the explosion expanded the base to fit snugly against the rifling grooves, scouring the fouling of the previous shot from the grooves. A Minié-ball rifle could fire many rounds before the barrel had to be cleaned. The rifle was used somewhat in the Crimean War (1853–1856), and, by the Civil War, most armies were retooling their muskets to fire the new bullet.

8. By 1864, a Union officer, William Tecumseh Sherman, had recognized that continued attacks into Minié-ball fire were getting nowhere. As commander in the western Union campaign, his aim was to occupy Southern territory and bring the war home to the Southern people. Therefore he avoided battle whenever possible, went around his enemies, and forced them to retreat. His was the strategy that actually won the war for the North.

9. The narrative in this section is drawn from Alexander, *Lost Victories*, 135–322, and *Lee's Civil War*, 33–167.

10. There *was* a partial answer available. In 1848, Prussia adopted the Dreyse "needle gun," a breech-loading, single-shot, bolt-action rifle that had considerably less range than the Minié-ball rifle, but could fire seven shots a minute to the latter's two. Its main advantage, however, was that soldiers could load and fire while lying on the ground. It's astonishing that no other armies adopted this weapon, because it could have reduced infantry losses greatly. But the gun was ignored by other armies, and its effectiveness recognized widely only in the Seven Weeks War in 1866 when Austrians were demoralized by fire from unseen Prussian soldiers firing from the ground. It's obvious the needle gun was most useful to troops on the defensive, but, if used widely, it surely would have stimulated abandonment of military formations in attacks and development of teams assigned specific targets or objectives, an advance that did not come until World War I. The needle gun had large design flaws. Gas escaped at the breech, and the paper cartridge had to be pierced by a needle driven by a spring to strike the primer located ahead of the gunpowder and behind the bullet. See Fuller, *Conduct of War*, 88–89; The Diagram Group, *Weapons* (New York: St. Martin's, 1990), 132.

11. Napoleon Bonaparte wrote in 1793 in *Le Souper de Beaucaire:* "He who remains behind his entrenchments is beaten; experience and theory are one on this point."

12. Jackson never wrote his memoirs. Although it's certain he reached this judgment in the Seven Days, it was not officially recorded till the battle of Fredericksburg, five months later. By that time he had distilled it into a maxim. Heros von Borcke, a Prussian officer on Jeb Stuart's staff, looking at the vast Federal army arrayed in front, turned to Jackson and wondered aloud whether the Rebels could stop so powerful an assault. Jackson replied, "Major, my men have sometimes failed to take a position, but to defend one, never!" After the battle of Chancellorsville in May 1863, Jackson, wounded, told his medical officer, Hunter McGuire, much the same thing: "We sometimes fail to drive them from position, but they always fail to drive us." Jackson also spelled out his theory to McGuire at this time. He told McGuire "that he intended, after breaking into [the Federal commander Joe] Hooker's rear, to take and fortify a suitable position, cutting him off from the [Rappahannock] river and so hold him until, between himself

and General Lee, the great Federal host should be broken to pieces." See *Southern Historical Society Papers*, vol. 25, 110, 119; Heros von Borcke, *Memoirs of the Confederate War for Independence* (New York: Peter Smith, 1938), vol. 2, 117; Alexander, *Lee's Civil War*, 38–39.

13. Lee did not tell Stonewall that his real motivation was to *maneuver* Pope out of Virginia, not fight him. This was the only time Lee adopted a maneuver strategy, brought on probably by his appalling losses in the Seven Days. Since Lee was thinking of maneuver, speed was not important, and he was more interested in leveraging Pope off the Rapidan River than in pressing him against the Blue Ridge or the river and forcing a desperate battle.

14. Lee actually planned to move around McClellan's flank after stopping his attacks, and convinced Jackson when he arrived from Harpers Ferry the day before the battle. But Lee had failed to reconnoiter the terrain in advance, and Jackson found only during the battle that there was insufficient space to permit a turning movement between the northern end of the field and a bend of the Potomac River. Lee's plan indicates he had been influenced by Jackson's ideas, but his behavior in subsequent campaigns shows his fundamental attitude had not changed. See Alexander, *Lee's Civil War*, 93–94.

15. Alexander, *Lost Victories*, 265.

16. Although the battle of Chancellorsville illustrates the principle of defend, then attack, it more closely follows the principle of blocking the enemy's retreat, and is so described in chapter 9.

17. The narrative on Gettysburg is drawn from Alexander, *Lee's Civil War*, 169–235.

18. E. Porter Alexander, *Fighting for the Confederacy* (Chapel Hill: University of North Carolina Press, 1989), 230.

19. Meade would have been compelled to chase after the Confederate army in exhausting forced marches. Anywhere along the way to Philadelphia, at any favorable position with open flanks, Lee could have stopped, built a powerful defensive position, and waited. Just as would have been the case at Carlisle if Lee had built a defensive position there (and subsequently was the case at Gettysburg, where the Federals did build a strong position), a force obligated to attack head-on would have been badly defeated.

20. E. Porter Alexander, *Military Memoirs of a Confederate* (New York: Charles Scribner's Sons, 1907), 424.

21. The defensive weapons we deploy today are extremely strong, superior to those used against us, and can be wielded in many cases by individual soldiers. Although the clashes in Afghanistan in 2001 and 2002 emphasized offensive weapons like GPS-guided smart bombs and AC-130 gunships, in fact defensive weapons are as effective in the American army as offensive weapons. A few examples: the handheld Javelin missile is lethal to all tanks out to 2,500 meters, the Stinger missile homes in on the heat of aircraft engines, rocket-propelled grenades allow infantrymen to fire explosives as powerful as light artillery rounds, TOW guided missiles can stop any armored vehicle out to 3,750 meters, and armored personnel carriers (APCs) and Bradley fighting vehicles protect soldiers from machine-gun fire.

Chapter 4: Holding One Place, Striking Another

1. The narrative on Gustavus Adolphus is drawn from Dodge, *Gustavus Adolphus*, 313–19; Fuller, *Western World*, vol. 2, 65–68; Paret, 52–55 (Gunther E. Rothenberg); Parker, 129–31; Livesey, 54–56.
2. The narrative on Jena is drawn from Fuller, *Western World*, vol. 2, 410–43; Maud; Paret, 131–34.
3. In the Jena campaign, because of the slow movement of supply columns, the Prussian army seldom marched more than twelve to fifteen miles a day. The French army sometimes averaged twice that. Marshal Jean Lannes's corps covered sixty-five miles in fifty hours. Because French troops largely got their food by foraging or requisitioning it from local authorities, their armies required far fewer horsedrawn carts and wagons than did the Prussian army. This increased French mobility immensely, and contributed much to Napoleon's success.
4. The narrative on the Kum River engagements is drawn from Alexander, *Korea*, 76–91.
5. Named after Lieutenant Colonel Charles B. (Brad) Smith, West Point class of 1939, who commanded the 1st Battalion of the 21st Infantry Regiment. Task Force Smith consisted of elements from his battalion, plus a battery of 105-mm howitzers from the 52nd Field Artillery Battalion under Lieutenant Colonel Miller O. Perry.
6. The battalion's K Company was pulled out of the line and sent to Taejon for medical disposition because of the mental and physical condition of the men.
7. Why the regimental commander had given this order is unknown. The records of the battle are silent on this point.
8. Although the main reserve force had been sent off to guard the open left flank, Company F was also in reserve. If it had attacked the roadblock from the north, while troops along the road delivered heavy fire on the position, the combined effort might not have broken the block, but very likely could have interrupted the resupply of ammunition to it from across the river. In the event, no unit north of the roadblock made any sustained effort.

Chapter 5. Feigned Retreat

1. Keeley, 44.
2. Legg, 43. His description of steppe peoples is the most complete and compelling in the English language. See Legg, 31–74.
3. Even the tremendous success of Alexander the Great's cavalry against Persia (334–326 B.C.) and of Hannibal's Carthaginian cavalry against Rome in the Second Punic War (219–202 B.C.) led only to brief emphasis on cavalry—and these horsemen carried spears, swords, and javelins, not bows and arrows.
4. The narrative on Manzikert is drawn from Friendly, 60–211; Oman, *Middle Ages*, vol. 1, 186–223; Fuller, *Western World*, vol. 1, 385–405; Legg, 184–211.
5. The Byzantines codified their military doctrines in two manuals: *Strategicon*, issued by Emperor Maurice in 579, and *Tactica* by Leo the Wise in 900. From Justinian onward, the policy of Byzantium was defensive. The realm was divided into military corps districts called *themes*, each protected by well-placed

fortresses. The Byzantines did not often seek battle, and retired to a fortress when attacked. Invading armies could seldom storm the fortresses, and, without an organized supply system, had to forage for food. Isolated foraging bands could easily be destroyed by Byzantines operating out of the fortresses. This was essentially the formula adopted by Belisarius in his campaigns in Italy against the Ostrogoths, and served the Byzantines well for centuries.

6. The narrative on the Mongols is drawn from Alexander, *Great Generals*, 67–94.
7. G. F. R. Henderson, *Stonewall Jackson and the American Civil War* (New York: Longmans, Green & Co., 1936), 333.

Chapter 6. The Central Position

1. The narrative on the Civil War campaign of spring 1862 is drawn from Alexander, *Lost Victories*, 40–94, and *Great Generals*, 123–42.
2. Johnston, of course, was *also* in the central position between McClellan on the peninsula east of Richmond and McDowell at Fredericksburg north of it. He could have left only a small screening force to hold McClellan, marched on McDowell with superior strength, and either defeated him or forced him into precipitate retreat. Johnston then could have joined with Jackson, turned back on McClellan, and tried to drive him against the James River and force his surrender. Such a move would, however, have presented the danger that McClellan might occupy Richmond, which, for political reasons, President Davis could not accept. Therefore Johnston was not in a situation to exploit the central position. What he *did* propose, however, was to withdraw his army to the doorstep of Richmond, draw as many troops as possible from the Carolinas and Georgia, then either attack McClellan or leave a force to hold McClellan and, with the remainder, march on Washington or Baltimore and perhaps beyond. But Davis, backed by Robert E. Lee, rejected this bold proposal. Davis did not want to invade the North, instead hoping it would tire of the war and grant the South independence, and Lee was focused on McClellan's army in front of him, not on a strategic campaign into the North. See Alexander, *Lost Victories*, 47–49.
3. The narrative on the Italian campaign of 1796–97 is drawn from Alexander, *Great Generals*, 95–122.
4. This illustrates the importance of commanders examining the whole situation before making a decision. It also illustrates the complexity of warfare, for Bonaparte's plunge between the two hostile armies offered opportunities to his enemy as well. The Austrian commander, Baron Beaulieu, should have seen that Bonaparte was in a potentially disastrous situation. The Piedmontese so far had not been defeated, and his own forces overall were superior in number. If he had attacked instead of retreating, he might either have driven the French into the arms of the Piedmontese, or forced them to retreat back through the Col di Cadibona. Instead Beaulieu did what many other commanders have done in like circumstances: he grasped at his security, not his opportunity. He protected his line of supply and communications, and thereby guaranteed his defeat. It is often the audacious commander, like Bonaparte, who succeeds—not because he has a perfect plan, but because his opponent does not have equal audacity.

5. The narrative on the Waterloo campaign is drawn from Fuller, *Western World*, vol. 2, 494–539; Creasy, 298–302; Chandler, *The Napoleonic Wars*, 134–39, and *Waterloo;* Blond, 469–99; Georges Lefebvre, *Napoleon: From Tilset to Waterloo, 1807–1815* (New York: Columbia University Press, 1969), 358–69. See also Colin, and Chandler, *Campaigns of Napoleon.*

6. Not a logical deduction. Wellington's supply base and port was Antwerp, north of Brussels, not the tiny Belgian ports along the Channel. Here is an example of a commander making a potentially fatal error on the basis of a judgment that was wrong on the face of it. If Napoleon had actually feinted with a corps westward toward the Channel, Wellington would have deployed his army in that direction, abandoned the Prussians, and, when Napoleon turned on his flank at Brussels, would have been hard pressed to retreat to Antwerp. Fortunately for Britain, Napoleon assumed Wellington would make the sensible decision and move toward Quatre Bras.

7. Fuller, *Western World*, vol. 2, 495.

8. On the morning of June 16, Napoleon had failed to order up Georges Lobau's 6th Corps, then at Charleroi, to Fleurus, just south of Ligny, or to Mellet, three and a half miles west of Fleurus. If Lobau had been at either place, he could have swung onto the right rear of the Prussians at Ligny, and Ney would not have needed to be called on. Napoleon finally ordered the 6th Corps to Fleurus late in the afternoon, but it arrived too late to play any role in the battle.

9. Napoleon was burdened throughout the Waterloo campaign in his selection of Marshal Nicolas Soult as his chief of staff. Soult was an able commander, but had never been a chief of staff, and performed his job poorly. Most notably, his written renderings of Napoleon's orders were often inexact and ambiguous. However, the crucial message to Grouchy, though badly worded, contained the essential instructions any responsible commander should have been able to follow: "push before you" the Prussians, and keep in touch.

10. It's clear Napoleon understood that this is what Grouchy should have done, because, on the morning of June 18, he sent patrols to the bridges at Moustier and Ottignies, on the Dyle River about halfway between Walhain and Waterloo, with orders to get in touch with Grouchy and report back prompt notice of his approach.

11. Fuller, *Western World*, vol. 2, 522; Blond, 491–92.

12. Seymour M. Hersh, "Escape and Evasion," *The New Yorker*, November 12, 2001, 52.

Chapter 7. Employing a Superior Weapon

1. In Afghanistan, 94 percent of bombs and other ordnance dropped on Al Qaeda and Taliban forces were precision-guided "smart" bombs, ten times the percentage in the Persian Gulf War of 1991. Of sorties by naval aircraft, 84 percent hit the target. See Vice Admiral John B. Nathman, "We Were Great," *Proceedings, U.S. Naval Institute*, March 2002, 95.

2. The narrative on Adrianople is drawn from Oman, *Middle Ages*, vol. 1, 3–37; Fuller, *Western World*, vol. 1, 266–76; *Ammianus Marcellinus*, vol. 3, 399–503; Jones, 92–95; Delbrück, vol. 2, 269–84.

3. The cataphract also carried a sword, a short spear or strong javelin, and an ax. In addition, the Byzantines fielded light infantry, who carried a compound bow and a quiver of forty arrows, a small shield, and an ax for close combat. The foot-archers were especially effective against the horse-archers of the Persians and other eastern enemies, since, being on the ground, they had good footing for accurate shooting. Even so, the foot-archer had to be protected by the cataphract, and he remained the major Byzantine warrior. See Jones, 96–97.

4. The narrative on Hastings is drawn from Oman, *Middle Ages*, vol. 1, 63–72, 149–68; Fuller, *Western World*, vol. 1, 360–84; Whitelock et al., 49–111; Creasy, 183–204; Davis, 113–18; Delbrück, vol. 2, 146–59; David Howarth, *1066: The Year of the Conquest* (New York: Viking Penguin, 1977).

5. In 1064, Harold had been captured on a visit to France by Count Guy of Ponthieu. William brought about his release. But apparently a condition William imposed was that Harold had to swear to support William's claim to the English throne. The Witan was in no way bound by this blackmail, because Harold had no authority to pledge the English crown to anyone.

6. The English army consisted of the housecarls and the fyrd, or national militia. On call of the king, every five hides (each hide was 120 acres of land) had to provide one fyrd member for two months. The housecarls wore steel caps with nasal pieces and long leather flaps that fell over their shoulders. Their principal weapon was the battle-ax. The ax man was supported by swordsmen and javelin throwers. Since the fyrd came from the whole kingdom, it was difficult to concentrate it on short notice. The fyrd's weapons were mostly spears, short axes, bills, scythes, and javelins. A few wielded slings to throw stones. See Whitelock et al., 92–93.

7. The narrative on Breitenfeld and Lützen is drawn from Delbrück, vol. 4, 147–83, 202–9; Liddell Hart, *Great Captains*, 76–152; Fuller, *Western World*, vol. 2, 40–75; Dodge, *Gustavus Adolphus*, vol. 1; Markov, 185–89; Parker, 121–31; Rabb, *Thirty Years War*; Koch, 28–38; Chandler, *Atlas of Military Strategy*, 24–29; Paret (Gunther E. Rothenberg), 32–55.

8. The matchlock fired when, by pulling the trigger, the glowing tip of a burning cord, usually soaked with saltpeter, plunged into priming gunpowder in a small metal pan. The resulting fire ran through a narrow vent to the barrel, igniting the propelling powder in the barrel.

9. Leonardo da Vinci may have invented the wheel lock; he illustrated the mechanism around 1500, but the pistol was not invented till around 1540. The wheel lock was used both for pistols and muskets. It was efficient but complex and expensive. On pressing the trigger, the pan cover slid forward, exposing the powder, which was ignited by pyrites struck against a small wheel as it turned by the trigger action.

10. The narrative on the war in the desert is drawn from Alexander, *Great Generals*, 236–75, and *How Hitler Could Have Won*, 71–80, 110–25.

11. The British also perversely divided their armor between relatively fast and relatively lightly armored cruiser tanks and slow-moving, heavily armored "infantry tanks," or "I" tanks, on the theory that the infantry needed tanks to assist in breaking through enemy lines. "I" tanks could move scarcely faster than a man

could walk, and were decidedly less effective than cruiser tanks in the highly fluid conditions of desert war. Even in cases where "I" tanks were on hand and could have intervened in a running battle, British commanders often insisted on reserving them for an infantry attack, even when one was not planned. For example, on November 20, 1941, in the opening rounds of the Crusader campaign, the German 15th Panzer Division attacked the British 4th Armored Brigade at Gabr Saleh in Libya and inflicted great damage on it. British General Alan Cunningham called on the 22nd Armored Brigade at Bir el Gubi to assist, but it could not cover the twenty-eight-mile distance in time. However, he refused to call on the 13th Corps's "I" tank brigade only seven miles away, because it had "infantry" tanks.

12. Basil H. Liddell Hart, *The Tanks*, vol. 2 (New York: Praeger, 1959), 103.

Chapter 8. Driving a Stake in the Enemy's Heart

1. Napoleon also faced the resistance of the people when he invaded Spain, and set off a guerrilla war that undermined French strength and permitted the British under the Duke of Wellington to drive French forces out of the country.

2. The narrative on Scott's expedition in Mexico is drawn from Eisenhower, 253–342; Bauer, 232–357; Singletary, 71–127; Nevin, 126–50, 169–93; Henry, 258–393.

3. Scott's army in theory totaled 14,000 men, but 2,500 were sick and 600 convalescing. It was organized in four divisions.

4. For a full analysis of Sherman's campaign through Georgia and the Carolinas, see Alexander, *Great Generals*, 143–67.

5. The narrative on Stalingrad is drawn from Alexander, *How Hitler Could Have Won*, 145–64.

6. The sea route to Murmansk and Archangel was a dangerous passage with atrocious weather, subject to attacks by German ships and by aircraft from German-occupied Norway.

7. F. W. von Mellenthin, *Panzer Battles* (Norman: University of Oklahoma Press, 1956), 160.

8. The narrative on the invasion of North Korea is drawn from Alexander, *Korea*, 228–373.

9. Secretary of State Acheson was especially culpable. He did not appreciate the magnitude of the Chinese threat, and dismissed it as a joint Soviet-Chinese effort to bring about the withdrawal of American forces from Korea. In his memoirs he wrote a long apologetic discourse disguising his abdication of responsibility. See Dean Acheson, *Present at the Creation* (New York: W. W. Norton, 1969), 466, 468.

10. Alexander, *Korea*, 247. MacArthur based this opinion on the fact that the United States had air power and Red China did not. He figured any advance by Chinese columns could be spotted from the air, and broken up by strafing and bombing. This shows MacArthur had paid virtually no attention to the structure of the Chinese Communist army, which did not rely on vehicles, but used the legs of its soldiers both to march into battle and to bring up weapons and supplies to the battle line. It was this enormous blind spot on the part of MacArthur as to the actual nature of the Chinese enemy that caused the disaster about to unfold.

11. Seymour M. Hersh, "The Iraq Hawks," *The New Yorker*, December 24 and 31, 2001, 59.

Chapter 9. Blocking the Enemy's Retreat

1. Though "advance to the rear" is how this operation is usually characterized, the commander of the 1st Marine Division, Major General Oliver Smith, with great aplomb, told a British correspondent that there could be no talk of retreat. After all, Smith contended, the marines and soldiers were surrounded, and therefore there *was* no rear, thus nowhere to retreat *to*. He preferred to call it a "breakout to the coast." See Alexander, *Korea*, 353.

2. The narrative on the Teutoburger Wald battle is drawn from Delbrück, vol. 2, 15–148; Fuller, *Western World*, vol. 1, 239–53; Markov, 76–80; Dio Cassius, 222–29.

3. Each German clan (a family-related division of the tribe) lived in a loose-knit village of 400 to 1,000 people. The clan's houses were huts of the roughest form, because the members changed their settlement quite often, in order to till fresh, fertile soil. Thus very few acres were cultivated, and even though the Germans were no longer nomads, they felt only a loose tie to the land. See Delbrück, vol. 2, 15–16.

4. Tiberius did not seek pitched battles with the German tribes. Instead, he split his army into columns, occupied and fortified all points of importance, and, by devastating the country methodically, reconquered the country by famine. See Fuller, *Western World*, vol. 1, 246.

5. Dio Cassius, vol. 4, 222–23; Delbrück, vol. 2, 90–91.

6. There has been much academic dispute about the precise location of the battle of the Teutoburger Wald. I have adopted the arguments of the great German military historian Hans Delbrück, who devoted exhaustive research to the question, and, in my opinion, conclusively proved that it was fought at and on the northern approaches to the Dören defile in the Osning Mountains (Teutoburger Wald), some twenty miles northeast of Paderborn. See his detailed arguments in Delbrück, vol. 2, 55–89.

7. The narrative on the Saratoga campaign is drawn from Lewis, *The Man Who Lost America;* Fuller, *Western World*, vol. 2, 279–309; Creasy, 351–72; Hibbert, 162–200.

8. Lewis, 105.

9. Howe's dereliction of duty is shown decisively in his response to a letter of May 18, 1777, from Germain, which Howe received on August 25 while he was in Pennsylvania. Germain's letter was in response to a message Howe had written him on April 2 in which Howe said he had given up all idea of an expedition "except that to the southward [to capture Philadelphia], and a diversion occasionally upon Hudson's River." Germain, in his May 18 letter, agreed with Howe's proposal (demonstrating Germain's total indifference to Burgoyne's upcoming expedition). But, realizing now that he had not sent Howe the March 26 letter, Germain covered himself by writing that he trusted that whatever Howe did, "it will be executed in time to cooperate with the army ordered to proceed from Canada." Responding to this letter, Howe wrote Sir Henry Clinton in New York

on August 25: "If you can make any diversion in favor of General Burgoyne approaching Albany, I need not point out the utility of such a measure." See Fuller, *Western World*, vol. 2, 281–82, 299. This proves that Howe was fully aware of Burgoyne's campaign, and deliberately chose to continue on with his useless campaign in Pennsylvania.

10. This in fact happened on September 18, when an American force occupied Sugar Loaf Hill at Ticonderoga and captured most of Burgoyne's supply fleet on Lake Champlain, severing British communications with Canada.

11. Creasy, 352.

12. It is passing strange that it took the British until 1781 to realize that the magnificent harbors of Hampton Roads offered their best chance to stamp out the rebellion. If well defended by strong naval squadrons, Chesapeake Bay and its rivers could have offered superb avenues to conquer not only Virginia and Maryland, but also to advance into Pennsylvania. At the same time, reducing Virginia would isolate the Carolinas and Georgia. If the middle colonies—Virginia, Maryland, Delaware, Pennsylvania, and New Jersey—were recovered, it would have been impossible for the southern colonies and New York and New England to coordinate their defenses. The British could have concentrated on each region in turn, and probably stamped out the revolt. The American Revolution is a wonderful example of a rebellion that succeeded in large part because the defending power was directed by incompetent leaders (in this case King George, Lord North, and George Germain, among others), and produced no first-class generals who could conceive and carry out a logical strategic plan.

13. The narrative on Yorktown is drawn from Hibbert, 314–31; Fuller, *Western World*, vol. 2, 310–40; Mahan, 152–73; Chidsey, *Victory at Yorktown*.

14. Actually, Washington wanted either New York or Hampton Roads to be invested by the French fleet. But Rochambeau privately informed de Grasse that he preferred Chesapeake Bay, and the French government had not furnished the means for a formal siege of New York City. See Mahan, 173.

15. Another flagrant example of the British failure to concentrate was a decision of Sir George Rodney, naval commander in the West Indies. When he received reports that de Grasse's fleet, with 200 homeward-bound French merchantmen, had left Martinique for Cap Français, he assumed that de Grasse would escort the merchant ships back to France, and would detach no more than twelve or fourteen warships for action off the American coast. As Rodney was going back to England because of bad health, he sent only fourteen of his own ships under Admiral Hood to cooperate with Thomas Graves (who had replaced Marriot Arbuthnot) at New York. Together they would be able to defeat de Grasse, Rodney decided. He then took the rest of the British fleet and escorted 150 British merchantmen back to England. This was a most unfortunate decision, because it relied on his enemy making the precise judgment he had made. De Grasse did not. He delayed sailing of the merchantmen, and—following a doctrine that fleets should be concentrated for maximum power, not dispersed—sent his whole fleet north. The British thus were inferior in numbers to the French off the Virginia Capes. See Fuller, *Western World*, vol. 2, 324.

16. The narrative on Chancellorsville is drawn from Alexander, *Lee's Civil War*, 135–67, and *Lost Victories*, 286–327.

17. *Southern Historical Society Papers* (Richmond, Va.: 1876–1953, 50 vols.), vol. 6, 267; Douglas Southall Freeman, *Lee's Lieutenants* (New York: Scribner's, 1942–1946, three vols.), vol. 2, 564–65; G. F. R. Henderson, *Stonewall Jackson and the American Civil War* (New York: Longmans, Green and Co., 1898; New York: Konecky & Konecky, 1993, two vols), vol. 2, 449.

18. E. Porter Alexander, *Fighting for the Confederacy* (Chapel Hill: University of North Carolina Press, 1989), 216.

19. Robert U. Johnson and C. C. Buel, eds., *Battles and Leaders of the Civil War*, four vols. (New York: *Century* magazine, 1887–1888; reprint, Secaucus, N.J.: Castle, n.d.), vol. 3, 161; John Bigelow Jr., *The Campaign of Chancellorsville* (New Haven: Yale University Press, 1910), 259.

20. Henderson, *Stonewall Jackson*, vol. 2, 431–32. Henderson's source was a personal letter from Jedediah Hotchkiss.

Chapter 10. Landing an Overwhelming Blow

1. The narrative on Leuctra is drawn from Buckler, 61–66; Davis, 23–27; Fuller, *Alexander*, 22, 45n; *Western World*, vol. 1, 83; Delbrück, vol. 1, 166–71; Dodge, *Alexander*, 116–24.

2. The narrative on Rossbach and Leuthen is drawn from Duffy, *Frederick*, 101–55, and *Army of Frederick*, 167–80; Ritter, *Frederick the Great*; Koch, 138–63; Delbrück, vol. 4, 278–79, 345–46, 369–70, 374; Fuller, *Western World*, vol. 2, 192–215.

3. Fuller, *Western World*, vol. 2, 196, quoting Colonel E. M. Lloyd, *A Review of the History of Infantry*, 153.

4. A musketeer could fire a maximum of four rounds a minute, but the average was two or three. The process of firing a musket was intricate, and required a number of specific steps. Thus the better trained and disciplined a soldier, the faster he could fire. See Koch, 141.

5. At Kolin, forty miles east of Prague in the upper Elbe River valley, the Austrians occupied a strong east-west position along a ridgeline south of the river. Frederick opened the battle by trying to sweep around the eastern flank of the Austrians, but the movement was spotted by the Austrian commander Leopold Daun, who had time to shift forces and stop the attack. This shift was shielded from Frederick by the crest of the ridge. He, thinking the flanking movement was going well, turned the bulk of his army into a direct assault up the hill to support the flanking move. Instead he ran directly into the emplaced Austrians, and suffered heavy defeat. This setback persuaded Frederick not to assume an operation was going well unless he could verify it, and caused him to be much more cautious in the future. See Duffy, *Frederick*, 121–31.

6. Actually the Austrians intended to go into winter quarters at Breslau, and move on Berlin in the spring. But this would have required the Prussians to keep a large army on guard, and diluted the forces Frederick could use to defend against other allied armies likely to approach Prussia in the spring of 1758 from other directions.

7. Fuller, *Western World*, vol. 2, 209, quoting Frederick from *Oeuvres Posthumes de Frédéric II*, vol. 3, 235–36.

8. The narrative on the battle of Trafalgar is drawn from Mahan, 236–51; Fuller, *Western World*, vol. 2, 376–404.

9. Four allied ships escaped to sea after the battle, but fell in with a British squadron of the same size on November 4, 1805, near Cape Ortegal, and all these allied ships were taken. See Mahan, 250.

10. Admiral Pierre de Villeneuve, commander of the allied fleet, fought bravely, exposing himself as recklessly as Nelson, and surrendering his flagship, the *Bucentaure*, only after nearly all his men were dead. He was taken to England, released, and left for France. Unwilling to face Napoleon, he killed himself at a hotel in Rennes, France, April 22, 1806. He left a letter to his wife apologizing for deserting her, and thanked the fates that he was leaving no child "to be burdened with my name." See Will and Ariel Durant, *The Age of Napoleon* (New York: Simon and Schuster, 1975), 525.

Chapter 11. Stroke at a Weak Spot

1. The English military historian J. F. C. Fuller's *Generalship of Alexander the Great* is the classic exposition of Alexander's methods. David G. Chandler, another English military historian, articulated Napoleon's methods most clearly. Two other outstanding military theorists, the Englishman Basil H. Liddell Hart, and the German Hans Delbrück, also understood Napoleon well, and both recognized the uniqueness of his accomplishment at Austerlitz in 1805. See Liddell Hart, *Strategy*, 125–26, and Delbrück, vol. 4, 434–35.

2. The narrative on Alexander is drawn from Dodge, *Alexander*, 125–70, 218–386; Fuller, *Alexander*, 147–80, 283–301; Liddell Hart, *Strategy*, 36–41; Hammond, 59–110; Delbrück, vol. 1, 175–219; Engels, 11–70.

3. Philip spent three years as a youth as a hostage in Thebes at the time Epaminondas was commanding the Theban army. The ideas of Epaminondas influenced Philip, and also influenced his son Alexander.

4. Neither stirrups (invented in India) nor the saddle reached the Mediterranean for another seven or eight hundred years. Hence cavalrymen could not use their horses' momentum to drive in with a long lance, as medieval knights were able to do. A cavalry battle in classical times therefore took the form of a thrusting melee.

5. After Issus, Darius fled to Thapsacus on the upper Euphrates River, abandoning his mother, his wife and children, and his treasury, which he'd foolishly left at Damascus. Darius wrote Alexander begging release of his family and promising friendship and an alliance. Alexander responded: "I am, by gift of the gods, in possession of your land. Come to me then, and ask for your mother, wife, and children, and anything else you wish. For whatever you ask for you will receive; and nothing shall be denied you. But for the future, whenever you send to me, send to me as the king of Asia, and do not address to me your wishes as to an equal. And if you dispute my right to the kingdom, stay and fight another battle for it; but do not run away. For wherever you may be, I intend to march against you." See Fuller, *Alexander*, 99–101, quoting one of Alexander's principal chroniclers, Arrian, book II, chapter xiv.

6. For a discussion of the battle of Castiglione, see Alexander, *Great Generals*, 109–14.

7. The narrative on Austerlitz is drawn from Chandler, *On the Napoleonic Wars*, 115–29, and *Atlas of Military Strategy*, 98–101; Duffy, *Austerlitz*; Horne, 83–193; Liddell Hart, *Strategy*, 125–26; Fuller, *Western World*, vol. 2, 407–8; Delbrück, vol. 4, 434–35.

8. Duffy, *Austerlitz*, 73; Horne, 135.

9. Duffy, *Austerlitz*, 74.

10. Kutuzov was sixty years old in 1805, and combined shrewdness, refinement, and extreme grossness all in one. He drank heavily and usually traveled with three wenches in his baggage train. On the eve of an important battle he would often summon all three. See Horne, 114–15.

11. Napoleon actually articulated this on November 30, 1805, when he rode up on the Pratzen with his marshals and looked out on the allied army moving across country toward them from the east. "I could certainly stop the Russians here if I held on to this fine position," he said. "But that would be just an ordinary battle. I prefer to abandon the ground to them and draw back my right. If they then dare to descend from the heights to take me in my flank, they will surely be beaten without hope of recovery." See Duffy, *Austerlitz*, 80.

12. Early on the morning of December 2, 1805, Czar Alexander approached Kutuzov, who was on the Pratzen in front of a column of Russian troops who were standing motionless. "Mikhail Larionovich!" the czar shouted, "why haven't you begun your advance?" "Your Highness," Kutuzov responded, "I am waiting for all the columns of the army to get into position." Alexander replied, "But we are not on the Empress's Meadow, where we do not begin a parade until all the regiments are formed up!" "Your Highness, if I have not begun, it is because we are *not* on the Empress's Meadow. However, if such be Your Highness's order." With no show of enthusiasm, Kutuzov now gave the command to advance. See ibid., 103; Horne, 151.

13. Chandler, *On the Napoleonic Wars*, 127.

Chapter 12. Caldron Battles

1. Keeley, 65–69.

2. Ibid., 74.

3. The narrative on Cannae is drawn from Alexander, *Great Generals*, 37–66.

4. The narrative on the Schlieffen Plan and Tannenberg is drawn from Fuller, *Western World*, vol. 3, 171–228; Liddell Hart, *The Real War*, 45–64, 70–71, 103–14, *War in Outline*, 23–45, 56–58, and *Strategy*, 167–77, 181–82; Keegan, 24–129, 138–50; Gilbert, 28–29, 35–77.

5. Fuller, *Western World*, vol. 3, 174.

6. Ibid., 173.

7. Liddell Hart, *War in Outline*, 24.

8. Fuller, *Western World*, vol. 3, 213–14.

9. On August 25, 1914, German radio operators intercepted a Russian message sent *en clair*, or not in code, which showed Rennenkampf's army was moving to besiege Königsberg, and could not come to the assistance of Samsonov in the near future. See Keegan, 148.

10. It will occur to readers that Samsonov *still* had a way out, even after François closed off his rear. The German 20th Corps was on his north, François's 1st Corps on his south, and Below's and Mackensen's corps on his east. But the Germans had *vacated* the region to the Russians' immediate west, and a forceful commander could have turned part of his army into a rear guard and backed out of the caldron to the west. This was all the more possible because the Russian 1st Corps, which had retreated back into Poland, was poised just south of the frontier, and could have provided a strong diversionary attack. In fact this corps actually did attack on August 29. François stoutly refused to give up his "blockade," however, and being unsupported, the Russians gave up and retreated southward again on August 31. Samsonov apparently never saw an escape route to the west, however, and neither did anyone on his staff.

11. The narrative on Barbarossa is drawn from Alexander, *How Hitler Could Have Won*, 81–109.

12. Heinz Guderian, *Panzer Leader* (New York: E. P. Dutton, 1952), 233–34.

Chapter 13. Uproar East, Attack West

1. Boats and rafts had been assembled beforehand and hidden in a nearby nullah, or deep ravine, now filled with water from the recent rains.

2. The narrative on the Quebec campaign is drawn from Fuller, *Western World*, vol. 2, 243–70; Liddell Hart, *Great Captains*, 207–74, and *Strategy*, 107–8; Chandler, *Atlas of Military Strategy*, 82.

3. This is the same French explorer who circumnavigated the globe in 1766–1769 with a crew that included astronomers and naturalists. Also the British flotilla included Captain James Cook, who later commanded three major voyages of discovery to the South Pacific, and sailed along the coast of North America as far as the Bering Strait.

4. Fuller, *Western World*, vol. 2, 266–67, quoting J. W. Fortescue, *A History of the British Army*, vol. 2, 381.

5. The narrative on the campaign in the west in 1940 is drawn from Alexander, *How Hitler Could Have Won*, 1–35, and *Great Generals*, 209–35.

6. Erich von Manstein, *Lost Victories* (Chicago: Henry Regnery, 1958), 103–4.

7. Basil H. Liddell Hart, *The German Generals Talk* (New York: William Morrow, 1948), 132.

Chapter 14. Maneuvers on the Rear

1. The narrative on Marengo is drawn from Chandler, *Campaigns of Napoleon*, 253–304, 381–412, and *On the Napoleonic Wars*, 82–98; Horne, 83–131; Duffy, *Austerlitz*, 37–51.

2. Jean Victor Moreau (1763–1813) was an early Revolutionary officer who helped General Charles Pichegru conquer the Austrian Netherlands (Belgium) in 1794, commanded the Army of the North in 1795, the armies of the Rhine and Moselle in 1796, and the Army of Italy in 1799. He was implicated in a plot against Bonaparte in 1804, but because of his high standing in the army he was allowed

to disappear into exile in the United States. He eventually returned to Europe, joined the Russians to fight against Napoleon, and was fatally wounded in the battle of Dresden in 1813.

3. Ultimately only 11,000 of Moreau's men in another formation, not Lecourbe's corps, got to Italy, and arrived so late as to play little role in the campaign.

4. Lapoype could not be reached in time, and his division did not take part in the battle.

5. The narrative on the campaigns in the Pacific is drawn from Liddell Hart, *Second World War*, 498–513, 613–31, 682–98; Weinberg, 632–55, 842–93; Keegan, *Second World War*, 290–307, 536–45, 554–85.

6. See Department of State, *Foreign Relations of the United States, Conference of Berlin (Potsdam), 1945*, two vols. (Washington: Government Printing Office, 1960), vol. 2, 346 and map opposite.

7. The 1st Marine Division and army units landed at Cape Gloucester, on the western tip of New Britain, in late December 1943. The operation was an unnecessary diversion of strength, and contributed nothing to the war, since the Japanese troops on the island had already been neutralized.

8. The Pacific Fleet's establishment of its mobile Service Force was one of the great innovations in naval history, and contributed mightily to American success in the war against Japan. It met all needs of the fleet and invasion forces except major repairs to larger warships. At first it consisted of tankers, tenders, tugs, minesweepers, barges, lighters, and ammunition ships. Later hospital ships, barrack ships, a floating dry dock, floating cranes, survey ships, pontoon assembly ships, and others were added. See Liddell Hart, *Second World War*, 510–11.

9. The narrative on Inchon is drawn from Alexander, *Korea*, 148–218, and *Great Generals*, 276–88.

10. J. Lawton Collins, *War in Peacetime* (Boston: Houghton Mifflin, 1969), 124–25.

11. Alexander, *Korea*, 172–73.

12. Omar Bradley and Clay Blair, *A General's Life: An Autobiography* (New York: Simon & Schuster, 1983), 544.

13. Alexander, *Korea*, 189.

14. Bradley and Blair, 556.

15. In March 2002 the Pentagon leaked to the press a scarcely veiled threat to North Korea (and other rogue nations) of just such a strike if it used a weapon of mass destruction, or tried to build a nuclear bomb. The leaked document was the nuclear-posture review sent to Congress in December 2001 that expanded the list of potential nuclear targets (beyond China and Russia) to Iran, Iraq, North Korea, Syria, and Libya, and disclosed that the United States was contemplating developing "limited" nuclear weapons for tactical use, such as blowing up underground stores of chemical weapons, or destroying nuclear research or production facilities. This was a shot across the bow of these states. National security adviser Condoleezza Rice said use of a weapon of mass destruction by any of them "would be met with a devastating response." See "What's New? The Pentagon's Nuclear Policy Largely Represents Continuity, Not Change," *The Economist*, March 16, 2002, 35.

Selected Bibliography

Alexander, Bevin. *Korea: The First War We Lost.* New York: Hippocrene, 1986, 2000.

———. *Lost Victories: The Military Genius of Stonewall Jackson.* New York: Henry Holt, 1992.

———. *How Great Generals Win.* New York: W.W. Norton, 1993.

———. *The Future of Warfare.* New York: W.W. Norton, 1995.

———. *Robert E. Lee's Civil War.* Holbrook, Mass.: Adams Media, 1998.

———. *How Hitler Could Have Won World War II.* New York: Crown, 2000.

Alexander, Yonah, and Michael S. Swetnam. *Usama bin Laden's al-Qaida: Profile of a Terrorist Network.* Ardsley, N.Y.: Transnational Publishers, 2001.

Amminius Marcellinus. *Amminius Marcellinus.* 3 vols. Translated by John C. Rolfe. Cambridge, Mass.: Harvard University Press, 1935, 1982.

Arquilla, John, and David Ronfeldt. *Swarming and the Future of Conflict.* Santa Monica, Calif.: RAND Corp., 2000.

———. *Networks and Netwars.* Santa Monica, Calif.: RAND Corp., 2001.

Bauer, K. Jack. *The Mexican War, 1846–1848.* New York: Macmillan; London: Collier Macmillan, 1974; Lincoln: University of Nebraska Press, 1992.

Becke, Capt. Archibald F. *Napoleon and Waterloo,* two vols. Freeport, N.Y.: Books for Libraries Press, 1971.

Bergen, Peter L. *Holy War, Inc.* New York: The Free Press, 2001.

Blond, Georges. *La Grande Armée.* Translated by Marshall May. London: Arms and Armour Press, 1995.

Brett-James, Antony, ed. *The Hundred Days.* New York: St. Martin's Press, 1964.

Buckler, John. *The Theban Hegemony.* Cambridge, Mass.: Harvard University Press, 1980.

Burke, James, and Robert Ornstein. *The Axmaker's Gift. A Double-Edged History of Human Culture.* New York: G. P. Putnam's Sons, 1995.

Chandler, David G. *The Campaigns of Napoleon.* New York: Macmillan, 1966.

———. *Waterloo: The Hundred Days.* London: Osprey Publishing; New York: Macmillan, 1980.

———. *On the Napoleonic Wars.* London: Greenhill Books; Mechanicsburg, Pa.: Stackpole Books, 1994.

———. *Atlas of Military Strategy: The Art, Theory and Practice of War, 1618–1878.* London: Arms and Armour Press, 1980, 2000.

Chidsey, Donald Barr. *Victory at Yorktown.* New York: Crown, 1962.

Clark, General Wesley K. *Waging Modern War: Bosnia, Kosovo, and the Future of Conflict.* New York: Public Affairs, 2001.

Clausewitz, Carl von. *On War.* Hammondsworth, England: Penguin Books, 1968. First published 1832.

Coleman, J. D. *Pleiku.* New York: St. Martin's, 1988.

Colin, Jean. *The Transformations of War.* Translated by L. H. R. Pope-Hennessy. London: Hugh Rees, 1912.

Coroalles, Anthony M., Major. "The Master Weapon: The Tactical Thought of J. F. C. Fuller Applied to Future War," *Military Review* 71 (January 1991): 62–72.

Creasy, Sir Edward. *Fifteen Decisive Battles of the World.* New York: Harper, 1951; Harrisburg, Pa.; The Stackpole Company, 1960.

Delbrück, Hans. *History of the Art of War,* 4 vols. Translated by Walter J. Renfroe Jr. Lincoln: University of Nebraska Press, 1975, 1980, 1982, 1985.

Diamond, Jared. *Guns, Germs, and Steel: The Fates of Human Societies.* New York: W. W. Norton, 1997.

Dio Cassius Coccianus. *Dio's Rome.* 6 vols. Translated by Herbert Baldwin Foster. Troy, N.Y.: Pafraets Book Company, 1905.

Dodge, Theodore Ayrault. *Alexander.* Boston: Houghton Mifflin, 1890; London: Greenhill Books; Mechanicsburg, Pa.: Stackpole Books, 1994.

———. *Gustavus Adolphus,* vol. 1. Boston: Houghton Mifflin, 1895.

Doubler, Michael D. *Closing with the Enemy.* Lawrence: University Press of Kansas, 1994.

Duffy, Christopher. *Frederick the Great: A Military Life.* New York: Routledge, Chapman & Hall, 1988.

———. *The Army of Frederick the Great.* New York: Hippocrene, 1974.

———. *Austerlitz 1805.* London: Leo Cooper Ltd., 1977; Hamden, Conn.: Shoe String Press, 1977.

Eisenhower, John S. D. *So Far from God: The U.S. War with Mexico, 1864–1848.* New York: Random House, 1989; Doubleday, n.d.

Engels, Donald W. *Alexander the Great and the Logistics of the Macedonian Army.* Berkeley: University of California Press, 1978.

Ferrill, Arthur. *The Origins of War.* Boulder, Colo.: Westview Press, 1997; London: Thames and Hudson, 1985.

Friendly, Alfred. *The Dreadful Day: The Battle of Manzikert, 1071.* London: Hutchinson, 1981.

Fuller, J. F. C. *The Generalship of Alexander the Great.* New Brunswick, N.J.: Rutgers University Press, 1960; New York: Da Capo Press, n.d.

———. *A Military History of the Western World,* three vols. New York: Funk & Wagnalls, 1954–1957; New York: Da Capo Press, n.d.

———. *The Conduct of War, 1789–1961.* New Brunswick, N.J.: Rutgers University Press, 1961; New York: Da Capo Press, 1992.

Gardiner, Robert, ed. *The Campaign of Trafalgar, 1803–1805.* London: Chatham Publishing, 1997.

Giap, Vo Nguyen. *The Military Art of People's War.* Edited and introduced by Russell Stetler. New York: Monthly Review Press, 1970.

Gilbert, Martin. *The First World War.* New York: Henry Holt, 1994.

Griffith, Paddy, ed. *A History of the Peninsular War.* London: Greenhill Books; Mechanicsburg, Pa.: Stackpole Books, 1999.

Hammond, N. G. L. *The Genius of Alexander the Great.* Chapel Hill: University of North Carolina Press, 1997.

Henry, Robert Selph. *The Story of the Mexican War.* New York: Frederick Ungar Publishing Co., 1950, 1961.

Hibbert, Christopher. *Redcoats and Rebels.* New York: W. W. Norton, 1990.

Horne, Alistair. *How Far from Austerlitz? Napoleon, 1805–1815.* New York: St. Martin's Press, 1996.

Jähns, Max. *Geschichte der Kriegswissenschaften vornehmlich in Deutschland.* 3 vols. Munich and Leipzig: R. Oldenbourg, 1912.

Jones, Archer. *The Art of War in the Western World.* Urbana: University of Illinois Press, 1987.

Karnow, Stanley. *Vietnam: A History.* New York: Viking, 1983.

Keegan, John. *The First World War.* New York: Alfred A. Knopf, 1999.

———. *The Second World War*. London: Hutchinson, 1989; New York: Viking Penguin, 1989.

Keeley, Lawrence H. *War Before Civilization: The Myth of the Peaceful Savage*. Oxford, England: Oxford University Press, 1996.

Kelly, Raymond C. *Warless Societies and the Origin of War*. Ann Arbor: University of Michigan Press, 2000.

Klonis, N.I. *Guerrilla Warfare: Analysis and Projections*. New York: Robert Speller & Sons, 1972.

Koch, H. W. *The Rise of Modern Warfare, 1618–1815*. Greenwich, Conn.: Bison Books, 1981, 1985.

Kolko, Gabriel. *Anatomy of a War: Vietnam, the United States, and the Modern Historical Experience*. New York: Pantheon, 1985.

Krepinevich, Andrew F., Jr. *The Army and Vietnam*. Baltimore: Johns Hopkins University Press, 1986.

Lawrence, T. E. *The Seven Pillars of Wisdom*. London: Jonathan Cape, 1927; New York: Doubleday, 1937; New York: Anchor Books, 1991. (First published privately 1926.)

Legg, Stuart. *The Barbarians of Asia*. New York: Dorset Press, 1990.

Lewis, Paul. *The Man Who Lost America*. New York: The Dial Press, 1973.

Liddell Hart, Sir Basil H. *Strategy*. New York: Praeger, 1954.

———. *History of the Second World War*. New York: Putnam's, 1971.

———. *Great Captains Unveiled*. Edinburgh: Blackwood, 1927; London: Greenhill Books, 1990; Novato, Calif.: Presidio Press, 1990.

———. *The Real War, 1914–1918*. Boston: Little, Brown, 1930, 1964.

———. *The War in Outline, 1914–1918*. New York: Random House, 1936.

Livesey, Anthony. *Battles of the Great Commanders*. London: Michael Joseph, 1987.

Mahan, Alfred Thayer. *The Influence of Sea Power upon History, 1660–1805*. Englewood Cliffs, N.J.: Prentice-Hall, 1980; London: Bison Books, 1980.

Mao Zedong. *Mao Tse-tung on Guerrilla Warfare*. Translation and introduction by Brig. Gen. Samuel B. Griffith. New York: Praeger, 1961.

Markov, Walter. *Battles of World History*. New York: Hippocrene Books, 1979.

Maud, F. N., Col. *The Jena Campaign, 1806*. New York: Macmillan, 1909; London: Swan Sonnenschein & Co., 1909.

Miller, Judith. *God Has Ninety-nine Names: Reporting from a Militant Middle East*. New York: Touchstone, 1996.

Miller, Judith, Stephen Engelberg, and William Broad. *Germs: Biological Weapons and America's Secret War.* New York: Simon & Schuster, 2001.

Moore, Harold G., Lt. Gen., and Joseph L. Galloway. *We Were Soldiers Once . . . and Young: Ia Drang—The Battle That Changed the War in Vietnam.* New York: Random House, 1992.

Nevin, David. *The Mexican War.* Alexandria, Va.: Time-Life Books, 1978.

O'Connell, Robert L. *Of Arms and Men: A History of War, Weapons, and Aggression.* New York: Oxford University Press, 1989.

Oman, Sir Charles. *A History of the Art of War in the Middle Ages.* Two vols. London: Methuen, 1924; London: Greenhill Books, 1991; Mechanicsburg, Pa.: Stackpole Books, 1991.

————. *A History of the Art of War in the Sixteenth Century.* London: Greenhill Books, 1987; Mechanicsburg, Pa.: Stackpole Books, 1987 (reprint of 1937 edition).

————. *A History of the Peninsular War.* 7 vols. Oxford, England: Clarendon Press, 1902–1930.

Paret, Peter, ed. *Makers of Modern Strategy.* Princeton, N.J.: Princeton University Press, 1986.

Parker, Geoffrey. *The Thirty Years War.* Boston: Routledge & Kegan Paul, 1984.

Perlmutter, David D. *Visions of War: Picturing Warfare from the Stone Age to the Cyber Age.* New York: St. Martin's Griffin, 1999.

Pimlott, John, ed. *Guerrilla Warfare.* New York: The Military Press, 1985.

Rabb, Theodore K., ed. *The Thirty Years War.* Lanham, Md.: University Press of America, 1981.

Rashid, Ahmed. *Taliban: Militant Islam, Oil & Fundamentalism in Central Asia.* New Haven: Yale University Press, 2000.

Read, Jan. *War in the Peninsula.* London: Faber and Faber, 1977.

Ritter, Gerhard. *Frederick the Great.* Translation and introduction by Peter Paret. Berkeley: University of California Press, 1974.

Singletary, Otis A. *The Mexican War.* Chicago: University of Chicago Press, 1960.

Stern, Jessica. *The Ultimate Terrorists.* Cambridge, Mass.: Harvard University Press, 1999.

Sun Tzu. *The Art of War.* Translated and introduction by Samuel B. Griffith. London/New York: Oxford University Press, 1963, 1971.

Tanham, George K. *Communist Revolutionary Warfare: From the Vietminh to the Viet Cong.* New York: Frederick A. Praeger, 1961.

Thompson, E. A. *Romans and Barbarians.* Madison: University of Wisconsin Press, 1982.

Warner, Oliver. *Trafalgar.* London: B. T. Batsford Ltd., 1959.

Weinberg, Gerhard L. *A World at Arms. A Global History of World War II.* Cambridge, England: Cambridge University Press, 1994.

Whitelock, Dorothy, David C. Douglas, Lieutenant Colonel Charles H. Lemmon, and Frank Barlow. *The Norman Conquest.* New York: Charles Scribner's Sons, 1966.

Young, Marilyn B. *The Vietnam Wars, 1945–1990.* New York: HarperCollins, 1991.

Acknowledgments

I am most grateful to my editor, Emily Loose, senior editor at Crown, for her relentless insistence on clarity, simplicity, and keeping me constantly on message. If this book is a coherent explanation of the rules of warfare, much of the credit goes to Emily Loose. I also wish to thank Caroline Sincerbeaux, Emily Loose's associate, who aided and abetted her in every way.

Index

About the Author

Bevin Alexander is the author of six books of military history, including *How Hitler Could Have Won World War II* and *Lost Victories*, which was named by the *Civil War Book Review* as one of the seventeen books that have most transformed Civil War scholarship. His battle studies of the Korean War, written during his decorated service as a combat historian, are stored in the National Archives in Washington, D.C. He lives in Bremo Bluff, Virginia.